Dear Hacker

Dear Hacker

Letters to the Editor of 2600

Emmanuel Goldstein

WILEY

Wiley Publishing, Inc.

Dear Hacker: Letters to the Editor of *2600*

Published by
Wiley Publishing, Inc.
10475 Crosspoint Boulevard
Indianapolis, IN 46256
www.wiley.com

ISBN: 978-0-470-62006-9
ISBN: 978-0-470-88978-7 (ebk)
ISBN: 978-0-470-88979-4 (ebk)
ISBN: 978-0-470-89020-2 (ebk)

Manufactured in the United States of America

10 9 8 7 6 5 4 3 2 1

Library of Congress Control Number: 2010926616

This book is dedicated to those people who always feel the need to speak out about whatever is on their mind. For my entire life, letter writers have been an inspiration to me. These are the people who actually make changes because so few of us take the time to compose our thoughts into a written form. Even today, when online forums are everywhere, it's those people who think it through and present their thoughts in a cohesive style who really wind up getting through to the rest of us. With all of this, it's no wonder that the individuals who have written letters to 2600 over the years to express their opinions, ideas, or outrage have comprised the most popular part of our magazine. It's this explosion of ideas that has made the whole thing so worthwhile.

ABOUT THE AUTHOR

EMMANUEL GOLDSTEIN (emmanuel@goldste.in) has been publishing *2600 Magazine, The Hacker Quarterly*, since 1984. He traces his hacker roots to his high school days in the late '70s, when he first played with a distant computer over high-speed, 300-baud phone lines. It didn't take long for him to get into trouble by figuring out how to access something he wasn't supposed to access. He continued playing with various machines in his college days at the State University of New York at Stony Brook. This resulted in an FBI raid, as he once again gained access to something he really shouldn't have. It was in the midst of all this excitement that he cofounded *2600 Magazine*, an outlet for hacker stories and tutorials from all over the world. The rapid growth and success of the magazine was both shocking and scary to Goldstein, who to this day has never taken a course in computers. Since 1988, he has also hosted *Off The Hook*, a hacker-themed technology talk show on WBAI 99.5 FM in New York City. In addition to making the hacker documentary *Freedom Downtime*, Goldstein hosts the Hackers On Planet Earth (HOPE) conferences in New York City every two years, drawing thousands of hackers from all over the world.

You can contact *2600* online at www.2600.com or by writing to *2600 Magazine*, P.O. Box 752, Middle Island, NY, 11953.

CREDITS

Executive Editor
Carol Long

Project Editor
Maureen Spears

Production Editor
Eric Charbonneau

Copy Editor
Maryann Steinhart

Editorial Director
Robyn B. Siesky

Editorial Manager
Mary Beth Wakefield

Marketing Manager
Ashley Zurcher

Production Manager
Tim Tate

**Vice President and
ExecutiveGroup Publisher**
Richard Swadley

**Vice President and
Executive Publisher**
Barry Pruett

Associate Publisher
Jim Minatel

Project Coordinator, Cover
Lynsey Stanford

Compositor
Chris Gillespie,
Happenstance Type-O-Rama

Proofreader
Jen Larsen, Word One

Indexer
Johnna VanHoose Dinse

Cover Image
Jake Tilson/Getty Images

Cover Designer
Ryan Sneed

ACKNOWLEDGMENTS

This book started off looking relatively simple but grew more and more complex as the sheer size of the project became apparent; we print so many letters in every issue of *2600* and we've been publishing the magazine since 1984, which means we had a huge amount of source material to draw from. On top of that, it was no small task to figure out the best way to sort them all into various categories and decide which of those would be the most interesting. Because of the size of this collection and the incredible number of pieces that it includes, many letters didn't make the cut despite each letter being precious in its own unique way.

In our last book, I thanked a whole ton of people who helped the magazine get off the ground, stay afloat through difficult times, and remain relevant to this very day. Without repeating those words precisely, I'd like to reiterate the tremendous contributions of *2600* cofounder Dave Ruderman back in our early years, cover designer and photographer Dave Buchwald who continues to add magic and creativity to every project he undertakes, our layout artist Mark Silverberg who makes the current issues of *2600* look sharp and attractive, and our office manager Mary Nixdorf who manages to keep the entire operation running smoothly, despite the odds.

We never would have succeeded without all of the writers, office managers, system administrators, HOPE Conference organizers, radio show participants, and artists that have worked with us over the years and helped to make this thing we do unique and unparalleled. Special thanks also go to Robert Barat, who helped sort through the many pages of letters in piles of issues to find the best ones. Finally, I must acknowledge the inspiration and encouragement of Kyle Drosdick, whose appreciation and skill in the fields of technology, history, and unbridled fun is a perfect summation of what the true hacker spirit is.

I'm pleased to have once again worked with the folks at Wiley, particularly Carol Long and Maureen Spears, who make it all so enjoyable. I also want to thank my agent, Cameron McClure, without whose diligent efforts, this book would likely never have come to fruition.

Last, but certainly not least, a big round of thanks to all of those many thousands of people who decided to put their opinions into writing and compose a letter to the editor of *2600*. Whether it was praise, hostility, the sharing of a personal story, or the discovery of some new security scandal, you're the people who created the magic of interaction that our magazine has become famous for over the years. I hope you continue to use the magic of words to get your message out.

CONTENTS

INTRODUCTION

After we put out *The Best of 2600* — a nearly 900-page collection of some of our best articles of the last quarter century — in 2008, you might be wondering how another large book has come to be published so quickly. It's an interesting story. In fact, the answer might surprise and even enrage you.

The fact of the matter is that all of that material, informative and provocative as it was, didn't comprise *a single character* of what has always been the most popular part of the magazine. Don't get me wrong—the articles have always been our backbone, and they have turned a great number of heads and caused a fair amount of whiplash over the years. We would be nothing without them. They endure to this day, and so much of our technology—and even bits of our society — has been irrevocably changed as a result of their publication. But...there's more. A rather significant amount, actually.

Any decent magazine has a variety of sections and/or features. And while articles represent the semiformal presentations of our writers on their particular fields of expertise, we had another somewhat more informal forum for those who just needed to get something off their chest or ask a quick question. I refer to the letters of *2600*.

I'm not entirely sure when we realized that this thing was taking on a life of its own. It was definitely within our debut year (1984). In fact, our very first letter was published in our second issue and, within a few months, letters to the editor had become a regular feature. Over time, it became our biggest and most popular feature.

For as long as I can remember, I've always liked the kind of discourse that's attached to the type of back and forth communication that you see in a letters section. As a kid, reading the letters in the daily newspaper was a bit of a thrill. I actually got my very first letter published in *The New York Post* at age eight! (I also collected baseball cards to retain some air of normalcy among my peers.) It just seemed so magical to be able to write something, have it appear on a piece of paper, and be read by an untold number of people somewhere. That was really my first foot in the door of publishing.

When I first got involved with computers in high school, I experienced the thrill of letters to the editor on a totally different level. Our school had a "high speed" 300 baud connection to a service called LIRICS Timesharing, a Board of Education operation that ran minicomputers for schools throughout Long Island. Using printer terminals (CRTs were still too new for us), we'd connect to the network and do various things with the computer. Some kids learned programming in languages like Basic, Fortran, and Algol. I liked to play games, use a "talk" program to send messages to other terminals throughout the network, and explore the system itself. (All of those activities were forbidden, incidentally. I found my niche almost instantly.) But there was another feature that attracted me right away. It was the Reply program. You'd first run the Question program by typing R QUESTION at the prompt (which, on the DEC-10 computer we connected to, was a dot). We'd then be able to enter a question for the system administrator. The question would be signed with the PPN (Project Programmer Number) for the school or class—ours was [410,3] and, later, [410,4]. Every day you could type R REPLY at the prompt and see answers to questions from the various PPNs around the island. If your question was actually replied to, you'd experience a brief feeling of elation. There's not even a hint of sarcasm here—we all took this very seriously. It was great fun to see someone get flamed for asking a stupid question, or to actually learn something interesting about the system through an answer. While not technically an editor, the system administrator was like a god to all of us. I found out later he was just another high school student from a different district who really knew his stuff.

Also in that same year, I was involved in an underground newspaper for my high school. It was called *Revelations*. In that publication, after becoming somewhat established and developing a bit of a following within the school, we started our own letters section. It was like a fantasy to see people actually start to write to *us*. Suddenly I was one of the people in the position of answering the questions, and not just someone hoping to get answered myself. The more we did this, the more people wrote in. It felt great.

All the while, I was always writing letters to various newspapers and magazines, everything from the local papers to *The New York Times* and *Newsweek*. Sometimes I'd write in to radio programs (yeah, you used to be able to do that) and hear my letter get read over the air. So few people apparently took the time to do this that it increased the chances of those who actually went to the trouble of putting their thoughts on paper. I never saw this illustrated better than the time in college when I decided I was opposed to the local school budget being passed and wrote a letter to *The Three Village Herald*, our weekly paper at the time, to express my thoughts. My letter was actually in reply to an editorial of theirs that supported the budget. In addition to printing my letter, they wrote a new editorial in that issue saying they were now convinced, as a result of my letter, that the budget should be defeated! And the next week it was. If I had *ever* doubted the power of the pen, those days were forever gone.

It shouldn't be very surprising then, that after getting involved in the launch of *2600*, my passion for this sort of thing would lead to more letters getting published, along with a great deal of back-and-forth with the readers. Only in the world of hackers, the enthusiasm was multiplied about tenfold. Everyone loved to write in and, in all our years of publishing, I've never met anyone who wasn't absolutely thrilled when their submissions were chosen for publication. There's just something magical about the whole process that continues to the present.

As the years went on, the letters became the most popular part of the magazine, partly because of the MTV generation's short attention span, but mostly because they gave the reader interesting dialogue and fun facts. If you knew a particularly weird phone number that you wanted to share, the letters page was more than happy to oblige. If you had a question about a computer system or needed to know how phone phreaks operated a particular function of the telephone network, odds were you would get an answer by writing a letter to *2600*. Sometimes, of course, you would get a somewhat sarcastic reply, particularly if the question came across as overly naive or laced with criminal intent. We were there to inform, but also to entertain. We tried never to be cruel or closed off to other people's perspectives. But we also displayed a healthy cynicism of any "facts" we were told, and we encouraged people to always question *everything* they heard.

Our attitude got a lot of people angry. Over the years, we've been accused of nearly every offense imaginable: being too political, too technical, not enough of either, left-wing, right-wing, protecting criminals, helping the government, etc., etc. It was a rush. If we were able to get so many different people angry at us for so many distinct reasons, we *had* to be on to something. We had great fun veering into topics that had absolutely nothing to do with hacking, including debating the proper names of controversial countries, 9/11 conspiracies, gun control, wars, history, even time travel. It all involved questioning beliefs and applying a default amount of skepticism to any topic. The hacker attitude melded very nicely with this means of communication.

Sometimes, people used the letters pages to simply gripe about something going on in their lives, most always related in some way to hacking or technological cluelessness. It was really important to know that we filled that particular need in our culture, because most of the time it's all about getting information out to people and making sure that someone hears your despair and frustration. Kids who got busted by their schools for opening a browser on the class computer, people arrested and sent away for ridiculously trivial crimes, whistleblowers needing an audience to hear about a company's transgressions involving privacy violations...there were just so many places in people's lives where we were needed to simply listen—or to offer advice.

We've received so many letters in our 26 years of publishing that it was a very daunting task to pick out the best ones. It's sad to think of the large number of really good ones that didn't make it into this collection, although they remain immortalized in our back issues. What's really interesting, though, is how the earliest letters combine so seamlessly with those of our most recent issue. Certainly the landscape has changed, but the tone and the attitude of the *2600* letter writer remains as healthy as ever.

This book is divided into nine chapters. It took a lot of agony to come up with the categories that worked and that were particularly relevant to the hacker culture. But I think we managed to nail it. Each of these chapters is divided up by year, so you can see how our world developed and changed within the confines of the chapter. Reading through each of them is a series of unique voyages.

We start with an examination of the many questions we've been asked since Day One (earlier, even). Questions, as you may know, are what keep hackers going, and it's what tends to get us into so much trouble with those people who are in charge and usually don't like to deal with a bunch of inquiries from curious and mischievous people.

Then we move into an arena quite familiar to all of us—the retail world. This is of significance to hackers because it's where the face off occurs between those who want to learn and explore and those who imagine themselves to be in control. It's that place where the mainstream of society meets the counterculture of hackers face to face. Retail outlets have become increasingly outfitted with technology since the 1980s, which makes them an attractive target for those seeking unique and somewhat humorous stories of technological applications and policies.

Because hackers tend to face all sorts of discrimination and injustice, the letters section became a natural sounding board for their frustrations. Our third chapter focuses on these challenges from the hacker perspective, everywhere from home to school to work. It's not easy living life as a hacker, but sharing it with compatriots makes it all seem worthwhile.

Technology has come so far in the last 26 years that it's almost unrecognizable today from what it was way back in "the day." Almost. Because despite the incredible advances, the huge amounts of storage that are now possible, and the lightning speeds of today, surprisingly little has changed. Back then, we felt that *exact* same passion that we feel today. The only things that were different were the numbers. I believe the letters in our "New Technology" chapter illustrate that from a firsthand perspective.

Then, Chapter 5 focuses on the corporate world. This is always fun, since their perspective of things is so very different than ours. We like to say that there's logic, and then there's corporate logic. They live in a very different reality, where things cost a whole lot more and where Orwellian fantasies bloom into nightmares. Naturally, the corporate environment is where many of our biggest fans reside, because we're able to live the lives they barely dare to dream about.

My absolute favorite chapter is the one that we devote to those people who are completely infuriated with one thing or another that we said or did. It's great to open up the floodgates and let the invectives pour forth. This is such a necessary part of any publication, but also one which tends to be neglected or avoided. Hackers, as a rule, love critique and debate. It's also a really good way of understanding why you believe in something if you must defend your position. And, of course, sometimes it was just fun to watch people destroy themselves with their own words.

This is then followed by Chapter 7, the saddest chapter—the one devoted to prisoners. It's both inspiring and depressing to see the large numbers of people who are locked up for various reasons flocking to our magazine because it gives them something to think about. We forget what a rare commodity that is in such a place. Here we find ourselves listening to what they have to say without judging them for what they may have done. That small action alone is far too rare an occurrence.

Chapter 8 provides a profile of the hacker as a rebel. This is really the heart of what we're all about. Everyone writing in has a hacker perspective of their own making. It usually involves questioning what they're told, pushing the envelope a bit, breaking the rules, and often getting into trouble. I think there's no better way to understand what makes a hacker tick than to study the words and thought patterns displayed here. All sorts of philosophies on our place in the world are shared, all manner of experiences related. What's truly amazing is that a letter writer from 1984 would have no trouble recognizing and appreciating the perspective of a fellow writer from 2009. The rebellious nature knows no time or age boundaries.

Finally, there are those letters that totally defy description. Over the years, we've attracted individuals of *all* sorts who felt compelled to write to us for a variety of reasons, some utterly nonsensical, others simply weird and unexpected. We've also gotten our share of misdirected mail, which we had no qualms about printing when the mood struck us. These letters added a great deal to the fun spirit of our pages, and we're including some of them here in the hopes that they continue to entertain.

The magic of letters to the editor will always remain with me. It's consistently one of the first places I look in any publication. The popularity of today's online forums underlines the desire of people to always be involved in the feedback process. Of course, having *no* quality control at all tends to dilute the final product, as is sadly the case in so many of the things we see on the Internet. In a printed publication, we at least have the opportunity to pick and choose. We don't publish everything we get and we remain quite selective in what actually makes it into the magazine. As the letters contained in this collection have also gone through a *second* selection process, you can be assured that these are the ones we *really* like. I wouldn't be at all surprised if you felt the same way.

Question
Upon Question

If for some reason you had to sum up the entire hacker culture in one single word, that word would simply have to be "questions." It's what we live for, what drives us, what always gets us into so much trouble. And it's one of the things *2600*, as a hacker magazine, gets the most of from readers. So it's only appropriate that we begin this collection with a sampling of some of the many questions we've received over the years.

They take on a number of forms, and you'll see common themes in the hacker world that have survived to this day, along with technical issues that might have been the norm at one time but which seem utterly bizarre and outdated today. Still, the desire to learn is what ultimately matters, and if our magazine somehow managed to date back another century, I think we'd recognize those components in whatever questions the readers might have asked back then.

So what sorts of things have people been curious about throughout our history? Well, there were those questions that we must have gotten asked a thousand times: What does "*2600*" mean? How do I become a hacker? Is it illegal to read this magazine? Can you show me how to hack into Hotmail?

The idea for us was to give people answers to the things they were interested in while teaching them ways they could figure it out on their own. Of course, there are always those questions that have nothing to do with anything we're about, and that's where you might see an instance of a sarcastic reply. Sometimes there was just no other way.

Looking back, it's amusing to see how people were so concerned about ways to make simple phone calls without going broke. In those early days, even local calls were expensive, so anyone who was able to figure out "alternative methods" of communicating was looked upon with great interest and even reverence. The computer bulletin board system (BBS) was growing in popularity as a means of meeting people, sharing ideas, and building the hacker culture. It also was the precursor to those first tentative steps onto the Internet. So many of the questions back then were merely about access, ways to get themselves connected so that they could begin the learning process, meeting that first challenge that gained them access into the marvels of the hacker life.

Of course, it wasn't just hackers who took an interest in all of this. The mass media, members of corporate America, law enforcement people, and even parents all wanted to know just what we were getting up to. And then there was the inevitable criminal element who saw opportunities through hacking to benefit themselves. We got questions from *all* of these groups, and we did our best to give as succinct and direct a response as we could, regardless of the source or the intent of the questioner. Because that's what the hacker world is always all about.

The one thing we never wanted to do was discourage someone from asking and, thus, learning. We were all too familiar with the ridicule new people often encountered when asking what some saw as naive or uninformed questions. Obviously, everyone had to start somewhere, and you could either guide them along to a place where they understood what was going on or drive them away and guarantee that they would look negatively upon the hacker community in whatever path they wound up going down. It was only when it was clear that a reader had no interest in actually being a hacker and instead simply wanted shortcuts and profits that we felt compelled to give them a dressing down. And sometimes that's exactly what they needed.

If there has been a significant change in the kinds of questions people have asked over the years, I think it's more along the lines of the specifics of the technology in use, and not so much having to do with the philosophy of hacking. This is why in the early years you see more questions about the phone network and beepers and stuff that we simply take for granted these days—or have completely forgotten about. In this day and age when *everyone* seems to be connected and making a free phone call is the norm rather than a crime, we still see the same sense of wonder in the questions we're asked, along with a hint of the rebellion and creative thinking that makes the hacker world tick.

1985 _____

Dear *2600*:

> *If I want to go trashing, am I forced to just attack my Central Office?*
>
> ANONYMOUS

There are lots of good places to trash besides phone companies. Look in the phone book under software companies, phone equipment, computer equipment, electronic equipment, or look at Radio Shacks, or GTE, MCI, or your local cable company. You will find loads of things, like free telephones, floppies, etc.

1986

Dear *2600*:

> *I have call waiting and a modem, so many of my calls are disconnected by the little tone that is sent that tells you someone is waiting on the line.*
>
> *What can I do?*
>
> DISSENTING OPINION

We would like to sympathize, but we don't get nice services like call waiting here. There are a few ways around it.

- *You can disable the call waiting, if you have "selective call waiting." You dial *70, then get a tone, and from this make your call. Then the call will not be interrupted.*

- *If you can set the amount of time that the modem can be interrupted for it to disconnect, this may help if you have a smart modem, but the modem at the other end of your phone may hang up anyway.*

- *If you also have call forwarding, you can forward your calls to another line. If you have two lines, you can send the call to your non-data line. If you don't, you can forward your calls to a local test number. Use one that gives you an eternal busy signal.*

- *If you are being constantly annoyed by someone who knows he is interrupting, then forward it to a test number that gives silence, a sweep tone, or a payphone somewhere. One way to solve the problem of being annoyed by a persistent interrupter is to call forward to the same number in a different area code where your number would not be valid and it would elicit a disconnect recording. The caller will hear "The number you have reached, XXX-XXXX, has been disconnected." It's also effective to turn the tables and call forward to another line in the harasser's house, or perhaps one of his relatives. He then winds up harassing himself.*

Dear *2600*:

> *How can I be like Captain Midnight? How about an AM carrier-current pirate radio station?*
>
> PV

We can't tell you what to do exactly, but we can say that it involves ingenuity, sneakiness, intelligence, persistence, and a youthful spirit. Mix those together and you should come up with something worthwhile.

There are many AM carrier-current pirate radio stations in existence. Too many of them try to sound like regular AM stations and few people notice anything different.

1987

Dear *2600*:

> *I am sort of a new kid on the block when it comes to hacking. So could you please indulge me if I am not of equal proportion to you. Could you tell me what steps I should take as a beginner in the field of hacking? First I would like to give you a background on myself if I may. I am 15 years of age. I am a known underachiever in my school. My teachers press me for answers but I refuse to comply with their methods. My hobbies are computers and basketball, mostly computers. My parents threaten to take away my computer which is an IBM PC if my grades don't improve and I tell them C's are average but they still want A's from me. The computer is half mine—I put in well over two thousand dollars. Well, back to hacking. First, what are some approaches that I can take in getting into another computer system to explore it for the wealth of information that I could use? Next, is there any device or gadget I can make to tell when my phone call is being traced? Third, I would like to know if you have some of the many phone phreaking devices known to us hackers? If so, I would be willing to purchase them for a reasonable fee. Also, do you have a program called a worm? I would like it for a BBS that sent a logic bomb in a program to me. This bomb wiped my TI's memory right out.*
>
> JS

If you read 2600 *enough, you should get a good feel for what kind of systems are out there and the "wealth of information" they contain. We can't condone breaking into any of them, but we can say that if you're determined and skilled, you'll most likely get into something. Hot water, in all probability.*

We know of no such device that could alert you to your phone being traced. Perhaps some government phones could do that, but we don't think it's possible at this stage in the game. Besides, how could it tell you that you were being traced before you actually got traced? It wouldn't do much good.

The 2600 *Marketplace is your best bet for finding electronic devices. Ads are free to subscribers. We don't approve of logic bombs, but we do want to show you what they look like. If anyone has one, please send it in. (On paper, please.)*

1988

Dear *2600:*

> *After months of agonizing over 2600's financial plight, I've figured out a way to return to the monthly format and solve another great problem that plagues BBSes all over the nation. How many times have you logged onto your favorite BBS and seen some message like this: "It has come to my attention that someone else is using my name, 'The Grim Reaper,' on other BBSes. Well, whoever you are, I'm the real Grim Reaper. I was The Grim Reaper months before you came around. You better not use my name any more, or I'm gonna kick your $#&*@ ass!!! You better think of a new name dude!!!"*
>
> *Well, the obvious solution to this common dilemma is to have a sort of "name registration," where individuals can register their alias with an authority—kind of like your given name when you're born. And who else would be the most likely authorization but the hackers' and phreaks' choice—2600! Think about it! You could charge each registration a nominal fee, like $3. For that $3, you will give the person a registration certificate, saying that he is the only one authorized to use a particular alias within a given limit, say, an area code. The person could get some little certificate to hang on his wall, and maybe even a patch to sew on his jacket.*

So the next time the loser user logs onto the BBS, he can now proudly assert: "By the power of 2600, I am the only Grim Reaper within the 212 area code. I am the only one certified and authorized to use that pseudonym. So be gone, you pagan!"

So, whadaya say? 2600 could be put into the black, and we would no longer have to put up with dueling 14-year-olds. We have a unique opportunity to help solve the hackers' two most serious problems.

ANONYMOUS

No thanks. There must be a better way to raise funds than to play big brother to dueling 14-year-olds. Besides, how in the world would the user be able to prove that he/she was the one with the certificate hanging on their wall? Computers still offer a degree of anonymity. Let's all try to enjoy that while we can.

1989

Dear *2600:*

How many subscribers do you have anyway?

THE APPLE WORM

Next to "Whatever happened to TAP?" that's the question we get asked the most. It's harder to answer than it might seem because 2600 isn't like most other magazines. We have around 1,000 people who get the magazine sent directly to them. But don't be deceived by that rather small number. Many others (random polls indicate at least four times that number) get what is known as a "secondary" copy, that is, one that has been copied by a friend or even electronically transcribed. Naturally, we prefer it when people subscribe directly because it helps keep us going. The most important thing, though, is to get the information out. Close to 1,000 more copies go to various newsstands and bookstores around the world. And whatever else is left goes to all of the people that order back issues in the future. So, to answer your question, we don't really know. The numbers just don't tell the whole story in our case.

Dear *2600:*

> *I am writing to inquire as to whether any issue of your magazine has information regarding access to long distance telephone calling card codes using AT&T or Sprint services without a computer.*
>
> *I used to have a calling card number that worked and billed to someone else, but it is no longer valid.*
>
> *I don't have a computer, so I need some way of finding a valid card number that works. From what I've read in one of your books, that isn't easy to do at random because AT&T is difficult to hack without a computer. I've tried using my old card and changing the last four digits, but it won't go through.*
>
> *If you have anything on this or know of a publication that does, please let me know.*
>
> MC
> Van Nuys, CA

What you want to do really has nothing to do with hacking or phreaking. There are lots of ways to make telephone calls. You discover them through individual experimentation. Using someone else's calling card is not the way to go. You victimize an innocent person and you also run a tremendous risk of getting caught. If you want to explore and manipulate the system, there's never been a better time. If you simply want to steal, you'll have to wait in line.

Dear *2600:*

> *How is it possible to publish hacking and phreaking information without those in authority changing those systems you expose?*
>
> WAFB
> Knob Noster, MO

Good question. Sometimes the systems are changed, sometimes some of them are changed, sometimes none of them are changed. But what we get out of it is the knowledge of how the systems operate and that's an invaluable tool which leads to our figuring out still more of them. In other words, knowledge and information are always advantageous and should never be stifled.

1990

Dear *2600:*

> Being a new subscriber, I was wondering what the 2600 represents in
> the title of your magazine?
>
> SNOOPY

2600 *hertz at one time was a liberating cry used by phone phreaks. By sending
a* 2600 *hertz tone down the line when connected to a long distance number, the
number would disconnect and you would have total control over the long distance
trunk. Not only that but billing was bypassed. This was commonly known as blue
boxing. These days that method rarely works, but of course there are many others.*

1991

Dear *2600:*

> I just received your Winter 1990 issue and was very impressed by the
> in-depth quality I read. I am writing mainly to find out what back
> issue of 2600 I should purchase for beginning hacking (phones and
> computers). I was taking a television/radio class in college a couple
> of months ago. In this class the teacher mentioned that anyone could
> pick up cordless phone calls on a scanner, and that it was legal. I
> knew this but nobody, I mean nobody else in the class of 50 knew this.
> Now I know what is meant when people like Agent Steal say, "Thank
> you to all the stupid people." I own a scanner and am just learning
> about devices to enhance frequencies via CRB research catalogs. But
> your issue is much more comprehensive by way of information. CRB
> is equipment. All this terminology is new to me also, so where do I
> turn? 2600 has opened some doors that I did not know existed. I own
> a computer also (no modem yet), but it is still such a fascinating tool.
> I want to be able to understand it inside and out. Not to mention
> phones. This is even more intriguing to me.

Just to let you know, I found out about 2600 through Sound Choice magazine. They put you on their list of fantastic catalogs. I can't argue with this. I think what you are doing with your catalog is a great example for other catalogs and people as well. Utilizing your First Amendment rights the way very few people know how. I hope that you can suggest some valuable reading material on phone and computer hacking. Thank you and keep up the good work.

S.C.
California

It's hard to point to a particular issue and say that is where you learn about hacking. It's probably better for you to read from issue to issue and glean whatever you can. If you find yourself wanting more info, try the previous year's back issues. If you like those, keep going.

Dear 2600:

I've learned through the grapevine that there is a computer program that automatically dials via a modem in search of carrier tones of computers that can be accessed. Apparently the program, without repetition, dials telephone numbers within a designated area code, and/or with a designated prefix, and stores those telephone numbers which provided access to computer carrier tones. Do you guys know of anything like this? I would really like to get my hands on a program like that. It would save many fruitless, red-eyed hours at the screen.

LH
San Diego

Your grapevine must be rather old. But that's okay—old as the information may be, it is still valid. Wargames dialers have been around since modems were first used. Some of the programs are in Basic, some in assembler, others in C. It's different for every machine. What you have to do is find someone with a program that will work on your machine. Ask on bulletin boards or check out our classified section. By the way, it's still open to debate as to whether or not scanning is illegal. Some phone companies will take action against scanners. We feel there's no harm in scanning, since you are not harassing any one person over and over but merely going one by one through a series of numbers in much the same way the phone companies do when they want to sell one of their overpriced services.

Dear *2600:*

> *I feel your publication serves a valuable purpose in today's technology-oriented society. Two questions, however. Isn't what you're doing somehow illegal? If so, have the cops pressured you for information about hacking/phreaking activities?*

> RA
> VIRGINIA
> (I'M NOT A COP.)

Congratulations. In answer to your first question, we publish a magazine about hacking. As long as the First Amendment exists, we're completely within the law. A magazine called TEL in California was shut down by the phone company in the seventies for printing similar information. We believe this action was illegal and in direct contradiction of freedom of the press. Since nobody has challenged it, their action stands as if it were legal. Fortunately, we haven't yet gone down that road in New York. In answer to your second question, no.

1992

Dear *2600:*

> *First of all, let me start by saying thank you for what you are doing. It is a service without quantifiable value. I have spent years in the shadows searching and scraping for information on the hacking field, generally only coming up with the occasional Phrack or Phun newsletter. Six months ago I was walking around the immortal East Village and I happened upon a little store called Hudson News. Inside, after an hour of hunting and browsing, I came upon a marvelous little document with a toilet on the cover. My computing life has not been the same since.*

I make no claims toward greatness in the pursuit of the hack, only that I understand the force that drives it, and that it is driving me. Unfortunately, your magazine is the only source of outside information I have been able to acquire on the subject (aside from that mentioned above).

I would be infinitely appreciative of your assistance in pointing me in the right direction, and giving a good shove. If there is anything I can do in return, though I could not imagine what, I would be happy to help.

Secondly, help! *I need to get Internet access that extends beyond CompuServe's meager mail facility (which I just found out about today). And I don't know where to begin to look. To the best of my knowledge, there are no colleges in Westchester County, NY, that are connected to the Internet and provide public access accounts, though I pray I am mistaken. Again, your assistance in this matter would be greatly appreciated.*

THE INFORMATION JUNKIE

We printed a hacker reading list in our Winter 1990-91 edition. Most of what is in there is still obtainable. Additions to this list will be printed in future issues.

If you can't find a college that provides public access accounts, then it may be worthwhile to actually enroll as a part-time student and gain access that way. Or for $30 a month, you can get PC Pursuit, a service that allows you to access modems in other cities. From there you can dial into other services that allow Internet access. As public access Internet sites pop up, we will provide the access numbers.

Dear *2600*:

Here are a few things I have been wondering about for a while, and I was hoping you could enlighten me. All of these observations are valid for the Atlanta, Georgia, area code (404).

1. *When I dial any number with certain prefixes, I always get a busy signal before I even hear a ring. It does not seem to matter which number I dial. Examples: 450-XXXX, 470-XXXX, 490-XXXX, and 670-XXXX.*

2.   One prefix always returns a fast busy signal (which I believe is the local reorder tone). This tone pops up after you dial the first three digits of the prefix (no additional digits necessary). Example: 430.

3.   For some prefixes, you dial a full seven-digit number and then you get exactly one ring and then a series of three or so single frequency beeps. Examples: 570-XXXX and 690-XXXX. In some extremely rare cases you will get something like an answering machine service after the first ring. The announcements are made by real people, and vary from number to number.

4.   Some prefixes require that you enter a number consisting of ten digits. After the second or third ring an announcement comes up and says something to the effect of: "Your call cannot be completed as dialed. Please read the instruction card and try again." Examples: 510-XXX-XXXX and 410-XXX-XXXX.

Since I have not made any progress figuring out any of the above stuff, I decided to see if you could help me out. Any information you can provide will earn you my everlasting gratitude. And if you cannot help, that's OK—I will still keep reading 2600 Magazine whenever I can lay my grubby hands on a new issue. I apologize in advance if any of this stuff has some simple explanation that has been common knowledge for years.

FD
ATLANTA

First off, never apologize for wanting to learn. It's far better to admit ignorance than to feign knowledge. And since 99 percent of the populace have no idea what we're talking about anyway, you're still coming out ahead.

We checked with the AT&T routing computer and all of the exchanges that you were getting busy signals on (450, 470, 490, 670) are not officially in use. They also cannot be accessed from outside the 404 area code. This could mean several things. These may be new exchanges that are still being tested. They may be special exchanges that the phone company uses for various things. We suggest exploring each of these exchanges every now and then to see if all of the numbers remain busy. Also, it can't hurt to have a local operator check the busy signal and tell you if the line actually exists.

Some exchanges (like your 430) are programmed not to accept any additional digits. It's more likely that this exchange is not being used at all in your area. To be sure, though, compare it to other exchanges that are not being used. Weird numbers like 311 are almost never used but so are a lot of other three digit combinations. Do they all react the same way? Keep a log and compare it every few months.

The 570 and 690 exchanges in your area are used for beeper services. When you get one ring followed by three or four beeps then silence, you have dialed some- one's beeper number and it is waiting for touch tone input from you. When you dial a sequence of numbers followed by the # key (optional), those numbers will show up on the beeper belonging to that number. If you get six or seven beeps that don't ever allow for touch tone input, you've reached what is known as a "tone only" number. The beeper will simply say that someone beeped but won't give any additional infor- mation. This is seldom used these days and is good only for people who get beeped by the same number exclusively (i.e., doctors who get beeped by their service). When you hear a voice message, you're reaching a service that is attached to someone's beeper. When you leave a voice message of your own, their beeper will go off telling them they have a voice message in their mailbox. Some of these numbers allow for either tone or voice messages to be left.

Since 510 and 410 are now area codes, this would explain why your switch waited for seven more digits.

On all of these numbers, we suggest you try prefixing with 1 or 0 or a carrier access code to check for variations. And we encourage people in different area codes to experiment in the same way and report their findings here.

Dear *2600*:

I have recently purchased your magazine and I like what I see. I don't have a computer yet, but I am interested in obtaining programs on disk that can copy application programs from a hard disk drive and/or flop- py disks such as WordPerfect 5.1, PageMaker, and CorelDRAW, even if they are under someone's homemade menu screen, under Windows, or both. Also, I would like information on telephone codes to make free long-distance calls (and any other phone tricks), a program to find the source code for any IBM compatible computer, and some type of beginner's guide on hacking that isn't technical. I was wondering could you tell me which back issues of 2600 deal with these subjects and could you give me a list of other sources—magazines, books, or people (addresses and phone numbers) that would have what I am looking for. I would greatly appreciate it. Keep up the good work.

BIRDMAN
TENNESSEE

Learning is a lot more fun and beneficial than making free phone calls and copying software. While the things we teach may enable people to accomplish these tasks, we believe they will at least understand what it is they are doing. You seem to want to bypass this part of it and that's something we cannot help you with. If, though, you're interested in more than just the end results, then you're in the right place.

Dear *2600:*

First of all, you have a great magazine so don't change a thing! *However, I just recently received a bunch of back issues, so pardon me if some of these questions are outdated or have been answered already.*

1. *How can I help 2600 grow (besides the obvious of sending you money)? I would like to do some sort of volunteer work for you guys, but that may pose a small problem since I live a few thousand miles from New York.*

2. *Is E.T. considered an honorary phone phreak?*

3. *What is the ANAC number for the 515 area code?*

4. *What can you tell me about your cover artist (Holly Kaufman Spruch)?*

5. *Please explain to me why it takes six weeks for you guys to process orders for back issues. It should only take about two weeks tops. And that's third class mail! If I decide to shell out maybe $75 for back issues, then I want the "invaluable" information (that I don't already know) as soon as possible, and don't want to wait a month and a half for it! This is very frustrating, and I would also like some other readers' opinions on this.*

6. *I sympathize with Kevin Mitnick in the Summer '91 issue. In plain English, he got shafted. I'm not saying that he's completely innocent, but the authors of the book Cyberpunk did write unfairly about him.*

7. *How about writing an article listing all of the known phreak boxes, what they can do, and if they can be used today. List all of the major ones like blue, red, green, and black boxes and then list the lesser known ones like the gold, cheese, diverti, aqua, etc.*

8. *Would it be possible to put together a big gathering of phreaks in some unknown exchange like the "2111" conference in the October 1971 Esquire article "Secrets of the Little Blue Box"? To me that is what phreaking is all about—helping other phreaks. By the way, I do know that you can't use a blue box to do this anymore, but you inventive folks should be able to come up with something that would work. If you did this, however, you would have to tell phreaks about it through word of mouth, as I'm sure many telco security personnel read your magazine.*

9. *I really enjoyed the "Hacker Reading List" in the Winter '90 issue. However, it was slightly incomplete—you forgot magazine articles. Below is a small list of hacker/phreak related articles that I have come across. A larger list is available at the back of the book Cyberpunk. Also, a very good book that Dr. Williams left out of the book list is called The Phone Book and the author is J. Edward Hyde. To find these, just go to your local library and see if they have the back issues. However, they might not have them as far back as '72, so you will have to use their microfiche. I personally found most of these at a college library.*

> **Esquire,** October 1971, "Secrets of the Little Blue Box."
> **Esquire,** December 1990, "Terminal Delinquents."
> **Ramparts,** June 1972, "Regulating the Phone Company in Your Home."
> **Ramparts,** July 1972, "How the Phone Company Interrupted Our Service."
> **Radio Electronics,** November 1987, "The Blue Box and Ma Bell."
> **L.A. Weekly,** July 18-24 1980, "The Phone Art of Phone Phreaking."
> **Rolling Stone,** September 19 1991, "Samurai Hackers."
> **Playboy,** October 1972, "Take That, You Soulless S.O.B."
> **Oui,** August 1973, "The Phone Phreaks' Last Stand."
> **Time,** March 6 1972, "Phoney Tunes."

CLARK KENT
AMES, IA

You don't have to be anywhere near us to help out. You can send us information, articles, and anything else that comes to mind. You can contribute to the discussion on our voice BBS and start other forums on hacking throughout the country. By letting people know there is a place for them to contribute, you'll be opening up a lot of minds that are just waiting to be liberated. It may not be quite that poetic but you get the idea. We don't talk about E.T., we will talk about the 515 ANAC when we find it, and we can't talk about Holly Kaufman Spruch. We agree that back issue orders take too long and we've taken some steps to alleviate the situation, including hiring people whose only concern in life is to speed the process. Keep in mind that it takes our bank up to three weeks to notify us if a check has bounced or is unacceptable for some other stupid reason. That's why we're not too keen on sending out back issues until we're sure we've actually gotten paid. We could send out cash orders quicker but then too many people would send cash in the mail, which is a pretty risky thing in itself. We're hoping for a maximum of three to four weeks from start to finish. Our authors and hopefully other readers have taken note of your other ideas. Thanks for the info.

Dear *2600*:

> *I run a BBS for the disabled called DEN (Disabilities Electronic Network). Until recently we had an 800 number accessing an eight-line hunt group. It was a very lively national bulletin board. Our 800 number is in limited service indefinitely as a result of our loss of funding. This has been the cause of a search for long-distance services that our users would make use of to access DEN. I found PC Pursuit by Sprint. PC Pursuit is a non-prime time service that allows 90 hours per month for disabled people and 30 hours per month for non-disabled people for $30. The service enables one to access many electronic services during non-prime time hours and weekends while not changing your present long distance provider. Are you, or anyone at 2600, aware of other such low-cost services? I'm desperate to find low-cost access for our users. We're a free service and it would be a shame if our phone companies' greed affected our ability to deliver a service to the disabled community.*

> TB
> NEW JERSEY

The call has gone out.

Dear *2600*:

> *How come your voice BBS is only open after 11 p.m.? Also, why do you give out an expensive 0-700 number instead of a real phone number?*
>
> PUZZLED

First off, the 0-700 number costs 15 cents a minute. A regular phone number would cost 13 cents a minute. While slightly more, this is not comparable to a 900 number or anything of that nature. We give out that number because right now the system doesn't have a set phone number; it sometimes shows up on different lines. It's only available at night because it's currently a single-line system and opening the BBS during the day would tie up the voicemail functions. Right now we're working on expanding the system so that it shows up on our main number and so that the BBS part is available around the clock with multiple lines. To do this, we need to find some flexible multi-line voicemail software along with some cheap computers. If anyone has any suggestions, please send them our way. For now. the voice BBS can be reached through AT&T at 0-700-751-2600. Most of our writers can be reached through the voicemail section of that number, which is available 24 hours a day. During business hours, the rate of the 0-700 number is 25 cents a minute. (Don't worry, we're not making a penny off of this!)

1993

Dear *2600*:

> *Ever since I've had a conscious knowledge of computers, I've wanted to hack. I haven't always known it was called hacking, but I've just had the mental inkling akin to hacking. The problem is basically I neither have the equipment nor the know-how needed. Right now I'm 15 years old and about to enter my junior year of high school and I feel that I'm almost past my prime for hacking (this may just be a*

*popular misconception). But, regardless of my age or scholastic rank-
ing, I feel I should start now. So I was wondering if you could steer
me in the right direction in terms of literature and an affordable, but
good, system.*

DARKHOLD PAGE
PITTSBURGH

We don't really recommend one system over another because everybody's needs
and tastes are different. What you need to do is play around on as many different
systems as you can in order to find out what you're comfortable with. We advise
using friends' systems or those in school or computer stores. Otherwise you run
the risk of getting something you don't want or can't use. Read some of the literature featured in 2600 in order to become more familiar with the culture. Any good
bookstore or library should provide you with much material. With regards to age,
you are hardly past your prime. Most hackers are young because young people
tend to be adaptable. As long as you remain adaptable, you can always be a
good hacker.

1994 _____

Dear *2600*:

*I am a new subscriber to 2600. The back issues I requested came in a
few days ago. I read every issue in a single sitting. The zine blew my
mind. 2600 is phat! Since I am a new member to the hack/phreak community, I find some concepts in your magazine hard to understand.
I've tried calling local boards, but the only users are kids addicted to
MUDs. Because I'm a 16-year-old kid living in a little Canadian hick
town called Medicine Hat (dumb name, eh?) with nobody to answer
my questions, I decided to use our messed up postal system to write
to you guys. Now, onto the questions:*

*What the hell is a PBX and how do I find an access number into one?
How do I find an authorization code for a PBX once I access one
and what do I do with it? I'd like to get onto some LD boards, but I
don't want to pay the high LD charges. I know you don't tell people to*

commit toll fraud, but you do tell how to. How would someone like me get toll-free planet-wide calls? Your contributors write about how they get on computer systems. I live near an army base and I know they have a computer system. How do I access the computers? Do I just phone up the number in the phone book or what?

My telephone company is AGT but most of the equipment is made by Northern Telecom. My area code is 403 and an engineer at AGT told me that my province is the first completely digital telephone system in Canada. I'm wondering if you have any info on how I can have fun with my phone system?

DrP
MEDICINE HAT, ALBERTA

PBX stands for Private Branch eXchange and it's basically a phone system run by and for a company. Oftentimes, security lapses allow people on the outside to access dial tones, voicemail, computers, etc. On many occasions, these are reachable through 800 numbers. Methods of making free phone calls abound here and in many other places. But that doesn't mean it's a particularly smart thing to do. We understand how difficult it must be for you trapped in the middle of nowhere but you do have to be careful. Your "completely digital telephone system" could easily monitor your activities. Learning and exploration should be your primary goals, not just getting things for free. Unfortunately, it's sometimes unavoidable to commit crimes, however small, in the process. You need to weigh the risks and decide what your priorities are. We don't suggest messing with your local military computer, at least not for starters. If there is a college in your area, do everything you can to get on the net. If you succeed, you will have eliminated the long-distance charges and opened yourself up to an unlimited world of knowledge and contacts. We wish you luck. And don't give up on Medicine Hat—there are probably other hackers there, too.

Dear *2600*:

You have mentioned that "hacking is discovering." Something bothers me and I would appreciate your help in clearing up my mind. I am trying to distinguish the difference between hacking and graffiti. Hackers who insert viruses into systems can be compared to the guy with a can of spray paint discovering how much destruction he can accomplish and how original and creative it can appear. Please tell me what you consider to be the difference between both forms of evil senseless destruction for no personal benefit other than pride in their destruction.

JV
NEW YORK

There is no defense for evil senseless destruction and we don't defend any form of it. Inserting viruses into systems is destructive; experimenting with their creation on your own system is not. Graffiti is destructive if something is destroyed in its creation and artistic if it improves what it replaces. Some of New York's old graffiti trains were true works of art. Both hacking and graffiti can be used in destructive ways but neither has to be.

1995

Dear *2600*:

Regarding someone's concerns over privacy of your subscriber list, section E211.4.2 of the Domestic Manual requires that publications sent by Second Class have a "known office of publication" open during "normal business hours where the publication's circulation records are maintained or can be available for USPS examination." A Second Class permit also requires that you tell the world, as you did on page 2 of your Autumn 1994 issue, the number of subscribers and newsstand copies sold (which impressed the heck out of me—I didn't know you were that big). So Big Bro is allowed to look at your subscription lists!

Have you considered mailing by bulk third class instead? The basic rate is 23.3 cents per piece (anywhere in the U.S.) which is probably not much more than you're paying now and there's no zone-based rate, no need to file a "Statement of Ownership, Management, and Circulation" or requirement to have a "known office of publication." Or how about offering the option (at a higher cost, obviously) of getting 2600 *by first class mail in a plain unmarked envelope? (I still prefer to buy mine at the newsstand, though.)*

Speaking of the USPS and the NCOA database mentioned on page 6, the USPS' database is now also being used to identify CMRAs (Commercial Mail Receiving Agencies, or "mail drops") to commercial subscribers (such as credit card companies who are concerned about applicants who use a mail drop as their "residence address").

Anonymous in MD

Protection of our mailing list always has been one of our highest priorities. While second class mailing allows the post office to look over your shoulder a bit, we don't believe we're giving them anything they don't already have. They don't have access to our subscriber lists. What happens is this: every three years or so a postal inspector comes by and picks ten names at random from our subscriber printout (they never get to keep or copy this rather large printout). We have to show that most of the ten people actually requested our magazine, usually by producing a subscription request. This doesn't concern us since the post office can get our subscribers' names and addresses by simply looking at the envelopes we send out. We don't believe they are using this rule to focus on hackers—a number of the ten names are usually large corporations. But it was admittedly odd that last time one of the names they picked at random was Kevin Mitnick. (We were unable to find his paperwork.) Even with this weirdness, we don't believe this is a threat since virtually every magazine in the country has to go through this. And, if it is a threat, we'll never know if we don't play along for a while. As for alternatives, first class mailing would nearly quadruple our mailing costs and third class would ensure that we're at the very bottom of the priority list.

Dear *2600*:

I personally feel that 2600 should revisit its apparent "print it all" policy dealing with letters/ads. For example, there is a seven line help wanted ad from someone who wants someone to write/call him and explain to him what an ANSI bomb is. Another wants you to send $3 to get a copy of an ANSI bomb detection program. I think it's important that as a magazine you help to educate those new to the community, but at the same time keep us from wading through letters *every month asking what a red box is, or why a certain person's red box doesn't work. I would at least suggest that right above the address to send letters, you put "RTFM." Just my couple of cents.*

LINCOLN

We certainly can't pull an ad because we think the person placing it needs to learn more. As for letters, we can only print a small fraction of what we receive. And a fraction of those will be from beginners who need some basic answers, not a harsh rebuff. That comes later.

1996

Dear *2600:*

I moved from San Antonio, TX, to a small town in South Texas and everyone here who sees me reading your magazine keeps asking me where they can get your mag. I tell them to subscribe but they are afraid their moms, dads, or wives will see it and think they are doing something illegal. I tried to explain that the information is not illegal—it's the "illegal use of" that is illegal. And it's this reason why I ask, "Where is the nearest place to buy your magazine south of Corpus Christi, TX?" In case you're wondering, I get my cousin to buy it and send it to me from Houston, and it seems to me that she is getting tired of doing this so I may be subscribing soon.

S6KILLER

Subscribing really isn't that bad an idea unless you live in the kind of place where your mail is opened before you get to it. All of our issues are sent in envelopes and the name of the magazine isn't printed on the envelope. As for where to find it, check any bookstore that carries a wide assortment of magazines. If you don't see it, ask. If possible, find out who their distributors are and tell us so we can contact them.

Dear *2600*:

> *OK, here is a* probably *stupid question. I have someone's IP address. I want to know if I can get more information on this person from the IP address. I grabbed this when I was using CU-SeeMe. I want to find out the person's email address and, hell, anything else I can get. I am new to hacking/phreaking/all that stuff. Sorry if I seem so stupid, but I guess you'll just have to deal with it. Thanks.*

> BEN

*Actually, the only stupid thing about your question was assuming it was stupid. Everyone who knows the answer at some point had to ask the question. Not asking out of fear is dumb but not nearly as dumb as ridiculing someone for asking. Many times the people who do this don't know the answer themselves! Anyway, as far as your question goes, the IP address will get you the name of their site. That info by itself, though, won't get you the username and, last we checked, CU-SeeMe doesn't reveal an actual username. If you have the IP and access to a UNIX prompt, simply type **nslookup** followed by the IP address and you will see the translation. (This will work in reverse if you are looking for the IP number.) To get a list of all machines on a site, type **nslookup** and hit Return, then **server xxx.site** (where xxx.site is the site name), and finally **ls xxx.site**.*

Dear *2600*:

> *I was wondering if you could help me with something. I want to know how to find information about people through a computer. For example, is there a database with everybody's profile I could get into and read? I hope you can help. I would really appreciate it.*

> RAUL
> HOUSTON

Yeah. Everybody's profile. Everyone in the world. No problem. The most interesting thing about your question is that in a few years people probably won't understand why we're being sarcastic.

Dear *2600*:

> *I was browsing through Barnes and Noble and came across 2600. I've never seen more underground info in a mainstream bookstore before. Is your zine legal just because the FBI hasn't bothered to leaf through it or do you sneak copies on the shelf when nobody's looking or do you play the establishment against itself or what?*
>
> DFW

What we do isn't illegal and no federal agency will be able to change that—at least, not without making a lot of other things illegal.

1997

Dear *2600*:

> *I just want to start out by saying I love your magazine! I am writing to express my concern about the attitudes of some hackers and wannabe hackers. It seems that it is getting harder and harder for newcomers to get pointed in the right direction and to have their questions answered. Some of my friends (who are newbies) have reported to me that even the slightest newbie-type question has quickly earned them the title of "lamer" and "wannabe." Come on, what is this crap? We were all beginners at some time. We were not born with these skills, people. All of us who know the answer at one time had to ask! It seems to me that the purpose of a hacker is to educate others and seek further knowledge for themselves. It now seems that more and more people are being shunned for asking a simple question. If we want to remain a powerful force we have to continue to spread knowledge, not shun others for asking for it. So I encourage newbies to keep asking and if someone treats you like crap and turns their back on you for asking them a question, they are the lamers, not you. In fact, they probably don't know the answer themselves.*
>
> ZeBoK

Dear *2600*:

I have an AT&T phone in my office. I've noticed at least once a day (normally between 12 p.m. and 4 p.m.) it will ring one time for about half a ring. Even when I get to it and pick up before it stops I get a dial tone. My main question is, is my phone being tapped or do you have any idea whatsoever as to what the problem is?

GRIM

Someone or something is calling you and hanging up. There could be thousands of reasons for this including a human error to a screwed up fax machine to a badly programmed phone system. It has nothing whatsoever to do with your phone being tapped.

Dear *2600*:

I read your mag as often as I can find it and it's definitely dope. Now the reason for my letter. I find myself in a potentially lucrative position at the moment and I desperately need sound advice. I figured that you guys would know enough about this to provide some insight. I have recently come into possession of what I believe to be very valuable information from a large pharmaceutical company here in Michigan. The info consists of a complete 1997 employee roster, a 1995 company directory complete with the names of all employees statewide, along with their phone numbers, fax numbers, and email numbers. I have diagrams detailing their entire voicemail system, along with support-ing documentation on their voicemail, and I have access codes and passwords to at least one computer system along with some miscel-laneous info. With this information a competitor could literally have a field day intercepting faxes, reading email, and targeting susceptible employees for solicitation.

I recognize that all this falls under the label of corporate espionage and I am aware of the risks. What I don't know is how to sell this info. How do I offer it to interested parties? How do I find out who is inter-ested? And most importantly, how do I approach them with my offer without scaring them away? What executive in a large corporation would I want to seek out? The CEO? Who? This letter is meant to go from me to you and not necessarily be printed in an upcoming issue. If it is, your advice will come too late. I would appreciate if you could send me a personal reply ASAP. Any advice would be greatly appreciated and if I found any of it useful in any way, I would feel compelled to make a "donation" to you fellas to lay out as you see fit. I estimate this info is worth at least somewhere in the low five digits. If I'm wrong, please tell me.

Mr. Swervon

You're wrong. But you're correct in saying that our advice will come too late. The only thing we have in common with you is that we are both, as you say, "dope" except you should have a capital D and write it on your mailbox. For those of you who are still within reach, please get it through your heads—we are not, never have been, and never will be into this criminal bull that idiots somehow equate with hacking! Corporate secrets bouncing around a computer system that's open to the world? Hey, that's fair game and they deserve the embarrassment of its discovery. But using this knowledge to line your pockets or, worse, using insider knowledge to get the information and then calling that "hacking" is an affront to any of us who hack for the sake of learning. These kind of people are remarkably similar to our biggest enemies in law enforcement: they refuse to see the difference between hackers and criminals, they twist reality to suit their well-defined purpose in life, they claim to be experts as to what kind of people we really are, and they're sleazy as hell. If only they would find each other.

1998

Dear *2600*:

I'm a Latin American hacker-wannabe, and I would like to know where can I find the software to do some damage over here, cause the damn government here is abusing on mostly all aspects of daily living and they have a few websites and I would just like to show them how the people feel about all their crap....

Sly

You sound more like a political prisoner-wannabe. You have to understand that this kind of thing could get you into a lot of hot water. Of course, if the cause is justified it may be a risk you're willing to take. But if you're just looking to play games, take a long hard look at how your government deals with such things before diving into it. If you're still interested, by all means search the web for security weaknesses, find mailing lists and newsgroups that deal with this kind of thing, and, assuming books are allowed in your country, learn as much as you can about how it all works. But please be smart—after all, the beauty of the net is that such political statements can be delivered from anywhere....

Dear *2600*:

> *I have seen your magazine and your website but I am still not sure what exactly your purpose is. Is the magazine for people who break into systems for the pleasure or profit of it, or is it for persons, such as myself, who enjoy learning about such intricate portions of the computing industry? I glimpsed through your latest issue at Tower Records and I noticed some stuff on IP addressing and such (which I enjoyed thoroughly) but then I saw the article on the guy who changed the system time on a virtual pet (which I felt was wasted magazine space, since he did not really get into the specifics) and it confused me a bit about the purpose of your magazine. I am thinking about purchasing a copy, but I don't want to find that after reading the magazine, it wasn't exactly what I was looking for. If you could summarize for me what your magazine is basically about, it would clear up my confusion and help in my decision about making the purchase.*
>
> *Forgive my ignorance, but what does 2600 stand for and what is with the payphone photos?*
>
> THE COMPUTER JUNKIE

If you've read the magazine and visited our site and you still don't know what our "purpose" is, you'll probably get even more confused by the other things we do and say. For the record, 2600 hertz is a magic frequency and we print payphone photos to cover up what's really on the back page. But we've said too much.

Dear *2600*:

> Alright. There are a few things that piss me off in this world. I don't
> like it when I am screwed over because of someone who feels they are
> better than me, I don't like when someone gets on your back for ask-
> ing something you don't know, and I don't like how newer hackers
> are treated in online society. I myself got interested in hacking about
> two years ago. When I started out, I had gotten a pretty bad rep in
> the hacker community. I didn't get caught doing anything, I didn't
> piss anyone off or do anything stupid, I just asked a question. Maybe
> some people would have thought that it was a dumb question too,
> but the fact that I was treated with no respect because I did not know
> something that they did really pissed me off. When I started out I knew
> that the hacker community was all about free exchange of information
> and exploring parts of the Internet that were confidential, merely for
> the thrill of breaking the rules. I did not figure the group to be a bunch
> of idiots about everything, I did not figure that I would be laughed at
> like I was an AOL member every time I entered an IRC hack channel,
> and I did not expect for anyone to treat me with any less respect than
> anyone else. Now, I do not think of all hackers this way, but I feel that
> these are the few that screw up the way that hackers are looked upon
> in modern society. Some people really have to mature. Just because
> you're a hacker doesn't mean you have to be a kid out of high school
> with nothing to do, because not everyone is like that. So for all of you
> hackers thinking that you "control" the lesser bunch, think again.
>
> PaKo

"Laughed at like I was an AOL member"? Sounds like you're guilty of the same gross generalizations you're accusing others of. But your accusations are quite justified—there are far too many snap judgments being made based on questions, names, or originating sites. Why is this? Mostly because people are insecure about their own images so they find it necessary to put others down for whatever reason as quickly as possible. The ironic part about this is that there are and always will be enough idiots for everyone to put down—this prejudging is completely unneces- sary unless, of course, the people judging fear for their own reputations. It's not worth blowing a gasket over—these people are what they are and you won't be able to change that. Letting it affect you will only give them more strength. And assuming this is what the hacker world is all about just makes it bad for all of us.

We're about asking questions. That's why we're all here. If you ask a stupid question, you can count on someone telling you that. But you should also be able to count on them answering it to stop you from asking it again.

Dear *2600*:

> *Two FBI agents were at the meeting in New York. They kept leaning in and listening to the conversations. Just a suggestion, but maybe if it were possible to move the meeting somewhere else? A suggestion is the World Trade Center. Directly in the middle of the two three-story buildings are a whole load of seats (out in the open) near a waterfall where tourists go. It'll look like we're a bunch of tourists. Good luck.*

TWISTED CIRCUITS

You're missing the entire point of our meetings. We're not trying to hide! That's why we meet in the middle of public areas. Understand? If FBI agents show up (and just how did you know they were FBI agents?), they're welcome to. Anyone dumb enough to do illegal things at a public meeting won't be getting our support anyway. And if the feds wind up doing illegal things, then we're more than happy to provide them with the arena in which they'll hang themselves.

Dear *2600*:

> *Does Janet Reno know what a kernel is?*

KRIS

Does 2600 care?

Dear *2600*:

> *While dialing an ex-girlfriend's number repeatedly (she owes me dead presidents and is running), I stumbled on an interesting phenomena. After about eight times of getting her voicemail, the number would come up busy or I would get her busy ("I'm on the phone right now")*

message. Then after another try or two I would get a strange dial tone and then a partial playback of a voicemail message. It lasted about 10 seconds and I assume the message was hers. After the message ended I would get disconnected. I tried back several times within a two-day period and always heard the same partial message playback. It happened five times and from different phone numbers. At the dial tone and during the message, pressing keys seemed to have no effect.

She is in the 201 (Northeast NJ) area code and subscribes to Bell Atlantic's Home Voice Mail. I am pretty sure that dialing the number repeatedly overloads the switch. I wonder if the overload could somehow give me access to more messages or perhaps the entire voicemail box or beyond? Let me know what you find out.

RepoMonster

We find it very unlikely that you could single-handedly overload the switch by calling back eight times in a row. What probably happened is that your stalking victim, while in some sort of a panicked state, tried desperately to make a different outgoing message to maybe hide her identity, failing in the process. Either that or she deliberately did this in order to confuse you, which she again obviously failed to accomplish.

Dear *2600*:

Why is Janet Reno on the cover of 15:2?

SMOKESCREEN

Sometimes you have to scare people to get their attention.

Dear *2600*:

I snail-mailed a letter to you without a return address, and I saw my letter in print in the next issue. My question is was there a reason I was given a new handle and my words edited to say the same first two sentences but the next couple altered? If this is because of monitoring

you guys are under and don't want to get your readers in trouble, I un-
derstand. But if it's not, wouldn't it be just like the censoring your mag is
against? If this thing is common just tell me, because it does make sense
to safeguard your readers. I'd also like to know if once you've given a
reader a handle if future letters are appended with the same handle. And
if I'm just dumb and paranoid and your response is that it was another
guy's letter, then why *is the reason why we only see his? You guys don't*
have to print this but at least reply to this via email.

RANT-o-MATIC

We can't reply individually to letters. Letters are signed with the handles or names
that we are given. We don't make substitutions. We have no idea what letter you're
referring to so we can't address specifics. We edit for clarity, literacy, and, in rare
instances, to protect the writer from revealing something damaging about them-
selves. It's pretty far from censorship.

Dear *2600*:

Please forgive my last email to your magazine. I was drunk at the time.

RANT-o-MATIC

1999

Dear *2600*:

I was wondering why your association is not writing any articles deal-
ing with the Y2K bug? I have been reading quite a few articles about
this upcoming problem and I am interested what the ramifications
would be in the hacking world. I was surprised in your last issue when
you didn't cover this and downright shocked when I picked up 15:4
and didn't see a peep about it! With the loss of most UNIX-based
systems, what will be left of the Internet as well as most of the com-
mercial systems based upon this dated OS? This is the biggest single
event in the computer genre since the microprocessor!

ZACK

It's also by far one of the most overblown events. We're being stirred into a panic by people who either have something to sell or some sort of agenda. The potential of the Y2K problem demonstrates nothing new—computers are always vulnerable to certain things and if you let your life be completely controlled by them you're pretty much asking for a rude awakening. It's far more likely that such an awakening will come when you least expect it, not on 1/1/2000. Oh and incidentally, UNIX systems will do just fine.

Dear *2600*:

> *Message: Please help me. I have been hacked on my geocities page. Is there a way to reverse this, or a way to hack it back?*

> TOPACE12

If you "hack it back," you may be committing a felony, depending on where you live. Be very careful. We suggest getting a book on HTML to avoid becoming a real legend in the hacker world. Putting up a web page before you know how to put up a web page is generally a very bad idea. The .gov sites are an exception.

Dear *2600*:

> *Great magazine! Anyway, I just wanted to know how I could start my own newsletter. I want to distribute it around a few schools nearby and at 2600 meetings. How could I start one? Should I just type it up on my computer and print it 300 times then put it where the school newspaper goes?*

> LeeTKuRp of HoC

This is one of the questions we're asked most frequently. The best advice we can give to any aspiring zine publisher is to focus on content and grow into your audience. If you look at our early issues, they were tiny but filled with material people were hungry for. As the years went on, we expanded. But we never could have started in the style we have now. We weren't ready for it then on many levels. For something like a school newsletter, the same basic rules apply. Make sure

you have something to say. There's nothing more important. Once you have that,
work on how you want it to look without draining your abilities. Then figure out
the cheapest possible way to get it printed and, before you know it, people will be
hunting for it. Good luck.

Dear *2600*:

> *OK I have some real serious stuff to tell but I need to be reassured that*
> *I can trust your company that you don't do this sorta thing just so you*
> *can turn people in then I will tell my very serious and true story for*
> *you but I must be reassured first please reply.*

> Anonymous

How can we lie to you? We published 2600 *for 16 years just so you would finally*
walk into our little trap. Welcome.

Dear *2600*:

> *Why are people so afraid of hackers? People in my school are afraid I'll*
> *do something to their credit or something, and I never even threatened*
> *any of them. I'm starting to wish I did.*

> Valen

Understandable but you must resist the dark side.

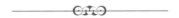

Dear *2600*:

> *In the main library of my city, I saw that they changed the old Windows*
> *NT computers to computers from Sun Microsystems running Solaris.*
> *The interface royally stinks and the keys are misplaced. I found out*
> *that if you press Alt+O and type anything you want, you'll get a gray*
> *screen that says: "Whatchew talkin' 'bout, Willis?" I wonder what*
> *is that?*

> Jack

From what we're told, this has something to do with the financial difficulties "Different Strokes" star Gary Coleman has gotten into. Since he gets a royalty every time that line is used, his financial standing will soon be restored. Your library will receive a bill every time you do that with the help of the secret locator chip that comes with all upgrades.

2000

Dear *2600*:

> What is it that 2600 does? (I know, I know, buy the magazine.) Where is the "About" button on your website? Everyone else has one... why don't you? I have heard of 2600 from co-workers, so I decided to check it out. After I checked out both "Free" and "Kevin" on the first page (to make sure they both went to the same place), I was unable to find any kind of history or explanation of what exactly 2600 is all about. Is it something to do with phones? It is, isn't it! How am I supposed to know?

> DAN WHEELER
> MSNBC INTERACTIVE

We're working on a special remedial site for the media.

Dear *2600*:

> I was thinking of starting a 600 meeting group at my college, just thought I'd see if it was cool with you guys. Is it?

> SCORCHMONKE

Fine with us. You might want to check with the people at 600 though.

Dear *2600*:

Why does "*resist" appear in the last bullet on the table of contents in the 17:1 Spring 2000 issue?

PHUCT

That's what is known as a printing artifact. It's a hazard of the digital age. Some people see small words and what appear to be significant comments hidden in their issues. Others see Jesus. As always, we apologize for the confusion and inconvenience.

Dear *2600*:

I was wondering how your old issues were originally distributed. They were just sheets of paper with holes punched. Did they come stapled together or in a wrapper or something? Just curious about the history of 2600.

AKOLADE

Originally, 2600 was mailed out as three sheets of paper folded into an envelope with loose-leaf holes punched in them. When we expanded to eight pages, we attached the paper so that it was two 11x17 sheets folded to fit in the same size envelope. We'd be interested in seeing recollections from original subscribers on the early days of 2600.

Dear *2600*:

When I first started reading your magazine I had no idea what the hell you were talking about. But my desire to learn the craft of the hacker and its ethics kept me going. Before I knew it, I was doing my thing because the first thing you told me was to read and not ask the dumb question "Can you teach me to hack?" Now all the magazines I read earlier are definitely worth my money. Thanks for your mentorship. I promise to teach and lead the next line of newbies as you lead me in the right direction.

DREYDAY _ 33
NEW YORK CITY

Dear *2600*:

> *What am I supposed to do to have an answer from you? I've wrote*
> *you an email and nobody answered me anything.*
>
> SoJo73RO

Many people take it personally when we're impersonal. But there's really no avoiding it. We get more email than most people could imagine. And while it may indeed
seem trivial for one of us to take a few seconds to answer you personally, multiply
that by many thousands and all of a sudden we've run out of time to put out a
magazine, run a website, do a radio show, fight lawsuits, and work on whatever
other project happens to be on the calendar. We've never had a U.S. president
return one of our phone calls and we have yet to take offense. We know they'd
like to, but there just isn't enough time. Of course, the real irony is that if you had
included your question, we might have been able to answer it here.

2001

Dear *2600*:

> *A colleague of mine recently went to a seminar in San Francisco*
> *regarding intrusion detection technology. These seminars are very*
> *popular now. His instructor, who claimed to be a previous security*
> *expert for AT&T (isn't everyone?) told the class to read 2600. But the*
> *warning given was to buy it from the newsstand and not to subscribe,*
> *otherwise "you will get checked out." I asked him who would be doing*
> *the checking. But since he didn't have the insight or forethought to ask*
> *his instructor, it is unclear as to whether the alleged checker-outer is*
> *associated with 2600 or an outside agency (possibly government?).*
>
> *So, in the interest of information gathering and because I am a sub-*
> *scriber, are you going to be checking me out?*
>
> BONEMAN

This would be unnecessary since we checked you out before you subscribed.
That's why we made sure you heard about us and followed the plan by subscribing.

Writing this letter, however, was not part of the plan and we will be taking corrective action.

Dear *2600*:

> Let me start by saying that I think your magazine is great. The first time I read it was the issue before the current Winter issue and now I'm hooked. Your blatant honesty about things is great. Anyway, I was wondering about a rumor a friend told me. Supposedly the government blacklists anyone who subscribes to your magazine or anyone who buys it in the stores using a credit card. Now I have no problem buying it with cash, but I was wondering if the rumor is true or not. I'm sorry if this is an annoying question and you receive it often, but I wanted the truth. Keep up the kickass mag.
>
> CYBERINFERNO

Even if it were true, do you think they would tell us? If they did, we'd certainly tell you. But most importantly, if such a thing were going on, the best way to fight it would be to challenge it by getting as many people on those lists as possible. Even the hint of such oppressive tactics should not be tolerated. (And don't forget to wear gloves when handling currency unless you want your fingerprints in the central database.)

Dear *2600*:

> I'm 12 years old and I've picked up your Spring 2001 issue. I'm now trying that decoding thing on the Windows encoder. I've got a couple of questions. What is the difference between a hacker and a cracker? Are there such things as "good hackers?" Do you guys focus on computer security or the opposite? And are there such things as computer whizzes who aren't nerds? If you ask me, I think that 2600 is the best, because I want to start a software company someday. Oh, yeah, why do you guys call it 2600 Magazine?
>
> ADAM J.

Where do we begin? How about before answering your questions, we remind our loyal readers that it's extremely important that questions like these get addressed patiently and as frequently as necessary. The people who ask them have obviously been influenced by all kinds of outside distortions and unless we take the time to correct them, they could easily become far more prevalent.

Now then, let's address these questions. "Cracker" is simply a word created by people who are tired of correcting misconceptions about hackers. The problem with doing this is that it preserves the misconceptions under a different name. By dismissing someone as a "cracker," we ensure that nobody knows any facts as to what the person is actually doing. Is the person damaging computer systems? Then he can be called a vandal. Is he using a computer to fraudulently bill other people's credit cards? Then he's engaging in credit card fraud. The point is we have plenty of ways of describing people who do bad things with computers or technology, just as we have existing laws to prosecute truly illegal activity. To answer your second question, if you believe that what hackers do is good, then there are quite a few good hackers. What hackers do is figure out technology and experiment with it in ways many people never imagined. They also have a strong desire to share this information with others and to explain it to people whose only qualification may be the desire to learn. There are quite a lot of people who call themselves hackers but relatively few who fit the definition. This is because our society doesn't seem to require someone to prove they're really a hacker— presumably because most people are so awestruck by the very concept and by the belief that they couldn't possibly understand what a hacker is, let alone question one. Suffice to say that if the "hackers" you know seem primarily interested in fashion, image, and putting down anyone who's new or of a certain age, it's quite possible they've simply latched onto a culture they themselves don't understand or appreciate.

As for your other questions, hackers need to experiment with—and appreciate—the concepts of computer security and security breaching. It's hypocritical to treat such things differently as your own situation changes. For instance, if your computer system gets breached, you should treat it as you would have wanted the security manager of the system you once breached to have treated it—however long ago that may have been. If you truly believe in the hacker spirit, then that should follow you through life, not end as soon as you "grow up." And yes, it's possible to be a whiz and not be a nerd. In fact, most any combination is possible.

As for our name, 2600 hertz was the magic frequency that people with blue boxes used to seize lines and explore the old phone network. Which brings up another important point—hacking is by no means confined to computers.

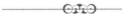

Dear *2600*:

> *I have a story that may interest you. However I'm afraid that if I published it, I wouldn't be around to see it if you know what I mean. Can I submit a story anonymously?*
>
> PHACEOFF

We know exactly what you mean. Many people submit stories to us and then go on vacation and wind up not seeing them when they're published. It's a very real fear that should not be ridiculed. And to answer your unrelated question, yes, by default all stories are submitted anonymously. Your byline is what you want it to be. Naturally, you should take steps to ensure that your outgoing mail isn't being monitored.

Dear *2600*:

> *Like most of the world I watched in horror as terrorists attacked New York and Washington last Tuesday. I am relieved to hear that the 2600 team is safe and I wish to express my sympathy to anyone who lost family or friends in the attacks.*
>
> *There's not much that I can do to help in this situation. I don't have any of the equipment listed as being required for the rescue operation. I'm overseas so donating blood wouldn't help. Is there any fund which I can donate to which will assist in restoring some communications in the disaster area?*
>
> THE _ CHAOTIC _ 1

Obviously, needs have changed since September. On the 11th, people were lining up for hours in order to give blood—but the sad fact was that not very many survivors were found. Don't think that this means such things aren't desperately needed. We heard of cases where people actually refused to give blood unless it was guaranteed to be used for WTC survivors! We can only hope that most people have come to realize how essential such donations are every day everywhere. If anything positive can come out of September 11, perhaps this is it.

2002

Dear *2600*:

> *I want to learn how to "hack" in such a bad way it makes me sick! I have the hunger for the information and a lot of time on my hands. I don't know how to even begin to start my hacker education, what books to buy, what progs or tools to get. I just picked up your mag in a bookstore and couldn't believe it. Finally answers or some type of help! I was ecstatic! Can you guys at least point me in the right direction? By the way, you guys rock!*
>
> MINGUS

We get about a dozen of these letters every day. So consider yourself honored that yours was selected completely at random. There are a couple of things that have to be understood. First, relatively few people are hackers, even though quite a few either want to be or walk around saying they are. Most of what constitutes hacking is the whole process of figuring things out. While we can offer tips and suggestions on specific applications of technology, we cannot tell you how to think. That's something you either develop on your own or not. If you keep an open mind and don't shy away from activities which most would view as a complete waste of time, you're off to a good start. And learning a little history is always a wise move—there are plenty of online resources in addition to our magazine which document the milestones of our community.

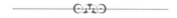

Dear *2600*:

> *I think my girlfriend has been cheating on me and I wanted to know if I could get her password to Hotmail and AOL. I am so desperate to find out. Any help would be appreciated. Thanks.*
>
> HSFK2

And this is yet another popular category of letter we get. You say any help would be appreciated? Let's find out if that's true. Do you think someone who is cheating on you might also be capable of having a mailbox you don't know about? Do you think that even if you could get into the mailbox she uses that she would be discussing her deception there, especially if we live in a world where Hotmail and AOL passwords are so easily obtained? Finally, would you feel better if you invaded her privacy and found out that she was being totally honest with you? Whatever problems are going on in this relationship are not going to be solved with subterfuge. If you can't communicate openly, there's not much there to salvage.

Dear *2600*:

> *My father passed away last year. Unfortunately he used my name and Social Security number in the past. Now I don't have a good credit report and I need help. Can you help me? I am the father of two baby girls and I would like to buy a house one day.*

LOP

Assuming you don't want to continue the family tradition and simply use your kids' SSNs, you need to clear your name. You seem to be under the impression that hackers go around wiping people's credit reports or creating new identities. Of the relatively few who do know how to easily do such things, hardly any would ever do it for hire. And we don't talk to them.

So the first step is for you to stop acting like you're guilty of a crime. Unless you are. (We still won't be able to help you but we'd at least respect your honesty.) If it happened the way you said it did, there are ways of dealing with it. Check with the Social Security Administration and the various credit bureaus and tell us what they say. If you're forthcoming with them and don't do anything stupid like ask people to help you get fake credit, you at least have a chance of setting things right. And even if that doesn't work, there are other channels which can give you a voice.

Dear *2600*:

> *I've been reading 2600 for, well, most years I could read and compre-*
> *hend what was written on the pages of 2600. It comes time now that*
> *I have a band and we have been ripping our brains out for names to*
> *call ourselves and finally I suggested "2600." My only questions are:*
> *Is this legal? Is this okay with the writers/editors of my favorite zine?*
> *I know 2600 is only a degree of megahertz used in phreaking, but it is*
> *a name trademarked by you. Is this all right?*
>
> DREW

It's hertz, not megahertz. While it's a very nice thought, we wouldn't be entirely
comfortable with a band going around with that name. What would happen if you
became really big and your music started to suck? People would forever associ-
ate the name "2600" with corporate rock and we'd probably wind up getting sued
by the giant record company that signed you. Imagine the irony. But seriously, we
have no say in this. You can call yourself whatever you want. We'd be happier,
though, if it were a reference of some sort rather than the entire name. After all,
there's always the chance that we're going to quit this publishing thing and turn
into musicians one day.

Dear *2600*:

> *I want to have a 2600 barbecue on my roof this summer. How can I*
> *advertise?*
>
> MARBLEHEAD

And just what in hell is a "2600 barbecue?" If you're trying to set up a meeting,
just look at our guidelines at www.2600.com/meetings*. It's unlikely having meetings*
on your roof would qualify though as our meetings are in public areas and usually
don't involve fire.

Dear *2600*:

> *In the Backtalk section of 19:1 you advised Mingus that "Most of*
> *what constitutes hacking is the whole process of figuring things out."*

Fair enough. However, you precede this statement by claiming that "...relatively few people are hackers, even though quite a few either want to be or walk around saying they are." Buh!? Granted, there are plenty of people who claim to be hackers despite having no knowledge of how to go about hacking and, more importantly, no interest in that knowledge. Nonetheless, if the hallmark of a hacker is the ability to figure things out, then surely a great many people are hackers, though most may not choose to classify themselves that way. It seems to me that the more constructive answer to the multitude of pests who ask to be "taught" to hack is to stress that anyone can be a hacker, but a true hacker teaches him/herself.

CZAR DONIC

Your way of saying it is certainly more constructive but it's also important to understand that while anyone can be a hacker, relatively few actually see this through and far too many attach the name to themselves for no other reason than wanting attention. What we're trying to say is that people need to work at it—like most anything else, it doesn't just happen because you want it to.

Dear *2600*:

> *Thanks for your kind information on your interesting website. I do not know where can I find an answer for my question but please trust me that I need to find a way to hack the passwords of one of the users of Yahoo! mail service.*

ALICE

OK, we trust you.

Dear *2600*:

> *I am living in Japan. I will be racing pro here and I would like to put the 2600 logo on my car. It will consist of the 2600 logo along with your URL. I will email you pictures of the car when the design is finished. I*

also have Jinx Hackwear going on the car. I think the more we can get
people to open their eyes in every aspect of life, not just the technology
industry, the better....

GARY

We have a logo?

Dear *2600*:

I'm not trying to piss off the magazine and all of the hacker community
by asking this question, as I too am a phreak, but the question is why is
it okay for us to snoop into other people's private files and though we're
not destroying anything, look around? I mean, I find exploring and
learning okay, but hacking isn't just the method of "checking things
out." It does involve eventually invading people's personal documents.
I really enjoy my privacy, but hacking and phreaking are like having
someone stare through my window and I'm morally supposed to be
okay with this? I'm not reprimanding anyone for hacking/phreaking
as I enjoy both and I love this zine, but why is it okay for hackers that
don't value the privacy of others, but when theirs is at risk, they can
freak out? Explain. Thanks.

ANONYMOUS

First off, it's not okay to violate someone's privacy, no matter what you call yourself.
Doing this is not, contrary to popular belief, one of the tenets of the hacker world.
That's not to say it doesn't happen—it most certainly does. But most people who are
involved in hacking have no interest in violating privacy and are, in fact, more interested in protecting it. The fact that massive privacy holes exist and that hackers are
the ones who often discover this doesn't mean that their goal was to violate privacy.
It's far more likely in such a case that the goal was to prove a system insecure, be
the first to figure something out, or demonstrate that a supposedly trustworthy entity
really isn't all that trustworthy. There are those who veer off the path and abuse
this just as there are those who steal when they realize how easy it is. To assume
that these acts are at all related to hacking is just plain wrong. But it's good to see
people trying to think it all through. Read on for another angle to this.

Dear *2600*:

> *I've recently discovered the joys of searching for *.eml files on Kazaa. Microsoft Outlook saves email messages as *.eml, even though they're just normal text files. Lots of people have emails saved which they don't realize they're sharing. So far I've gotten instructions to call the American embassy in Lebanon, two moms cursing up a storm about some other mom who goes to their kids' hockey games, some home-wrecker begging the "if it wasn't for* her *could you have feelings for me?" question, lots of product registration codes, and lots of pictures of ugly strangers. It's fun! Just be warned that lots of these are viral, since I guess people want to save viral messages as evidence or something. Lots of Nimdas, Klezes, and stuff. Even worse than that, though, are the massive amounts of cheezy forwarded jokes you'll get.*

> Rob T Firefly

Now this is clearly an invasion of privacy. But it exists because of bad design and lack of education. It's unreasonable to expect people to not look at something that is literally in the public domain simply because it's supposed to be private. That's just human nature. It's more reasonable to expect people to learn from this and do a better job designing systems and keeping their own files private—scenarios made all the more likely because someone played around with a system and figured something out. Again, we don't condone this kind of abuse but we also don't believe it warrants an hysterical reaction with all kinds of retribution. At least now there's a better chance that people will be aware of this.

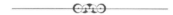

2003

Dear *2600*:

> *How can I get a copy for myself? By the way I am living in Iran.*

> KAYVAN

We do offer a special "Axis of Evil" incentive for people inside participating countries. Simply mail us something of interest from your country and we'll respond with anything from a single issue to a lifetime subscription, depending on how interesting what you send us is. Just another way to annoy the authorities.

Dear *2600*:

> *Now that I have had an article published, is there someone that I could send future articles to through a more direct means? I have no problem submitting them like everyone else. I am just blatantly trying to jump the line.*

> No Name

No line jumping here, sorry. Every submission is judged on its own merits, not the name(s) attached to it. But it was probably wise of you to leave your name off of that question.

Dear *2600*:

> *Why do hackers refer to a hacker that is not causing a problem with the system he or she is observing a "white hat" and the one who is committing a crime a "black hat?" You would think a group of ultra-liberal free spiriters would be less driven by color. Don't say it doesn't matter what color is chosen for the term because if it doesn't matter then reverse the terminology. I'm personally getting tired of white people associating crime, evil, and bad things with my heritage... especially when the white people in our society are committing most of the crimes.*

> Ken

To begin with, hackers are not the people coining the "black hat/white hat" phrases and using them. Rather, they are used by the people who have money to make by creating an atmosphere of fear mongering so that people buy their products or attend their expensive conferences. As to the problems you have with the actual colors that are being used, that's a language issue that goes far beyond anything we can address here. But you certainly don't help matters by continuing to label races albeit in a different direction. And finally, please don't label hackers as being allied with any one particular political view. We certainly have our opinions here but they are just that—our opinions. They may or may not reflect what most other hackers agree with. Individuals are free to make up their own minds.

2004

Dear *2600*:

> *I realize that most of you don't agree with projects like TIA or Big Brother, but at the same time you want all information public. How do these two coexist? Would you agree with Big Brother if anyone could access the information it collected? Keep up the great work.*
>
> TCHNPRGRMR

Actually we know of very few people who want all information to be public. We believe information, particularly that of a private nature, needs to be protected. Often this isn't the case and one of the best ways of determining this is for systems to be constantly tested for security holes. This leads to the messenger frequently being blamed for the message. Hackers who uncover unprotected private information are treated as if they created the weak security when all they did was figure out a way to defeat it. The media portrays them as the threat to your privacy when in actuality hackers do much more to protect it. We consider their actions to be responsible, especially when they reveal their findings to the world.

Meanwhile, all kinds of corporate and governmental entities seek to invade our privacy on a constant basis for reasons ranging from surveillance to marketing. While it would solve nothing to give everyone access to the information these entities collect, it's extremely important to understand exactly what they're doing and how, as well as ways to protect oneself from such intrusions. This is something else they don't want you to know.

Dear *2600*:

> *I'm thinking of starting a meeting in my city. Unfortunately, I've never had the opportunity to actually attend a 2600 meeting. Can you tell me what basically happens at these meetings? Are they organized by any one person and if so, how are they run? How many people are usually in attendance (on average)? I just want to make sure that if I go ahead with this, I do it right. One way that I would like to survey the interest in starting a meeting here is to print inserts and put them in the 2600 issues in my local Chapter bookstores, requesting that those interested contact me to assert their interest. In order to get the inserts in as many issues as possible, I'd like to do this as soon as an issue comes out. Can you tell me when the issues hit newsstands?*
>
> N,COW

Meetings are open to everyone and there is no set agenda. To many, "gathering" would be a better description. We don't tolerate any kind of disruptive, exclusionary, or illegal behavior and many are surprised by how little of that we've had to deal with. You don't have to be an expert in any particular field but curiosity and open-mindedness are essential if you want to get anything out of a meeting. More info can be found on our website (www.2600.com/meetings). You can also find out when an issue is about to hit the stands on our main page.

Dear *2600*:

> *Hi my name is Ashmit. I guess you already know that lol. Anyways, I got your email from the www.2600.com website. The reason I am emailing you is because I was hoping you could help me out with a little something. I need to know whether you can gain access into a web server and its databases. If you can then we are set. Basically, here is the deal in a nutshell. I need someone with the abilities to get into my school server and change a few things. I have saved up $3500 over the past year for this and am willing to pay it in cash, as I am from the Winnipeg area. You do not have to worry about getting caught because I am sure as long as you erase your traces, there is no way of either one of us being caught, guaranteed. I hope you can help me out because I am extremely desperate.*
>
> ASH

"Desperate" doesn't begin to cover it. Whatever your problems, and we certainly won't try to minimize them, they are nothing compared to the world of hurt you'll enter if you do stupid things like offer complete strangers money to help you do illegal things. But even if you weren't a complete stranger we would tell you the same thing. And just where did you get this distorted view of the hacker world where this is the kind of thing we do? Yeah, we know—the mass media. It's still no excuse. There should be something in your genetic code that alerts you to the fact that you're doing something extremely stupid and wrong.

So we're clear, the offer was in Canadian dollars and not American, right?

Dear *2600*:

> *I have acquired info of a possibly useful or at least informative nature that could affect multiple governments. I acquired this info after being arrested for crimes related to it by the Secret Service. I am still going through the courts. Do you want this information?*

LeStat

You have to ask? That's what we're here for!

2005

Dear *2600*:

> *I'm just one lame kid from Serbia who wants to learn all of the techniques. I know a lot about hacker history, LOD, MOD, Kevin Mitnick, etc. Please help me to learn how to become an elite one day.*

TAMSTO

The first thing to learn is never to use the word "elite" as a noun. In fact, don't even use it as an adjective. It's radically lame. If you're really interested in learning, there is much you can ingest through these pages and by investigating on the net. It's not about doing things the way everyone else does. It's not about one particular form of technology or a series of steps. Rather, it's a state of mind that you can apply to almost anything in your life. It involves questioning, experimenting, persistence, thinking outside the box, and, above all, avoiding those people who latch onto the hacker community to be trendy. These are things you must develop within yourself; there are no magic answers to memorize. Once you have a hacker mentality (which comes quite naturally to many in the hacker world), you can then apply it to whatever you already have an interest in and begin to break new ground. Good luck.

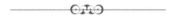

Dear *2600*:

> Just wondering why 2600 isn't a monthly or bimonthly publication? Thank you for your time and keep up the good fight.
>
> JASON

We're not monthly or bimonthly for the same reasons we're not weekly or daily. We're quite comfortable in the quarterly lifestyle.

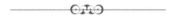

2006 ⎯⎯⎯⎯⎯⎯⎯⎯⎯⎯⎯⎯⎯⎯⎯⎯⎯⎯⎯

Dear *2600*:

> I have written an article that I am interested in publishing anonymously. I do have some concerns over the protection of my identity should the company I am writing about demand it of you. I have been a reader for about eight years now and would never have considered writing the article to begin with if I was not confident that your organization would keep my identity anonymous, but I guess I am just looking for a little reassurance before submitting it. I have sought legal advice on the topic and was told that if the company were to invest in identifying me and if they were to successfully identify me they might have a case for revealing corporate secrets. To be honest, even as I am writing this I seriously doubt this particular company would care to invest in finding me.... Then again....

Also, I know there are no strict guidelines for article submission as far as length, but my article is a little over 2000 words. Is that cool?

NAME REMOVED

First, we sure hope that wasn't your real name you used in that letter if you're this worried about keeping your identity secret. We can keep our mouths shut but many others can't. In all of the years we've been publishing, we have never given out the name of someone who didn't want their identity revealed. There have been unfortunate instances where information in the name someone used was enough for their employer to track them down and take action. That's why it's so important to not give away details of your location, name, appearance, or anything which someone could use the process of elimination in order to come knocking at your door. We take confidentiality very seriously, even if other members of the media don't. But you also have to take precautions on your end, such as not submitting something under the same username that people already know you by. If you wish to remain anonymous, just say so and we won't use any name at all to identify you. But even this may not be enough if you're sending email from an insecure location, such as your school or workplace. As for length, that's not something to worry about if your subject matter is interesting, which we suspect it is.

2007

Dear *2600*:

We're a group of young hacktivists from Canada and we are going to be starting our own printed mag. We're going to be breaking ground with some top notch articles and I'm sure a few of our articles will mention 2600. When they do, I'll email you again to let you know, as we would love to reference and tell people about your mag. Here's the thing: I am interested in hearing a short story about how 2600 got started and put on the stands all over. Any tips? Thanks in advance for the advice.

ALEXANDER CHASE

It sure wouldn't be a short story. The thing about starting a magazine is that it takes a really long time to develop from scratch. We began very small and grew to a size we were comfortable with. That's the most important bit of knowledge we can share with any new publication. If you start too big, you will burn yourselves out and go broke in the process. That's assuming you aren't already big with lots of money to invest. But then you're not really a zine. The key is patience and determination, coupled with a good dose of insanity. We wish you luck and look forward to seeing what you come up with.

Dear *2600*:

> *I just realized upon Googling my past screen names that a letter I wrote a while ago was published in your magazine but I didn't receive my free subscription! This is probably because I stopped checking my last email address and moved on to other emails.*
>
> MARCIO

It's also probably because we don't offer free subscriptions for letters. Look at how many letters we get! We would go bankrupt extremely fast. We offer free subscriptions for articles, which generally go into far more detail than letters. If, however, you were to send us a two-paragraph article and expect a free subscription for that (as many do), it would likely get converted into a letter if it were to get printed at all.

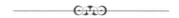

Dear *2600*:

> *What OS do you prefer: Windows, Linux, or Mac?*
>
> DAVIS

We don't discuss religion here.

Dear *2600*:

> Given that there are no guarantees in life anyways, what would you
> say to a curious one who wonders approximately when the deadline
> is for letters to the editor for the next issue? Thanks!
>
> OMID

We would say that you made the deadline. Congratulations.

Dear *2600*:

> Hey guys. Are you interested in Polish payphones? Well, if you are I
> could take some photos. Just tell me.
>
> suN8Hclf

While this somehow feels like we're entering into a drug deal, yes, we are inter-
ested. Hook us up. Thanks.

Dear *2600*:

> Do you have any surveys which show the most popular computer
> companies? Under each company what is the most popular computer?
> What is the most popular OS? Who has the best customer service? Do
> you have anyone who can write a program starting with DEBUG?
> Do you have anyone who does assembly language programming on a
> DOS/Windows OS? If so, what books does he recommend to help me
> learn this language?
>
> FK

Do you ever write anything that isn't a question? Most of what you're asking has
nothing to do with our subject matter, is way too general, and is really stuff that
you get to learn on your own after playing around with computers for a while.
You will find plenty of people willing to give you advice once you get involved.

2008

Dear *2600*:

> I always thought 2600 came from 2600Hz. Today a friend told me that Amiga 2600 was meant. Now we have some money on this question. Can you help me out with the proper answer?
>
> JAN

We can say with certainty that our name has nothing to do with the Amiga 2600. You probably meant the Atari 2600. We had nothing to do with that either. Nor did our magazine, whose very first headline on our very first front page in January 1984 shouted out "Ahoy!", have anything at all to do with the Commodore computer magazine named Ahoy! which started publication the same damn month. ("Ahoy!" incidentally is the correct quote of how Alexander Graham Bell used to answer the phone, despite what you might learn from certain televised cartoons.) Now that we've gotten all of that sorted, perhaps we should discuss what percentage we will receive of the bet we helped you win.

Dear *2600*:

> I'm a huge fan of 2600 and frequent visitor to your site. I've been reading the magazine (when I can find it) for over a decade now, since I was a freshman in high school.
>
> I'm writing to ask if you, or anyone who runs the site, knows the exact date the first issue of 2600 was published. I know it was January 1984 and that it probably actually hit the shelves of stores within the first week of the month, but I can't nail down any one day to credit the event to. I run a little blog called The Great Geek Manual where I write a daily chronology called "This Day in Geek History" and, as a fan, I would like to include the first publication of your magazine. In fact, I would love to include all the major milestones in the history of both your magazine and website, if anyone has any dates handy. It's not a very popular blog, just a few dozen readers, but I would really appreciate any help you could give me. Thanks!
>
> ANDREW

We didn't hit any shelves until years after we started publishing. In 1984 we were a fledgling monthly newsletter that only had three sheets of paper. Our first issue in January went out to several dozen people and was mailed sometime in the middle of the month. Those of you early subscribers may remember that we fell into the habit of mailing each issue on the 12th of the month for some reason. We hope that helps.

Dear *2600*:

> *How can I use the services of a hacker?*

ETSJOBS

Whereas most religions require you to pray or do some sort of penance in order to obtain the goods and services you desire, with hackers you have but to ask and pay our nominal fee. Obtain any password, change any grade, even travel back in time when necessary! Your wish (plus the fee) is our command. Now go tell all your friends.

Dear *2600*:

> *Tell me how much one of your hackers would charge me to delete my criminal record from the Texas police database.*

[NAME DELETED]

Well, we would start with erasing your latest crime, that of soliciting a minor to commit another crime. (Your request was read by a small child here in the office.) After you're all paid up on that, we will send out the bill for hiding your identity by not printing your real name, which you sent us like the meathead you apparently are. After that's all sorted, we can assemble our team of hackers, who sit around the office waiting for such lucrative opportunities as this to come along, and figure out even more ways to shake you down. It's what we do, after all. Just ask Fox News.

Dear *2600*:

> I have a lot of hacking-related pics on my phone and I was wondering how I should get them to you in a usable format since I do not have anything that will hook up to my computer to get the pictures off of the phone. Any advice would be very helpful.
>
> ERIK

It seems odd that you have a picture phone with no means of sharing pictures. If you can use email on your phone, you could always email them to us. If that doesn't work, you're just going to have to send us the phone. (And don't forget the charger.)

Dear *2600*:

> I'd like to publish two articles; can I meet a staff member?
>
> MUSIQUE MAISON

Not so fast there. You don't get a personal visit until you publish 20 articles! Nice try though.

Dear *2600*:

> What is the point of the meetings?
>
> DANIEL

Since we apparently won't fool you with the obvious reason, we can tell you the real one: to get people out of their homes on the first Friday of the month so that the monitoring devices can be installed.

Dear *2600*:

> Is it true that a subscription (paid by credit card) to your magazine would probably get you on an FBI watchlist?
>
> WYLLIE

If you believe such a thing exists, then making that list as large as possible is the best known way of fighting it. We have strong doubts that a list of this sort is out there, as we've heard all kinds of different versions of this fear expressed over three decades and we have yet to see any real evidence that supports the theory. But the danger of our surveillance state eventually reaching this degree of accountability certainly isn't beyond the realm of possibility and it almost seems as if there are members of the public who actually want something like this. Clearly, we represent those people who don't, and it's only through education and constant vigilance that we can stave off such a nightmare for the foreseeable future. People being intimidated into not getting a copy of our magazine only moves us closer to the oppressive scenario dreaded by so many.

2009

Dear *2600*:

> *My name is Tuyishime Aimable. I live in Rwanda. I joined the 2600 community a few months ago. I like what you are doing. The problem is that I can't attend any meeting or any other event because I live very far from you. So I would like to ask you if you could help me to grow in that community otherwise or help me promote the 2600 in my country.*
>
> AIMABLE

Contrary to popular belief, you don't have to live in the Western world or even have access to high tech in order to be part of the hacker community or to spread the enthusiasm of the hacker culture. If we look back at the really early days in our own country, hackers did just fine playing with rotary dial phones and glorified electric typewriters. While technology is often at the heart of it all, it's actually not just about the technology in the end. It's about the thought process. If you learn to think like a hacker, where you are and what you have access to will become secondary. By questioning everything—human or machine—and by constantly experimenting and sharing your findings, you'll be able to apply this hacker mind-set to almost any situation and, in so doing, find other like-minded individuals. This is another reassuring fact. There are always other people, no matter where you are, who will share your curiosity and passion. It's just a question of reaching them. So our advice is to use this distance as an opportunity to start something fresh and to be a real pioneer in your country. Just because you're far away from us doesn't mean that you can't start running your own meetings or events. Of course, every country is different with regards to rules, what is tolerated, and how individual thinkers are dealt with. So make sure you're familiar with what you're up against and what you're willing to fight for. As hackers are almost always heavily involved in freedom of speech issues, the reaction against them can sometimes be a bit heavy handed. This is true of any authority figure. So be aware of this, keep reading a lot, and always maintain a level of curiosity. You will find the hacker community all around you.

Dear *2600*:

> *First of all, I recently subscribed to 2600 and I love it.*
>
> *I was thinking of starting my own small quarterly magazine and was wondering if you had any advice. Thanks!*
>
> MICHAEL

We assume you're talking about starting an actual printed magazine as opposed to something online. Going print is a lot harder and has many challenges but we find the printed word is more enduring, if only because it requires a certain commitment that oftentimes doesn't exist in the glut of electronic prose. Naturally, there are exceptions on both ends of the spectrum but print is in our blood so we're naturally going to feel its magic.

The best advice we can offer you is to let your zine grow into a rhythm. Most new zines either overdo it and get burned out (or lose a ton of money) or don't put in enough effort and wind up never really going anywhere. You need to gauge your readership and figure out where your content is coming from and how much of it you can manage for each issue. These things take time and you will almost certainly not get it right from the start. The important thing is to realize that you will be putting effort, money, and material into this project and you may never wind up in the black. If you can accept that and work it out so that in the worst case scenario you don't lose a fortune, then you have a much better chance of evolving into a regular publication that might, at the least, break even. But, no matter what, having that printed object in front of you is an achievement you will be proud of for many years to come. That's why it's always better to try and fail rather than avoid failing by not trying.

Dear *2600*:

> *Hello. My name is Ray. I am visiting Honduras, and for way too long. A year too long. Is there any way that I can enter the Honduran database to alter my date of entry and my port of entry? Thank you for any help that you can give me.*
>
> Ray

So you'd like for us to erase a year off of your stay in Honduras? There's bound to be a good story in here somewhere and we'd really like to hear it. We have a hunch it might be a little more complicated than simply changing dates in one country's database. We'd probably have to change a second country's database, too. And mess with the memories of the people who were supposed to have seen you for the past year. It could get a little tricky. And, oh yes, expensive. But we've said too much.

2

Tales from the Retail Front

Hackers tend to involve themselves in every aspect of society, so it was inevitable that the retail world would become one of the more commonly addressed targets of their observations. Naturally, this didn't sit particularly well with the retail world.

In our earlier years, most of the attention focused primarily on phone networks and computer systems. The people playing with technology were mostly... well, *us*, and those people who were trying to keep us from playing with technology. Those would be the folks who *ran* the phone networks and computer systems. The Internet wasn't around and phone calls were still very expensive. If you were at a university, maybe you had a shot at playing with something a bit more advanced. Such opportunities were few and far between, though, for the masses.

But then the 1990s were upon us and all of a sudden technology began to explode all over the place. It was no longer something for the privileged few; everybody was getting in on the act. Where once it was a rarity to see even one bank machine, like a mutating virus they began to pop up everywhere, as did all sorts of strange payphones and other electronic gizmos for the consumer. People moved away from the BBS scene and into the world of the all-encompassing network, specifically the Internet, which became more and more commercial as the years went by.

A dramatic change was also noticed in the stores. First, *every* retail outlet now had computer systems for its own use, for the convenience of the customers, or simply to sell. So naturally, the hackers of the world descended in droves on the malls and wrote to us to share their experiences. Some were funny and some were painful. But they all represented the quest for knowledge and the desire to share information. It aggravated the retailers no end, but that was the cost of doing business in the technological age.

Stores like Radio Shack had *always* been an attractive target for hackers. It was, after all, one of the few places where you could just walk in and buy a computer in the early days. And Ratshack also had this really annoying policy of insisting on getting customers' names and addresses for each and every purchase, even if you were just buying a single battery! Always out to subvert the system, hackers figured out all kinds of ways to screen that little routine up, one of which was to always provide the corporate address of Radio Shack as their own, or even that of the very store they were standing in, no doubt so that it too would receive one of its own catalogs in the mail. Eventually, bad publicity and consumer outcry forced the chain to change its policy, and I can't help but wonder if hackers played some small part in that.

With the advent of electronic kiosks for everything from designer greeting cards to job applications, the hackers' playground expanded immensely. We like to believe that the mischief makers simply tried to figure out how to get around restrictions, like enabling a boring product search terminal to jump out and start surfing the web. Overreactions on the part of the managers were inevitable, but occasionally there were those who chose to listen and learn from what these intelligent pranksters were doing.

Of course there were those people who got the wrong idea of what it was all about, the ones who thought that stealing was cool or that the only interesting thing you could do with technology was break it. I can only hope that our words of admonishment to those types jolted them off the path they were heading down. If not, at least everyone else understood our position in no uncertain terms.

We also found ourselves increasingly taking on the role of consumer watchdog in some of these retail outlets, printing accounts of privacy intrusions being practiced by some of the major stores, or software being used by employees and repackaged as new, and even allegations that a major bookstore was keeping issues of our own magazine out of the hands of potential customers. Oftentimes these allegations led to rebuttals from employees and executives at these very chains, as well as the occasional legal threat. A truer exchange of ideas could not be found anywhere else.

1995 _____

Dear *2600*:

> *I was in Ratshack the other day and bought a 43-141 modem pocket tone dialer. It was the last one they had and they had it on sale for seven bucks. The next day I came in and tried to buy a 6.5536 mhz crystal. The guy looked on my "account" on the computer and saw that I had purchased a pocket dialer. He asked what I needed the crystal for and I told him that my dad needed it for a scanner. Then I saw*

a sign on the service desk that had a picture of the Ratshack Shack president and it said that they only wanted your phone number and address for sending out catalogs. I asked the guy about it and he said that he couldn't sell me the crystal. So the sign is just bull, I said, and he said that they also keep records to monitor possible illegal activities. I was wondering if I might possibly have a case of false advertising or something if I get the guy's voice on tape telling me that when the sign just says they want your info for a catalog.

AFRICAN HERBSMAN
LEXINGTON, KY

It's more a case of a blatant invasion of your privacy, one which should be followed all the way up the corporate ladder of Radio Shack. We'd be most interested in any responses. The most important lesson to be learned here is that nobody with any expectation of privacy should ever give his name and number to any retail outlet.

Dear 2600:

> *I was at Fry's (a large Silicon Valley electronics megastore chain) a couple of Saturdays ago with my sister, and it was really busy and as I was walking out, this security person said, "Excuse me, can I look inside your backpack?" I was taken aback and said, "What?" She then said, "It'll just take a moment. Let me look in your backpack." I said, "No," and continued to walk out the store. The nerve. I never once opened my backpack or removed it from my back while I was in the store. I didn't want to leave it in the car for fear of theft.*

> *I was at CompUSA (a computer megastore chain) the other day and once I walked into the lobby area (past the automatic glass doors), I started looking at their current newspaper ad posted on the wall. The security guard came up to me and said, "I need to look in your backpack." I shook my head and said firmly, "No." The guard was taken aback and then meekly pointed to this "sign" which said CompUSA reserves the right to search blah, blah, blah, etc. I just said, "Nope." This really ticks me off. I mean, if they saw me steal something and called the police, okay, then maybe they can look in my backpack. What are they thinking?*

This all seems like a great intrusion into what's left of my civil rights. Has any of this sort of stuff been covered in 2600?

SAM
BERKELEY

You're absolutely right—this is a great invasion of our rights. But we have nobody to blame but ourselves. We've created the type of suspicious society that begs for paternalism and doesn't mind if some rights are stepped on in the process. The sad fact is that an increasing number of stores are getting away with this kind of abuse, thinking that if they put it on a sign, they can do whatever they want. Some stores won't let you in unless you check your bags. Whether or not you agree with this method, it works much better since you simply aren't let in if you don't agree to their rules. By attempting to search your bags after you leave, there is no out for the customer except to create a scene. If you do create such a scene, you will win in the end since no store in its right mind will search customers against their will and risk massive lawsuits. It is also effective to "advertise" these policies when we find them. The future of such things is really in the hands of people like us.

1996

Dear *2600*:

> *Just last week I went to my neighborhood Costco (Price Club). They always have a screen saver and a password on each computer. I asked the guy in that department why they did that and he said some hacker would probably come in and erase everything on the computer. I wasn't too happy with this, so when he went to the bathroom I shut the computer off. It came back on in Windows 95 and I was able to make my own account. Then I looked at their screen saver. It said "Welcome To Costco" (because it was at the front of the building and everyone who came in saw it). I decided to change it and put in a new password. Now everyone who comes into the store sees a screen saver that says in big letters "Hack The Planet, Read 2600." When I was leaving, I saw the guy trying to guess the password. He'll never get it. It's BernieS.*

JAMEZ BOND

1997 ─────────────

Dear *2600*:

> *My Barnes and Noble store uses four AT&T PCs for looking up books. If the ISBN number X50 is entered (Author COFFEE, I; Title COFFEE), all coffee sales for the past year are shown. I haven't tried X[1-49] yet, but I thought you'd like to know.*
>
> BLACK JAGUAR

Anyone who can manage to publish a book with that title and author name stands to make a pretty penny.

Dear *2600*:

> *Keep up the great work! Your magazine has helped me out a lot. I'm a Barnes and Noble bookstore employee and I'm writing because I felt it was time to dispel some misinformation about the chain, as well as shed light on their proprietary computer system. First of all, in response to Ford's letter in Autumn '95, no, there is no concerted effort to hide copies of 2600. The shelves, and the magazine section in particular, are often in disarray, and due to the small format of 2600, it almost always winds up in the front of the rack. Paris Modeling was most likely left there by some dumb pre-teen. I know we would always put magazines like* Big Beautiful Women *(overweight centerfolds) and* Body Primitives *(really graphic piercings and tribal stuff) right in front next to* Knitting Monthly *to aggravate right-wingers. No, B&N doesn't track purchases of 2600 or any other zine (though it's always better to pay cash—heh-heh).*
>
> *Now to the phun stuff. As you have noticed if you have been in one of the B&N stores, they have a mess of dumb terminals where people look up books and do other stuff. This is mainly in contrast to Borders', whose info runs on a dedicated Windows box, where the OS is always accessible! B&N uses a slew of terminals in a star topology which downruns to two or more so-called "nodes." These will usually be in the back, generally one in the manager's office and one or more*

in the stockroom. These are garden variety 486SXs which run 95 percent of the store's computing horsepower, and which are configured to run blinds, i.e., without monitor or keyboard. The majority of the superstores, including all new locations, task an opsystem called "Wings" which handles title lookup, inventory receiving, all register functions, password management, and other bookish functions. The main screen is a char-based menu, consisting of "Title Lookup", "Customer Orders", "Cashiering", "Receiving", "Manifests", "Utilities", and "Quit". All of these require a two digit ID number and an alphanumeric password eight characters or less. When you have shoulder-surfed a login (preferably from a manager, because they have the greatest access) you are in business. (There is at least one default password which is to be used as a backup.) Try accessing "Customer Orders", F7 for "Old", then type in someone's last name, first (no space) to see what J.Q. Random is ordering. Or place new orders for your friends. Imagine their surprise when a hapless employee calls them in two weeks and explains that their copy of Coping with Irritable Bowel Syndrome *was delayed at the shipper and do they still want it? Accessing the cashiering functions requires both an id/login as well as a unique manager's id/login, but if you get this far, well, I hope you're looking over your shoulder, because this is thin ice. Doing any of this stuff requires some obvious computer usage which is supposed to be restricted to employees, so it might be a good idea to wear a shirt and tie or skirt as appropriate and carry some books (there are always new temps who nobody knows), or else come in a maintenance suit with a clipboard and some wrinkled work order.*

There is a secret configuration screen that most booksellers know nothing about (they are incredibly computer-illiterate), and which doesn't require the id and login. Pressing Alt + Shift (left) + Shift (right) simultaneously will open a complete diagnostic menu, which controls the screen, the keyboard, the menu display, and other niceties. Some fun can be had here. Press E to exit when done. Soon the system will be updated to include access to the Nationwide Books in Print Plus database from any of the dumb terminals, which'll be a handy reference to have at your fingertips.

The total sales figures, inventory adjustments, and other official hoo-doo is transmitted via modem through the ISP computer ("In Store Processor"—a 386 or better box which talks directly to New York), so that if the power fails all transactions are retained, etc. This is most likely some permutation of the store's fone/phax bridge; I really don't know. Good luck.

/DEV/THUG

Dear *2600*:

After reading /dev/thug's letter to you in Volume 14, Number 1, we had to send in a reply. We at the Barnes & Noble's support desk would like to thank him for the wonderful laugh.

In his letter he wants to dispel some misinformation about the store. He failed miserably. First off, the system is not proprietary. B&N likes using standard hardware and configurations because it makes supporting the system easier. As for the operating system, our friend must not be familiar with UNIX or DOS because that's what runs most of our stores. Only a few stores at this time are running Windows NT and I hope he knows how to recognize that!

/dev/thug must have picked up a computer dictionary somewhere and neglected to read the definitions of the big words he was trying to use to impress your publication. Not all our stores use a "star topology." A lot depends on the number of registers and nodes. The star topology is used in very small stores. Another thing: the main server does not "run blind." It has a monitor and keyboard. This is where the store runs the openings, closings, and other managerial functions.

The operating system he talks about is not called Wings. The operating system is QNX, a version of UNIX used for point of sales applications. Wings is just a label given to the system. As for the "secret configuration" screen of the DTs, it's not a secret. Anyone with any kind of computer knowledge knows that DTs and PCs have CMOS screens and that's all this is. There isn't much fun in playing around with these settings because almost any change made will either freeze the screen or make it go to a blinking cursor. This can be reset by hitting D to reset the defaults, S to save them, and F9 to exit. There is no E command as /dev/thug stated in his letter. He must be out of the info chain as far as development goes because the idea of putting Book In Print onto the store system was scrapped over a year ago. Instead B&N has chosen to create their own Title database that will be incorporated into the new system. And the best part... the ISP (In Store Processor) is a glorified word processor. The ISP has only two real functions: one is to keep track of the store's magazine inventory and the other is to let the store managers read their administrative messages (a cheesy form of email). It's not even a backup to the nodes. There are no modems connected to it even though sometimes one of the store modems is labeled "ISP modem." If the wiring is traced it goes nowhere near the ISP. There is no "fone/phax bridge"—it's two modems on the node. One is for polling and the other is for the store to shop vendors.

If /dev/thug had taken a few minutes to call us at Westbury, we would have gladly answered any technical questions he may have had. We don't mind taking time and going over the system. Having people in the stores who are educated on the system makes our job easier.

BARNES & NOBLE FINANCIAL CENTER
WESTBURY, NY

You may be getting a lot more educated people in your stores than you can imagine. Thanks for the info. We've now published letters from three different Barnes and Noble employees, all of whom are cool enough to share info rather than restrict it. Surely such people exist at other large chains....

Dear *2600*:

I was at a Kinko's copy shop doing some self-serve copies and I accidentally knocked the key-counter off the workstand two or three times. After I made the first batch of copies, I had to redo two pages. When I went to the check-out counter, the key-counter only had two clicks on it. I figure when the counter hit the floor, it must have unlatched the reset mechanism.

VIRTU-AL

We expect lots of key-counter dropping at Kinko's.

1998

Dear *2600*:

I just read the letter from your 15:2 issue from Greyhare about Software Etc. employees being able to take home games and bring them back to sell at full price. I would just like to confirm. I was best friends with a Software Etc. manager for a while. He could take any game home for two week periods, providing that they had enough copies left at the store for the customers. When he returned them, they would shrink-wrap the plastic back around the box and sell it as "new." Software Etc. and Electronics Boutique still have a "7 day no questions asked" return policy anyway, so there is no need to become an employee to take advantage of the "freeware" program. As far as I know, that's nationwide.

ENTROPIC

Well, it didn't take long for our readers to confirm this practice, which seems to be widely known in the software industry. Just further proof of the hypocrisy the software police call reality.

Dear *2600*:

I am writing in response to the letter in 15:2 written by Greyhare about being able to get software for free while working at Babbage's and Software Etc. I used to work for the company which owns Babbage's and Software Etc. and can confirm that you are correct, sir. Allowing the sales associates to take home any piece of software is considered an employee benefit. Under this system, employees are allowed to take home two products but must return them in three days. The product would then be wrapped again and put back on the shelves for sale. This was the system back when I left the company in '95. Another thing to note is that back when I started with the company, software was still primarily on 3.5" floppy diskettes and this policy was in effect. Their belief is that an employee is supposed to remove all the files that were copied or installed when they were finished checking out the software. Now whether it is legal or not, I do not know. This does bring up some *interesting legal issues because where I live, there are some video stores in the area that rent computer games. Another thing to note is that representatives from the software companies will come to the store and talk to you about their products to try and find out what you know about them. If you're nice to the reps you can receive a full legal copy of their software for either an extremely cheap price ($5 to $10) or even sometimes for free.*

FIGARO

None of this surprises us. But we find it amazing that organizations like Software Publishers' Association cry bloody murder when anyone else does similar things. SPA is strangely silent on this issue yet they emphatically state that schools aren't allowed to copy software they've already bought and individuals face a $250,000 fine and five years in jail for every piece of software they "illegally" copy. And they're talking about after you already paid for it! After all, they reason, when you buy software, you aren't really buying the software—you are only buying the right to use it! And we all know how Microsoft was crippled by all those people who made illegal copies of their products. Clearly, such policies are greed-motivated. How much money can possibly be brought in from the sale of the same copy of software? And how much will this go up if fear and intimidation are factored into the equation? Fortunately, there aren't all that many people who take these threats seriously—the employee policies of the retailers simply add further evidence to this.

1999

Dear *2600*:

The other day my friend and I were purchasing a few parts at a local Radio Shack store. We were browsing through the diodes looking for a 36-volt zeiner, when we overheard the manager talking to a new trainee. The manager said, and I quote, "The software on this computer is completely secure. You don't have to worry about anyone screwing it up." Being an avid reader of your magazine, and remembering the article "Screwing with Radio Shack and Compaq" from issue 15:3, I decided to correct the manager who, apparently, is not an enlightened reader of 2600. Just as they were leaving the Compaqs, I walked up and dropped the demo (you can Ctrl-Alt-Del when you get the start menu up and end the demo outright). I then opened up a DOS prompt, set the prompt to "These are not that secure,", and went back to shopping. Before I could purchase a few parts, she came up to me, her security pride shattered, and asked me to leave the store, never to return again. I guess some people can't stand being proven wrong.

PALADINE

Dear *2600*:

I am sure you have all seen the credit card boxes in most stores. They have an LED message bar at the top, a numeric keypad, and a place to swipe the card. I have seen them almost everywhere, including Blockbuster, Wal-Mart, and Ingles. They are out on the checkout counter for all the patrons to use. The heart of these machines is a simple modem setup. Hmmm, modem. The modem calls the store's system, wherever it may be, each time a credit card is used.

Here's the kicker. The setup program for each modem is accessed through the credit card boxes! I found this out by accident one day while messing with the box in Blockbuster. After trying different key combinations, I was prompted with the setup options on the little green LED screen! I reset the modem, and the system hung. The idiots working there were like "What the heck happened?" As it turned out, they apologized for a "power surge" (heh) and gave us our rentals for free!

So I know what you are thinking, "That's great, but how do I do it?" Well, the answer is simple. Every one of these machines is made by the same company, and therefore there is a default key sequence that will enter setup on most any machine. By default, no password is requested, however I have encountered machines with password protection (in Wal-Mart). To enter setup you must press the upper right and lower left keys simultaneously, then the lower right and upper left keys simultaneously. This should get you into setup on 90 percent of all boxes. If you find that the box is password protected, often it is the store number, which is on all receipts. I have rarely encountered protected ones. Apparently, most stores think that all the protection they need is an obvious key sequence. Typical.

Once you are in, there are plenty of options, such as changing the number to dial, resetting the modem, setting the baud rate, and even better stuff. I am not telling you this, though, so that you can steal credit card numbers; this is to simply give you more knowledge. If you steal credit card numbers, you are reflecting poorly on yourself and the hacker community, so don't. Have fun with this, and keep information free.

WillyL. AKA Yerba

This is an excellent example of what the hacker community stands for. In the eyes of the ignorant, there is no other use for this information except to commit a crime. There is nobody at our office who upon reading this didn't immediately head over to the 24-hour supermarket to try this out. It's what you do with the knowledge that determines what kind of person you are. There are those who would already condemn you for telling us and certainly they would condemn us for telling the world. Playing around with such a system may get you into trouble but it's little more than curiosity and experimentation, both healthy things. Now, if you rig the thing to call a number and approve your fake credit card, you become a thief as soon as you start stealing. That defines where we draw the line: at the actual commission of a crime. Not the spreading of information, not the theorizing, not even the experimentation. Vandalism and theft are easily defined yet our critics want to muddy the waters by extending their definitions to encompass speech and simple mischief. All this will accomplish is to create a whole new population of so-called criminals. Unfortunately this seems to be a growing trend.

Dear *2600*:

Recently I was in Borders Books and I really wanted to get this Linux book with a three disc set but it cost 70 bucks. I only had $30 on me. It just so happened that there was an older edition of that book that was only $29.99. I swapped the price tags. When I went to the front counter, the lady didn't even think twice when she asked for 30 bucks. I started to get really curious about this. I came back the next day and found another expensive book but this time switched the price tag with a book on a completely different subject. I went to the checkout and the lady said it was the wrong tag and she had to look up the real *price. A few days later I was at CompUSA and they had two versions of Visual C++: professional, which was $450, and learning, which was $80. I switched those tags and it worked.*

SenorPuto

Good one. Now try this. You can avoid the hassle of paying entirely by simply running out the door while holding the item you wish to take. This may result in loud noises, shouting people, and sirens of various sorts. We suggest experimenting as much as possible and keeping a log of what different stores do. And if by some bizarre twist of fate you wind up in a courtroom, show the judge this letter. They need to laugh, too.

Dear 2600:

As a 43-year-old computer abuser who has been around since the day of the 8086 dual 360 floppy CPM, green monochrome screened speed demon, I have something to get off my chest. Although I don't usually share this information with anybody, but I just had to let you know I pinched your magazine from Borders Books just because I was curious and I dig the rush. I can't remember a magazine I have enjoyed more or learned more from than yours. I sincerely hope that you were paid up front or have your books on consignment with these chain stores, because I feel guilty as hell for taking something so valuable. It's not that I couldn't afford the book, I just wanted to take it out for a test drive.

pArtYaNimaL

We've always looked down on stealing simply because of the inherent dishonesty involved. People who think that's somehow what hackers are about just don't get it. But in this case, you hurt us as well since stores stop carrying us if issues get "pinched" and, most especially with the smaller publishers, zines wind up paying for missing issues. So, if you want to hurt us and tarnish the image of hackers at the same time, just keep doing what you're doing. Otherwise we hope you find some other way to show your distaste for corporate America.

2000 —————————————————————————————

Dear *2600*:

> I was in Blockbuster a few nights ago and when I was waiting for
> them to ring up the movie, I was messing around with the credit card
> machine—you know, the one they let you slide your card in and punch
> in the numbers yourself. Anyway, I started messing with it, and when
> I punched in enter and 1, I got a setup message. It would let me set
> up new passwords and all, but I was more interested in the baud rate
> setup for it. My question is what can I do with this info.

CASHMOLIA

*Depending on what kind of person you are, you can either learn how their system
operates or really screw things up and probably get in a mess of trouble. Hopefully
the people running these systems will also learn how incredibly badly they're set
up in the first place.*

Dear *2600*:

> Cheers to all those people out there who have enough courage to come
> forward and expose the secrets of so many chains. We should all ap-
> plaud the risk they are taking and their willingness to do it nonethe-
> less. Hopefully, all those stores that have been overcharging us, the
> consumers, for years will finally see that if they don't change their
> ways the consumers will strike back. I hope you, the good people at
> 2600, will continue to print these articles as well as ignore the idiotic
> requests of these stores.

GAS FUMES

*More like demands, you mean. But we don't print information for the purpose of
revenge. We print information, period. We like to learn about how things work. We
don't advocate using what we print in a destructive way, even when it may appear
to be justified.*

Dear *2600*:

This is to all of you out there who enjoy McDonald's. I work at McDonald's and during my three months of flipping burgers I have uncovered some very interesting information about their computer systems.

The managers at McDonald's have a three-digit clock-in number. Most managers use their three-digit clock-in number as their system op code, which is a six digit number. For instance, Sue, the imaginary manager, has the clock-in number of 106. She is not too bright. Sue uses her clock-in number twice over to make up her six-digit password, like 106106. All employees have a three-digit number but if you are not management then your number is a double digit represented with a 0 in front like 061.

In each McDonald's, there is a main server in the manager's "office" which controls the entire store. Every order that beeps on the screen is controlled by the system. This system can easily be accessed from a remote location by knowing the number of the store. Here comes the tricky part. It has to ring five times in order for the system to pick up. Easily solved by knowing what time they close. Just call at like three in the morning. (After the store closes people stay around three more hours to clean up.) Once connected you are prompted for a password.

Now we are stuck with the dilemma of not having a manager password. You can get this a couple of ways. First, every Sunday night McDonald's does a system dial-up. This task is completed by the lazy manager before closing. What happens is the manager sends info to the company through dial-up and it prints out a long sheet of receipt paper containing all the hours each employee worked that week and (aha) each employee's clock-in number. To obtain this sheet you must do some trashing and get a little messy unless you have connections. The second way to get a manager's number is eat a lot of McDonald's food and wait for an employee to go on break. When the employee orders food they get a half price discount and they need a manager to type in the code so they can get their munchies. Just lean over and flirt with an employee about the same time the uncaring manager types in their code.

BIG MAC

Dear *2600*:

> *I am a Barnes and Noble employee and I would like to state my opin-*
> *ion on what some readers are saying about Barnes and Noble being*
> *against free information for all. That is a fallacy. Barnes and Noble*
> *will order any book that you want. But we do apply the age regulation*
> *laws for selling pornography. 2600 is not a pornographic publication*
> *and therefore can be sold to a person of underage status. There was a*
> *letter in 16:4 from a former B&N employee stating that the memo of*
> *Tom Tolworthy meant that if deemed inappropriate, it could be put*
> *behind the counter. Tom Tolworthy meant Playboy, Penthouse, and*
> *controversial books such as the work of Robert Mapplethorpe and*
> *Sally Mann, not 2600!*
>
> *In the B&N I work at, 2600 is right in the computer section on the*
> *second shelf in full view. There has never been any debate of 2600*
> *being put behind the counter. The fact is that my bosses do not know*
> *what 2600 is. To them it could be a comic book.*
>
> *This is a company that put the South Park soundtrack on the music*
> *section listening stations! This is a company that sent the store a CD*
> *for an in-store play, and there were cocaine references in one of the*
> *songs! Give the company a break! They pay my bills and give me*
> *medical insurance!*
>
> ANONYMOUS BARNES AND NOBLE MUSIC SELLER

But what would happen if your bosses did know what we were about? What would
happen if they themselves didn't approve? Our reading of the memo makes us fear
that individual managers, or even clerks, could relegate us to behind the counter if
they felt we were unsuitable. This kind of power is too easily overused and abused.
We've gotten letters about this sort of thing in the past and we'd appreciate spe-
cific details from our readers if they encounter this at any store from any chain. This
will allow us to pursue the matter with the store or chain and, in the worst case sce-
nario, at least know not to send any more issues there.

Dear *2600*:

It has come to our attention that you have published an article, alleg-edly written by a former employee of Staples. The article itself concedes that it is written by a former disgruntled employee who is volunteering trade secrets and proprietary information of Staples. The clear intent of this article is to encourage malicious destruction of property and stealing. Should you choose to continue to provide assistance to this individual's criminal activities as well as criminal actions by others, you are, of course, subjecting yourself to liability.

In addition, in publishing obviously misappropriated trade secret in-formation, you are open to liability for any damage we may suffer. While you are certainly free to publish any publicly available informa-tion, the publication of obvious trade secrets and misappropriated pro-prietary information obtained in breach of fiduciary and contractual obligations is not protected by the First Amendment.

Staples is a strong supporter of the World Wide Web and the benefits of the Internet. However, the protection of confidential and proprietary information and the maintenance of the integrity of passwords and other security devices is essential to the functioning of the Internet. Just as you would protect the privacy of your subscribers and their confidential information and keep your own and other confidential information safe from hackers, we have an obligation to maintain the integrity of our trade secrets and proprietary information. As a legal matter, we cannot tolerate the publication of trade secret information as it puts in jeopardy very valuable rights of Staples.

If you reflect for a moment, you must recognize that as a publisher, you have similar interests in protecting the integrity of the security of pri-vate information and passwords. In failing to respect these rights you stand to lose them. Should you find yourself a victim of a disgruntled employee or hacker who seeks to damage or destroy your business through revelations of proprietary secrets, or private information of yours or your subscribers, you would find yourself without a remedy at law due to the defense of "unclean hands." Your enemies, hackers or disgruntled employees or subjects of your publications will undoubt-edly take the position that you are barred from protecting rights that you violate.

Under all of these circumstances, we have no choice but to insist that you remove from any material you continue to publish any of our trade secrets, including passwords and confidential information concerning our security systems. In addition, we hereby demand that you identify the author of the article "Messing with Staples" so that we may pursue our legal remedies and take appropriate action against this individual. We hope to avoid the need to include you in any legal proceedings. However, in order to maintain the important protections of our property, we have no alternative but to vigorously defend our trade secrets and proprietary information. Consequently, you can be certain that we cannot simply let this matter drop. We hope that you will respond responsibly and immediately, but if we do not receive a satisfactory response to this letter by 5:00 pm on Friday, January 28, 2000, we will pursue our legal rights.

Jack A. VanWoerkom
Senior Vice President,
General Counsel
Staples

Thanks for the friendly advice on freedom of speech and protecting our privacy. It really made us think. While we were doing this, we realized that we've been publishing this magazine for longer than Staples has been in existence. And while we appreciate the suggestions on how to run our business, we feel your needs would best be suited if you simply minded yours.

You claim to have the "obligation" to protect sensitive information. Why doesn't that obligation extend to implementing proper security? Or are threats and intimidation the only methods you know of to protect privacy?

In the interests of space, we'll overlook your repeated misuse of the word "hacker." But one thing we're really curious about is what the so-called "trade secrets" are that you wish to keep quiet. The fact that one of your stores used a password of "password" on a publicly accessible machine? (You do use different passwords at different stores, don't you?) The previously unknown "Ctrl-Alt-Delete-End Task" trick to drop into Windows 95? Or the fact that we exposed the true identify of Fred Klein?

There is nothing in the article that any reasonable person would consider to be a trade secret. Of course, we've wandered into the corporate world again, haven't we?

And as for your "demands," you really should know better. We will never reveal a source without that source's explicit permission. And we won't cave in to threats of any sort. You may think this is a good opportunity since we're already embroiled in a lawsuit filed by the entire motion picture industry. That would be another mistake to add to your already impressive list.

2001

Dear *2600*:

After reading Jeff's letter in 18:2, I had to chime in. While in college I worked for Radio Shack. I was fired for allowing my phone number percentage (the amount of phone numbers required for maintaining a position at the Tandy retailer) to fall below 92 percent. Since I only worked on the weekend, if more than one customer asked me not to include their information, then I immediately fell below the quota. I suppose I could have found some malicious way to find retribution but instead I landed a six-figure position in the tech industry and am alive and well in LA.

As a side note: Each Radio Shack collects customer information on a daily basis and uploads it to a secure server at the home office in Texas at the end of each night. This is done via a dial-up 56K USR point-to-point connection when the store manager closes out for the evening. As part of the process, the manager is given a printout that includes the activity for that transaction which is typically filed away for safe-keeping. As time goes by these printouts become cumbersome and are supposed to be shredded. In my experience through the four stores that I had worked at, the managers typically just throw them out.

The collected data is used for a myriad of things. The management always told us that when confronted by customers as to why we ask for this we were to "just tell them that it's collected so that we can send them a catalog." We know that this is an untrue statement since you have to either make a purchase to get a "free" catalog or make a formal request. I can only imagine how valuable this user list would be to other vendors. Ever notice the arrival of a Crutchfield catalog after making a purchase at Radio Shack?

Needless to say, they take collecting this data very seriously. The next time you go in to buy a capacitor and are grilled for ten minutes on where you live and what your favorite color is, refuse and watch the clerk's temperature rise. There is so much pressure put on these folks to gather data that they will often add fake customer info to your receipt if you decline so that they can come back to work the next day (a practice that I refused to do and thus was released from employment). What do you expect from a company that pays its employees $4.25 an hour?

HANOVERFIST

2002

Dear *2600*:

Recently I was in Toys"R"Us and was walking by their "for employees only" computer station. The inventory (I'm assuming) program was moved off to the side of the screen and I noticed the all too familiar blue "E" Internet browser on the desktop. The Start button, My Computer, etc., buttons were not present, but clicking on Explorer got me access to the local drives, etc. Just for giggles I entered "www.2600.com" and was surprised to see that there was an active Internet connection. Joy. I had my wife and kid with me so I saved the "old 2600 masthead" as the desktop and closed the Explorer window. On my next visit that computer station was powered down, but the adjacent system was on. You can't minimize the inventory program, but you can drag it out of the way and play around if you like. I left a token of my esteem on that desktop as well and out of curiosity I flagged down an employee and asked if the computer that was powered down was for customer use. He said no, both were for employee use. I asked if it was broken or anything because I could repair it for a modest fee. He said he didn't know but the assistant manager might.

The assistant manager told me they had powered down the system after "a hacker broke into it and left a virus" and that they had an outsourced contract company coming to look at it. I acted astonished and told them I hoped they could straighten it all out. I suggested they should make some changes to their system to make it harder to get into. The assistant manager in all his infinite computer knowledge assured me "if a hacker wants in, there's nothing you can really do to stop them." Wow, maybe that's an untrue stereotype we should get behind!

MOON KNIGHT

Dear *2600*:

I just finished your Spring 2002 issue. I was shocked to read the letter "The World of Retail" on page 37. I didn't know anyone else did that sort of thing. At the B&N near me, 2600 along with Adbusters are relegated to the back of a shelf. At first I thought it was a mistake just like TheDude did—not so. Minutes after moving 2600 and Adbusters to their deserved and prominent positions, they were once again subverted, this time beneath an overhanging shelf. At this point my friend and I took it upon ourselves to make a decisive change. Having about 15 or 20 of each in our hands, we proceeded to place one magazine in front of every other magazine on the rack. It really looked nice and I've been back to the store several times to find both Adbusters and 2600 in the very front at eye level of their respective sections. Unfortunately this is the only place that sells either or both of the magazines in my area, but a tragedy was certainly averted.

SIGNAL9

There's a difference between poor placement and placement specifically designed to keep us hidden. We're obviously more concerned with the latter as it's a deliberate attempt to silence our words. We appreciate your efforts but encourage readers not to disrupt operations at your local store by making a mess of their system. If you suspect foul play, get as many specifics as you can and let us know. It's made a big difference in the past.

2003 _____

Dear 2600:

An interesting thing happened to me yesterday. I had gone to Office Depot to try to find an organizer for school and was waiting around while my mother looked throughout the store. I saw the computer section where all the floor models were being shown off and decided to have a little fun. I went up to one of the computers (they were all running Windows XP) and logged in to the guest account to play around a little. After a while I got bored of this and decided to see if the Administrator account was open. (Any Windows OS based on Windows NT has a default Administrator account with no password.) I logged out of the guest account, then tried first to log into the OfficeDepo account (which was a password protected admin account). Since I couldn't get in that way, I decided to try the default Admin account. From the login menu I held down the Ctrl and Alt keys and pushed Del twice, thus bringing up the Windows 2000-style login box. I typed "Administrator" as the username and left the password box empty, then clicked "Log in." Sure enough, the store had not set the password for the Administrator account and had left it completely open. So I decided to play around a little with the user accounts. I opened up the User Accounts control panel and changed the Office Depot's Guest account to Administrator level, then took the password off of the OfficeDepo's admin account. As I was doing this, one of the store employees walked by and asked if I was finding everything to be satisfactory. I said "yes" and he went on his way, paying no attention to what I was doing. I was amazed at how blind these people could be at times, but continued my tinkering.

I decided to change the Administrator account password, and as I was changing it, another one of the employees walked up and said "trying to change the password, huh?" Freaked out a bit by his inquiry, I told him that I was "just seeing what the system could do." His next remark surprised me, though. He smiled with a smug expression on his face (like the "I know something you don't know" look) and said "Go ahead, change it. I'll show you a little trick." Well, at this point it was obvious to me that he wasn't going to kick me out of the store or anything. It seemed that he was challenging me to lock him out of his own computer. So I complied with his wishes and put a password on the Administrator account. He then asked me what the password was and I told him, and I then explained to him that I had accessed the hidden Administrator account, which by default has no password. I told him all I knew about it and he was surprised by this information, as he hadn't known of this vulnerability before.

After I told him how it was done, he proceeded to log in to the OfficeDepo account and remove the Administrator account password by changing that account in the Users control panel. I knew of this trick but was surprised that it worked on the default Administrator account. After the little demonstration I chatted for a while about computer security and the failure of the Blaster worm and left the store encouraged and smiling. I figured most people would overreact to what I was doing, but instead the man had actually treated me civilly and kindly and even talked with me about security. I'm glad that not everyone in this world has unjust misconceptions of hackers. I just hope that I'll meet more people like this in the future. The man even waved and said "have a nice day" as I left (though it's possible that's just a part of his job).

theXorcist

This goes well beyond someone just doing their job. That person had a very healthy outlook towards technology, one we would all do well to imitate. He wasn't afraid of what you might do to the system because he understood the basics of how it worked and he was confident in its overall design. He was also willing to listen and learn something new, an attitude that results in people (especially hackers) explaining what they know, as you did. This kind of thing happens all too rarely but it's always good to see it take place.

Dear *2600*:

In 20:3, C.B. Cates wrote a good article about ripping off Blockbuster by way of calling in a wrong-store return. Actually quite intelligent, but Blockbuster has been aware of this possibility for quite some time and they're starting to train their employees to treat every wrong-store return as if it were a fake. There's a distinct and meticulous method and systematic answer-and-response now that sounds more like exchanges between KGB diplomats half a century ago than employee interaction at a rental store. Also be aware that any employee (and certainly manager) with any sense will know the store numbers and addresses of most every store in the district. And, if not, they're all listed by the telephone in the first place. Best of luck, but know that the prospect of this working is dropping quickly, especially with the amount of shrink many stores are getting.

POETICS

We're glad they got the wake up call.

2004

Dear *2600*:

A few issues back a reader of yours talked about how many stores with computers on display use the store ID as the password. If you think that's low security, try shopping at CompUSA! Only took one guess to get into their forbidden account. I got on one of the Macs there and attempted to switch from "Customer" to "Compusa," which gave me a prompt for a password. Just as I was doing this, an employee came over to sell me something so I entered "compusa" as the password and started to walk away because I thought the employee would get peeved when he saw the prompt but it logged right into the employee account whose desktop looks identical to the customer one so he didn't even notice. I've since gone back and tried this on the other display computers. All of them use the compusa/compusa login! They're overcharging for the speakers I wanted to buy so I decided not to say anything. By the way, great magazine and radio shows!

ERIC M.

Dear *2600*:

> *This is an update to the "coupon trick" article printed in 20:2. I was so intrigued by the article that I immediately began making up some coupons for a test run at a local department store chain called Fred Meyer. I knew they had recently installed self-checkouts and was eager to see if the trick worked. Well, it did work but I found myself wanting more. In the original article the author discovered that a 30-cent coupon had the numbers 3030 in the barcode and that by changing them to 7575 the coupon was instantly a 75 cent coupon. The problem is that his basic method is limited to a cents amount, or a maximum of 99 cents. I wanted to make up coupons worth dollar amounts. After clipping every coupon out of the Sunday ads I compared all of the $1 coupons and all of the $2 coupons and so forth. Well, it was very easy to figure out that all of the $1 coupons had the exact same code as each other and all of the $2 coupons had the exact same code as each other and so forth. I searched for the coupon with the highest value and ended up with a $7 coupon for Crest whitening strips. I merely wrote down the two digit code used to represent $7 and applied that code to a coupon I had for a box of Tide laundry detergent. I printed up the coupon and used it on an $8 box of Tide and sure enough it subtracted $7 and gave me a grand total of $1. Happy shopping and enjoy!*
>
> CLINT

Let's once again make it clear what the difference is between hacking and stealing. Discovering the vulnerability, figuring out the system, and testing it are examples of hacking. But you seem to have vaulted over to the stealing community, which really doesn't involve much in the way of skill and simply turns you into a dishonest person. And don't try to use the "unfair prices" logic as the people (most likely in the store) who have to cover the difference are probably a lot more innocent than you. We only ask that you do us one favor. When you get caught and prosecuted, don't go telling the authorities that you hacked the system. All you did was mess around with one part of it in a very crude manner.

2005 _____

Dear *2600*:

> *I hope LabGeek (21:4) was told the truth and Wal-Mart is paying $2,000 per anti-theft shopping cart! At Food 4 Less in Southern California nobody knows, but best guess seems to be $500 with two locking wheels.*
>
> *There is a yellow line around the store but the triggers for the wheels (which lock up very nicely) are wires buried in the asphalt or under the sidewalk. I tried going around the yellow line and it locked up where the wires had been put in the pavement.*
>
> *A manager said they have lost no carts in the three weeks since they got the system although it does seem anybody with a couple of wrenches could swap out the locking wheel for the non-locking ones pretty quickly.*
>
> *The manager said they had a sort of remote control key that could unlock the carts easily so it is probably an RF trigger. I know a compass shows nothing funny around the lines so it is not a simple magnetic device.*
>
> *This does lead to the question of what frequency and if it is coded....*
>
> OWA

Dear *2600*:

> *I recently bought an item at Wal-Mart in another state and decided I no longer wanted it. So I returned it at our local Wal-Mart (as they nicely allow us to do). The catch, however, is that the tax rates differed between the states by 2.5 percent. When I purchased the item, I paid roughly $63 with 6 percent tax. When I returned it, they calculated the price with the local tax information (8.5 percent) and gave me back roughly $65. I'm not sure if anyone else had this happen to them, but I found it amusing.*
>
> NETSURF

Dear *2600*:

Re: "Best Buy's Uber Insecurity" in 21:4, I'm going to have to either call a bluff on this one or say it's a fluke.

As an ex Best Buy technician I can tell you that the hack that was described would not be possible in all Best Buy locations. The network the writer most likely connected to was one of the "geek squad," which is on a VLAN of the store's regular network. Web access is restricted through the use of a proxy server (168.94.74.68:8080). All Best Buys are uniform in setup. The wireless network that the remotely located registers are a part of have to go through the proxy server.

Therefore the writer must have connected to the "geek squad" network (which needs proxy address anyway) or the writer was in a new Best Buy location that is different from the other 650 or so. Changing blocked ports wouldn't necessarily allow access to the web. The biggest indication that I have that the writer connected to the GS network and not the store network is the 192 address. BB corporate-controlled networks are 10.10 networks.

Interestingly enough, once on the store's internal network any employee's credentials give access to many different things. Even the logins of terminated employees or those who have quit still work sometimes.

One of the interesting hacks that we pulled off while I worked there was exploiting the punch in/out process. We used a simple application to punch in and out. The app verified your time in/out with the system's clock! The system's clock was verified by the bios clock. The bios was not password protected. So... if you get my drift, punch in anywhere, find a terminal that you could get to bios from, alter bios clock. Ten minutes' work just turned into ten hours' work. Easy to catch if you're doing it in large increments.

Obviously the way to protect against this is to lock the bios out with a password and write software that checks a controlled clock.

KAOS

Dear *2600*:

> *I recently went to Disneyland and noticed something interesting. Disneyland now has a bag check like at the airport. If you have a backpack, they ask you to open the pockets. The first check I went through, the lady gave a quick glance and let me pass. At first I laughed. If they were checking for bombs, this made no sense. Why be so brief? I then suspected they were checking for food, so I did a quick experiment. I put a can of soda and some chips in my bag the next day. Again the lady quickly looked at my bag and let me pass. Near the end of our trip, my sister got a teddy bear in a large box. The box had a small hole in it and as the lady checked it, she looked in the hole and gave it one shake. Why is Disneyland wasting so much money on such laughable "security?" We may never know. I just wanted to know what you guys thought of this.*
>
> *By the way, great mag. I am 13 and I love it though I don't understand half of the code.*
>
> S<small>AM</small>

Disneyland is a microcosm of the United States. The same silly security practices they use there can also be found in many other places. It's really all designed just to give an illusion of safety. And maybe also to make us laugh.

Dear *2600*:

> *I am in an interesting position. I am currently an employee of a McDonald's, the only job I could get in the area at 17. I used to be a computer repair tech with a company in my hometown and I've been hacking my computers, commercial radios, and vintage cell phones for years. In a few days at 10 p.m., the McDonald's restaurant where I am employed will be shut down for system upgrades until around 5 a.m. All computer systems, routers, network switches, point-of-sale equipment, modems, UPS systems, printers, and racks will be pulled out and replaced with new equipment as the McDonald's Operating Corporation sees fit. I already have an agreement with the store manager and a representative of McOpCo allowing me to collect any equipment I feel I can use or resell.*

If you've never been an employee of McDonald's you would be shocked at how the management treats the employees and the things that go on behind the scenes. Employees are monitored 24/7 with cameras and microphones. (I'm not imagining this. Electret condenser microphones dangle from the ceiling panels and I have already written chapters of information on the security system.) Add to that the McPropaganda posters everywhere in the bowels of the restaurant, the overall Orwellian feel to everything, and you can probably see where I'm going with all this.

I'm going to be bringing home thousands of dollars' worth of computers loaded with proprietary software. I'd just like to get a sense of the interest in an article exposing the entire system. I've already done a write-up on the Internet-accessible surveillance setup that the store managers use to watch us from home.

To keep all of this on the legal side, after the article is written, some of the hard drives will be formatted and most of the formatted equipment will be sold on eBay, minus what I want to keep. Being an amateur radio operator, I have a hobby that takes a lot of money. If I get fired for this, I really don't care. Unlike my sad little managers, I'm actually going to college.

JON

Our interest in an article like this is of such a magnitude that we doubt expressing it in words would adequately convey our enthusiasm. We will be waiting by the mailbox. (We also took the liberty of removing your last name, call sign, and location from your letter as that most certainly would have gotten you fired. This is one of those rare occasions where we've chosen to err on the side of caution.)

2007

Dear *2600*:

A few months ago I wandered into a Cingular retail location and wanted to find out how much information about my account they had access to. I acted as if I wanted to pay my bill and had some other questions about my account. I told one of the sales reps my cell number and he punched it into the computer and up came all of my info, including my address, date of birth, last four digits of my Social Security number, and call history. I watched the screen as he looked at my account. Unfortunately, the rep didn't even know who I was since he didn't ask me to identify myself nor did he ask for the passcode *I explicitly told Cingular to put on the account when I first got service. More astonishingly, the passcode was displayed in plaintext on the computer screen in red color! I assume he was supposed to ask me to confirm it. Oops.*

Disturbed by this, I next went to one of the Cingular franchise stores instead of a corporate store like the first one. Again, I simply said I had some questions about my account, gave the woman my cell number, and she pulled up the record and allowed me to look at it. She didn't ask who I was or confirm any account information or the passcode. The only difference was the look of the web-based application she was using, and the fact that she did *ask for my ZIP Code when she first punched in the cell number. Recently I found out that the franchise stores now need to put in the last four digits of the SSN to access the account. Still, the passcode is displayed in red for them to see.*

I'm really disappointed to see this easy availability of my cell phone records, especially after the scandal last year in which anyone could pay $100 to get a call history through pretexting. I didn't even have to pretext to get this info. I could've been anyone going into the stores and giving them any phone number since they didn't verify my identity. Then I could've called customer support with the passcode that I could see onscreen and do whatever I wanted. The big question is why does an in-store sales rep even need access to accounts that have already been set up? Their job is to sell and activate new phones. They could still accept bill payments without having access to existing customer accounts. Allowing in-store sales reps to have account access is much less secure than having that info available only in a call center. For one, the interaction isn't being recorded, and the store reps are open to bribing, whereas call center reps are much less likely to be able to accept bribes due to logistical reasons.

On the Cingular webpage they state:

> *"As you may have read or seen in the media, a number of web-sites are advertising the availability for sale of wireless phone records. Please know that Cingular Wireless does not sell customer information to, or otherwise cooperate with, these companies, and we are working aggressively to combat their practices.... Cingular is supporting efforts to criminalize the unauthorized acquisition or sale of wireless phone records. In addition, Cingular has a variety of safeguards in place to protect against unauthorized access to customer information, and we continue to evaluate and enhance these safeguards. If you wish to better protect your account from unauthorized access, contact us at 1-866-CINGULAR (1-866-246-4852) and ask that a passcode be placed on your account."*

Well, they can start the criminal investigation with their own in-store sales people.

As a side note, I also saw a small colored graph of some kind on my account's main page, which indicated how much revenue I brought in relative to other customers. I asked the rep what it was and that's when he got uptight and said I wasn't even supposed to be looking at the computer. I guess this graph tells call center reps how valuable I am as a customer.

DAVE

As long as there are human beings in the equation, security holes like this are going to exist in one form or another. Education, not automation, is the answer.

Dear *2600*:

> *I'd like to respond to "Target: For Credit Card Fraud" from 24:3 with a bit of skepticism. First, I cannot see how he has done "more good than harm" by exposing this info about hacking into Target's internal network by not doing anything for "over a month" and then writing*

an article about how he illegally played around in it while he worked there and not showing any evidence of reporting this security flaw to any Target authority. I am not trying to bash on 2600 for publishing it, but really, should these kind of articles get published?

I mean this guy is writing an article to a hacker mag a month after being an employee of that company reporting a flaw in their network and pretending to be a bad-ass, remaining anonymous, and pointing out how this information is only for advice to the company to change their security system.

He did not mention what position he held, but we can assume he did not have an authority position since he mentioned that he played around on the internal network from registers to computers in the employment kiosks along with managers' and backroom computers, therefore implying he was a ground worker without an office (therefore not part of the tech group) and that he did not do his job, but rather played around with people's information like a little kid writing amateur DOS batch files to retrieve this info.

A big concept that slipped my mind when I first skimmed through this article is that, if this kid knows all of this "techie" knowledge, why in the heck was he working at Target in the first place? Obviously this kid is either exaggerating or lying about the "break-in" he actually employed on the network. Discouragingly, this kid did not last long enough to explore the whole entire network. Oh golly! What a shame! He couldn't steal more credit card info or at least feel like he was stealing some valuable information that anyone can get access to. Come on, registers? In no way are they involved enough in the network to even have employee info. I've worked with registers in similar stores. You have no access to anything except a big calculator for retards.

In summary, this kid is either exaggerating on what he found or he is flat out lying. I've learned never to trust a source unless others can back it up and this is a good example of it.

Kid, I suggest you stop child's play and start doing what they pay you for and let the real techies worry about security breaches.

> It just sickens me how anyone can write a BS article such as this and get it published. In no way is this article helpful to the readers, the mag, or Target for that matter. Don't wait a month to write a vague article on a company's poor security unless you report the flaw to the company first! If you don't, then you are indeed doing more harm than good, and shouldn't include the BS about "please do not use this info for malicious purposes." People like this make a bad name for hackers.
>
> F33DY00

Do you really believe that there are no intelligent people working at Target who have "techie" knowledge? There are people everywhere who know things that may be a lot more than what's needed for their jobs. And regardless of whether or not this writer should have reported the information to his local supervisor before revealing it to the world, what's important is that the information wasn't kept secret. We've seen plenty of examples of how reporting something to your boss or teacher or even to someone you have no connection to can backfire and wind up causing you all sorts of problems. It's a microcosm of the hacker getting blamed for the vulnerability that he didn't create but merely exposed. And in this particular case, there are likely many other companies making the same mistake who will read this and learn something about what they're doing wrong—before it's too late. So while you may only see the evil that can come from disclosing such information, there is always a benefit to discussing these mistakes.

Incidentally, the system at Target may have been changed since this article was printed. In fact, we received this letter from the author of the piece after we had already put the article into the issue:

"I appreciate that you are going to publish my article, but I believe that by the time it is printed, the information will no longer be accurate. It has come to my attention that the deadline for PCI compliance is very close (http://www.pcicomplianceguide .org/). If Target is following the standards set forth by PCI compliance, then their security setup would have changed. I have no way to verify any changes have taken place, but I can only assume they have tightened up their security. I am requesting that you do not publish the article. I don't want to propagate false information and put the reputation of your magazine at risk."

2009 _____

Dear *2600*:

> *Alamo and National Rental Car companies allow customers to sign up for their frequent renter programs at their websites:* alamo.com *and* nationalcar.com. *If a customer has rented before, they can search by name and driver's license number to find their record. Alamo's search page asks for name, license number, and date of birth, but will return a match with only a correct last name and license number. National's page asks only for name and license number, but will also return a match with only a correct last name and license number. Once a match is found, it pre-fills the registration form with name, address, phone number, license number, date of birth, and frequent flyer numbers which have been previously used by the customer, all from their database.*

> *Obviously, this is a huge security flaw, since with only a last name and license number, anyone can obtain the address, phone number, date of birth, and frequent flyer numbers of a customer who has ever rented from one of these companies. With Alamo, even if you search with an incorrect date of birth and incorrect first name, the site will pull the correct date of birth from the customer database and populate the field with this information. National Car allows the customer to sign up for the "Emerald Club" program with this form, which means that an identity thief could sign up and change only the address to which the Emerald card would be mailed. Once in possession of the Emerald card, they could then make reservations under the customer's name, date of birth, and driver's license number. National's website does require a credit card number for a $1 authorization verification, but it does not use AVS (address verification system) to authenticate the billing house number and ZIP Code.*

> *This also opens the companies' customer databases to the possibility of serious corruption, since all of the information in the pre-filled registration fields can be changed, and then submitted. This apparently updates the companies' main databases, since a new search on the search page at* alamo.com *with the "old" last name and license number then returns no matches, but a search with the "new" information returns*

a statement that the customer is already registered. Customer support at these companies say that there is no way to remove any customer information from their databases or to make them not searchable on the website. On the upside, this feature did allow me to overwrite the information that these companies had about me and therefore protect my information and privacy to some degree.

Unfortunately, this is just another example of how virtually nonexistent strong privacy laws are in the United States. We need legislators to pass strong privacy protections similar to the laws in other countries, which stipulate that companies can only maintain information as long as is necessary to provide the service for which it was originally collected.

NONE NONE

Thanks for so clearly pointing out where the true threat to our privacy lies—not from hackers but from companies that don't take their customers' personal information seriously enough to protect it sufficiently from all sorts of prying eyes. This is the root of so many of the security problems we face today.

The Challenges of Life as a Hacker

Like all humans, hackers encounter many different sorts of problems as they journey through life. However, unlike most people, hackers find problems that often venture into the arena of the unbelievable. That's because hackers are always pushing the limits and exploring in places where others have too much sense to wander. Most of the hackers' difficulties are caused by this insatiable quest for knowledge coupled with the rest of society's inability and unwillingness to understand them. And whenever that happens, sending a letter to *2600* is the best way to vent and also help get the word out.

Over the years, we've been a sounding board for all manner of injustices and, in more than a few cases, I think it's made a real difference in changing things for the better. While there are still plenty of horror stories that go on in schools where smart kids are penalized for knowing more than the teachers or for finding security holes in their computer systems, we see increasing instances of teachers and administrators who listen to and respect the knowledge of the kids. And, as a side note to this, our forum has helped reach out to these same kids to let them know what's acceptable, what is constructive behavior, and what is not.

Of course, the problems don't begin or end in the schools. They're everywhere. and hackers are constantly running full force into them. It could be a confrontation with an obstinate mall cop. (I remember one time getting thrown out of a mall in St. Louis with a bunch of other hackers because we dared to challenge their crazy rule forbidding people from wearing their hats backward!) It could be a run-in with a credit card company or one of the phone giants. Or someone facing prison time because of an overzealous prosecutor or a badly written law, each of these in existence because of the lack of a true understanding of the technology in question. Oftentimes we heard from kids who were facing persecution inside their own homes at the hands of their hacker-fearing parents. We also frequently received mail from people being unfairly disciplined in the companies that they worked for, often for something as innocuous as accessing a web page or bypassing a filter. Injustice was literally everywhere and our letters column was the one place where a sympathetic ear was guaranteed.

There would also be a fair amount of what we considered to be "silly" problems— to put it nicely. People who were blowing a gasket over something that happened to them in an online forum such as IRC. Or those who believed that they were being targeted by some technical super-being because their phones would ring and their lights occasionally flickered. The letters pages have always been a magnet for the super-paranoid and for anyone with some sort of an agenda to push. As the ones holding the magnet, we've always been eager and ready for these sorts of submissions.

We also had our own close-to-home issues with the prosecution and imprisonment of friends like Phiber Optik, Bernie S., and Kevin Mitnick. We found ourselves hauled into court because we joined in a movement to spread computer source code that allowed equal access to DVD technology, regardless of what operating system an individual was running. (We lost the case primarily because of the power of the Motion Picture Association of America and the lack of understanding of the technical issues in both the mass media and the courtroom. And also because we were easily demonized as a hacker magazine, one of the reasons why they chose us to sue out of the many thousands who were doing the same thing.) These became causes célèbres that the community focused intently upon and helped spread word of throughout mainstream society. Oftentimes, we'd hear about the penalties these brave souls would have to pay as a result of daring to speak out. But by sharing this with the rest of our readers, the message became stronger and still more people were inspired to do similar things. I can't help but believe that this really did end up changing the landscape.

Increasingly, our concerns became those of the average citizen and, within a short amount of time, hackers were helping to fight consumer fraud by exposing certain dishonest schemes put on by the phone giants, credit agencies, and the like. We found that people were willing to set aside their preconceived notions about hackers if it meant that their overall concerns were addressed with regard to privacy abuses and rip-offs by various companies. Oftentimes, we were the only ones who were taking their complaints seriously.

But there would always be a fair number of misguided individuals out there who assumed that the only things hackers were good at were breaking into computer systems, changing grades and credit scores, finding out the passwords of their cheating significant others, and exposing every conspiracy known to man by simply accessing a secret system that held all of the damning evidence. Obviously, there was an awful lot of TV watching going on in the world and we had our hands full dispelling the various myths that continued to be bandied about. At least we had fun doing it.

1985

Dear *2600*:

I recently got a notice in the mail from Mountain Bell. Me and 4 other guys roomed together in this apartment and one skipped town after he disconnected his phone. He didn't pay his final bill, so Ma Bell is threatening to have our phones *cut off because of what* he *did.*

The lady at Ma Bell says it's cause this guy left his final billing address as ours, so as far as Ma Bell's concerned, he still lives here and gets phone service by using our phones. Can you believe it?!!

P.S. We are now having to pay $20 a month extra to keep our phones connected. People! If you're living with someone and are going to disconnect your fone, give Bell a fake final billing *address so this doesn't happen to you!*

MAD AS HELL

It would be amusing if someone were to give a large corporation's address as their final billing address. Theoretically, everybody there would get a threat similar to yours. Realistically, it probably isn't quite that easy. But this is nothing new for telephone companies. We've heard many similar stories and a good deal of them have to do with college students. The telephone company gets away with murder when it comes to dealing with students in dormitories.

1987

Dear *2600*:

Have you ever been talking on a payphone and had your time run out? First the phone collects your money and then the nice man asks you to deposit a nickel for another five minutes. You reach into your pocket and all you have is a quarter. You deposit your quarter and are left alone for only another five minutes! It seems quite unfair that no matter what you deposit is treated as a nickel. I can understand that under primitive central office equipment the phone just checks to see if there is a coin ground. But today since most big cities have a majority of their central offices cut over to ESS, why can't someone at the phone company modify the switches to accept dimes as dimes and quarters as quarters?

MARY M.
COMLAND, IOWA

Why indeed? Let's hear some "explanations" for this one from the folks on the inside. If we don't get a satisfactory answer, you may be looking at next year's project to combat consumer fraud.

1989

Dear *2600*:

Here's a note of possible interest.

Congressman Kweisi Mfume (D-MD) introduced a bill (H.R. 1504) that would make it a criminal offense for persons under the age of 21 to possess a beeper. Presumably, this is because many drug dealers use beepers to keep in touch with their customers. But banning the use of an innocent piece of telephone technology by the young is a pretty screwy way to deal with the drug problem. Also, why age 21 instead of 18? What happens to college students and others trying to earn a living as messengers, field technicians, or some other job requiring the use of a beeper? Maybe we should lobby against this bill. (H.R. 1504 was referred to the House Committee on Energy and Commerce.)

PHIL

We certainly should lobby against this bill. It's another crystal clear example of high tech phobia. This time, instead of trying to figure out why drugs have become such an essential crutch to so many of us, the authorities think that making a small bit of technology illegal will somehow solve the problem. For one thing, beepers don't make drug deals. People do. Beepers are a tool, like telephones, notepads, pocketbooks, and automobiles. Should all of these be made illegal to certain people who might use them to deal drugs? More importantly, these well-meaning clods are overlooking a grossly obvious fact. Dealing drugs is illegal. So how can they expect anyone who illegally deals drugs to suddenly honor the law and not carry a beeper? The only people who will be inconvenienced by this law will be the law-abiders, who obviously are not the targets of the law!

1991

Dear *2600*:

> *I thought I'd share with you a story, and a tribute to the downward spiral of our society.*

> *I am enclosing a clipping from the course descriptions for my high school. When I read the description for a computer technology course, I said to myself, "Cool, I can finally use my school time to expand my knowledge of something useful." I talked to the counselor and he arranged for me to be interviewed by the teacher who asked me a few general questions that alluded to my character, which I answered quite well, and he asked me why I wanted to take this "select class." I told him I wanted to learn more about operating systems and software that I haven't yet been exposed to. He next asked me what I knew already. I told him I'd programmed in BASIC and C and was familiar with UNIX and MPE XL operating systems. He told me I'd be considered.*

> *As you may have guessed, I was not allowed to enroll in the class. A friend of mine with far less technical knowledge than myself was, however. A few days later, my friend talked to the teacher about me and the teacher said, "I got the impression he was some sort of hacker dude; he'll probably just try to crash our networks."*

> *Why do they fear me? Do they fear my knowledge? My political alignment? My attitude? What? Do they dislike males with long hair? Why do they associate hackers with game players?*

> *If I was in their class, I would not have crashed their networks. I would have enjoyed building them. But I am pissed off now. Really pissed off, and you can bet your mother's ass I'm gonna crash 'em now.*

> PETER THE GREAT

Treat people like criminals and they will act like criminals.

1992 —————————————————

Dear *2600*:

> *Congrats on a cool 9:2 issue; 2600 has to be the most relevant zine in press. I've got a request for help. Nothing drastic, but my credit is getting hacked by a major corp. Used to work for Motorola, doing s/w for new chips.*

> *When they started drug testing, I spoke out along with others and filed a lawsuit. Eventually, we won the suit and eventually I quit. But in the meantime, Moto also pulled nasties like losing paychecks, making drug accusations while I was under cross-examination, having an exec "remind" me that people can get "hit" for only $300 in this part of the country, etc.*

> *Over a year later, just after participating in a second lawsuit against Moto, I got a notice from AMEX about "my new credit card." I hate AMEX and never do biz with them. Sure enough, a card had been issued in my name and the papers came from Motorola, applied for by one of their local managers five days after my second suit had been filed. I got the card stopped, no charges on it so this won't cost me money. I checked with AMEX and they claim it's all my fault because I'd been a Moto employee and had given them my SSN for tax forms. The manager claims it's just a database error and that all employees were supposed to get corporate cards, my employee records hadn't been purged, etc.*

> *The above statements may be true, but they lead to interesting questions. First, I'm more than a little pissed that the police wouldn't even listen to the case, AMEX won't reveal my credit application forms, and so far no lawyer will even touch this issue without major bucks, which I can't afford. If you or I had hacked some corporate exec's credit this openly, we'd be in a jail now. Ergo, another example of corporate immunity from laws designed to nail individuals.*

> *Second, how many years have to pass before use of my SSN by a former employer is no longer considered a "mistake"? Can all of my former employers file credit applications in my name without legal*

recourse, ad infinitum? Are there federal statutes which apply against the keeping of database records for "fraudulent purposes"?

Third, should I just drop this and catch up next time it happens?

I mean, I can file a lawsuit for a "cease and desist" order against Motorola's use of my SSN without a lawyer, but are there any other actions recommended?

I realize this may not be quite your domain to answer questions, but I thought you might be familiar with the issues.

PACOID

Americans are slowly waking up to the fact that the current credit system is horribly unfair and arbitrary. We believe if an agency is going to make money selling information about you, you should have the right to see it and correct any errors without having to go to a lot of trouble. Currently, the consumer has to do all of the work. And a lot of consumers would correct their credit reports themselves if they knew how. But, in today's world, accessing and correcting your own credit report (which was started without your permission) would be a violation of the credit agency's privacy.

Concerning the problems above, the solution is to be loud and vocal and send lots of certified letters. We cannot access people's credit files for them nor can we recommend people who can. We would suggest filing a court order against Motorola to prevent them from using any of your personal information. We welcome other suggestions.

1993

Dear *2600*:

The unpleasant incident which occurred to the attendees of the 2600 meeting held in Pentagon City Mall in D.C. is too upsetting. If the mall cops hadn't bothered the meeting, they might have caught a few shoplifters or someone who was clearly breaking a law.

The news of the incident spread fast, though. I first read it on the Internet, then in the zine. I think the hackers did a good job when they contacted the media (The Washington Post) and several other organizations (EFF, CPSR, ACLU) after the incident. Spread the word around, let more people know, and maybe we won't have any more chances of dealing with the S.S. men in our local malls.

Keep up the great work!!!

Knight Klone
Atlanta, GA

The D.C. events are a perfect example of what transpires when hackers stick together and use their resources. It also serves as a model of what can happen when authority figures overstep their boundaries and then try and cover the whole thing up.

Dear *2600*:

First off let me say that The Hacker Quarterly *is one of the best publications I have read in a long time. It talks of all the things that Mr. Computer Science Prof should have told you but wouldn't, most likely because it might endanger his/her control over students. However, I am sending this mail mainly because our neo-Nazi sysadmin (I don't really know if he is a Nazi, or just scared of free access to information) has so severely restricted our access to the Internet that most of the newsgroups are academic related or tea-time conversation topics. Anything that might pertain to socially deviant behavior (hacking, learning something not government regulated, etc.) has been deleted. In fact this morning more than 1,000 newsgroups have been screened out from our system. Is there any way for a person to get around sysadmin control over net access for users or access Internet before the screening process goes into effect?*

I have tried to get more info on Internet, but even anything more than a story-like explanation of the system is impossible around here. Shameful, doesn't even trust his own computer science students.

Any help would be greatly appreciated.

Lost and regulated in
NB, Canada

Your story is not unique, unfortunately. Oftentimes, people in charge feel the need to restrict or cut off access. Apart from making sure we never turn into people like that, the best thing we can do is look for ways around it. Since you already have access to the Internet, it shouldn't be too difficult to telnet out to another site that isn't as restrictive. Perhaps you could trade accounts with a student at another school or subscribe to a cheap public UNIX system. With the Internet in its present form, anything is possible.

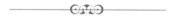

1994

Dear *2600*:

Your editorial on the fate of Phiber Optik was dead-on. Your statement that "Basically, they succeeded in sending a few friends to prison for trespassing" sent a chill of recognition down my spine. A few years ago, after getting off a late shift, a friend and I were arrested while walking alongside some railroad tracks owned by Southern Pacific. The short version of our story is that the sheriffs had nothing better to do, and needed a "big" arrest for their records, so they charged us with felony attempted train derailment. They stole personal possessions from us during the booking procedure, set bail at an outrageous $5,000 each, and falsified the arrest records to support the felony charge. Of course, the prosecutor read the law and withdrew the felony charge; the charge was supposed to be applied to anyone who placed an explosive within 1000 feet of a switch!

The sheriffs did not want to be embarrassed, however, so they convinced the prosecutor to replace the felony charge with a misdemeanor trespassing. Now, the tracks we were walking along were only 20 feet from a major street, in an area that was not fenced off, posted trespassing, or sensitive in any way. Yet, we were technically trespassing, and we were prosecuted, coerced into pleading guilty (mostly because we couldn't afford a lawyer, and the public defender never even appeared at our hearings), and I actually served 30 days jail time and

1000 hours of community service. All this because I walked along some train tracks.... The negative ramifications of this event took years to overcome, and cost thousands of dollars in lost wages, bail bond fees, and legal fees.

The point is, once law enforcement officials begin an investigation or make an arrest, they will do almost anything to avoid the embarrassment of having all charges dropped or the "suspect" going free. Better to lock up a couple of kids for nothing than admit they shouldn't have arrested them in the first place. Unfortunately, when it comes to hacking, law enforcement is clearly as unjust and absurd as it is in the rest of America, if not worse. Phiber Optik has my sympathy, and the police have my contempt.

RACER X

Thanks for sharing that. Such experiences need to be told to others so we can all be on the lookout for injustice.

1995

Dear *2600*:

I'm writing to warn others that there really is no such thing as freedom of speech in American universities today. Unfortunately, I learned this sad truth the hard way. I had a hacker/phreak web page running on a web server at my school. It wasn't all that much, but I was proud of it. I had some lame outdated exploit source, and about fifty box schematics online and available to the public.

The web page was online for several months, and then it was shut down. A self-righteous and clueless admin took it upon himself to disable my account on the web server. In spite of the fact that, at least according to some more intelligent admins, the questionable source code was so obsolete as to render it useless.

After the web page was finally axed, I was told that my job at the computer lab was threatened, because I was, as my boss told me, "giving people ideas." Imagine my gall! Spreading ideas at a university!

All and all, the whole thing was a very frustrating experience. Not only did I see something I put some real effort into get taken away, but I had no success in explaining to admins at my school why freedom of speech is important. As far as I can tell, however, there were two good things which came out of anything I put online. The first of which being that, according to the access logs, many users in Eastern Europe were able to access the h/p info I put online. I'm proud to think that I had even a small part in the positive changes which are going on over there.

The other positive thing that came out of my web page experience occurred to me after a train ride. I had to call my parents, and the only phone around was a broken payphone. The phone wouldn't accept any money, and the old woman in front of me was really in a jam. She had to call her son so she could get a ride home, but she couldn't call him because the phone was broken. Luckily, I had my red box with me and I was able to place the call for her in spite of the difficulties with the phone. Needless to say, the old woman had never seen anything like that, and she was more than a bit shocked and thankful. If it weren't for the information which I had on my page, I would not have known how to box that call, and both of us would have been stranded at the train station.

There's a tremendous amount of good which can come from knowledge. Unfortunately, as I found out, there are many people, even in universities, who don't see that as good. They only see a status quo which they feel it is their duty to defend. I honestly believed that an American university would be safe from such people. Unfortunately, I was wrong.

ROGER BLAKE

But it sounds as if this university is teaching you a great deal about the state of affairs in today's world. Good luck.

Dear *2600*:

> *I am sick of seeing tangled cords at payphones. This is probably the result of people switching sides during their conversation, thus making the receiver do a 360-degree revolution. If people would put back the receiver the same way they found it, things would be a whole lot easier.*

> STICKMAN

All it takes is one to ruin it for the rest of us.

1996

Dear *2600*:

> *I was reading your article on Ed Cummings in the Autumn 1995 issue and I stumbled on a fact that I personally was not aware of, and frankly find appalling.... This is Title 18, USC Section 1029: "possession of a technology which can be used in a fraudulent manner..." What's next? In a year, will carrying a pencil in your pocket be considered concealing a deadly weapon? It's amazing that the people supposedly representing us in Congress could pass such an anti-citizen law. How in the world can they make it illegal to distribute information of any type? How can they make it illegal to own a device that maybe, if someone feels like it, could possibly, if they wanted to break the law, be used in a fraudulent manner? Is it actually true now that having a copy of BlueBeep zipped up on my hard drive makes me a felon? This is unbelievable. However, it seems like a law that will disgustingly stay on the books. Is there anything we can do about this? I don't think so! I have already written to my congressman. Is the constitutionality of this law being challenged by anyone yet? Please, give me a minute—I have to recover from shock, and then go and clean off my hard drive and hide my red box that has been lying in a desk drawer for a year.*

> *I never thought I'd see the day where I'd have to fear arrest for talking or writing about something. I'm nauseated.*

> TcP
> DENVER, COLORADO

We're getting letters like yours every day. People are realizing the implications of this law and it's well worth getting upset about. So far, one person is challenging the constitutionality of this law: Bernie S. The problem is that it's very difficult to do this when the Secret Service keeps throwing him into prison. It's a fair bet they're aware of this fact.

Dear *2600*:

There was quite an interesting letter in the Winter 95-96 issue from J.R. A lot of what he wrote is fact and is going on as you read this. I hope 2600 does take the time to investigate what he says. It would truly be a public service.

I, too, have heard from reliable ex-military sources that the CIA (among other agencies) is implementing such measures to track U.S. citizens. Of course, when it comes time to make the public aware of this bit of technology it will be, perhaps, said to make life easier for us in terms of keeping one's medical records "on file" to expedite treatment. Or to make it easier to renew your driver's license, or to register to vote, or whatever. They will surely try to have us think that our government has its citizens' welfare at heart. Even as J.R. states, we'll be told (perhaps initially) that the chip is to keep track of child molesters and drug dealers.

There are idiots out there who refuse to see past their noses and will readily accept the given reason(s). Perhaps it won't even occur to them that their privacy is in jeopardy. The behavioral science people doubtless know the type of people who are most likely to accept the "reasons" for the chip. The initial "advertising" will target this group.

How about 2600 actually getting involved in (1) doing whatever it can to investigate our claims, and (2) actively joining the actual fight against these aims?

D.Q.
Stamford, CT

By printing your letters, we've become involved. And you can bet that whatever we find out we'll share.

Dear *2600*:

> *Well, I read your magazine every chance I can get, but just about a week ago my parents found a copy (the one where it talked about the stealth trojans and a little about a red box). Well, I made one and they found it and took it to a computer dude they know and they asked him what it was and they got pissed off and took away my laptop and all of my 2600 booklets. They even told the school to not let me on the computers unless I want to type a document and if I do they stand behind me the whole damn time. Now I am in even more trouble because my mom told my English teacher to look out for what I am reading in class and my friend had the brand new copy of 2600 and he let me borrow it while I was sitting in class and she took it away and called my mom. What should I do? There is no possible way to get hooked up to a computer without someone constantly on my back.*

> ZERO

The primary obligation of any prisoner is to escape. Whether that means actually leaving or simply figuring out a way to handle things so you don't go crazy is up to you. It seems that you should try to figure out a way to gain trust among your parents and teachers before doing anything else. Once you do this, you have a shot at convincing them that hacking and, for that matter, reading aren't inherently bad things. This won't happen overnight and it may not happen at all, but it's worth the effort.

1997

Dear *2600*:

> *I have a rather interesting story that you may be interested in. I'm a junior in high school and our school has several COCOTs. So like any curious student I spent my study hall hours playing with the phone. One day I decided to dial the 11xx and 11x numbers. When I got to 118 and hung up the phone, the payphone started ringing. When I picked up the phone I got a message saying your call could not be put through. I would dial 118 several times a day and the same thing would*

happen. Well one day I was dialing and I saw my principal eyeing me suspiciously. The payphone did the usual thing of ringing after I hung up. Later that day during my history class I got a pass telling me to come to the main office immediately. When I got there I was escorted into the principal's private quarters where I was greeted by a police officer. The principal grinned at me and said something to the effect of "We finally got you—this time we outsmarted you." I expected to have them yell at me for phreaking the phone or something but to my surprise they told me that they were going to charge me with prank calling 911! This was quite a surprise considering I had dialed 118 and nothing else. They then told me that 911 had been receiving calls from the school all year long and that one came in at the exact same time I was playing with the payphone from that very phone. I told them about the 118 and, to make a long story short, they checked the PBX records for the school and found that 911 had never been dialed from the school. So I was let off the hook and it turns out that there are multiple numbers that trigger the 911 system but they don't make this information public. Why they have multiple numbers and why they don't make it public remains a mystery to me, but the moral of the story is don't dial 118.

Socrates

It's entirely possible that this COCOT and/or your school had a speed dial entry for 118 that went to the police for some reason. Try it from some other part of town to see if this is the case. Congratulations on escaping the combined wrath of your school and the cops.

Dear *2600*:

What the hell is this world coming to? I tried a phf exploit in Netscape the other day, and I just randomly picked an address, then I was taken to a screen that said some smart-ass remark like, "Smile, you're on candid camera!" Why does everyone who writes an article on phf forget to mention that there is a new version of phf which isn't always so blindly installed on the server? The newer version looks to me like it tells the server when you tried to use their phf and your email address. There might be a few more things that it writes down in the log, but then again this is only a guess. Remember this the next time you try this because I don't know all of the details. Can anyone tell me if using phf in any way is illegal?

THE HEMROID

We don't believe testing a security flaw is something that people should get in trouble for. But rules vary depending upon where you are and who your enemies are. In theory we live in a fair-minded democracy but in actuality our nation is comprised of smaller sections where democratic ideals are not necessarily held in high esteem—such as your school, your workplace, or Tennessee.

Dear *2600*:

Two people in my area (Ocala, Florida), have been caught for talking, that's right, just talking to 13-year-old girls and making the mistake of letting them know exactly where they were going to be at a particular moment in time. While you may think this is "wrong" at first, buying into the socially acceptable and popular concepts of what is right and wrong, think first of the implications.

These two people have been arrested, not for their actions, but for what they have said. These are two people who do not have the resources for great lawyers that would eat the government alive for issues such as free speech and entrapment... but two regular people, much like ourselves were arrested for just speaking to a minor. Think about that: just speaking to someone online is enough to get you arrested and have the media speculate grossly about the so-called "porn" they've found on your hard drive. Talking to a minor and possessing legal pornography are enough to get you arrested with trumped up charges that "protect" the children.... I contend that it is the parents' responsibility to teach their children not to meet strangers, etc. They should teach the children logic instead of trying to shirk off their responsibility to the government to the detriment of the rest of society.

ANONYMOUS

All of the sensationalism in the media has helped create this paranoid and suspicious society where the worst is always assumed of everyone. There are dangers to children and they should be addressed. But somehow, this kind of reactionary thinking is far scarier for all of us.

Dear *2600*:

> *I recently found myself in a disturbing situation. I was at a shopping mall and needed to make a phone call. I went to a payphone, inserted the proper coinage, then I used my Sony Magic Link as a phone dialer and proceeded with my call. Minutes later, I was approached by two mall security guards. One grabbed my Magic Link and the other grabbed the phone out of my hand and hung it up. They told me they were detaining me until the police arrived. At this point my head was spinning, when I asked them for what reason, they told me it was for illegal use of the payphone. I could not understand what they meant. When I asked, they stated that I used an illegal electronic device to steal telephone service. Then they proceeded to turn on my Magic Link, however, it was password protected. They told me to enter the password. I refused, stating that to do so is in violation of my right to privacy. Then they proceeded to escort me to the security office like a common criminal. When the police arrived, a videotape was reviewed showing me approaching the phone, inserting money, then using my Magic Link. When the officer saw this, he told them there was nothing that he could do and that it was incorrect to have apprehended me in the first place. They told me to leave. On my way out, one of the security guards yelled to me, "Don't let us catch you with that thing in our mall again!" What I really want to know is, was it actually a violation of my rights asking me to enter the password? Doing so would give them access to all of my personal information. Any help is much appreciated.*

> X-Ion Noize

You absolutely do not have to show these idiots anything that's password protected. They can pursue it but to do so would involve their having knowledge of some sort of a crime having been committed. In this case, they had nothing.

What's more, what they did to you could easily get them fired and the mall they're "protecting" sued for a very large sum. You have every right to use your device on these phones and we encourage you and others to do this whenever you wish. If you expect trouble from this, make sure there are witnesses and that everything you do is above the board, regardless of what they may do. This kind of thing happens far more often than most people think.

Dear *2600*:

> *My name is [obliterated] and I am hoping you can help me with a problem I have been having for 2 ½ years. I saw an article in* Newsday *on Sunday, June 8, about hackers. At the end of the article, a women called the radio show about someone billing calls to Bangladesh to her calling card. We are having the same problems.*
>
> *About two and a half years ago, our phone bill contained more than 300 calls to adult sex lines and it hasn't stopped. The account is in my husband's name. Our phone number at the time was [obliterated]. We blocked access to these numbers but more things came up. We were billed for international, long distance, calling card, and collect calls, all to our bill. Companies like Pilgrim Telephone, Telemedia Billing, and others showed that we called long distance using these carriers. We called all the companies, NYNEX, AT&T, to tell them we did not make these calls. They all said they were directly dialed from our home. Our children are small, we had no one home for many calls, but they practically called us liars and my husband a pervert. We have gotten NYNEX's recourse department to take off the calls, which eventually were over $700 and sent them back to the independent companies for billing. We are now being pursued by collection agencies. By the way, in August 1996 we moved from our home and had our number changed to an unlisted number in an effort to stop this. We had the lines checked, we have blocked everything possible to block but to no avail.*
>
> *Since reading the article on hackers, I am convinced that a hacker is somehow getting these calls billed to our account. I am begging you to help us solve this problem. We cannot call long distance anymore,*

use a calling card, or call collect. We are at our wits' end to solve this. Please, please help us, or get the word out to your fellow hackers to please leave us alone and go on to someone else. The article stated that hackers usually do this to reveal the flaws in computer systems, but this person, or persons are illegally billing their calls to us. NYNEX will not admit a problem. Also, calls were being charged to our credit cards. I have canceled one card, and changed the number on the other but it is still happening. Help!!!!!

[Name Obliterated]

First off, let's clear something up. Whoever is doing this to you is not acting as a hacker. Just because someone has the ability and is capable of figuring something out does not mean that they are the culprit. Now, concerning your problem, it seems relatively clear that you are known to the perpetrator. Otherwise, this wouldn't follow you to another location, another number, and a credit card. It's up to you to figure out why. As for how, that's pretty easy. There are bugs in many of the major long distance companies and almost all of the smaller ones that allow people to bill all kinds of things to other numbers and make it appear as if those other numbers made the calls. We've seen cases where sleazy companies just ignore third number billing blocks and collect call blocks and bill using those methods anyway. It's possible to make weird things happen by dialing into an 800 number using an operator who has gotten an ANI failure—the number you tell the operator then follows you around on whatever calls you make through that 800 number. We're certain there are an almost unlimited number of ways of doing this. If the phone company is serious about tracking this down, they should put a pen register on your line so they can see this happening live. Yes, they can be used to help customers as well as spy on them. Demand it. And don't be afraid to launch a criminal investigation. This kind of thing does none of us any good.

Dear *2600*:

I've got a real problem here. My truck was broken into right after Christmas and my one-year-old's toys, his clothes and food, along with juice and milk were stolen out of it. The bastards didn't take my tools, my radio, or anything else in the truck—just my kid's stuff. That really pisses me off stealing from a kid. I have a description of the car,

make, model, color, year, bla bla bla. I was wondering if you could be
so kind as to show me the way to tracking these guys down. Do it for
the children, man. I've tried searching the WWW but can't find it.

Jakob14246463526390210

Don't you have a gang of men with guns in your town who prowl around all the
time? They usually take an interest in this sort of thing. Plus they're a lot better
equipped to handle crimes like this.

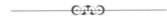

Dear *2600*:

I was recently on the IRC channel #c when I noticed someone using
the nickname "Mitnick". I asked them about it, and they claimed to
be the son of Kevin Mitnick. A few minutes later he said it was "time
to go back to his cell" and logged off. The fact that someone can pre-
tend to be Kevin Mitnick, or his son, and has the audacity to do so,
contributes to the downfall of the computer underground.

Archmage

The fact that someone takes IRC so seriously contributes to their own downfall.

Dear *2600*:

For the last month and a half, I have been planning to start 2600
meetings in my town. All the publicity has been done and the meet-
ing is set. The problem is that my mother doesn't want me to go—I
can't tell her I planned it, but I need to be there. How can I get her to
change her mind?

xxxxxx

We put x's over your fake name so that nobody could ever figure out who you
really are and jest you about this for the rest of your life (or theirs, depending on
how upset it got you). Your parents should be proud of you for organizing some-
thing in the first place. But keep in mind they watch TV and they probably believe

everything it says. Those are the images you will have to disprove. Perhaps show-ing them our meeting guidelines (available by emailing meetings@2600.com) *might be enough to sway them. Failing that, consider the unthinkable—bringing them along! It happens a lot more often than you think and we find a diverse crowd makes for a much better gathering. People who go to meetings just to hang out with their friends are missing the point of them. Plus it can never hurt to have big people around when the security guards start getting bitchy.*

Dear *2600*:

> We recently attended a 2600 meeting in Dallas. We were surprised to see only small children who knew nothing of importance and had little discretion as to the purpose of the meetings. We propose a new meeting location in Lewisville, TX. This we hope will increase the local following and adult attendance, or at least those of us who are out of the seventh grade. We will anticipate a direction from you, oh lords and masters.
>
> THE PHRKMAN AND CYBRTHUUG

First off, you mailed us this letter in all caps and it was really annoying. Second, rather than run away from these "small children," why don't you stick around and share your ideas with these people? They might even teach you something.

1998

Dear *2600*:

> I'm a rather new reader of your magazine and I love it. I went to my local Barnes & Noble for the latest issue and searched the stands for a copy, but I couldn't find it anywhere. Then I noticed that there were drawers below some of the stands, and sure enough, I found about 20 copies there. I was rather pissed that they weren't on the shelves, and when I asked a couple of employees, they claimed they'd never even

heard of the zine. Well, after a little bit of complaining, I got them to put the zine out where it normally goes and then put some up by the registers, so hopefully, you should get a few more sales from them. Well, I just felt like sharing.

JAVELIN

Thanks for the support. We depend on our readers to keep an eye out for this sort of thing. Always remember to be polite, though. Otherwise, next time they'll just burn the issues upon arrival.

Dear *2600:*

Your magazine captivates. It shows not only that there is a clearly defined line between "hacking" and "using a DoS attack to impress my buddies." However, I guess I'm bowing to the inevitable when I say that I still get disgusted at idiots who insist on being malicious for no reason. If you do this kind of shit, you need to rethink yourself.

Taking aim at average computer users who are ignorant when it comes to things like this is bush league. Just because you can get on IRC and type "/whois joe" doesn't give you the right to go slam a lame OOB down the poor guy's/gal's throat, especially since they don't know what's going on, and then flaunt about it. You probably didn't even write the program that did it.

It's not funny. It's stupid. Just because you can send broadcast packets by typing a command in your shell account doesn't make you "elite" or "scary." It does, however, make your "penis smaller" and your "gapped front-teeth wider."

I'm sorry if I seem a tad irate—this was just inspired while I was taking a magical journey in IRC-land (which is becoming more and more the medium of dysfunctional communication) and watching these morons come and harass people who were actually trying to enjoy themselves (however that works on IRC). Just think before you do something next time—is it really worth doing?

Also, your site was recently added to our web proxy server to be blocked, much to my disputing. Unfortunately, there's no way around this as it's done right in the Livingstons that we dial up.

DAVE
WRECKER OF UNIVERSES
DESTROYER OF WORLDS

While what you say is true for the most part, you must also remember that this is only IRC and that IRC is only part of the Internet, neither of which can be considered "real life." Half the problems we face are caused by people who want to apply "real life" solutions to matters of the net. So don't burst a blood vessel over what the little ASCII characters on your screen are doing. Yelling at the TV is far more productive.

Dear *2600*:

I own a large apartment complex (100+ units) and in the past 3-4 months I have had reports and documentation of calls to 900 numbers (sex lines) from several residents' apartments. The calls are being billed on the customers' RBOC bill from third-party billing agencies. The calls take place when the residents are not home and in one case the resident was out of state.

I can't believe that someone is getting into the apartment with a master key as they are tightly controlled and the events are all during daylight hours. We have lots of nosy neighbors and a service crew of four people who ask questions of anyone who is not a resident.

Each resident has a portable phone. Could someone be accessing their phone line through the portable phone? I was able to listen to the caller's voice as it was recorded by one of the billing companies. It was too clear to be coming from a portable phone. This leads me to believe that the hacker is getting into the E5 switch and fooling Ameritech's equipment as to the source of the call. Is this possible?

Please give us a clue as to how this may be happening. The residents to whom this is happening to are not wealthy people.

COL PETE

First off, you do not need to be a hacker to do this. Hackers will explain to you how it works, unlike the phone company or the people who want to continue getting away with this. For some reason people think that because we understand how these things work, we're the ones responsible when things go wrong. Anyway, your problem is simple. And it's extremely common. To give you an idea, over the years we've had at least a dozen phone lines that don't belong to us pop up in the 2600 office on unused jacks. In fact, we have one right now. It happens to lots of people all the time and the phone company doesn't want you to know this because if word got out that your phone number actually appears in multiple locations, they would have a hell of a time convincing people that "if the call comes from your line, it must be coming from your house." There are numerous points where a line can be compromised—junction boxes, basements, even central offices. We know of cases where phone lines for an entire apartment complex were accessible in one tenant's closet. In your case, someone obviously has gained access to all of your lines and is simply clipping onto them at will. In all likelihood, the point of entry is somewhere on your property. Check your basement, garage, even individual apartments if all of the lines run through them. If each of your residents has the exact same type of portable phone, it's possible a weakness is being exploited there. Most modern cordless phones have protection against this type of thing. In either of these above scenarios, your culprit would have to be fairly close.

1999

Dear *2600*:

> *I really need your help. A few days ago, I sent a not-so-nice email to a Klan address at kkk.com. Since then, an anonymous Klan member has been sending me hateful messages, and I would really like to get back at him. Do you share my views on anti-racism? (I hate KKK and all they stand for.) If you could help me I would greatly appreciate it, and I'm sure a lot of people would as well.*
>
> DVS

What exactly is it you hope to achieve by picking a fight here? Such groups are always going to exist, both on and off the net. By engaging them, you give them both the attention and motivation they would otherwise lack. If they do something to you or your friends, by all means react, but to strike out at them first seems rather pointless.

Dear *2600:*

> *My mother has America Online and I have my own ISP, but sometimes when I'm bored, I go on AOL and talk to some friends. I recently received an email which I believe to be fake, but I need some reassurance. I got it shortly after talking to a friend of mine about hacking the CIA mainframe.*
>
> > *Subj: This is encrypted mail from the Central Intelligence Agency*
> > *Date: 12/28/98 6:33:23 AM Pacific Standard Time*
> > *From: nobody@nowhere.to (Anonymous)*
> > *To: XXXXXX@aol.com*
> >
> > *Hello US citizen we understand that you and another AOL member by the screen name: XXXXXXXXXX are conspiring to hack into the CIA mainframe and destroy the United States National Security, although we are sure that you can not breach security on our mainframe we are going to be setting up survailence around both you and XXXXXXXXXX to secure the fact that you will not break into anything the CIA or any other government branch needs to keep away from the public eye. If you try to breach survailence or national security I can assure you that there will be no trial you will be scentenced immedialey and killed by armed forces within your neighborhood, I strongly recommend that you stay calm and not try anything for the good of your family and of you.*
> >
> > *Sincerely,*
> > *Central Intelligence Agent #23642*

SINCERELY,
LIQUIDCACHE

Well, they sure do have the lingo down. But if there's one thing we've learned from our encounters with federal agencies, it's that they know how to spell surveillance. Odds are someone close to you is laughing.

Dear *2600*:

I am an avid reader of your periodical and have been involved in computing for many years. I would just like to rant at how annoying it is to see all these "bad asses" who use three's for e's and so on. This is ridiculous. This does not help how people view hackers. If we want respect, we need to be professionals at what we do and how we act, including our opinion. Besides that, it is annoying to read. If you think you are worthy of the title of hacker, then you would know not to use the spellings. In addition, before you voice your opinions, make sure you know all the facts. Opinions are valid only if they are researched. Granted, you will not know everything, but at least try to find out as much as possible. Just a reminder, you are not "elite" if you exchange letters with numbers. It is annoying as hell, besides proving your ignorance.

ICE BREAKER

W311 $a1d.

Dear *2600*:

I was flipping through channels and I saw a report on a local news station in the Dallas/Ft. Worth area about "the hacker threat." The title they used for the main show was "techno terrorists." I couldn't believe the backdrop they had as the blacked-out hacker talked—it was the "Free Kevin" image as seen when you first enter the 2600 site. First of all, where did we get the name "techno terrorists" from? Do we make chemical bombs and threaten the free world? Do we massacre world centers without reason simply for giggles? Second, why in the hell did they pick the "Free Kevin" banner?

SHINOBI

We don't even massacre world centers WITH reason! Reports like this are all too common and exist mostly to shock and outrage people without actually informing them of anything. When you see crap like this, complain to the offending station and spread the word so the whole world can see what idiots they are.

Dear *2600*:

> *Today I was looking to rent the movie* Hackers *from my local video rental store and to my dismay, they didn't have it at all. I went across town to an identical store and they didn't have it either. At this point I was getting suspicious. Why would a video store have so many old and, in my opinion, bad movies, and not have this one movie from less than five years ago? It seemed a little too weird to be a coincidence. I checked two other video stores in my area and after about an hour of searching found it at a Blockbuster. I may just be paranoid but it seems weird that a movie about a group of young "computer enthusiasts" such as ourselves would suddenly disappear from video store shelves soon after Clinton declared war on "cyberterrorism." My friends think I'm just being paranoid, but I can't shake the feeling that all such media will slowly be swallowed by the abysmal vortex of ignorance and the public will be uneducated as to the essence of hacking and will only live with the terrible misconception that is infecting our society. I just thought I would let you guys at 2600 know about this, as it could soon become a problem.*

> FeuErWanD

You can blame Clinton for many things but not finding Hackers *at your local video store probably isn't one of them.*

2000 _____

Dear *2600*:

> *First of all I would like to say I am a new reader of 2600. I was referred by a friend of mine. I must say to all of the staff at 2600 that you do a great job and have educated me more then I expected. At any rate I*

was writing this letter to ask you about an error I have found on your front cover. The error is in the Date Section. The date reads as follows. Volume Sixteen, Number Four Winter 1999–1900.

Now I was struck by this. A magazine of such elite skill would not let something like this slip past, but then again no one is perfect. I just thought I would point this out to you. Keep up the good educational work in the magazine.

AssMonkey

Dear *2600*:

Well, I just have to start out by saying that I am very angry about Kaplan's decision against you guys, but I really believe that this case can only be decided by the Supreme Court. I think we will prevail in the end. Now, while browsing the MPAA website today I stumbled upon a quote in the FAQ section: "DeCSS is akin to a tool that breaks the lock on your house." Now what is this garbage they are posting? They make it sound like DeCSS is a tool which can (in their eyes) break into any home, but in reality, DeCSS would be a tool letting you break the lock on only homes that you own, as DeCSS can be used to only rip DVDs that you already own.

MaD-HaTTeR

There's no need to even accept any house analogy since it's completely inappropriate. A DVD is a commercial product that, once purchased, should not be subjected to further restrictions on its private use. The MPAA has defined this as a piracy issue, which it most definitely is not.

Dear *2600*:

I agree with you guys and gals, we should be able to copy DVDs. What sites can I go to to get the info to copy DVDs?

DAN

It's amazing how we didn't get any letters like this until the mass media started reporting that the MPAA had defeated a bunch of DVD pirates in court.

Dear *2600*:

I just wanted to say that I appreciate the efforts that you are putting forth in your legal battles with the MPAA. You're fighting a battle that is highly important for all of us and I thank you.

aUD10phY|

If anything has shown the value of what hackers are about, it's this case. It has strengthened our resolve beyond description. Thank you, MPAA.

Dear *2600*:

I don't see this as a real problem, because there's a simple solution: Get a site hosted in the UK or some other country. On that site they can have pages redirected to the pages with "illegal" material. Basically, use that site as a "proxy" for your link to the site with the offending material, and voila, you're back in business with links and everything.

I mean, really, are they going to come after you guys for links to links of illegal material? Probably, but let's see how far we can take it.

Pete Davis

While many have suggested everything from leaving the country to operating our website off an oil rig in international waters, we think the best move is to stay right where we are and fight. Changing the playing field would be a temporary solution at best as oppression tends to go looking for new lands to conquer.

Dear *2600*:

Just thought you'd like to know that on the 10/25/00 episode of the WB show Felicity, *they had a character who wore a 2600 baseball cap. Of course, he was a whacked out sysadmin/tech support person who named his computers and thought they were female. Too bad they didn't buy an anti-MPAA shirt instead. Now that would have been a statement!*

Mistral

We consider that an example of fair use and we've never tried to deny anyone the right to use our stuff. At the same time, when studios sue us and then ask to use our stuff in one of their films, it gets a little annoying.

Dear *2600*:

> Is there any reason why it's Fall of year 0 on page 33 of issue 17:3 but not on any of the other pages? How come this page gets to be special and display "Fall 0" while the rest show "Fall 2000"? Is page 33 an outcast or just being defiant?
>
> Anyway, do you use automatically generated footers on each page like MS Word creates or do you type each footer by hand? Just wondering. Well, it's an awesome mag so however you're creating your footers, keep up the good work.
>
> Paper

Like we've said—repeatedly—we've been working on getting the Y2K kinks out of our systems. We're making available substitute footers for page 33 that can be pasted over the noncompliant ones until we complete repairs. Watch for details.

Dear *2600*:

> Our systems were hacked today by www.2600.com, or so the email said. I got an email with the subject "US PRESIDENT AND FBI SECRETS" and an attachment. As soon as I clicked on the attachment, my Outlook went on a rampage, emailing everyone in my email system with this attachment, and some with jibberish words. I have to say, it made me laugh but then about two hours later, it wasn't as funny because I couldn't get any work done. All in all, you guys are funny, but at the same time you suck.
>
> Agentskye101

It's truly stunning how many people believe that just because somebody put our web address in an email that we have anything to do with it. We've gotten all kinds of threats because of this and we'll continue to ignore each and every one of them. In the meantime, we suggest you stop using programs like Microsoft's Outlook as that seems to be the common factor in all of the problems people have been experiencing.

2001

Dear *2600*:

> *I have an interesting story that everyone who enjoys privacy should read. I am a student at Northeastern University in Boston. Today I was visited by two policemen who wanted to talk to me about the content of websites that I was viewing. They claimed that certain materials and or sites are flagged and that they know every website I have been to. When I asked what specific sites were "flagged" they said I was being "evasive." When I asked if they will keep harassing me if I kept going to these sites they said "maybe." I still have yet to know the URL of a single "flagged site." I am wondering if this is true or not. I hate to think that my college tuition and money paid for Internet service is used to pay some person to spy on us. What should I do?*

> NATE

The first thing to do is find out just who these clowns are who visited you. What kind of "police" were they? Campus, city, state, federal? Or were they even cops at all? Once you have that established, demand to know what specifically they want and don't be afraid to raise a stink about this. Being a college student, you also have the advantage of possibly being around people who still believe in freedom of speech. Use that idealism to the fullest and don't be afraid to get others involved. Be prepared for any site that you may have visited to be made public—they may also try to make stuff up which is why keeping logs is a good idea. This kind of thing happens far too often and it's only by loudly challenging these people that anything will change.

Dear *2600*:

> *While reading an online article about your recent court ruling to remove linking to DeCSS code, the article stated that linking to the material was considered illegal. This is what caught my attention. Now not only distributing this code is illegal; but the mere act of inserting a link into a web page to this information is illegal. It would be like you asking me where you could buy a gun. I tell you Dick's Sporting Goods and then you kill someone. Am I responsible for any wrongdoing (keeping in mind that I didn't provide you with the gun but only the information on where to buy one)? It seems to me that the ruling is extremely unfair and unconstitutional.*
>
> *31337*

We prefer to avoid gun analogies almost as much as house analogies. What we need to remember is that we're talking about speech, something far more valuable—and powerful—than any weapon. Many reasonable people are sickened by the proliferation of guns in our society. But to see speech as a threat—that requires a distinct hostility and fear toward the openness we've always been taught to value. You don't need an analogy when the actual event is so blatantly wrong.

2002

Dear *2600*:

> *Your site is blocked on my school's network. My school happens to use a filter program called X-stop. The program is the masterpiece of a company called 8e6 Technologies. I went to their site and requested that your site be unblocked. The following is what was sent back to me:*
>
> *"The site is currently blocked in our Criminal Skills library and does meet our criteria for blocking."*
>
> *I think this is total BS. You guys aren't criminals and your website is nothing more than a news/information site. Keep fighting and good luck on the DeCSS case.*
>
> NICK FURY, AGENT OF S.H.I.E.L.D

We'd appreciate it if everyone involved in making software purchases sends people like these a periodic note saying "Your software has been blocked from our purchasing department because you meet the criteria of Close Minded Morons."

Dear *2600*:

> *Unsolicited commercial email (spam) is crippling the effectiveness of the Internet. Roughly 80 percent of the mail arriving in a typical email user's mailbox is spam. This is an incredible drain on users, involving millions of dollars of lost time for businesses, frustration for users old and new, and the clogging of system bandwidth and disk space.*
>
> *Technology has not solved the spam problem, nor is it likely to. Filtering technology has been ineffective. Government will not enforce the laws that have been enacted until citizens start to demand action. So far, they have done very little. And the UCE industry has demonstrated a blatant disregard for the law of the land and common decency.*
>
> *Therefore, we, the users of the Internet, are declaring war on spam. This war will continue until the UCE industry obeys the existing laws. We demand that the UCE industry provide functional opt-out proce-dures, stop forging return addresses, label advertisements in the subject line, and comply immediately with "do not contact" requests.*
>
> *The FTC has announced that it is "collecting" spam. You can refer spam to* uce@ftc.gov*. Since the government refuses to take action to enforce the laws, we will send every piece of spam in our inboxes to the FTC until they take positive action. There is a small underground movement of users who are already doing this on a case by case basis. The goal of "spamwar" is to amplify this and give it a focused stra-tegic goal.*
>
> *We will conduct this war email by email, making the lives of the spammers hellish until they surrender unconditionally. It is time for the users to take back the Internet.*
>
> BRUJO

Before you get too carried away with your epic struggle to liberate the masses, you should understand a few things. Bombarding a federal agency with redirected spam—even at their request—is unlikely to accomplish anything except to waste even more resources. By calling for government action, you may one day actually get your wish—and live to regret it. The last thing you should want is government regulation of something like the Internet. It would wind up extending far beyond commercial email. All aspects of online speech could be endangered by having an overseeing body. Spam does need to be fought but we believe it can be done using available technical means. We also think that with a little imagination, we can make it pretty uncomfortable and unprofitable to be identified as a commercial spammer. Ideas are welcome.

Dear 2600:

> I have a problem and thought maybe you or my fellow readers could assist me. Every day I receive ten annoying phone calls that say long distance on my display. I pick up and there is no one there! I have tried yelling and screaming and punching my phone and nothing seems to work. Today within a timeframe of five minutes I received probably 20 phone calls from the same long distance number. The difference with this one is that instead of silence there is a beeping noise every so often. What can I do about this huge annoyance?
>
> ADAM FROM ONTARIO

We're surprised that screaming and punching the phone didn't work. That usually does it for us. But let's explore an alternative method. It sounds to us like this is a fax machine calling you. The beeps usually indicate this. Since you have the phone number, you might be able to figure out who it belongs to, either through a reverse directory lookup or by calling a variation of the number—if it belongs to a fairly large organization you might find their main number ends with "00" in the same exchange. Sometimes fax machines also pick up with humans or voicemail systems that give you the name of the company/person. You could even try hooking up a fax machine and receiving the fax yourself! That's a sure way of getting some info. If all else fails and you still wind up getting these calls, contact your local phone company's annoyance call bureau and get them to deal with the situation. This is a free service unlike the *57 rip-off that many phone companies will try to get you to use.

Dear *2600*:

> *So I was there waiting in line at the local FedEx for my laptop to come back from being serviced. I was behind three gentlemen of Middle Eastern nationality. Two of them were at the counter talking to a lady who worked there. I think they were trying to figure out when a package was going to arrive at its destination. Anyhow, while I was looking at my slip, I glanced over at the very quiet third man who was sitting in a chair in front of me. He had a piece of paper and a manila envelope in his hand. On the white piece of paper he had written everywhere "INS.DA.DOJ.DO?" (I couldn't make out the last character). This was written everywhere, on both sides too. Then he flipped his hand over and on the envelope he had a bunch of words written like a list or address. The only words I could make out were [something] Middle School. That's all I could get before he got up to leave with the other two men. I don't think the envelope had been sent yet because the stamps didn't appear to have been crossed out yet by the post office. There were big stamps on it with pictures of a man with a hat on like Eddie Murphy wore in* The Golden Child. *The first thing that came to mind when I saw the characters on the letters were those letters with the anthrax. I didn't get their license plate for further tracking but they were driving a late '80s silver Honda Accord. My second thought was why the hell would an international terrorist just walk into a building holding "evidence?" So what the hell do I do? If I let it go and they kill someone, I am a bad person. If I call the police and he turns out to be practicing his English or he was just sending money to his family, I am a bad person. I haven't judged yet, but what would you do? I turned to you guys because you're probably the most neutral people I know. Any input would be appreciated.*

Lectoid

This may be the first time we've ever been called neutral. It's important in a case like this to take a step back and look at the conclusions you've already reached. People of Middle Eastern descent are considered suspicious by default. Would you have given the same amount of scrutiny to someone who looked more like you? This guy being quiet also made you suspect something. But what's so unusual about someone being quiet while they wait in a chair for someone? As for the letters he was scribbling, are we really to believe that such a thing is a suspicious activity? Even if he was writing down the name of every government agency he knew, so what? Having the words "Middle School" on an envelope really isn't that unusual either.

We're not faulting you for having this thought process. What we're doing is asking you to examine it and try and understand why these simple actions could somehow plant the seeds of suspicion in your mind. Then imagine the entire country thinking along the same line.

The fact is you will not know if someone is up to something evil unless you know them very well or are highly trained in spotting such activity. There are a few lucky exceptions to this but they tend to involve rather large clues, none of which were apparent here.

You can rest assured that you didn't do anything to make you a bad person.

2003

Dear *2600*:

> *I am an engineering student at a Canadian university. As I am sure is the case in many post-secondary institutions nowadays, professors at my school are increasingly turning to the Internet to dispatch course information. Early this semester I was looking for one of my course web pages. Having lost the syllabus, I had only the first assignment from the class to guide me. I typed a few of the more interesting words into a Google search box and hit go. Much to my surprise, two links emerged: one to the assignment and another to the solution (both postscript files). Quite intrigued I clicked on the link to solutions. Rightfully, as the assignment is not due for another week, the link was dead. However, Google keeps a cached text version of the postscript files it encounters and it was broadcasting these solutions to the world. Now I know there are a lot of people in my class that would love to get their hands on this information—hell, some of them would probably be dumb enough to print it off, put their name on it, and hand it in. My question is how do I get it taken off the web? If I contact Google would they be willing to remove it? How would I alert my professor*

without appearing guilty (but still remain credible)? Or should I just
tell him to do some damn work and come up with a new assignment
every year instead of just recycling them?

EIGENVALUE

It would be ridiculous to bother Google with this. Your professor is lazy, plain and
simple. If he gives out the same assignment every year, surely the possibility of a
previous student passing on the solution to a current student must have crossed
his mind. If you think you'd be somehow held responsible if you told him of this
hole (at the same time offering to complete a different assignment), then we sug-
gest going the anonymous route, either letting him know the specifics through
some kind of anonymous note or telling the entire class in the same way.

Dear *2600*:

> *Al Jazeera is the cable network in Qatar that has acted as the propa-*
> *ganda mill for Osama, Saddam, and any other Arab with an anti-*
> *American story to tell. Ironically, it is owned by the same rich fatcat*
> *who built us a giant airbase in Qatar so we would protect him from*
> *his rough neighbors. Here are the results of some basic reconnaissance:*
> *[output of whois lookup deleted].*
>
> *Spams away!*

ANONYMOUS

We didn't print this data only because it would have taken up way too much space
and it's very easily obtained by simply looking up the owner of the domain.

Even if your facts were accurate—which they are far from—your way of dealing
with those you disagree with really stinks. How about providing some intelligent
dialogue to back up your argument rather than merely attempting to silence dif-
ferent perspectives (through spam, harassment, denial of service, or whatever
else you're willing to engage in)? As you probably know if you've read our pages
before, we have some major issues with entities who abuse power and intimidate
individuals. But we would never condone an attack that would silence those who
disagree with our way of seeing things.

Dear *2600*:

I am so glad that you publish your magazine. Especially for poignant editorials such as "Not in Our Name" from the Spring 2003 issue. I feel such an affinity to the concepts and ideas expressed. Especially the importance of the fact that "We may not like the message, we may not agree with it, but if what we allege to stand for is to have any value, we have to do everything possible to ensure it isn't silenced."

I am an idealist but I see some dangerous holes in the above stance. For example, I volunteer for a nonprofit media group that has a public website where anyone can anonymously post news and anyone can anonymously post comments.

Recently we had a lot of hateful speech and threats of all sorts toward women and men who post to the site. This open board got so full of altered and reposted photographs, violent threats, anti-Semitic comments, anti-gay comments, etc. that many posters felt physically in danger and didn't want to use the site anymore. Other concerns such as being dragged into a criminal investigation by the police as well as investigation and monitoring by the government feed my nightmares.

The group decided to post a letter about why we thought this was wrong and removed the open board posting on the website. We all regretted doing this and promised to return the open posting ASAP.

How can these practical concerns be addressed and not silence any message whether we agree with the content or not? Are there any limits? Is true equality exploitable?

Your thoughts would be really helpful.

Brian

You are not silencing anyone by removing the open board posting scheme. You're simply not playing host to opinions you find offensive or destructive by permitting them on your site. We find that sometimes people feel the only way to be fair is to allow everyone to say whatever they want in any forum without any sort of control. All that ensures is complete chaos and the eventual destruction of whatever community has been built.

It's essential to not restrict expression and opinions in our society. But that doesn't mean you have to allow others to destroy what you're trying to do. For instance, if we printed everything that was sent to us, the message of 2600 would soon be lost in a lot of gibberish. Are we denying freedom of speech to those whose words we choose not to print? Not at all—they still have their freedom of speech. If their words were made illegal by the government or if they were otherwise silenced, that would be a clear abridgment of their rights which would be of concern to anyone regardless of whether or not they agreed with the speech itself.

All that open board posting does is dilute what it is you want to put out and make it so much easier for hostile forces to shut you down. What you offer is not a finite resource. Others can run their own boards and websites. Now if you were a broadcaster using public airwaves that are most definitely finite, then you would have the obligation to give others access. At least in theory. The way things have gone in our society lately, that freedom has been pretty much bought and sold. But that's another story.

Dear *2600*:

> *I was sitting at home the other day, minding my own business, and the phone rang. I went to pick it up and it was the trademark telemarketer nuisance call. As some of you may remember from the past few issues, there have been some articles that describe how telemarketers work. Occasionally telemarketers' computers will call more people than they have available telemarketers. When this happens, they hang up as soon as somebody picks up. That's called a nuisance call. What was interesting this time was that Caller ID actually reported a number, rather than "Anonymous" or "Unavailable." When I called it back, it said something like "Code 1563" and promptly hung up. I didn't write down the exact code, but it was something to that effect. I was curious so I called it back again and it just rang. Does anybody know exactly what this may be? I'm assuming it was a telemarketer. However, it was odd that it actually gave me a number on the Caller ID. The phone number was 702.889.08XX. It was a harassing phone call, so I have no hesitation about posting the number.*

> PATRICK

This is getting a bit silly. Your phone rings once and you're ready to declare war on whoever dared to dial your number? We agree that telemarketers are a royal pain and should be dealt with harshly when they annoy people. But this could have been an innocent wrong number, something that used to not be a big deal in the days before Caller ID. If you get an actual sales pitch attached to a phone number, let us know and we'll print the entire number. And before anyone starts to scan out all the numbers to fill in the above Xs, the number was disconnected when we called it. We can only speculate as to why.

Dear *2600*:

> *Point me in the right direction for some software programs. The reason I am asking is that I am having some trouble with a person in a newsgroup that is "spoofing" me. I have actually been able to take the information back to the ISP, but when I make a complaint to the ISP they ignore it even with complete headers of the messages.*
>
> *As it stands I am being hit with threats from other posters about posts made from this person "spoofing" me and them thinking that it is me doing it. I can live with this if I can get this person to stop doing this, but again the ISP refuses to do anything.*
>
> *Now I have seen some people who are able to actually get the names and addresses of people through their posts and this is what I would like to be able to do. No, I will not use this to attack this person, as all I want to do is send them an email through an anonymous remailer just to warn them I know who they are and what they are doing and ask them to cease. I know this sounds "farfetched" but I really have no desire to harm anyone. I just want this person to cease.*
>
> *I have asked some questions about this in chat rooms and even the alt. binaries.2600 newsgroup, only to be laughed at and be told that if I asked such a stupid question again, my personal information would be posted all over the net. Personally, I don't see what I actually did wrong. Nor why I was being treated like I just demanded the keys to the Internet backbone. So far what I have learned about tracing an ISP I learned at* geektools.com *and by using smartwhosis.*

Now you see why I would like to know how to actually get the name and address of this person so I can get him to stop. Heck, I would even send you the headers if you would give me this information just to prove to you that I am not out to hurt anyone.

A little help here, please? Some names of the programs that do what I ask would be great as I could locate them on my own.

Thanks guys, your magazine is great!

DANIEL

The Internet is comprised of all kinds of people ranging from morons to geniuses. And there are very few among these who don't enjoy watching reactions when certain personalities clash. When you ask for help, you will invariably get mocked by people who either want to provoke more of a reaction or who simply like to be obnoxious. Many times this turns the original poster into an hysterical lunatic and their progression into eventual institutionalization becomes a source of entertainment all around the globe. You can avoid all of this by not taking it all too seriously or, at the very least, not appearing to take it too seriously. If you find out about a fake post that went out somewhere, post as yourself and make it clear that this wasn't you and you'd appreciate it if someone would help you figure out who it actually was. Depending on software and methods used, this is usually not very difficult and someone in all likelihood will step forward. If they don't, there's no point in making an issue of it. An ISP has better things to do than get involved in something relatively minor like fake postings. But there are plenty of people out there who will lend a hand if you don't come off as a nut. And if you show no outward signs of being upset at what's going on, whoever is behind it will eventually get bored since there's no longer any entertainment value.

Dear *2600*:

I am being stalked by a computer! A computer driven by a cowardly poor excuse of a man. When I lived in the apartment above his, he used sound to drive me crazy and vibration to make me go to the bathroom. He would go in his bathroom when I was in mine and tap some signal letting me know he was listening and at a later level he would leave feces at my apartment door.

This Ahole took all my messages off my message machine, of which in my time there I had three. He probably listened to my phone calls. There were always clicks in my walls when using my latest phone/ message system. He changed my voice messages and took my messages off. He got into my TV and I cannot use my menu screen. He took the caption off and lowered my sound among other things. I don't care how he does this. He stays up all night with no lights on and works on his computer. I moved—that was great! No. Somehow he's here doing the same things. After two months, he is still a pain in my ass and causing me to be very sick.

Can I stop this, short of having his fingers cut off? How do I do this?

LILY

We assume you're asking us how to stop this and not how to have his fingers cut off. We strongly suspect you're the victim of a rather large practical joke and/or an overactive imagination. We get many such letters and they all go along pretty much the same lines. Someone is terrified of a person who can do anything to their technology and who is unstoppable. It's a great plot line for a movie but in real life it's not so simple. But what is simple is getting someone to believe that such all-encompassing magic is possible. Once that's achieved, you are completely under the person's control because everything bad that happens will then be blamed on this person, thus making him more powerful with each technological misfortune. The symptoms you describe (apart from the feces and pipe tapping) are all quite common in everyday life. His being on a computer all night is almost certainly irrelevant to your problems. And it's likely he will stop whatever provocations are aimed at you once you stop reacting as if he were evil incarnate. Such a perception tends to inspire many such performances.

2004

Dear *2600*:

Currently I have someone stalking my family from a location in Ohio. Making a very long story short, he calls my house and my Caller ID shows a "token" telephone number. He can call back in a minute and the Caller ID will show a completely different number across the U.S. He has gone as far as to call the local police department and pose as a member of my family claiming to have murdered the entire family. Needless to say the SWAT team showed up and the rest is history. My research shows that this perpetrator has done this before numerous times. The Ohio state police department is aware as is the local police department where I live. He has served time in prison for assault and drugs, so he is capable. I am trying to protect my family.

My question looks to you to figure out how to identify where he is calling from. Is there a way? I would so appreciate any help. Prior investigations have deadlocked at that point. Thank you!

ALI

Let's see if we have this straight. The police departments know who this guy is and he has yet to be prosecuted? Why aren't they tracing him themselves? They certainly have the ability. There are also all kinds of clues you can uncover if he is indeed stalking you, such as why you were selected, things he's made reference to, hints as to location, etc. But again, if you already know about his record (and presumably his name), then it should be easy for anyone with access to law enforcement to track him down. Without that access it becomes trickier but by no means impossible. Every case is different, which is why we can't give you a surefire answer. But it sounds to us like you already have something to go on here.

As for spoofing Caller ID, as we've said before it's quite easy and can be done in a number of different ways. Unfortunately, people still believe that this information is secure and infallible. As your case demonstrates, it is far from either.

Dear *2600*:

When did it become wrong to search for information on technology? After reading your article in 20:4 ("Paranoia vs. Sanity"), I was compelled to write my senior English paper on hacking, which I got approved by the teacher. I covered the origin, famous hackers, previous court cases, current laws, and current security issues, all while trying to encompass a main point that hackers are not the evil twisted madmen the media makes them out to be. During the research for this paper my high school implemented content filtering software from Lightspeed Systems. This new filtering system made searching on the Internet difficult. As a result, I, along with other students, began to search for information on how the filter worked and ways to bypass it. Our searching led us to discover that the filter did not block secure connections or connections running via a proxy.

A few weeks later I was called into the principal's office and questioned about my use of Google to find ways around their new filter. I tried to reason with the administrators that what I was doing in no way harmed the school computers and that it was breaking no laws or school rules. I attempted to explain that my only goal was to investigate and learn about the filtering system. Despite the arguments from myself, other students, teachers, and my parents, I was given punishment. I was to report to in-school suspension during two of my three computer-related classes during the next week. Even more bizarre was the fact that I was allowed to use my personal laptop during my suspension.

It seems that the paranoia has hit my school administrators with full force. Now that two more students have been issued time in suspension for the same acts of merely searching for information about the filtering system, I can't help but ask when did it become wrong to research the flaws in a piece of software? At no time did any student cause harm to the school's systems or data. So much for trying to educate yourself in a public high school!

PCRACER51

At some point you ought to let the geniuses who run your school in on the fact that their actions probably led to hundreds or even thousands of other people (our readers) pursuing the very knowledge they thought was so dangerous. If they understood this "risk" from the start, we bet they'd be a little more careful about stepping on people's rights.

Dear *2600*:

I was minding my own business being a good citizen going through customs in Newark when the customs agent looked at me, looked at my passport, looked at his computer screen, and mumbled something like, "That's not you." I was then separated from my family and told to follow a TSA person to the INS processing center. Very curious as to what the problem was, I proceeded to wait in a small room with about 40 people who appeared to be foreigners trying to enter the U.S. I heard one of the INS officers on the phone telling someone how short staffed they were and how it would be hours before something could be done. So I settled down for a long wait. Luckily, one of the agents spotted my passport and said, "Hey, that's an American one. Hand it over to me—I'll get it done." I am certainly glad I wasn't an immigrant coming through Newark that day. A few minutes later I was called up and was just told "Sorry, but you have one of those names that is very common." He apologized for the delay but offered nothing else. I thanked him and left to rejoin my family.

I'm sure this has happened to others. I haven't decided whether to feel more secure because they are taking things seriously enough to pull me aside for a few minutes, or whether to be annoyed at the inconvenience. I am leaning toward the former but I haven't discounted the latter.

Anyway, just sharing some experiences. Thanks for continuing to print such a useful publication. Happy 20th!

Jynx

"One of those names that is very common?" Are they saying your full name is that of some terrorist somewhere? And that many other people have that exact name? Or that people with common names are by nature suspicious? Perhaps only one of your names was the same as a terrorist's. Does this mean they stop everybody with that one name? You're entitled to know precisely why you were held, regardless of whether or not they ever choose to tell you. By the way (and you didn't hear this from us), we have it on good authority that the terrorists are getting very close to figuring out how to use fake IDs.

Dear *2600*:

Something very scary happened at my place of business today. I work at a small computer store in Tampa. Nothing big, just a small mom and pop place that fixes Macs and PCs. Someone came in and introduced himself as a senior computer analyst who works for the Department of Homeland Security. He said that our company was in a unique position to see "sensitive " data on people's computers and wanted to know if we had seen anything unusual lately. When we tried to probe the matter further as to what would be "anything unusual" he avoided the question totally—but it was pretty obvious as to what he meant or at least what I thought he meant: anything written in Arabic or something to do with bombs or terrorism. The scary thing is the agent said if we ever came across something that we thought they should have a better look at, they could have someone over to our store within 20 minutes to clone the drive and bring it back to their labs for further investigation with no warrants! It seemed like I was the only one this scared the hell out of. We have government agents wanting to look at people's hard drives and when I told others about this, they just brushed it off and said that this is the world we are living in today and called me crazy for thinking twice about it. I do not care what I find on someone's computer when I am trying to fix it—it is none of my business and it should be none of the government's business either. Sad that this is the beginning of the end of privacy.

oo

We're well beyond the beginning. If we're ever to start moving in the other direction, we'll need lots more people like you watching out for and reporting any abuses like this. Be sure to get as much information from these people as you possibly can before making it clear that you have no intention of cooperating with them. And then be sure and report this "suspicious activity" to anyone who will listen.

2005

Dear *2600*:

> *Been a reader of the magazine for some time. Just had to write to tell you that I got pulled over tonight. My license is suspended and I just got off of house arrest and am now on probation. I happened to have a copy of 21:3 in the glove compartment when the cop searched the car. As I stood in front of those wonderful blue flashing lights, he came back to me with the 2600 in his hand. I was thinking that I was about to get a hard time because I had a magazine that said "hacker" in the car along with three old computers in the trunk awaiting my repairs. As he stood in front of me flipping through the pages with this "I know what this is all about" look on his face I explained to him that I'm a network security/administration major. He then revealed that he used to be a network engineer but had to take up being a cop because of the pay (or lack thereof) in the state I'm in. Driving on suspension, on probation, and driving home at 1 a.m. after picking up some software from a friend, the cop let me go. Kind of nice knowing that that type of authority respects what we're all about. Just thought I'd share that. Keep up the great work.*

MLG

We understand the relief you must have felt. But it sounds as if there was absolutely no cause to search your vehicle and even less to judge you on your reading material. Despite the fact that this turned out OK and that the cop appeared to be a decent person, this sort of thing is more than a little frightening.

Dear *2600*:

> *Typically, at least from my school's filter, trying to go to www.2600.com would yield that the site was blocked because it was "Illegal." So imagine how strange it was to go to www.2600.com and find that it was blocked because of profanity. (Of course, I have yet to find anything outright profane about it.) Going to www.2600.net produces the ex-*

pected results—blocked, the reason being "Illegal." However, going to www.2600.org *takes me straight to the website with no problems.*

Just thought it might be interesting to know.

FxChip

We really think we deserve more than a one word categorization. Morons.

Dear *2600*:

In response to Public Display's letter about his school password/user-name system in 22:1 in the Utter Stupidity section, I have had the same dilemma. In my school your user ID is your graduating year and then four random numbers. Graduate in 2008, 83456. Now the passwords are something random: tree, date, note, paper, etc. But all the admin accounts, which you can find by going into the security option of the C: drive, are simply just username and password the same, like SA and SA. Now, my friend and I found this out. When you are on the account, you have access to grades, principal/teacher files, student files, and so on.

All my friend and I did was look around and then we left a .txt file in the tech guy's folder which said "Hey, found a hole in your system, here's how to fix it, etc." When they found that, they traced it back and we were given ten days out of school suspension and banned from further computer access as long as we are in the school's district.

Now I think that's a little extreme, don't you?

FALLEN

It's extremely stupid and indicative of administrators who have no control over their systems and punish the first person who tells them this as if they were the ones responsible for their own ineptitude. As they have already unfairly prosecuted you, we suggest letting everyone in the area know the specifics of the case until they're shamed into apologizing for their irrational reaction.

Dear *2600*:

Keep up the great work, guys! This is what I got back when I submitted your site for approval from our work's filtering service.

"Thank you for submitting a website unblock request to our Filter Review Team! This website is blocked because it contains information regarding militias, illegal weapons, bomb making, terrorism and similar sites. Please review our filtering criteria located in the support section of our webpage.

Thanks again for your feedback.
Filter Review Committee
Site: http://www.2600.com/

PUKETHECAT

And we hear that the people who run bsafeonline.com are a bunch of child molesters. See? We can accuse people of things, too.

2007

Dear *2600*:

My local library has turned into a Nazi dictatorship. They just put on a blocker program called WebBlocker. I'm unable to download from a free gaming site. It gives an error that the connection has reset. I do not think the router has done this but rather the blocking program. Are there any easy hacks or web tools for someone who has no under-standing of code of any kind?

Also, is there a group out there who hack in the spirit of common good or in the name of our country the USA? I mean are there or have you heard of anyone that has hacked bank accounts, servers, websites, and such in the Middle East that support terrorist groups or dictatorships? I would think that there would be people out there. I'm just wondering because this would be a great story to tell.

BARRON

So on the one hand you're upset that someone has decided to control your access based on who and where you are while on the other hand you're interested in learning how to disrupt the activities of others on the net based on who you believe they are? How do you propose concluding whether or not someone deserves to be taken off the net or otherwise attacked? Your opinion? Someone else's? What your government tells you? This is not what hacking is about. What you're interested in is doing the bidding of one group of people in order to defeat another. This is what the military does. And every time something contentious happens in the world, members of our military try to get hackers involved in the fight for their version of justice. By even considering such requests as legitimate, we tarnish what hackers have always stood for which is free and open access to thoughts, ideas, and technology. People are free to do what they want on their own or as part of some other organization but please don't assume hackers are about to become another branch of anyone's military.

Dear *2600*:

> After receiving the newest issue of 2600 I started going through my stacks of back issues. This wasn't what I was looking for but I came across an all time great article in 20:3 entitled "Infidelity in the Information Age." Normally I'd just skim this article and move on but last May my wife broke the heartbreaking news to me. I'll leave out the juicy details but she told me she broke off the affair and wanted to fix our marriage. Having your spouse tell you this is the worst kind of agony. I can say there is nothing more painful or life changing that I've ever experienced. Within the next few weeks I changed from being an all-trusting husband who never questioned his wife's faithfulness to an obsessive, overly jealous man who had to know where she was and what she was doing at all times. Atoma's article was about the information he was able to pull up off his girlfriend's computer from deleted and hidden files. He was not only able to find this information but he was able to put everything together and create a very detailed timeline of everything she did including phone calls, bank withdrawals, and addresses she went to.

I am not so lucky. My wife is aware of my computer skills and if she wants to do something on the Internet that she doesn't want me to know about, she'll use one of the Internet accessible computers at her college. When I wasn't pacing or going nuts in some way, I was on the web trying to find out everything I could: Where was she now? What was she doing? How long had she been there? What was this guy's name? Where did he live? Where did he work? What was his email address and phone number? Did he have a criminal record? Was he a sex offender? Was there a warrant for his arrest, hopefully?

www.blackbookonline.info has links to several sites looking up criminal or government records. With this site and others I was able to answer all these questions. Atoma said he was shocked that he was able to get all the information that he did. I can easily say the same thing about what I found off the Internet: my wife's college-issued student identification cards that worked similar to credit cards. You deposit money and that amount is credited onto the card. This allows you to use these cards to pay for anything while on campus. This information is then put on the college's website so the students can view their account balance and history. Through this website I was able to see when she arrived by the coffee she purchased before her first class and when she left by paying the parking fee for the parking garage. The college email account allows you to forward all incoming and outgoing emails to another account so you can view them in your preferred email provider. I had no trouble setting this so I could monitor her online communication. I had access to her class schedule, room numbers, times, teachers and their email addresses as well.

Our home phone and cell phone providers are also available on the Internet. I cannot only make monthly payments online but I can view the call history going back several months. I was able to see everyone my wife talked to on our home phone and her cell phone. If she deleted something from the history on either phone, it would not be removed from the online records. Using Firefox, I found an extension that helped me find street addresses. All I had to get was a name and city. www.skipease.com gave me access to the extension "People Search and Public Record Toolbar." This gave me several links to websites including www.zabasearch.com to do my searches and made it very easy to not only get me this guy's home address and phone number but also his wife's name. After a few searches I not only had the information I wanted but I also had names and addresses of him, his wife, and his mother-in-law. Family tree web pages gave even more details: children's and parents' names, birth and marriage dates and locations. Driving by the house gave me the chance to see their cars and license plates. I found www.dmv.org—*this website gave me links to my local state's online pages to see what I could find with the license plates.*

Many cities and counties offer websites that allow you to check records to see if someone is an offender or has a criminal record. Some states even have prisoner inmate lists on the Internet. These government sites are free and available for use by the public.

On my wife's flash drive I found a good-bye letter that was more of a love letter. It gave me more information allowing me to add Google Earth to my toolbox and gave me a picture of where they'd been and where they talked or dreamed about running away to. I was also able to visit websites giving details of each of these locations including some of the available intimate activities for the guests.

There is a ton of information on the Internet and once it's there you can bet that info will never be erased. If you doubt that, go to www.archive.org. *I created a website and removed it over seven years ago and they still have every detail of it. Once someone gains access to the Internet, it's like installing a new hard drive with all of this information. It's all right there. You just need lots of patience and to know how to look for it.*

During this last year things have improved. What started with the news led to me being severely drunk on a regular basis and my wife living with her family in another state for two months. I've also been nearly impossible to live with, but it's shown me that she's truly committed in making our marriage work. Things with us are better now but we are still in the process of healing.

A Broken Husband

While it's understandable to be completely distraught over what happened, you also demonstrate why people should be genuinely afraid with all of this information about them so readily available. Stalkers, lunatics, and people with overall bad intentions have all sorts of power to inject themselves into your lives and it's very difficult to escape their intruding eyes unless you have a decent plan to protect your privacy. The vast majority of people do not.

Dear *2600*:

> *Thanks for the great publication. I love it. I have been reading it since I was 12 and really enjoy it. I have had some problems lately that I think you great geeks can figure out or give some advice about. Here is my problem. I have been receiving a bunch of calls from the "Secret Service" lately and it is getting really old. I highly doubt that the Secret Service likes prank calling people, and I would like to know who is behind the problem. It is a private number which is the trouble. And I can't block all private calls because some of my friends have blocked Caller ID by default. So how should I go about stopping the calls and/ or figure out who is calling me? I figure they are just from some other more immature 14-year-old not too different from myself. I am getting the calls on my cell phone which is the worst part. They call about six times a day and call between 3 p.m. and 11 p.m.*
>
> Beachedwhale

Let's not be so quick to assume that the Secret Service doesn't like to prank call people. But you mention that this caller managed to block Caller ID, which right there puts them at a level of sophistication beyond that of the Secret Service. So what you're dealing with is an entity who is calling you over and over again without identifying themselves. Back in the old days, this sort of thing happened all the time. Today it's so much easier to identify incoming calls even when they're blocked. There's no more running to the central office while trying to keep the caller on the line and taking 20 minutes to figure out what part of the country the call is coming from. These days it's all logged somewhere. If the Caller ID is blocked, then you (the called party) simply aren't able to see that information. But your phone company can. Those are the people who can help you put a stop to this. There are other more tricky ways such as forwarding your line to a service that reads the ANI data rather than the Caller ID data. A few years ago, a company named Z-Tel inadvertently provided this service to their customers when forwarding calls to another line. Someone could call your landline with their Caller ID data *blocked, the Z-Tel service would ring your line and after a certain number of rings would forward the call to a second number that you had designated as part of a "follow-me" service, and the caller's actual number would appear as the incoming number on the second phone regardless of blocking status. This little feature was discovered and "fixed." But there are undoubtedly other ways of doing this and we're sure our readers will send in suggestions. For now, simply don't pick up blocked calls and return the phone calls of anyone you know who calls you with their number blocked. When the people behind this stop getting anything other than your voicemail, they will grow bored and move on to something else like physically attacking you. And then you'll know who they are.*

2008

Dear *2600*:

> This a message for people out there that I need help on undernet server #translate. There is a person who needs to have a reminder about abusive actions taken on #translate. They have banned people because they think that there was a spam going on by me and they need to remember that if they use mirc for illegal purposes that they should be charged and banned from mirc for life.
>
> Their name is @moniq so remember this name and let this person know about it.
>
> And this is a global message to all 2600 fans out there so please come in ASAP and thank you for the help.
>
> MORGAN

Have you been outdoors at all this year? There's a whole world beyond IRC, trust us. And even if there wasn't, it would be extremely difficult to figure out how we could possibly care less about any of this. We hope we were able to help.

Dear *2600*:

> *Not really an article, but unsure of where to send this to.*
>
> *Did you guys know Borders in NSW, Australia are selling 2600 for 18 bucks an issue! I know it's great that they sell it at all, but makes me glad I've subscribed through the website.*
>
> ROUTE

It's almost not really a letter, too. But it's an interesting factoid. The Australian dollar at press time is worth 95 American cents so it's almost exactly even. Even with all of the various charges that go into overseas distribution, charging nearly 200 percent over our cover price doesn't seem justified. Someone's making a lot off of us. And it ain't us.

2009

Dear *2600*:

> *I am being bothered by two people. Can you help me?*
>
> LEONARD

No. We could have maybe handled one but you had to go and complicate things.

Dear *2600*:

> *I want to place an order on your store and I would like to know if you ship to Australia. My method of payment will be credit card. So please let me know if you can assist me with the order. And please do not forget to include your web page in your replying back to my mail.*
>
> *I will await your prompt response as soon as you receive this mail. I will be very glad if you treat this email with good concern.*
>
> FRANK MOORE

This one almost got us but it actually is part of a scam. The "good concern" is what seemed a little fishy so we checked online and, sure enough, there are thousands of almost identically worded letters floating around on the net. What's the scam? Well, first of all, printing our reply in a magazine pretty much defuses the whole thing right away. However, were we to respond to this person via return email, we would undoubtedly get a followup asking for a list of products we sell. (That in itself is a bit strange since someone should already know this if they're interested in ordering something from us.) They would then send an email ordering a large number of items, and somehow the only way to make the order go through would be to involve bank transfers to third parties once their payment to us had been received. We would be enticed by having the amount they pay to us be substantially more than what we needed to transfer to the third party, most likely an additional amount for our "trouble." Needless to say, their payment to us would turn out to be fraudulent and any money we sent out would be lost along with anything we sent them in the mail.

It's hard to imagine people falling for such schemes but it happens all the time and the fact that even for a moment we thought this was a real letter indicates that these con jobs can, in theory, still work.

Incidentally, yes, we do ship to Australia.

Technology

Seeing how technology has changed over the years has been one of the more fascinating and sometimes frightening side effects of putting out a hacker magazine. The frightening part is partially the incredible speed with which everything has been transformed. The computers we were working with only a few years ago are by today's standards absurdly slow and outdated. Now imagine what machines were like a quarter of a century ago!

The other frightening aspect is how our attitudes have changed concerning things like privacy, surveillance, and "security." That last one is in quotes because the increased security we're faced with every day in buildings and airports and schools is really nothing more than the *illusion* of security. We've come to accept being spied upon constantly and we even willingly give out information that we would have clung to defensively in years past. Still, much of the hacker world remains healthily skeptical of these trends and I think if there's to be any sort of salvation from this pit, this is the community to turn to.

While the ingredients and the surroundings have changed, I believe the hacker spirit is still pretty much as it was when we first started to publish in 1984. In those early days, there was so much more attention paid to phone phreaking because it was our backbone. There was no Internet, no Skype, no easy way to communicate with people who weren't already within shouting distance. And that's really what was driving us back then: the desire to communicate. You see, it had been made so difficult and the people in control were so monolithic, that you sort of *had* to figure out a way to get around them. That's why coming up with methods of making free phone calls was so important. And as the world of phones began to change in the wake of the Bell breakup, there were suddenly a whole lot of new ways of doing this. "Blue boxing" had, of course, been the standard choice of illegally routing calls through the Bell System itself. But with the advent of new phone companies, the implementation of "equal access" (which allowed customers to choose alternate carriers), and the use of all sorts of gizmos like extenders, PBX systems, voicemail, and the like, there was a plethora of new worlds to explore. We couldn't have started publishing at a better time.

One invention that was first published in our pages probably turned out to be the biggest thorn in the side of the Bell operating companies in their entire history. That, of course, would be the guide to converting a Radio Shack tone dialer into a "red box." The tone dialer was simply a little box Radio Shack sold that emitted touch tones for completely legitimate purposes. With a little modification that most anyone could manage, the circuitry was altered to emit the special tones that made a payphone believe that you had just inserted money. Every kid in the country was using one of these converted boxes and the only thing the phone companies could do about it was completely change the insides of each and every payphone. It was an absurdly simple system they had designed (one beep for a nickel, two for a dime, five for a quarter) and its cracking was a victory in the fight against artificially high payphone rates. We don't think of it today, but back then "long distance" was anything more than 20 miles away and the rates were astronomical.

But naturally, phones weren't our only obsession. Computers were changing just as fast and people were starting to actually get their hands on ones they could bring home and play with. So all of a sudden, it became less essential to dial into someone else's computer (with or without permission) to play around and experiment. People began to put together their own systems and words like Linux began to be spoken with enthusiasm. Once it became easy to actually communicate via email on the fledgling Internet, the need to call far away BBSes to accomplish this became much less of a necessity. So much of the illegal nature of hacking faded away because we wound up getting what we wanted: cheap/free communications and lots of technology to experiment with.

None of us could have ever conceived of our device-crazy society of the present, where everyone seems to have a computer and a cell phone. Well, maybe we saw it in our imaginations, but I don't think any of us really believed it would come true. New technology certainly didn't solve all the problems, and all sorts of new ones wound up being created as a result of its prevalence. There were legal issues, privacy concerns, even the fun of the Y2K bug that was fodder for all types of discussions in the hacker world.

If there was a device of some sort, you can bet somebody wrote a letter to us about it. Everything from traffic lights to garage door openers, from surveillance cameras to grocery carts—the letters section was the place to theorize and share knowledge.

Granted, we didn't always have the answers—one writer's assertion that a grocery cart cost $2,000 went completely unchallenged (they actually cost around $75)—but we did our best.

I think you'll find that the tone of these musings on the new technology of the time is pretty standard for the hacker mindset: discover, mess with, share results, and move on to the next toy. That's really how we managed to get so far in such a short time.

EDITORIAL NOTE

Some letters in this chapter may contain URL addresses that are no longer active.

1984

Dear *2600:*

A few exchanges in my vicinity have recently upgraded their switching equipment. On 11/5/83, 914-268 switched from a step-by-step to a Northern Telecom DMS100. 914-634 and 638 also switched from a Number 5 Crossbar to a DMS100 on 6/9/84.

Through trashing, 99XX scanning, and "social engineering," I have found out the following: The suffix 9901 is a "verification" recording. In 268: 9903, 9906, 9909, 9911, 9912, and 9913 are all various recordings.

Another neat function on DMS100 is that you can hear the MF tones after most calls. New York Telephone calls this the sound of their new system helping to serve you better.

Also, these COs are under New York Telephone jurisdiction. Yet, they bought from Northern Telecom DMS100 instead of a "nice" ESS system from Western Electric. Could this be the breakup at work?

This equipment offers ESS functions such as call waiting, call forwarding, "dial tone first" fortresses, etc. My question is: What type of toll fraud equipment is standard or optional for the DMS100? Does it record everything like a pen register? Etc...

Curious

First off, our compliments on your ability to notice the changes that most people miss. As far as your 9901 discovery, many exchanges in your area have been known to do that. If you dial XXX-9901, you'll hear a computer read the exchange and area code. It doesn't really serve much of a purpose. But interesting things can always be found in the 99XX area, if your company uses it.

Concerning the DMS100, it is the breakup of the Bell System to an extent. New York Telephone has been buying equipment from Northern Telecom for some time now. But since the divestiture, they've become a little more flagrant about it. You'll see quite a bit more experimentation with products from other suppliers in the near future. The DMS100 is a very good switch, but it's got certain drawbacks as far as phone phreaking is concerned. It does have certain "devices." These don't work exactly like a pen register, but they wind up having the same effect. What is done is this: if you happen to send a 2600 hertz tone down the line, DMS100 will make a computer record of whatever you did in the surrounding time. They automatically investigate your line if this is detected more than an undetermined amount of times. This is where the pen register comes in. The system is already equipped to handle a pen register through a special box in the exchange that's set up entirely for that purpose. This box ties into their automatic surveillance equipment. So it's kind of a two-step process, but the DMS100 makes it much easier.

So far, we haven't been able to find any advantages (or bugs) in a DMS100. We will continue to look, though. Regarding the MF tones, they're simply not being filtered as they are in most places. The GTD#5 (made by GTE) and the DMS100 both, as a rule, only filter about ten percent of the MF tones. They also don't filter out rotary outpulses, whenever they exist. Perhaps it's a way of cutting corners.

DMS100, as you know, sounds just like ESS. About the only way you can tell if you've dialed into one is if you hear absolutely no clicks or pops when the party answers, as you do with ESS, crossbar, and step. Instead you hear a real faint, mild tick. When dialing out on one, you won't hear any clicks either.

Dear *2600:*

Here's the latest info on phone scramblers.

Phone scramblers/descramblers are a type of device that allows one to communicate over the phone without anyone being able to hear your conversation in between the source and the destination of the call. They are perfectly legal to own and operate, but there is one catch.

(The following information was obtained from a phreak who worked with an ex-CIA agent—to verify the validity of this statement.) The CIA, working in conjunction with AT&T, has the right to legally tap up to 600 phone lines in the U.S. The way that they are able to do this is that Bell Telephone can "test" your line any time it likes to see if it is working in proper order. Under the new ESS telephone system, finding scramblers/descramblers is very easy and, once you are found, an instant file is generated on both the sender and the receiver of the call. They (CIA) will also do their best to try and crack your scrambler code. I have been told that they are extremely good at this. My advice to those of you out there thinking about building such a device is to seek other ways and for those of you currently using them to stop. Using these devices is simply waving a flag to AT&T and CIA saying, "I've got something important to say, and I don't want you to hear it."

AGENT ORANGE

Thanks for the info and for the warning. While you're most probably correct about the powers that be taking a strong interest in any person using such a device, it seems absurd that we should have to constantly live in fear of having our privacy stripped, simply because we desire a little privacy?

We face some real problems in the near future if surveillance continues to grow and not enough is done by individuals to curb it. Technology is a deadly weapon— for anyone.

Stay alive, awake, and indignant—you can't lose. Thanks for writing.

1985

Dear *2600:*

I've been staying awake nights lately wondering why whenever someone gives out a nationwide toll-free number (in an advertisement or a radio show) they always give out two—one for callers outside their state, and one for callers within. Why can't the phone company give them one number for both? It might be cheaper the first way, considering that in-state calls are often discounted separately from cross-state calls, but even rich folks like IBM have a separate 800 number for the in-state calls. You'd think that they would rather pay more for one number and confuse their public less. Or would they?

INSOMNIAC

It has to do with tariffs. In some states, things get so ridiculous that the United Parcel Service has to ship packages to another state in order for them to be delivered within the same state! Similar antics are the rule with phones, especially now after the breakup. Generally, if an 800 exchange ends in a 2 (i.e., 522, 932), it's likely the exchange only works within the state and not nationally. In other words, it's been the telcos that have been setting the rules of two numbers for the same thing. That's been changing, though. ESS allows practically any number to be used as an 800 number regardless of exchange. This allows for lots of letter-numbers (800DIALITT, 800TELECUE, etc.) and also allows the same numbers to be used all over the country. So it should start looking less confusing. Now get some sleep.

Dear *2600:*

When will it almost be impossible to use long distance services? It is so easy to phreak off them and they never catch the majority of us, but when will it stop?

PUZZLED

Only when the world is a burnt out cinder will it stop completely. As technology changes, so do phone phreaks. Blue boxes used to be the only way a phreak made free phone calls. Now there are extenders and alternate carriers. We don't think extenders are going to die out anytime soon. Alternate carriers (Sprint, MCI, etc.) will get harder to abuse as equal access moves in, but there will always be a way. We love to hear about new methods.

Dear *2600:*

Is it true that blue boxing is on the way out? I hear it has something to do with CCIS. What exactly is this and why is it so troublesome to phreaks?

WORRIED PHREAK

Blue boxes are indeed a dwindling resource. But there's no need to throw them out yet. They aren't going to be totally useless for quite some time.

Basically, AT&T is converting gradually to CCIS trunks. These don't allow boxing.

In-band signaling is the only kind of trunk signaling that supports boxing. It is by far the most prevalent at the moment. Basically, in-band uses a 2600 hertz tone to indicate that a trunk is idle, and thus can accept routing instructions from an "outsider."

To box a call, the criminal blasts 2600 down the line after making a long-distance call. The line thinks it's idle and waits for routing instructions. Now the criminal puts a KP tone and an ST tone around the number that he's trying to get through to. These comprise the routing instructions. Thus, the line thinks it's idle, then it receives the routing instructions, and routes the call to wherever the person sent it. Now, his central office (CO), which does all billing, still thinks he is making the call to wherever, so it keeps on billing him at that rate. If it happens to think he was making a toll-free call, it won't bill him at all!

Another form of signaling is out of band. This uses control tones out of the normal band of telephone transmission (approximately 800 hertz to 3000 hertz). The idle tone is 3200; others shifted upward as well. So why couldn't you just make a new box? Don't forget, it's out of band. These tones aren't in normal transmission, so the local CO and customer interface loop just don't bother to transmit them. You can blast all the 3200 you want—it won't go through the CO to the trunk. But this is not the "death of boxing" as it has several disadvantages to the telco too numerous to mention.

The real death of boxing lies in Common Channel Interoffice Signaling (CCIS). This is a direct connect data line going from one ESS switcher to another at speeds up to 4.8 kB (usually 1.2)—incredible speeds. All routing instructions are sent through these lines. It isn't looking for control tones on the trunk; it's getting them elsewhere. This means that you can blast 2600 hertz tones all you like. It won't make a difference because the equipment is no longer listening for them. This kind of signaling is being phased in all over the country. Look for one in your neighborhood.

Since CCIS has benefits for really high-volume trunks, you can try looking for long-distance trunks to Canada, or rural states. These probably won't be phased in for a long time, if at all. (Remember, very few companies just invest in new technology for new tech's sake; even AT&T won't be able to do this for long.)

1986

Dear *2600:*

I'm a new subscriber and would like to contribute some interesting information.

First, there's a computer at 8005387002 that accepts a ten-digit DTMF sequence and speaks them back at you. The input must be ten digits with *, #, A, B, C, and D tones accepted but not pronounced, and is more forgiving than most COs as far as frequency tolerance goes. Tape recorded DTMF inputs will decode fine if your tape speed and audio levels are up to par.

I'm employed by the cellular telephone industry and would gladly write an article on cellular phreaking if there's any interest. The article will have to be a bit on the technical side however, and the techniques outlined will require a knowledge of electronics and hexadecimal math and access to a PROM programmer.

BERNIE S.

The number you gave belongs to a company that sells equipment that generates speech and is activated by touch tones. It will be a good tool for those who need to decode phone numbers. Radio Shack sells a chip that is called a touch tone decoder; maybe one of our electronically proficient readers can produce a schematic to make this chip work for us.

With regard to writing articles: please write about cellular phones, but write two articles. The first should be an overview of how cellular phones work, how calls are routed, and how we can call a cellular phone. Include some sample phone numbers or perhaps a directory of numbers to call. Try to answer simple questions that people who have not had a chance to use cellular phones may ask.

Then you can tell us how we can phreak them. If it is technical, try to give some reference sources. Try to make it interesting so, even if we lack the education and resources to practice cellular phreaking, we would want to read it.

Dear *2600*:

This comes from a Pacific Bell bill insert:

"A new prefix, 811, will soon be available for you to call your Pacific Bell business office toll-free from any area served by us. All our business office numbers will be replaced by toll-free numbers with an 811 prefix.

"If your PacBell business office numbers changed to an 811 prefix, the new prefix and number will appear on your telephone bill.

"After this change, you only dial 811-XXXX from any PacBell area in the state to reach your local office toll-free. However, if you are calling from an area where 1+ dialing is required, you must continue to dial the 1 before dialing the seven-digit 811 number.

"Some of you who have specialized equipment could have a problem in dialing the 811 prefix. You may need to contact your vendor. Until equipment modification is made, you may continue dialing the old business office numbers available from 411.

"This change will save you the cost of a toll call to PacBell when a call is made to all non-local offices. (Today, calls to our BOs are normally toll-free from a customer's home or business area.)"

Reader on the Pacific

Something else which is popping up in many places is the ability to choose your operators. Generally, dialing one "O" will get you your local operator, i.e., New York Telephone, New Jersey Bell. Dialing "OO" will get you an AT&T operator. The local operators are used for making collect, third-party, and credit card calls to local areas whereas AT&T operators handle longer distances. We presume they both have the same capabilities, equipment-wise.

1987

Dear *2600:*

> *Congratulations for beginning to publish articles on cellular telephones! The only thing wrong with the article was the title—"a look at the* future *phreaking world." Cellular telephone phreaking is not in the future. To my knowledge, cellular telephone phreaking has been going on for about four years in at least one major metropolitan area. The lack of detailed information on cellular telephone phreaking in this publication has thus far placed 2600 in the dark ages.*
>
> *Computer assisted blue boxing is still essentially the same as blue boxing in the dark ages of 1961. The same MF tones were used in 1961 and the phreakers were* very *successful. The advantages of using cellular telephones for phreaking and hacking instead of using landlines is outstanding. Cellular phones are the most immune to tracing even if used from a fixed location and it is virtually impossible to be nailed if you use one from a different location every time and for short duration or while you are traveling on a highway.*
>
> THE NEW AGE PHREAKER

We have yet to hear from a group of cellular phreakers, although we don't doubt they exist. By the way, have the Newspeakers among us begun saying celtels yet?

Dear *2600:*

> *Here's some interesting information that 2600 readers might be interested in.*
>
> *US West has introduced their new MPOW (Multi-Purpose Operator Workstation), which converts any IBM-compatible PC into a complete TSPS console with advanced capabilities. I'm sure many 2600 readers with PCs will find this concept intriguing. Perhaps there is a way to obtain and copy the board(s) and software.*
>
> *Mitel's new telco product catalog describes several interesting products, including MF tone generators and receivers, and a dialed-digit recorder. The latter is capable of "blue box detection" and detects and*

prints out all 2600 hertz and MF tone activity in red, triggers external alarms, and prints out all other line activity as well. No doubt phreaks have been busted with the help of this device.

Radio Shack now has a budget version of this for under $100. Their compact device prints out all dialed digits (touch tone and pulse) as well as the start and end times of all incoming and outgoing calls. Until now, nothing coming close to this in capability was available for under $1000. Law enforcement types will undoubtedly be using this updated version of the pen register in various "fishing expeditions." It's interesting to note that the use of such equipment by police does not require a warrant, which means they can (and do) use it to snoop on whomever they choose to without worrying about wiretapping regulations.

On a more upbeat note, I've discovered that the Mitel S200 PABX where I work is externally programmable by modem, and can be programmed to forward calls, among other things. I suspect many businesses with WATS lines and newer electronic PABXs are vulnerable to this "roll your own" approach to WATS extending. PABXs are fascinating—they're amazingly complex, versatile... and vulnerable. With a programming manual and a little inside knowledge or hacking skill, one can manipulate a company's entire telephone system from afar. Definitely worth checking into! I'd be interested in finding out what other 2600 readers have discovered about this subject.

BERNIE S.

Thanks for the info. We must add that the new Radio Shack toy is, to say the least, incredible. Is it really true that the police don't need a warrant to use that instrument? Where do they attach it? They must need some kind of permission from someone to either climb a telephone pole, install the thing inside the central office, or plug it into the side of a house.

Dear *2600:*

No one makes the following for the Apple:

1. *A combination speech generator, clock, printer buffer, and copy card. Maybe even some ROM memory.*

2. *A 110, 300, 1200, 2400 baud modem with European and American tones for 110 and 300 baud, autodial.*

3. *A card for interfacing an Apple to almost any hard disk. Also needed is a way around the ProDos limit of two 32 meg disks per slot.*

4. *A coprocessor/accelerator card that has all three major processors on one card: FAST 6502, Z-80, and 6800 plus 64K RAM.*

   Any takers?

   JOHN NIX

1988 _____

Dear *2600:*

> *Our small liberal arts college recently switched over from its old cross-bar system to the AT&T System 85 early this year. In the old days, you subscribed to Wisconsin Bell (like all Wisconsin residents), had your name in the phone directory, were available through directory assistance, and could use your long-distance service with the 1+ option. That has changed since then. If technology is supposed to make life easier, it doesn't and it also makes it a hell of a lot more expensive.... To make a long distance call, we now have to dial the 800 port (I use Sprint) and use a calling card to place the call. For those of you who use software for your modems, try programming a 20+ sequence! Then we also are charged a 50-cent surcharge for placing the call! And if you're like me, that really adds up. We are unable to call 950s, "toll-free" Wisconsin Bell lines, and we are unable to turn off call waiting for an incoming call. Good if you are trying to run a BBS from your dorm room. There are only 37 outgoing lines, and 27 incoming. So during normal business hours (the school's business office is also on the system), you will be unable to place a call! Someone from AT&T also forgot to program all of the reachable prefixes in our area! Even some of our faculty cannot call home! For a system that is supposed to be "smart," it sure isn't. If I were to call myself using the prefix that*

the school is accessible through, the phone system doesn't even know to just use an internal switch. Instead it goes ahead and wastes an outgoing and incoming line while I talk to myself. So to prove to the school that something needs to be done, we're getting 37 people to call themselves during busy business hours, and make the system paralyzed... for about four hours. That should teach them what they refuse to listen to. Like all systems, no one cares until it happens to them....

CRAY-Z PHREAKER
SKUNK WORKS

The bug you're about to exploit is probably the easiest part of the system to fix. All they have to do is block out that exchange like they've blocked out others. But the point is you have to get the college and the phone company to listen to you, the end user. You must do whatever you see fit. This means being loud and specific as to what problems you're faced with. Remember, you have the same right to telephone service as anyone else in this country. Being at a college does not mean you're signing away this right. Demand answers and if you don't get them, make sure everybody knows it.

And a message to AT&T: This is the second time in as many issues that we've heard major complaints about your System 85. Last time it was the House of Representatives. Who will it be next?

1989

Dear *2600:*

> *Columbia University has recently installed a new digital ROLM system to replace the old Centrex. This change has angered many students for the following reasons:*
>
> *The system is incompatible with modems and answering machines and the university charges "rental fees" for data-comm equipped telephones as well as for space on the Phonemail voice message system.*
>
> *They've blocked all access to 976 and 540 numbers simply because the billing software on their "state of the art" system is not able to track them.*

They slap a $5 surcharge on every collect call received.

You have to dial nine digits (91 + Personal Security Code) just to get an off-campus dial tone.

They impose a $100 limit on the Personal Security Code (PSC). If your account runs over $100, they turn your PSC off, even if it's in the middle of a billing cycle, and even if they didn't bother to let you know that your account was nearing $100.

The system bills you for a call 45 seconds after you stop dialing regardless of whether or not the call goes through. If you call long distance and let the phone ring more than a few times, you're billed for it even if the person doesn't answer.

The local calls are now timed as opposed to the untimed trunks we used to have.

There are only 400 trunks for over 8,000 phones. Reorders are not uncommon.

The Phonemail answering machine type service does not have enough channels. You could find the message-waiting light flashing on your station, but you might have to dial the message retrieve code 15 or 20 times because you can't get a circuit.

Is there any FCC ruling that the university is violating by imposing these restrictions on us? Their attitude is more one of "Well, that's just the way it is. If you don't like it, pay New York Telephone to draw wires into your room." Indeed, I have put in a private line. But there are a lot of people who just cannot afford to do that, and are being shafted right up to their tonsils. Any advice?

GMW

If you haven't already, read our Spring 1988 issue where we describe how such a system was installed at the State University of New York at Stony Brook with a lot of the same problems. Not much has changed there; in fact, many things have gotten worse. Frequently, every phone on campus appears to be busy because the university refuses to buy enough incoming trunks. Outgoing calls are often just as hard. A recent test revealed a wait of 25 minutes just to get an outside operator (it had nothing to do with the NYNEX strike). Outside operators refuse to bill to the originating number because the exchange isn't recognized as an actual telephone company exchange and they have no way to verify your identity. And ROLM can't handle call supervision so everything bills after 45 seconds, even international calls, where it can easily take that long just to get a busy signal. For a corporate setting where individual preference really doesn't matter, ROLM may be bearable. But for a university setting, no system could be worse, that is, for the students. We happen to know that Stony Brook makes money from the phone system now because the bills they send to students are much higher than the bills that come from the phone companies. In other words, New York Telephone doesn't charge the university for uncompleted calls. Yet the university charges the students. Where does the money go? It's getting to the point where some universities are as sleazy as AOS companies.

At least Columbia offers you the choice of putting in your own lines. Stony Brook offers no such freedom. The wimpy student government thinks they accomplished something by winning the right for a student not to have a phone at all, rather than winning the right to choose one system over the other.

A company called BITEK has moved in to handle billing. They developed a notorious reputation for ignoring student complaints about bills. Finally, someone broke into their Phonemail account (which they never changed from the default password), and changed the outgoing message to "Hello. This is BITEK and we don't care about your problems!" They've also just installed a "state-of-the-art" automated billing computer that sounds like it belongs on Lost in Space.

As far as we know, there's nothing illegal about what Columbia and Stony Brook are doing. But it's damn immoral to rip people off and make already chaotic lives even worse. There are ways of getting even, like scanning out the entire Phonemail system and clogging up the system with junk mail (not using your own extension, of course). Or calling someone on campus and sending a symphony of touch tones. The ROLM switch will dutifully keep the line open until the concert is over, rendering the recipient's phone useless. But the most effective way is to complain until you're blue in the face and to let those responsible know what's being said about them.

Good luck.

1990

Dear *2600:*

> Since the foneco strike in New York, the outdoor payphones that were
> vandalized and are now repaired do not *allow red box usage. Even
> after putting in the first coin, using the box results in a recorded request
> to deposit the balance due. They must have done something with the
> coin detect relay setup. Indoor phones in building lobbies and stores
> still seem to work okay.*
>
> CURIOUS

Throughout most of New York, a new relay system known as MARS has been
installed over the last year. You may have noticed a difference in the way
the dial tone appears. Some phones may not have been switched over yet.
We're looking for more information on this, as well as ways of bypassing the
disadvantages.

Dear *2600:*

> From what you know about the Caller ID systems that are gradually
> being introduced, do you think it would be possible to build a circuit
> or add-on box to your own home phone to send a false number to the
> party you are calling? It would seem to be the ultimate defense against
> the invasion of privacy while at the same time giving the appearance
> of cooperation without a "P" for privacy showing up on everyone's
> Caller ID screen.
>
> PETE
AKRON, OH

Absolutely. We hope to see someone do this soon.

1991

Dear *2600:*

> Kudos to Noah Clayton for that most excellent Autumn 1990 article, "Converting a Tone Dialer into a Red Box"! I found this article to be among the best on this subject and Mr. Clayton's genius is unsurpassed in considering and actually designing a successfully working red box out of a tone dialer—both in terms of styling and simplicity—not to mention effectiveness! It sure as hell beats using a converted Walkman for the purpose!

> But, speaking of payphones, I am very much interested in learning more about employing these phones for channeling to other numbers. . I am aware of using internal corporate loop lines for such action, but in one of your previous issues, you made mention of employing payphones to call out to other numbers. Could you recommend to me where I could find this information out?

> TG
> PA

Any phone line can be modified to forward to another number. Payphone lines are not supposed to be able to do this, but they certainly are not totally immune. Such modifications generally require access to phone company computers, which we frequently make reference to in these pages.

Dear *2600:*

> I'm not sure if you've covered this or not; I'd expect you probably have. Caller ID is the greatest thing to come along since caffeine pills. The Caller ID blocking system they have in my area is bullshit. It will not work if you run the whole gamut of options available. Reason: though the number displays as P or PRIVATE, you can still add the number to your Priority List or call back directly, in which case you can tap your line to see what numbers are being dialed. I haven't tried this; this is an assumption that the numbers are stored in the box, and not

in some memory hole in the bowels of C&P. Am I right? If so, don't tell everybody! If the authorities realize this we're screwed.

I also have a question. My home answering machine is the hackable kind that recognizes tones. Something weird, though: at my office we use a phone system with AT&T HFAI-10 phones, and I can't retrieve my messages directly using these phones. It's as if the tones aren't recognized. But if I take another nearby extension, and press the buttons so that the tones on phone #2 come out the earpiece and into the mouthpiece of #1, they're recognized. What would cause this? I know we have standard tones because I can use them for most voicemail applications. I've tried (my bank account, etc.). Any comments?

BK
BETHESDA, MD

As there are still relatively few areas of the country that have Caller ID up and running, we cannot give you a definite answer. But you should not be able to call a blocked number under any circumstance. That seems pretty logical. If you find that you can, please tell us. The authorities are liable to realize this if it's true—they don't need us to tell them. Regarding your touch tone problems: you probably just have lousy sounding tones. Either they're not loud enough on one particular instrument or they're not long enough. This is a common problem with the newer phone systems. Get a tone dialer (white box) to overcome this no matter where you are. (It's always sad to see technology marching backward.)

Dear *2600:*

One of the great values of your mag is that the back issues I have saved are always full of things I didn't understand a year ago but are invaluable now.

Case in point: your article on UNIX was mostly irrelevant to me in the winter of 1989, but a newly acquired Internet account makes it now altogether essential.

CH
NEW YORK

We've always put out the magazine so it doesn't become outdated. While operating systems may change, the basic frameworks will remain intact. And the spirit of hacking links it all together.

1992

Dear *2600:*

> *A friend recently passed along a copy of your Autumn 1991 issue. I particularly liked the discussion about the postal system, but there are a couple of recent developments that I think merit some follow-up investigation.*
>
> *Over the last year, the USPS has been installing new sorting machines that can read barcodes placed in the address block, rather than only in the lower right corner. (The USPS refers to this as "wide-area" barcoding.) Some of the questions raised by this new system are:*
>
> *If the barcode is placed in the address block, does the letter get sorted by the BCS or the MLOCR?*
>
> *Does it make any difference in sorting whether the barcode is placed above or below the address or in the traditional lower-right-corner location?*
>
> *If a letter is barcoded with only a five-digit ZIP Code, does it get fed to the MLOCR to attempt to find the ZIP+4? If so, is there an advantage in using the address block barcoding so that the MLOCR's nine-digit barcode doesn't overlap the earlier five digit?*
>
> *Further, quite recently the USPS has announced that it is using ZIP+6 coding. For street addresses, apparently the additional two digits are the last two digits of the house number. (For example, 1234 Main Street, Fooville, USA 12345-6789 will now be ZIP+6 encoded as 12345-6789-34, with the check digit adjusted accordingly.) The additional two digits will show only in the barcode, not in the printed address.*
>
> *What about P.O. boxes? Will they be ZIP+6 encoded? Most boxes already have a unique ZIP+4.*

What about apartment buildings that have a unique ZIP+4? Will they have the last two digits of the street number appended, or the apartment number, or neither?

If you are as intrigued by these questions as I am, I look forward to your follow-up article.

LM
BERKELEY, CA

The Face Identification Marker (FIM) determines whether or not a letter is processed by a BCS. If FIM A or FIM C is present, then the letter will go to a BCS regardless of where POSTNET is located. In fact, as long as the appropriate FIM is present, the letter will go to a BCS even if POSTNET is not used at all.

Our understanding of MLOCR is that it uses various elements of the address block to determine what barcode should be sprayed. The MLOCR will always try to spray the most accurate address information. For instance, if a letter has a regular ZIP, but the MLOCR determines the location's ZIP+4, then it will spray the more accurate barcode instead.

As far as we know, there is no advantage to using "wide-area" barcoding. It is an example of USPS actually responding to the needs of businesses, many of which use window envelopes for expedience. Wide-area barcoding simply makes it easier for those businesses to make the transition to POSTNET.

Eventually, MLOCRs will be upgraded to use ZIP+6. As a small business, 2600 awaits this increased complexity and confusion with delightful anticipation. In any case, your suggestion of a follow-up article will be mailed to those responsible.

Dear *2600:*

Ever since the California DMV decided it would be a good idea to slap a magnetic strip on the back of their driver's licenses, I've been itching to get into mag strip hacking. Of course, mag strips have been around for some time on the backs of our credit cards, ATM cards, and student ID cards, among others. But now there is an additional motivation. A driver's license is a whole new ball game.

From what I've heard from other mag strip hackers, the data encoded on the California driver's license is basically the same as the info printed on the card. Not too exciting. But the media is saying that in the future the DMV wants to encode your driving record on the card. Now that would be something worth modifying.

Imagine getting pulled over on Sunset Boulevard. The cop asks for your license, looks you over, and goes back to the car. While you sit there confidently, the cop zaps your card through his portable mag strip computer. No violations show on your record. Of course, the cop gives you a speeding ticket, so he encodes it straight onto your card and gives you a paper copy as well. But once the cop pulls away, you whip out your laptop computer and homebrew mag strip reader/writer from the back seat. A few strokes on the keyboard and your driving record is clean again—at least on your magnetic strip.

But even while there is no driving record on the card as of yet, it would still be useful to modify the info on the mag strip. Say sometime in the future you attend a large political protest, and you are arrested along with hundreds of others. In order to process this volume of people, the cops are using mag strip reader ticket printers. They zap your card, enter the violation, time, date, etc., and it prints out a citation for you. Of course, the cops aren't paying enough attention to notice that the information on your magnetic strip is different from the information printed on your license.

That was mostly fiction. Now here's some fact. In order to get in on the ground floor of the mag strip scene, I purchased a used mag strip reader from Marlin P. Jones and Associates of Lake Park, FL. The model was the Taltek 727. Cost only eight bucks. I figured out how to power the device, and by gosh it worked!

The unit is powered by a 12V AC supply. It has a RAM, ROM, a telecom microprocessor, and a 16-character alphanumeric display. Two phone jacks are on the back as well as some sort of serial I/O jack. It has two keypads. One has standard DTMF style keys and the other has keys for specific functions. The unit has several functions and was apparently used by a gas station of some sort. The most useful function by far is its ability to read the numeric track of a magnetic strip and display this info on its screen.

To do this, turn the unit on and get the "swipe card" prompt by hitting the "check" key, for instance. Then hit the # key. Now swipe the card and listen for the unit to go "bleedunk." Now hit the "CE" key. You will see the contents of the numeric track of the mag strip on the screen. Use "CE" to scroll through all the digits. Wala! Eight dollar mag strip reader. I have read credit cards, ATM cards, a university ID, and airline frequent-flyer cards.

This unit has another interesting feature—a built-in 300 baud modem. To use this, connect the unit to a phone line. Hit the "function" key, then hit 9. Now enter the number you want to dial and follow the instructions. The unit will dial the number and attempt to connect at 300 baud. You may want to monitor on an extension.

In addition, if you hit the "reset" key while the initialization message is still present on power-up, the unit prompts for a password. Haven't been able to hack that yet. Plus, if you can find no other use for this unit, it has a "calculator mode." Hit the * key twice to use that. Overall, a pretty nifty little gadget. I guess now it's only a matter of time before the hackers of the world encode viruses on their magnetic strips and hold the California DMV hostage.

Mr. Upsetter

Dear *2600:*

I have a complaint. I have been out of the BBS scene for several years, but recently I decided to break out my old 300 baud modem and call some of the local boards. I was surprised to find that not one of the local boards would let me log on using "only" 300 baud. Now, call me a Luddite if you want, but I remember not too long ago when 300 baud was the standard, and my modem served me quite well then. Now it seems that 2400 baud is the standard, likely to change again to 9600 baud in the near future. Exactly why shouldn't I be able to log on at 300 baud if I am perfectly satisfied with that speed and have neither the money nor the desire to buy a new modem every two years? This sort of baud rate supremacy and the very concept of planned obsolescence nauseates me to no end.

Henry H. Lightcap
Seattle, Ecotopia

To understand why people aren't overly thrilled with slow modem users, consider that they wind up tying up lines for much longer than most other callers. It's unfair that we all have to keep upgrading to stay with it, but that's the nature of rapidly developing technology.

Dear 2600:

You might have seen a television advertisement from Bell Atlantic promoting their package of optional features, namely Call Waiting, Call Return, and Caller ID.

The basic story of the commercial is that a husband at work calls up his very pregnant wife who can't make it to the phone before he hangs up. But no problem, she has Call Return so the phone will "remember" and return the call. And he, at work, has Caller ID so he knows it's her calling.

An hour later, she starts having labor pains and calls him again. He can't leave work, so he calls a friend (thanks to Call Waiting which "lets important calls get through"). Interestingly, there are two versions of the commercial at this point—one of them simply has the friend calling out. The other has a voice-over which says "Tone Block" keeps anyone from interrupting your important calls.

At the end, husband and wife are in the hospital with new infant, and they get an incoming call from their friend who used Call Return to get back to them. However, if you think about it, in most cases hospital PBXs will not send out a "proper" ANI. (Nor, for that matter, would other businesses.)

> DANNY
> NEW YORK

It's not the first time that phone companies have resorted to lies and deception to make a quick buck. It won't be the last.

Dear *2600*:

> *I have spoken with college telephone administrative assistants. I've called AT&T technicians. None have answered my questions. Now it's time to speak to the experts.*
>
> *As a college administrator at a small school in Colorado, one of my responsibilities involves responding to students who are victims of harassing phone calls. This past school year has seen a drastic increase in the kind of heinous phone calls that put college women in fear for their lives. (We're not talking about cute prank calls here.)*
>
> *Here is the technical background: The college phone system works around its own PBX allowing "on campus" calls to be dialed with only four digits. Calls to phones outside the PBX require a "9" to "get out."*
>
> *The college phone system has voicemail as an option. The voicemail system not only records the caller's message, but also tells the date, time, and* most importantly *it records the caller's extension if the call is from on campus.*
>
> *The question: I want to catch the caller(s). Doesn't it make sense to you that since the voicemail system is able to record the caller's extension if he/she leaves a message, that there is a way to note the caller's extension if the "callee" answers? Suggestions?*
>
> *Of course, a technically savvy caller could dial 9 to get off campus and then call his/her victim by dialing all seven numbers. The voicemail system is only able to note that the call is coming from "off campus." This leads me to my second question: There are apparently 50 lines into the college's PBX. I am told that the only way we can know the source of a call is to have "phone traps" placed on all 50 lines, and then find the source by matching the time of call. What do you think?*
>
> *ANI is not an option for the near future; legislative and corporate hang-ups are still clogging up the system.*
>
> *2600 is by far my favorite 'zine. Keep up the good work.*
>
> CB
COLORADO

Your system sounds like a ROLM. Whether or not it is, the same logic will apply. First off, it's possible to block the 9+ feature to the college, especially if your college owns the entire prefix. If not, individual numbers can be blocked in this manner. It's also possible to log all calls that are made in this fashion. But, more importantly, your telecommunications department needs to be more upfront with you. Don't settle for assistants; speak to whomever is in charge. Obviously, if the voicemail system is receiving information on which extension is calling it, the capability exists for that to occur on non-voicemail calls. It's only a matter of setting it up. There are special display phones on most systems that show this information on a screen. (On ROLM systems, they're known as 400s.) We suggest attaching one of those onto the lines that have the problems. As far as anything coming from off campus, you will need cooperation from the local phone company. We'd be extremely surprised if they weren't using ANI in this day and age.

If all else fails, try forwarding the problem lines directly to a voicemail message that sounds as if a real person is picking up. This may trick the caller into leaving a message thinking they're speaking with a person. Then if they're on campus, you'll have the number. And if that doesn't work, try to trick them into calling something that WILL log their number, like an 800 number.

Dear *2600:*

> I have just picked up my first issue and I really like what I see. I don't consider myself to be a great hacker, but I do have some very basic electronic skills and some fairly extensive programming skills.
>
> Recently, while I was flipping through the UHF channels, I picked up a very interesting phenomenon: phone conversations. My TV doesn't normally receive UHF channels, in fact, there isn't even an antenna hooked up to the UHF input, only VHF. My TV is a fairly old (very early '80s) model. It has a rotary knob for VHF and UHF, plus individual tuning rings on the outside of both knobs.
>
> I have noted that there are as many as four conversations at a time and they seem to be in my neighborhood. They only appear at the very end of the dial, around channel 83, however it requires a lot of tuning to even get it with a lot of static. If I get lucky, it sounds as clear as if you were on an extension. After one person hangs up, the signal jumps and I end up having to retune it.

About the only possibility I've been able to come up with is that the shielding is ineffective on our neighborhood connection post at the edge of the street by my house.

Now I have heard stories about people getting images on monitors from others due to RF interference. In fact, our beloved government was in a panic over this issue not long ago. What I would like is your opinion about this phone interference. Also, could you tell me what the frequencies in this area are and if I could get hold of some kind of radio equipment that could receive these frequencies?

SITTING DUCK

What you're experiencing has nothing to do with ineffective shielding. The upper UHF channels on older TV sets happen to cover the same frequencies that are now used for cellular telephones! And every time you listened in, you were break-ing a federal law. That is the extent of "protection" that is given to cellular phone calls. You can buy a scanner that covers the 800 MHz spectrum which is where cellular calls can be found. Buying such a scanner is legal. Owning one is legal. Listening to those frequencies is illegal. By the way, if anyone happens to tape any broadcasts over those public airwaves, please send them to us. We promise not to listen. (Make sure you don't either.)

Dear *2600:*

I just started reading your wonderful periodical two issues ago. I saw your Autumn 1991 issue at a local bookstore here in town. I picked up the magazine and was very excited. You see, I have been BBSing for a few years now, and have always been interested in everything you guys cover.

I've got a story. My father used to use my current bedroom when I was little as his office. When he moved into a real office, he had the separate line for the room disconnected. Soon after, I moved into the room. I didn't pay much attention to the outlet in my room because I thought it was just hooked up to the main house line. About eleven years after we got the line disconnected, I decided to see if it worked. I called a friend and was excited. I thought to myself I could now have a phone in my room. I then called my house line and it wasn't busy. My mother picked up the line and we talked for a while.

From what I could tell, Ma Bell just forgot to unplug the line and never charged us for it. This was all before I knew any better and before I got into hacking.

Then one day I picked up the phone to call a friend and there was a guy on the line. I didn't say anything until I think he said something to the effect of "Jeff, is that you?" I replied back that I wasn't Jeff and hung up. I was kinda scared to use the line for a while, but a few weeks later I really had to get hold of somebody and my sister was on the house line. I picked up the phone in my room and there was that same guy on it. I never got a chance to use the line again because a few months later my parents gave me a phone line for me to use in my room. When the new line was all hooked up, the old line wouldn't work. I didn't think about it all that much until recently.

My question is, does this happen a lot? I mean is Ma Bell really so big that they can forget about a line for over a decade? If I was older, or if I knew any better, I could have really raised some major hell.

THE PSYCHEDELIC SLOTH
OREGON

This kind of thing happens all the time. In fact, odds are if you move into a new house and plug in a phone, you'll be connected to someone else's line. That is what happened to you. Your old line was disconnected. The phone company does not "forget" about phone numbers for ten years. What they do instead is hook wires (cable pairs) together at a junction box, serving area interface, or the frame itself so that the same line shows up in two different places. Why? Because they make lots of mistakes. It's happened here at 2600 twice in the past few years. A good clue is when someone beats you to answering the phone when there's nobody else around. Or when you start getting messages for nonexistent people on your answering machine. Keep this in mind next time the phone company claims that you're responsible for anything dialed on your line. And remember that any conversation, wire or radio, can be easily monitored, accidentally or on purpose.

1993 _____

Dear *2600:*

> Here is a tidbit you may want to share with your readers: the AT&T
> calling card lets you call without any surcharge from any phone booth,
> hotel room, etc. for ten cents a minute under the following conditions:
> 1) You subscribe to Reach Out America ($10 month includes one hour
> of free out-of-state, off-hour calls); 2) Your call is made to a number
> which is in a different state than the one you are calling from; 3) You
> call off-hours (weekends or 10 p.m. to 8 a.m.).
>
> Concerning the ongoing issue of lack of security and verification pro-
> vided by various institutions (banks, telephone companies, etc.), I lived
> for many years in European countries (Poland, France, Switzerland,
> Great Britain), where you are not trusted by anybody. Every action re-
> quires positive verification. This may prevent some errors but it makes
> life very difficult for citizens who do not want to abuse the system.
> Making a collect call or third-party call takes twice as long because
> everything has to be verified. All contacts with authorities have to be
> done in person as nobody trusts a phone call. Even a letter is suspect.
> Coming to the United States, where you are in general trusted by the
> authorities, was a big relief.
>
> CL
Holmdel, NJ

*While the AT&T plan is better than nothing, there are still far too many restrictions.
What we need are inexpensive, surcharge-free, and easy ways for all of us to
make coin-free calls from anywhere in the country. Any phone companies out
there interested?*

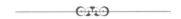

Dear *2600:*

> I have two questions. First, I have recently bought a $20 radio trans-
> mitter from a mail order place that advertised in the back of Popular
> Science. What I was wondering about was, would it be possible to send
> data from a modem over the airwaves via the transmitter? And just
> have the people listen in, connect their modems to a radio receiver,

and watch as the data is fed onto their screen? Next, could you try and settle an argument I am currently in with my friend? On New Year's Eve, while my friend and I were waiting for a ride to pick us up, I tried to explain to him that television cable was transmitted over the phone lines. He doesn't believe me, and although I do believe I read it somewhere, I am not certain either. Think you could clear things up for the both of us?

THE WINGED PLECENTA
OREGON

It certainly is possible to transmit data over airwaves. WBAI-FM in New York did this a number of years ago. Of course, most listeners felt compelled to change the station at that point. If your transmitter is delivering a clean signal, you should be able to do the same thing, however, your range will be very limited. Cable TV can only be transmitted over phone lines if the phone company controls cable TV. It's considered the wave of the future to have this happen, as well as to have cable companies delivering alternative dial tones.

Dear 2600:

In the process of gearing up for the 1996 Olympics, Atlanta city officials announced several months ago that they were going to begin to upgrade the city's traffic lights. By far the majority of the traffic lights here are "dumb" lights, with no pressure plates or flow sensitivity at all.

This announcement got me thinking. Anyone out there have any experience in hacking traffic light controllers? I find myself extremely curious about how these damned things work. Especially the "intelligent" ones.

LONE WOLF
ATLANTA

Traffic lights can be a lot of fun to play with. Many people aren't aware of how the sensors work or even where they're located. More recently we've heard of traffic lights that can instantly turn green when exposed to a strobe light. This is supposedly to allow ambulances to get through intersections more easily. We've heard rumors of rapidly flashing headlights having the same effect which could definitely lead to some interesting traffic situations. It goes without saying that if you're going *to hack traffic lights, you should be very careful not to put anyone's life in danger. So we won't insult our readers' intelligence by saying it.*

Dear *2600:*

> Enclosed is a copy of an advertisement for Modem Mate I and Modem Mate II. "Modem Mate I secures your modem by foiling the hacker. By attaching Modem Mate I to your existing modem, you make your computer system virtually undetectable. When a hacker attempts to call your modem, Modem Mate I intercepts the call by answering with a realistic sounding 'Hello.' The hacker will simply hang up, not realizing that a computer system even exists on the other end. Only someone who knows the proper codes and procedures can gain access to the modem." Modem Mate II only allows predefined calls using Caller ID.

> JULIAN
> CLEVELAND

Would we love to hear that "realistic sounding hello."

1994

Dear *2600:*

> The article, "2600 Robbed of Touch Tones" interested me for several reasons. In 1978, I brought a touch tone telephone from Chicago to my parents' house in a backwoods area of the Pacific coast that still runs crossbar equipment. I plugged the phone into the old style modular to four-prong adapter, dialed a couple of numbers, and, lo and behold, I was doing that touch tone thing! (We were probably the first in that community to have a touch tone phone.) My mom made me call the phone company to see if it was all right to use a touch tone phone. I hit the "0" on the touch tone keypad and talked with the operator. The conversation went something like this:

> Operator: "Hello, may I help you?"

Me: "Hello. Yes, you can, I'd like to know if I can just plug in a touch tone phone and use it without any problems?"

Operator: "No, we have to put more voltage on the line and then charge you $1.50 extra each month."

Me: "Uh. Oh, okay, well we'll call you when we go to touch tone phones, thanks."

By my calculations, my parents have saved about $270 now by not allowing the phone company to steal an extra $1.50 a month for doing absolutely nothing.

I know what a hassle it can be to have to go back to pulse, but I learned a great trick while living in Brazil that makes me appreciate pulse abilities. Most of the phones were rotary (as a matter of fact, I only came across one touch tone phone in the span of a year). To lock the phones from unauthorized use because you get charged for even local calls, they would put a locking mechanism on the dialing rotor of the phone. A kid I happened to be with showed me how to toggle the "on-hook" mechanism to simulate the pulses. Phone numbers with a lot of 9s and 0s are a little tedious, but with practice, even those numbers will be a breeze. By pushing down and up on this mechanism quickly, we were able to make all the phone calls we needed and then some!

I've got a cheesy phone with a dead keypad, so I keep in practice by using that phone to search for new loops and such while watching TV. Sure, a pocket dialer would do the same thing (unless you're in the 2600 office in New York!), but you never know when the batteries are gonna die or something. So whenever you see one of those locking covers on either a touch tone pad or the rotary portion of a phone, make an extra special effort to try out the technique!

PowER SPIKE

An old trick that still works. By the way, it looks like we may have figured out a way to get free touch tones for 2600 or, at least, not be charged an additional fee for them. A service known as Intellidial allows subscribers to have a limited number of PBXish features (call transfer, call pickup, hold, etc.) for a fairly low price. Touch tone service is automatic for anyone using Intellidial—we're still waiting for the day when it's automatic for everyone.

Dear *2600:*

> Last week I had to use a Scantron for my finals. I wanted to know
> if there are any marks I could place on the paper that would tell the
> computer to give me a better score. I think that the computer they use
> is some IBM model. Also, could you tell me how to write a program
> in BASIC that would get me into a system like the Internet? I have my
> local college's number and have gotten to the front door but when it
> comes to really getting in I have no means of doing it. I have also tried
> going in from the college itself but I have to be a student or something
> to get use of the computer.
>
> Thanks for your help....
>
> BRIAN

*Those little test papers have been the objects of attention for decades of frustrated
students. We've yet to hear a surefire way of defeating them. As for access, remember that the Internet is a lot more than a system; it's a rapidly expanding means of
travel to systems all around the world. If you're near a major city, you should look
for cheap Internet outlets or public UNIXes. Computer stores or user groups are
good sources of information. If you decide to go through your local college, it may
be worth your while to take a class there if that qualifies you for a free account.
If this is impossible, you can always go through somebody else who attends the
school but doesn't have an interest in the net.*

Dear *2600:*

> In response to a letter from Martin regarding features disappearing
> from AT&T Public Phone 2000s, I never saw one of these phones
> working. I made several calls and finally got someone at AT&T to tell
> me the story. Seems the phones were fielded, and AT&T upgraded
> the software in them. FCC noticed that they had stuff in there (like a
> modem to call an info service) that was not permitted in the tariffs.
> No word on how the FCC missed that on the initial release. So, AT&T
> was forced to disable those features until they get permission from the
> feds. I was told that the TDD still worked, but I never checked it out.
> There is also an RJ11 jack on the phone that will allow you to connect
> your own computer device.

Frankly, I find this very amusing... every time someone says that we'll soon be sending faxes from the beach or making videophone calls like in the AT&T commercial, I just relate this story and assure them that we've got a 20-year wait before they can deliver any of that stuff. Unfortunately, the promise of things to come has shut down a lot of people who would have actually delivered some of this stuff. And I thought Bill Gates was the ultimate vaporware salesman!

FRED

Have you ever gotten tired of hearing those ridiculous AT&T commercials claiming credit for things that don't even exist yet? You will.

Dear *2600:*

I read in the Winter 93-94 issue Owen's concern about LoJack. This device is used for tracking "stolen" cars. It works by sending telemetry information about the car to specific receivers placed around the area. The theory is that if the car is stolen, it could be traced to the stripping shop.

In reality, it transmits telemetry information tracing you to your favorite shops, hangouts, etc. All the time. Many insurance companies require LoJack-type devices on certain cars (usually high-performance sports cars, Saab, Porsche, etc.). Potentially, the insurance company could ask the LoJack company the average speed of your car, and appropriately adjust your rates. If money is tight at the LoJack company, they could sell your habits to marketing companies. There is a huge risk for anyone using the LoJack device on their car.

I believe the LoJack device is easily defeated by yanking out the antenna. These are little loop antennas. There are two intersecting loop antennas about an inch in diameter. They broadcast in the 900 MHz area shared by amateur radio operators. (If you are a ham and you interfere with the LoJack freqs, expect a call from the FCC!) These people are really nasty, and are quite difficult to feel treated fairly by.

TOMMY B.

We believe that manipulating any kind of surveillance or tracking device is not only acceptable but necessary. Stolen cars are nothing compared to what these things will do to us.

Dear *2600:*

> *I am writing in response to A-$tring's letter in the Winter 93-94 issue requesting information on UNIX-like operating systems for DOS boxes. One of the best UNIX clones I have seen is Linux.*
>
> *(Excerpt from the Linux FAQ)*
>
> > *Linux is a free, copylefted full-featured UNIX for 386 and 486 machines which use the AT bus. It is still in "beta testing" (the current version number of the kernel is less than 1.0) but is being used worldwide by thousands of people.*
> >
> > *Free means that you may use it, change it, redistribute it, as long as you don't change the copyright. Free does not mean public domain. Linux is copylefted under the GNU General Public License. Linux is a freely distributable UNIX clone. It implements a subset of System V and POSIX functionality, and contains a lot of BSD-isms. Linux has been written from scratch, and therefore does not contain any AT&T or MINIX code—not in the kernel, the compiler, the utilities, or the libraries. For this reason it can be made available with the complete source code via anonymous FTP. Linux runs only on 386/486 AT-bus machines; porting to non-Intel architectures is likely to be difficult, as the kernel makes extensive use of 386 memory management and task primitives.*
>
> *(End of excerpt)*
>
> *As you can see, the best part about Linux is that it is* free! *Linux comes in many "flavors" depending upon the distribution you acquire. I recommend the Slackware distribution: it is very easy to install and is the only Linux distribution approved by J.R. Bob Dobbs.*
>
> *The Slackware distribution is available on the net at its official distribution site of* `ftp.cdrom.com`*. For those without net access, it can*

be ordered on a 30-disk set on CDROM from Linux Systems Labs for $59.95. However, these folks and many like them who distribute software under the GNU Public License don't actually send any of their profits back to the authors or to the Free Software Foundation. To be honest, I spoke with the folks at Linux System Labs this morning and they said they were considering sending 10 percent of their profits to the FSF, but they weren't sure yet.

Be prepared to either get a new hard drive or repartition your hard drive before installing Linux. It is a complete operating system with its own file system. You will need a 386 or better with at least four megs of RAM to run Linux itself, eight megs minimum to run X Windows. The full distribution with X Windows takes up about 90 megs of disk space. However, that includes X11R5, all TCP/IP utilities, UUCP, GNU C and C++, joe, Tex, vi, emacs, four shells, kermit, mail, elm and pine, Sound Blaster compatibility, all the man pages, and full source code for everything.

I think it's a great way to teach oneself UNIX system administration and just about anything else you want to know about UNIX.

Toaster

Narragansett, RI

Dear *2600:*

This letter is about Xam Killroy's article on "Build a DTMF Decoder" in the Spring '94 issue.

I, for one, am an avid Commodore 64 user, as are several million people worldwide. Although the article was not completely negative, it did, in fact, state several bad points. First of all, the Commodore is not a "toy computer which currently serves as a doorstop."

Although the 64 is not as powerful as today's PCs, they are very user friendly. We don't have to worry about installing a program wrong, having IRQ conflicts, or hoping that the device we just hooked up to our COM port was in the right one.

The 64 is user friendly and very simple to use and very inexpensive. So you're probably saying, "Geez, this guy must live in the stone age." Actually, I own a 486 DX 33, and am sad to say that the only things I find better on it (over the 64) are some of the games. Sure, I might *have a base memory of a measly 64k, but the 64 can be upgraded also, just like my 486. Furthermore, millions of people can't be wrong about the 64; you don't hear much about it today, but rest assured, the 64 users are still out there.*

Just one slight correction: Commodore 64 can be had from $20 to $40 from most sources, and Vic 20s are all but impossible to find used.

All in all, it was a very good article, and I would like to see more done with this "toy computer."

By the way, this letter was composed with my 486... what a bargain. I spent $1200 on a machine to do this, while my $30 64 can do just as good a job.

COMMODORE HACKER

So why didn't you use it?

1995

Dear *2600:*

Came across this article in the San Diego Union-Tribune. *The system was compromised on August 13, 1994—the same day as the HOPE Conference in New York. Somebody's work that weekend did not go unappreciated. There was also an article back in August about "a mission" to hack the new New York subway toll machines made by Cubic here in San Diego. Keep up the good work.*

MR. PINK
SAN MARCOS, CA

The Metrocard system in New York has been meeting stiff opposition from the public. Not only has there been no expansion of the system to more than a fraction of subway stops, but the Transit Authority has barred the use of the cards by more than one person per trip. So, in other words, if you have a card with $2.50 on it, you're not allowed to use it for yourself ($1.25) and then let someone else use it for the remaining $1.25. Seems there was some kind of security problem....

Dear *2600:*

> *A while back, I was with a friend of mine in his car. We were deliver-ing a package in some old guy's driveway. I waited in the car and my friend's garage door opener was just sitting in front of me. The thing looked very tempting, so I picked it up and pointed it to the old guy's garage door. Just to see what would happen, I pushed the button. To my surprise, the garage door opened! Well, I quickly pushed the button again so it would close the garage door. I just wanted to know if you guys could maybe do a section on garage doors.*

> THE LAUGHING COW

It's quite simple really. The devices come with a default code. Many people never change the code so there are lots of us with the exact same code. A little common sense would make this security hole a lot harder to find.

1996

Dear *2600:*

> *Hi, I'm an 11-year-old hacker who loves this mag. OK, to the point: there's a trick where I live where you dial 984 plus your last four digits, wait to hear the dial tone, hang up, then pick it up again. You hear a high pitched whine, hang up once again, and the phone rings. What the hell is this?*

> VITAMIN X
> BETHLEHEM, NH

It's called a ringback and they're quite common although the first three digits are often different from place to place. It's for phone company testing which means you're not supposed to know about them. But we know of nobody in the history of the world who's ever gotten into trouble for using one, except for maybe annoying people inside their house by constantly ringing the phone.

Dear *2600*:

I have a comment and a story to relate. First, my comment: Keep up the good work! I don't know if I really consider myself a hacker as such (I'm a scientist), but I love learning about the technology around me. I firmly believe that knowledge, like anything else, can be used for good or evil; my son can verify that. I hereby salute you for providing knowledge to the masses!

Secondly, I want to pass on this story. My wife and I were driving around Leesburg, VA on Route 15 and we came to an intersection with something funny going on. All four stop lights were red and each had bright white strobing lights blinking on and off very quickly. In addition, traffic was beginning to pile up on all four sides. Understandably, nobody wanted to go through a red light. Neither of us had ever seen anything remotely similar to this before. Luckily, I remembered reading about how the police and fire departments change the lights green by using an infrared strobe and I might be able to simulate this by flashing the brights. So, I told my wife to flash the brights. What did we have to lose? Well she did it and only our traffic light turned green! Needless to say, that little trick gained me much respect in her eyes and got the traffic moving again. Those other folks might still be sitting there! Too bad for them. Maybe they should read 2600!

Dr. Bob
Germantown, MD

Dear *2600*:

I stopped war dialing for about a year and recently I got back into it. I soon realized that war dialing was not going to be as easy as it used to be. The first number I dialed, a voice picked up and said, "Hello? Hello?" This is what I was used to. As soon as my computer hung up the line and got ready to dial the next number, I received an incoming call. It was the guy I just war dialed. I was surprised—Call Return (*69) had totally slipped my mind. I have tried to war dial a couple of times since then but the same thing happens. The modem is not able to dial out because the line is tied up with all the angry incoming calls.

I am able to block Caller ID with the handy *82 disable number, but what can I do about Call Return?

Ty Osborn
Guy At The Desk

Since you're obviously in a part of the country where blocking (*67) does not disable *69, we have an alternate solution. Get call forwarding on your line so that when people call you back, it goes someplace else and doesn't interfere with your dialing. That's a marketing angle the phone companies are unlikely to pursue.

Dear *2600:*

When walking around a strip mall, I heard a beeping sound. It sounded like a beeper, but faster. I looked around and no one was there. But there was a NYNEX payphone! It was beeping. I picked up the receiver and it stopped. So I dialed my friend's house and I heard the "Thank You for Using NYNEX" recording. It didn't ask for any money, the call didn't go through, and when I hung up the phone, it started beeping again! What could this be?

PoT-UsA

Sounds like one of NYNEX's new phones was in some sort of trouble. These models are almost exactly like COCOTs and a number of them cut off the touch tone pad after only a few digits. When you pick up the receiver, you hear a fake dial tone. After you actually dial the number, the phone grabs a real dial tone and makes the call. It sounds like this phone was having trouble getting a real dial tone so it started screaming for help.

Dear *2600:*

You may have noticed that in newer models of cars, many come with remote control unlock/lock transmitters. They do a variety of things— the Mercury minivans can even be started remotely. Now, since there are only a certain number of frequencies, some will overlap or share.

I have noticed that with my remote I can walk down the rows of cars at malls or other parking lots and open a car every so often by continuously clicking on the button. So far, I have had the best luck with Dodge cars and trucks.

TheFetish To Heresy

1997

Dear *2600:*

I was thinking about the millennium bug (computers supposedly will not be able to tell the difference between 2000 and 1900 due to an error in coding, and they might interpret the change of 00 at the end of the date as 1900 instead of 2000 which will in turn cause a majority of systems to shut down) when I realized a quick fix to this might be a Morris worm program to correct the problem on a widespread basis. Anyhow, if the hacking community presents this even as a workable solution at the very least it might improve the public perception of us, especially for something we took so much sh*t over in the first place (worm).

Steven

Sending worms out all over the net to fix software is probably not the best way to make friends.

1998

Dear *2600:*

I went to a nightclub the other night and the security guard had a new ID verification machine. I unwittingly gave my ID to the guard—he "zipped" and up came all of my info. It looked like a Trans330 (credit card authorization box) but all it did was read the mag stripe on

the back of my ID and then verify that it was valid. There was also
an antenna hanging off the side. So now someone somewhere knows
simply that I drink or go out but where does it go from there? Does it
know about outstanding warrants or unpaid parking tickets?

THE MEDIK

It certainly could if it were programmed to do this. What we need to find out is what
information this thing is currently looking for and what records are kept of each
query. While it may not be a privacy invasion yet, there is little to prevent it from
becoming one in the future.

1999

Dear *2600:*

I picked up my first issue of 2600 (15:3) when it was printed last year,
and after reading skwp's "Back Orifice Tutorial," a great sense of relief
and of closure washed over me.

You see, last summer, in the guise of being my friend for several months
(and via my own stupidity) a person using the BO software comman-
deered my machine. At which time he/she then proceeded to format
my hard drive, all the while raving something about my having at-
tacked this person (claiming to be female) in the university parking lot
that I was attending. I was angry and shocked—quite near the verge of
outright openmouthed silence. In all my years, I had done my best to
stay out of flame wars, and the BS that can wrap up and engage your
full attention on the Internet if you let it, and now, here I was sitting
at a nothing screen because I had let down my guard—despite all the
literature I can remember reading (and still do) stating the obvious
of what can happen if I should decide to take that risk; despite all the
hype that the local news likes to drudge up on everything from child
porn to hacking The New York Times, etc.

Although I had all but forgotten the incident, I'm glad I ran across
(albeit somewhat belatedly) skwp's article. At last I understood the

technical side of what happened to me and my machine, giving me a sense of freedom from that ghost that occasionally haunts in the Coke-induced buzz-haze of the wee morning hours. Understanding, if not in whole, then in part (for after all, who can understand the lunatic ranting of those who just need help) can help rebuild and make a new person of you, as it did me. So without further ado—I realize of course, this was a long-winded way to say it—thank you. Thank you very much. I shall look forward to future issues.

MADE IN DNA

You really do understand what it's about. It would have been easy to blame hackers for creating the program or for explaining how it works as so many do. You chose to listen instead, and to learn.

Dear *2600:*

In the letters section of your Spring 1999 issue (16:1), the editorial response to the question concerning the Y2K bug was mostly dismissive. I do agree that the "threat" of this bug has been blown out of proportion, however the very media frenzy that is creating this scare can be used to great effect by a knowledgeable hacker.

First, even though many systems are Y2K compliant, the media has most people expecting problems. If files (such as log files, etc.) mysteriously change or vanish on January 1, 2000, most people will credit this to Y2K, be thankful that it wasn't worse, and not look any further.

Second, there will be some systems affected by the bug (most likely legacy systems and older versions of some software). Searching through revision histories of software packages often reveal at what point a particular software company "fixed" any Y2K bugs. Systems running prior versions of software may suffer some problems on Y2K. (The usefulness of this depends entirely on the software, system, and the specific effects of the bug on the software.)

I would also like to add a small tidbit of information relating to the "Adventures With Neighborhood Gates" article in your Summer 1999

*issue (16:2). Many models of visitor dial boxes call the resident's phone.
The resident then may choose to let the visitor in, and open the gate
by dialing "9" on a touch tone phone. When the resident answers,
the dial box mic usually remains active. A tone dialer held up to the
mic can usually be used to send the same signal to open the gate. If
a resident wants to give someone access through the gate without the
resident being present, they can record the appropriate tone onto the
outgoing message of their answering machine. Anyone calling the resident from the gate when the resident is gone will get their answering
machine. The machine plays back the recording (which has the tone)
and the gate opens.*

R.B.

*Good luck finding an answering machine these days that will allow you to record
a touch tone. With regard to Y2K, we're going to remain rather dismissive on this
one. What many people fail to realize is the fact that these so-called Y2K disasters
can occur at any time if computers are involved and adequate backups are not. At
least with Y2K, we have a date with doom or, at worst, an approximation. Any computer system can fail without warning for reasons that we haven't thought of yet.
Assume that and work within those parameters—we bet you'll survive just fine.*

2000

Dear *2600:*

*I've been enjoying the current discussion on school IDs and wish to
contribute my school's little story. Our faculty wisely decided to make
all of us wear necklace badges every day, and, as could be expected,
there was widespread resistance. Tweeter, in issue 17:3, mentions his
plan to organize a total boycott of the ID system, and I am happy
to report that our school's doing just that rid us of our ID problem.
Nowadays, the IDs are only used for admission to pep rallies and
wearing them isn't required. Our school also took the wise step of
removing the SSNs from the badges and replacing them with numeric*

birthdates (010203 for January 2, 1903). Of course, it leads many of us to wonder why the IDs still exist, but schools' mentalities are clearly not something for "ordinary" humans to fathom.

SEKICHO-SENSEI

And when they come up with a reason why having your birthdate on these cards is necessary, let us know.

Dear *2600:*

Just walking on campus, and what do I see but a group of elementary schoolers with barcoded photo ID cards. How infinitely sad.

DATA REFILL

Wait till you see the tots with imbedded chips.

2003

Dear *2600:*

At school we went on a walking field trip to some play or something, and on the way we saw an ATM. And I told my friends that I had read an article in 2600 that said if you press the right buttons you can get to a hidden menu. So I went over to the standalone ATM and pressed all four corner buttons and the menu came up and it started beeping (like a PC does). It beeped eight times. All my friends were laughing and we still make jokes about it to this day. Thanks for the laughs, 2600!

SATCH379

We're always happy to provide amusement. And the fact that you probably have no idea at all what your field trip was supposed to be about is just icing on the cake.

2004

Dear *2600:*

After reading all the letters about insecure systems in the previous issue, I wanted to write to you and share the wonderful experience that I had in setting up my voicemail at school this past year. I go to Rensselaer Polytechnic Institute (www.rpi.edu) and everyone who works there is stupid beyond belief for a number of reasons. One of those reasons is the handling of the voicemail system. In order to initialize your voicemail, you have to pick up any phone on campus, dial the voicemail number (6006), then dial your phone number (for instance, 4002), then input the default password (122456), then use the menus to enter a real password, set your greeting, etc. The problem with this system, as I'm sure you've already guessed, is that anyone can set up anyone's voicemail. When I first set mine up, I accidentally dialed the wrong number and set my own password and greeting to my neighbor's phone. I could easily have gotten to school a day early and set every voicemail on campus to profanity or something equally juvenile and damaging. The point of this is many large organizations like schools and corporations seem to go instantly stupid when issues of security come up. The fact that voicemail exists is apparently good enough for them. Any concerns about security or impersonation are just ignored.

MANIACDAN

Even 20 years ago this would have been considered absurdly dumb. But we're impressed that they deviated from the 123456 default password string. We smell a Darwin Award.

Dear *2600:*

I was recently at a Wal-Mart in Mountain View, California, and I noticed that they had gotten some shiny new carts for the customers to push around. On the left front wheel of all carts is a very boxy cover that none of the other three wheels has. On inspection of the *new cart, there is a notice that the cart won't go past the yellow line in the parking lot. I assume that this is an attempt to prevent theft of what I'm told are $2,000 shopping carts (sounds a bit high, doesn't it?). Anyway, out in the lot I played with a couple of the carts to try to determine how they knew they were crossing the yellow line and inspecting the method of preventing movement past (metal skid drops over left wheel). I found that the silly things work via a simple optical sensor tucked under the big wheel cover that I assume detects the color yellow and engages the metal plate to stop the cart from moving forward. Does this sound stupid to anyone? All you'd have to do to avoid the wheel lock engaging is trick the sensor into not seeing the yellow line with, say, a piece of tape or aluminum film or aluminum foil over the sensor or maneuver the cart around the line somehow? Just thought I'd mention this to everyone. I don't expect to ever try it as Wal-Mart does a very good job of protecting their assets and there is no shortage of outside cameras.*

LABGEEK

This might explain why people have been spotted carrying Wal-Mart grocery carts over their heads in the parking lots. If you really want to cause some mayhem, a nice yellow line painted right next to the store will certainly accomplish this.

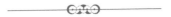

Dear *2600:*

Started using Google AdSense several months ago. Here's something that all webheads should know—lawyers like to get clients, especially on cases where they know that their odds of winning are very good. For that reason alone, lawyers really spend a lot on Google AdSense words like asbestos, cancer, or mesothelioma, etc.

Mesothelioma pays out big—we're talking like 20 clicks can get you near one hundred dollars! Here's another neat thing to know: if you sign up with the Google search thing via AdSense and put the search on your site, you can search for those high paying words and click on the first Google ads that come up on the search and then you can pull up the keywords that you want to when you want, not having to wait for the ads to rotate up to your site for clicking. If you are using a proxy server to do all of that, it's possible that it may be a little harder for them to follow your IP address back to you!

Please note that some folks overdo this or do it stupidly and get their accounts shut down, but if you are careful, you can succeed at this pretty profitably for the long term. Never thought that lawyers would be filling your pockets with cash for free, did ya?

JEFF AFFILIATE

And somehow we still don't.

2005

Dear *2600:*

Recently I was taking the placement test at Mercer County Community College here in New Jersey and made a very disturbing discovery. MCCC uses a web-based testing system called "ACCUPLACER" (which is approved and normalized by the College Board). The client machines were standard Windows 98 machines, accessing the ACCUPLACER system via IE (obviously this may be different at other locations).

Before the test begins, you are asked to enter your personal information into ACCUPLACER. While entering my information, I noticed a drop-down box appeared as I entered the first letter of my name. It took a second to realize I was seeing a list of people's names who took the test on this particular machine which started with the same letter as mine. Curiosity getting the better of me, I skipped down to the "Address" field and entered a 1. Sure enough, I saw every address starting with a 1. After a quick chuckle, a sudden realization struck me as my eyes drifted to the Student Identification Number (which is usually the person's Social Security Number) field. I entered a 1 and, sure enough, I saw a list of every SSN that started with a 1 that had been entered on this machine. Now, keep in mind that you are given paper and pencil for scrap, and most of the time the proctor was either not in the room or not watching closely.

It would be trivial for somebody to sign up for the placement test (after verifying over the phone that ACCUPLACER is an option) at their local college, which may be free, and generally carries no obligation to actually sign up for classes afterward, and leave with a few dozen SSNs written on a scrap of paper in their pocket. All the person has lost are the two hours the test takes.

So who is to blame for this? Primarily, I would say it is a lapse in security on the client machines. Disabling all Cache and AutoComplete features would fix the problem on the client end. However, you have to question the wisdom of ACCUPLACER using SSNs as identification for a simple placement test in the first place.

Just thought I would get the word out for anyone who may be getting ready to take their placement tests that, for their own security, they may want to avoid ACCUPLACER if given the choice.

MS3FGX

Dear *2600*:

I've read several of your magazines so far. I will admit I am not actually much of a hacker, but by reading your magazine I have become a little more aware of things that could be exploited. I was at the airport the other day and I was helping my grandparents get to their airplane by pushing their wheelchairs. I wanted to push them to the gate so I was given a special ticket. The ticket allowed me to go with them, while not allowing me to board a plane. There was one problem though. As I was going through security, they only glanced at my ticket. Suddenly I realized that one could take a picture of the ticket and edit and use it again to get back to the gate area, provided the edited copy was well made and the checker didn't ask for the disabled person you were helping. I'll leave it to you to speculate about how this could be dangerous. Even more surprising, when I left the airport, no one ripped up the ticket or had me throw it away. I could have taken it home, scanned it, and edited it to produce numerous tickets such as this.

The second thing I noticed were the payphones. I had an urge to fool around with the phones, but did not for fear that I would look like an idiot. However, I noticed that some of the individual areas where the phones should have been had been covered by a sheet of metal that was attached with some sort of weak adhesive. With relative ease, one could pull the sheets off the wall and get ahold of the cords that the phones had once connected to. Again, I'll leave you to speculate about what one could do with a hole in the wall and potentially the cords that had once connected to the payphone. Thank you for your time.

ANONYMOUS

If they were the old fashioned Bell payphone lines, all you would be able to do at most would be to use that line in payphone mode. If it was a COCOT line, there might be some other possibilities. But this is so frequent a scenario that it's not that big a deal. Also, you would likely draw quite a bit of attention by pulling metal sheets off walls and connecting your instruments to the wires.

As for your first scenario, this is probably something the airport people would take seriously. But remember that it wasn't too long ago when going to the gate with a passenger wasn't anything to be concerned with. We're not convinced that "world events" have changed anything but the paranoia level in various officials. After all, anything you could do at the gate if they let you through without a ticket could also be done simply by buying a ticket. So where exactly is the increased security? We suspect it resides in a few minds but not in many other places.

Dear *2600:*

On a recent trip I had a layover in Houston. While at the airport there, a lady came over the PA system and said "Threats, suspicious activities, and inappropriate jokes will not be tolerated and will result in jail time." I can understand the first two, but we can't tell jokes now? Yes, you read that right; it's apparently illegal to tell off-color jokes in an airport! Anyone know what happened to the First Amendment?

On the plane leaving Houston, I took the opportunity to experiment with the phone in the back of the seat in front of me (a Verizon service).

I had noticed that you can reach the operator for free (normal calls require a credit card transaction). Having already forgotten about that encouraging message over the PA at the airport, I told the guy next to me it would be funny to dial up the operator and tap out SOS in Morse code. He said you had to pay to reach the operator. I showed him differently, and once I was connected to the operator I typed out SOS three times. Then I held the phone up to my ear. To my horror, I heard "Stay on the line for 20 seconds and we'll land the plane." I hung up and freaked out for the next 45 minutes.

I know sending out an SOS in a post 9/11 world was stupid and immature, but this system seems incredibly ludicrous to me. I'm guessing this "feature" was implemented after 9/11 since many of the passengers were smart enough to call home using the same type of phones. It must have been created under the guise of safety, but I doubt it could ever protect anyone since I don't know many people that can translate SOS into Morse code, and I haven't found anyone else that knows about this setup. One final concern: How did Verizon come to control which planes stay in the air and which ones are grounded? Aside from incompetence and virtual bribery, why would our government entrust our safety to a phone company?

Dr. Apocalypse

There's really nothing new about the joke thing. But by "inappropriate," they mean jokes about security, hijacking, etc. that might make people really nervous if there's the perception that you may not be kidding. This has been the policy for decades.

As to what you heard, you didn't mention if it was a recording or a human. We'll assume it was the latter in which case we'd bet it was an operator attempting to ascertain whether or not this was a true emergency. By giving you that warning, it sure got you to stop in a hurry. Verizon obviously doesn't have the power to land planes but after receiving an SOS signal from an aircraft, they're certainly in a position to pass that along to the relevant authorities. We trust you learned a valuable lesson here and hopefully kept many others from venturing down this path.

2006

Dear *2600:*

> First keep up the awesome publication. I read it to stay sane.
>
> I was frequenting one of my favorite forums when I happened upon a link to http://www.privatephone.com. This intrigued me beyond belief. The way it seems to work is that you choose a state, an area code, and then a city. It'll generate a number for those specifications and then all you need to do is provide a valid email address for this messaging service to work. This seems extremely interesting and looks like a lot of fun could ensue, especially along the lines of remaining anonymous in this day and age when that's becoming increasingly harder.
>
> I wouldn't mind some more information on this service if anyone out there knows anything about it. And I certainly hope I'm not poking at something that has already been discussed. Though I don't believe that I am.
>
> CRAPINAPLE

These services are popping up all over. The result is a phone network that has almost no similarity to the one where geography actually meant something. Now we can each have dozens of phone numbers from all parts of the country and confuse the hell out of people who want to know where we really are.

Dear *2600:*

> Last night my girlfriend and I were at a local Meijer super store. Most times I'll just go to the register to check out. The employees are usually friendly enough. We were in a bit of a hurry this time, so we went to the U-Scan. I had some cash on me and she had her debit. I assumed that because after I put in my cash and the "other payments" option was still on the screen that the programmers of the U-Scan were bright enough to figure out that if a card is swiped to only charge the difference. No dice. Instead, the machine flips out! The under-trained

employee didn't ask us what happened. He just simply canceled the order and printed a receipt. Apparently the machine didn't even record that I put money into it. Or, if it did, he deleted it. Regardless, all he did to do this was touch the corner of the screen, type 27, then type 240. I'm assuming one of the numbers is a store number and the other is his employee ID. The menu was very simple; a monkey could navigate through it. With a bit of a distraction it seems like you could start printing your own receipts! This is stealing and illegal, so don't! But it's always fun to play with Meijer employees.

CHEMDREAM

2007

Dear *2600:*

My neighbor's burglar alarm went off this morning and after it kept going for a while I walked around their house to see if anybody was going to do something about it. Apparently my neighbors weren't home because there was no sign of life, but they had several "Protected by Brinks" signs on the lawn. So I called Brinks to see what they had to say. After navigating their automated phone system to get to an operator I was asked to enter the phone number of the location where the alarm is installed. Since I didn't know my neighbor's phone number I had to enter "#" several times to get through to a person. I explained to the Brinks representative that my neighbor's alarm was going off. When they asked me for my neighbor's phone number I explained that I didn't know it but I gave them my neighbor's address. After checking their records they happily informed me, "Oh, that address isn't monitored." Nice! What if I had been a burglar casing the neighborhood to find unmonitored alarm systems? It wouldn't take a genius to social engineer these idiots who are all too eager to tell you which addresses are monitored and which aren't.

ARCADE ONE

Dear *2600:*

I am writing about possibly getting an article posted. I believe that this would make a worthy article for its controversial nature and its unending curiosity. I have always found the idea of time travel plausible. It has always been on the back burner in my mind trying to figure out how and why. So I am asking that you give a moment of your time to read a story/theory about time travel. I think it would be worthy of readers' time as well. After the publishing of H.G. Wells' book The Time Machine, *science has embraced a new study. Throughout time they have become more and more aware that this might not be so far-fetched. Scientists are believing that they are getting closer to unlocking the mystery and making it possible to indeed time travel. Many theories have been presented over the years and I would like to share mine with you now. First off, I would like to eliminate the idea of using a DeLorean car (as in* Back to the Future) *to time travel. I would also like to eliminate the idea of a time machine that can travel both forward and backward in time. I state that because time is a constant. It is always moving forward. Chronological events in history easily verify this. Now that I have cleared up those little misconceptions, I would like to move on to the bigger picture. To make time travel possible we are going to need a vessel that can carry us. This would look no different than your average space shuttle with minor alterations. For example, the engines may be different and the gas chambers larger to hold the amount of fuel that is going to be needed to make this a reality. Now with our shuttle built, we need to discuss how it is going to be used. Assuming that the shuttle was built to execute our plan, we are going to need to travel away from the Earth at a speed faster than the Earth is traveling. Time on Earth is only relative to the speed the Earth is traveling. We manage our time due to the spinning. By traveling this speed (assuming that there is enough fuel to propel us that fast and for the amount of time), we are able to create a difference in our time and Earth's time. Time now having a different factor for us, we can imagine that the Earth is aging more than we are at a faster rate. It is as if we are slowing down time due to our speed. Without precise calculations we are not able to determine the amount of time we would be exceeding during our travel in space. Upon returning to*

*the Earth, assuming that the theory is correct about time being differ-
ent for moving objects and the speed they are traveling, we can infer
that the time we have aged would be less than what the Earth has aged.
It may not be the fountain of youth, but it is a step up. Remember
that this is only a theory. There are kinks and ideas that are subject
to change. Thank you for your time.*

JESSE

*It's good to hear that scientists are exploring the possibility of time travel without
the use of a DeLorean as they are rather expensive and difficult to get a hold of.
We also are indebted to you for confirming that time travel is indeed a one way
street. This easily explains why we have not met any time travelers since they
would have to come from the past where it hasn't been invented yet. We look forward to future reports from the laboratory.*

2009

Dear *2600:*

*I have been in the electronic security industry since the early 1990s, at
first installing and later designing and selling CCTV, access control,
intrusion, fire alarm systems, and integration packages. I think that
your fine magazine should be mandatory reading for anyone who
works in any security field. I've been a reader for so long that I forgot
when I started.*

*All of our security systems have a computer/network component. It
always amazes me that my industry "peers" seem to know so little
about computer networks and less about network security. I always
ask people in my business if they read or know what 2600 is, and the
answer is almost always no. It is no wonder that IT managers cringe
when they see us pulling into their parking lots!*

*I want to remark on an editor's response to a letter by Estragon in
the 26:1 issue concerning CCTV systems in supermarkets. This same
remark can be applied to many surveillance system installations.*

Large CCTV installations in supermarkets are very common. Many "mega-stores" may have 64 or more cameras and four or more DVRs connected to RAID arrays to collect and archive video (to be stored for years in some cases). The reason is not to stop you from shoplifting a steak or some dairy products, although this deterrence is a side benefit. The main issue is the store protecting itself from fraudulent "slip and fall" personal injury lawsuits.

You have to sell a lot of lettuce to buy a $30,000 to $40,000 CCTV system, but if you prevent one fraudulent lawsuit, the system has paid for itself many times over. Supermarkets which operate on a notoriously low profit margin are able to win discounts on insurance for having these systems installed. Video images are sometimes stored for the length of time allowed to file a lawsuit against the store. This is years in many localities. Hence, the RAID array.

Reading a book by its cover can be misleading. In the example shown here, the motive is purely economic (could even be greed). Yes, storing images of shoppers (including me) grates on me, but in many cases, these stores need this protection to stay in business.

Just thought a view from a different angle might be enlightening.

THE SECURITY DEPARTMENT

We thank you for showing us a different perspective on this.

Dear *2600:*

What happened to all the 10-10-XXX long-distance prefixes? It seemed at one point, about ten years ago, you couldn't go a minute without seeing or hearing an annoying ad for one. It seems like they all of a sudden disappeared. Now I don't know what to do with all those promotional refrigerator magnets....

MARK C.

They do still work but with all of the other means of communicating that are available these days, the seven-digit Carrier Access Codes (CACs) don't get nearly as much attention. Incidentally, the 10-10-XXX format is really a 101-XXXX format. Leading zeroes were a part of the newer four digit codes (known as Carrier Identification Codes or CICs) that replaced the old three-digit codes (10XXX). So AT&T under the old system was reached by dialing 10288 and now it's reached by dialing 1010288. It's hard to imagine the need for 10,000 of these codes throughout the country or that the old limit of 1000 was ever reached. But apparently every small and obscure company in any part of the country was assigned a code and they rapidly filled up, even though the extra digits seemed to serve very little purpose to customers. Perhaps our readers can share some stories on some of the more unique carriers that must be out there somewhere. Also, the question nobody seems to ask is why was it necessary to add the second "one" in the dialing code? 101-XXXX would seemingly work just as well with 10-XXXX since we have yet to find any use of 102, 103, 104, etc. as prefixes. Perhaps they're actually planning in advance for that dark day when there will be a need for 100,000 different carrier codes.

Obviously, it's a rather silly system that few people even use anymore and that only makes the entire method of dialing a whole lot more cumbersome than it needs to be. Add to that the disaster of area code splits that wound up destroying the geographic representation of phone numbers, and one has to wonder if we should consider just starting over and doing it all properly.

The Magic of the Corporate World

We've always had a very special relationship with our friends on the corporate side of the aisle. We like to laugh at them and they pretty much want to eliminate us. It's been like this since Day One.

We've rounded up some of the best exchanges about and between hackers and corporate environments of various sorts. You'll find that the dialogue varies quite a bit over time and as the playing field changed.

In the early days, it was almost all about the phone company. Companies, actually. In fact, *that's* what made it all so fascinating. The monopolistic Bell System had just been broken up and the entire telecommunications industry was in turmoil. What was once one phone company was now seven regional companies and one long distance company. Brand new non-Bell companies were emerging all the time. It was a hacker's dream.

Throughout it all, we were the ones in the midst of figuring out what kinds of security systems all of these new entities had to keep people from what was then the ultimate goal: a free phone call. This was why they hated us so much. But if you take a look at what it used to cost in those days to simply communicate, was it any wonder that people were eager to figure out alternatives? And as time went on, the marketplace eventually reached the same conclusion and communications became dirt cheap—even free under many circumstances.

But our role wasn't simply to figure out their security systems. We also became a de facto watchdog of corporate America. Why? Because we had a whole lot of very observant people writing to us who understood how technology worked. They called things as they saw them—and very often what they saw they didn't like. You can bet that any malfeasance whatsoever on the part of the various phone companies would eventually find its way onto the letters pages of *2600*, whether it was unfair collaboration between companies that used to be part of the Bell System, or fees being charged for nonexistent services, or privacy abuses of one sort or another. One of our readers even laid the blame (quite properly) for the 1973 coup in Chile on a phone company called ITT. The phone companies were still getting away with all kinds of things, but now at least there was a centralized place where people could talk about it.

The new kids on the block were anything but exempt from this. We came down hard on COCOT (Customer Owned Coin Operated Telephone) and AOS (Alternate Operator Service) companies because of the widespread price gouging they were engaged in. There were exceptions, and we'd even hear directly from them on occasion. But the sad fact was that they were simply an exception to the very unpleasant rule.

As time marched on, we became well acquainted with other corporate dramas. One of the more interesting ones centered on an online provider named Prodigy that drew a lot of unwanted attention when it was suspected of intentionally copying users' private data off of their personal computers. The accusations and defenses played out right there on the letters pages, culminating in a letter from Prodigy explaining it all from its side. It was good to know corporate America was paying attention.

But that also became a problem for us. Because corporate America was paying so *much* attention to us, they felt compelled to come after us in force in 2000. It's not that we were doing things to them specifically; it's that we *represented* a world they really didn't care for. That's why the Motion Picture Association of America, with the backing of every major Hollywood studio, the big American broadcasting networks, and even some professional sports leagues, took us to court for challenging their lock on new technology, specifically the emerging DVD market. We lost the case but we won the argument. Through this action, the world became aware of how the industry intended to keep control of technology out of the hands of the consumer. It was a black eye they have yet to recover from. It also segued very nicely into the battle the music industry was engaging in with the public. The Recording Industry Association of America also had no idea how to deal with new technology. Their only answer, like the MPAA, was to use the courtroom to desperately cling to the world that they were used to. That battle continues to this day.

The letters column was the place where "corporate logic" got to be laughed at and where the individual had the final say. We had an almost infinite supply of material showing the abuses and cluelessness, whether it involved privacy violations through consumer credit reports, technology being crippled in the interests of profit, mega-mergers, an unhealthy obsession with licensing everything under the sun, or even examples of the corporate mentality making its way into schools and homes. Probably the best part of all of this was getting letters from people *inside* the corporate world who saw what we were doing and absolutely *loved* it. Anonymously, of course.

1985

Dear *2600:*

> Please help me settle something I've long wondered about. Do telephone employees get free phone service or discounts on their phone bill?
>
> SJ

From what we've been able to find out, free telephone service is given to management employees and also to those employees that have been around for 30 years or longer. Usually there's a usage allowance of around $35 which includes service charges and local calls. Any charges above that allowance get billed to the employee. Anyone who works for the phone company for more than six months is entitled to a 50 percent discount. These rules, though, probably vary greatly throughout the country.

Dear *2600:*

> I live in the 215 (Philadelphia) area code and made a directory assistance call to 609 (South Jersey) to get an Atlantic City number, and then placed the call to the actual number. The actual call naturally appeared on my AT&T portion of the bill. But the killer is that the directory assistance call, supposedly one of an allotment of two free DA calls via AT&T, came up as a 50-cent charge on the Bell of Pennsylvania portion of the bill! Apparently, Bell of Pennsylvania owns a special exception to the interstate rules and handles calls to three neighboring New Jersey counties. Since directory assistance is probably handled out of Trenton, my DA call got handled and billed by Bell of Pennsylvania. You won't believe how AT&T handles this situation—you have to call them up and they look you up to make

sure you made the equivalent required call, then credit your AT&T account! Since this is a totally manual operation, and since we the public have never been told of this strange hack, chances are good that Bell of Pennsylvania is collecting gobs of half dollars which their customers really do not owe. Furthermore, when a watchful customer does go through the requisite manual process, it seems as if Bell of Pennsylvania ends up with AT&T's money. AT&T also seems to be able to see the Bell of Pennsylvania portion of the bill on their computer terminals. Why do I get the impression that AT&T is not as severed from the operating companies as they would have us believe? Hmmmm...

ANONYMOUS

Dear *2600:*

I recently had my telephone disconnected due to the fact that my roommate had forgotten to pay the bill. I have no dispute with the billing, however, my question is this. My PacTel bill was around $15. We had paid off $85 of our bill, leaving a balance of $82. Therefore, I would assume, we had paid our debt to PacTel and only owed money to AT&T. Now at the bottom of my monthly long distance statement, it says that the billing is only provided as a service to AT&T, with whom Pacific Telephone has no connection. If this is the case, under what authority did they cut off my telephone service? If I fail to pay my MCI bill, would PacTel cut me off? Shouldn't I just be cut off from AT&T's lines, and collecting is their problem? Just a little more confusion resulting from the breakup.

NO NAME

Nobody should really be surprised when two companies that were once one do each other favors. We've heard quite a few similar tales and would like to hear more. Perhaps we could gather them together and go to the right person and get these companies in a big pile of trouble. Nothing like phreak revenge, they say.

Dear Twenty-Sic Hundred En: [sic]

Is it something we did or didn't do that might be the reason you haven't used Easylink lately? If so, please let me know.

Just contact me at (516) 938-5600 (or drop a note in my Easylink mailbox 62661080) and I will be more than happy to answer any questions that you may have.

Sincerely,
JOHN SENGELAUB
WESTERN UNION

Please leave us the hell alone. You people are fools.

Dear *2600:*

I've seen piles of examples of inaccurate billings from alternative long distance companies (mostly resulting from a lack of called party supervision control). Automated data calls are the biggest culprit—where the other end didn't answer or was busy and the modem took about a minute to time out (typical setting for a long distance call). The calls charged as if they had been answered in each and every case. There are many more mundane cases that are generally known—the C-SPAN cable service had some problems since they let the phones keep ringing on their talk shows until they are ready to put people on the air. Thus, the phones might ring for five or ten minutes or more, and many people just got ringing and eventually gave up. Guess what? The people calling via alternatives discovered that they had gotten billed for those calls—even though they were non-answered. Lots of them. Now if a company wants to make it a policy that you pay for all calls whether they are answered or not that exceed a certain duration, I guess that's OK, but nobody doing this has ever admitted publicly that that's what they do! In fact, if you confront them with the question, they deny it as often as not (most likely because they don't understand what you're talking about because they've never been told what's going on!).

The little guy who makes a few long distance calls a week doesn't have to worry about calling up the alternative's business office once a month to clear off a couple of bad billings. But many businesses are in exactly this sort of situation, and needless to say they can get a bit tired of it pretty quickly.

ANONYMOUS

We'd like to compile a list of long distance companies that charge for unanswered calls and busy signals. It could prove invaluable to consumers who are shopping around. If you want to help us on this, call or write us. We'd also like to know how much of a hassle each company creates for removing wrong numbers from the bill.

1986

Dear *2600:*

Why are there different subscription rates for "corporations"?

CORPORATION

Ideally, we are trying to make 2600 available to anyone who wants it. This means that the subscription price must be low. The individual subscription price barely covers the cost of printing, mailing, layout, and other costs that are involved in producing a monthly publication. One solution is to charge more for those who either have a lot of money, will make lots of copies for their employees, place copies in their library on public display, or stand to gain financially from reading 2600 (those who earn a living beefing up security).

Although we do not copyright our issues, we would prefer that companies refrain from making copies and regularly distributing them. We are told that many do— especially certain telephone companies.

The amount we currently charge for people who represent businesses is rather small compared to many other newsletters and security publications which can actually be in the hundreds of dollars—and many of these are quarterly or bimonthly.

Finally, for those who have not asked, the corporate subscribers receive the exact same edition of 2600 as do all other subscribers.

Having different subscription rates is a solution that should not hurt anyone. The higher priced subscriptions help us maintain the same service for those who have less money—who are largely the same people who write the articles that appear in 2600.

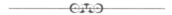

Dear *2600:*

Thanks much for providing lots of useful information. Here is an ironic little announcement about the new president of the Coalition for Open Systems.

From Courier *published by Xerox, Palo Alto, California: "The Corporation for Open Systems has named Lincoln Faurer, former director of the National Security Agency, as the group's first president. Faurer was chosen on the basis of his extensive experience in the standardization process and in negotiations with vendors. Membership in COS currently stands at nearly 40 companies."*

ᴋI

Those are not just 40 little companies either. They include Bell Labs, Boeing, DEC, Kodak, NCR, Northern Telecom, Xerox, and others on the executive committee alone!

We are sure that Mr. Faurer will enjoy running future discussions of data encryption and other standards with the rest of the coalition.

Dear *2600:*

Congratulations on the apparent success of your newsletter. I learn something from each issue. Your points on the power of computers and the information that is processed on them are correct. And you provide a valuable service by attempting to educate your readers and (sometimes) chide those who would use the information improperly.

I work on the other side of the fence—data security for a large corporation. I don't always like what you say about the condition of my profession—because it is usually too painfully true!!! I also have the nature to try, test, and explore new areas to see what happens. But I wouldn't proceed to the point of "crashing" or "disabling" a system as was stated on page 3-42 of your June issue. Finally, the point of my letter!

Please don't tell people how to crash a computer system. It may prove your technical superiority, or that you can read a technical manual. However, just as the lives of many innocent people connected with your BBS and others were unjustly and adversely affected by raids by uneducated and unqualified intruders, crashing a major (or minor) computer system has serious consequences to innocent people, directly or indirectly. And, unless you know the effect you have on my business (retail, oil, banking, public utility, medical care, etc.), you are just as naive, over-your-head, and dangerous as the authorities that confiscate a BBS.

On a lighter note, we don't need your help anyway. We crash our systems on an irregular basis. Unintentionally, of course. Which helps explain why you see so few computer professionals loitering in pool halls these days. They are too busy trying to recover from the latest/ greatest technology.

Keep up the good work.

The Stopper

Please note that those people who confiscate BBSes get the full support of law, unlike those who crash mainframes.

On whether or not we will stop printing system shutdown procedures... that is something we shall consider. Our main point is to show how easily it can be done by anyone—a computer buff or a saboteur.

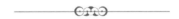

1987 _____

Dear *2600:*

I live in Pasadena, a few miles from L.A., and have been having trouble with the local 818-350-1028 Metrofone port. They have just upgraded to better software making it almost impossible to hack the system. I have heard that US Sprint has bought the company and they're going through serious changes that may affect us all. Rumors are that prefixes will be added to the codes and maybe more than that. I also have found some weird codes that give carriers and call unknown homes/businesses and the Metro operator. If you or anyone could explain what is happening or list some local ports, I would be very thankful.

HEX CONVERTER

First of all, GTE Sprint bought US Tel and, thus, changed their name to US Sprint. As far as we know, they're not interested in acquiring Western Union's Metrofone service. Second, every independent carrier has gone through a phase of making their authorization codes a little harder to guess. Metrofone is simply one of the last to finally get around to it. It doesn't mean the end of the world by any stretch of the imagination. And finally, almost all long distance companies have "weird" codes that hook you up to special numbers. In most cases, it's either an internal office at the company itself or a special "toll-free" service provided to the people whose phone you wind up ringing. Simply ask customer service what kind of "toll-free" service they provide to understand it better.

Dear *2600:*

Enclosed is a tabloid article about access code toll fraud on Texas college campuses. Hope you guys get some use or laughs from it.

It mentions a number set up by Texas Tech for students to turn themselves in for toll fraud. Has anyone ever considered doing the following?

"Hello, (insert name of long distance company)? I would like to turn myself in for toll fraud. My name is (insert name of some person you wish revenge on)."

You can guess what happens from there....

Technocracy now!

THE HOODED CLAW

What you suggest is immoral, unjust, sneaky, disgusting, and horrible. It's also incomplete. The number to call is 703-641-9292. It belongs to the Communications Fraud Control Association, that scary organization that gathers information from all of the long distance companies and that recently plastered Texas Tech with posters warning students of jail time for making unauthorized long distance telephone calls.

Dear *2600:*

> *I think we agree that in coming years, phone literacy is going to be as important for resisting the police state as computer literacy. One example is the British disarmament movement, CND, whose members have been fighting a running battle for years over malfunctions that always seem to happen to their heavily tapped phones at crucial moments. Another concerns the fall of Allende in 1973: in the early hours of the fateful morning as Pinochet's tanks began rolling towards the Presidential Palace, it appeared that the phones of about 2500 of Allende's closest associates in government had gone dead. In his book on the Allende "destabilization," the U.S. ambassador at the time marvels that this could have been accomplished in a few hours by only two phone technicians. Gee, GTE? No, ITT.*
>
> AUDIE O'SIRKIT

We never did trust them anyway.

Dear *2600:*

> *Here is a question you might have one of your staff try to answer for the newsletter readers. It's a problem I have and I'm sure others do too. Being I only have one phone in my house, how can I run a PC through a modem with call waiting?*
>
> KM

Call waiting is a very annoying problem for anyone with a computer. The beep of a second call coming in frequently interferes with data flow. As a result, the phone companies are "introducing" a service that should have been available from the start, and in some cases was. There are a few different names for it, but basically it allows you to turn off call waiting for one call, usually by dialing *70 or 1170 before making a call. In many areas, this feature always existed but was never publicized. Now that people are expressing an interest in it, you'll hear about it and also get charged for it. History just keeps repeating itself.

It might be advantageous to drop call waiting altogether and just get another phone line with tripover from your first line. In most places, there is no charge for this feature, at least not yet. And it gives you the freedom of talking on the phone and sending data at the same time. A two-line phone will deliver most of the features the phone company charges monthly fees for: call waiting, three-way, speed dialing. The charge for a second phone line will just about equal all of the little charges they throw in.

Dear *2600:*

> Recently you mentioned beeper companies not yet being raided by the police for phone numbers. They don't have to raid them! According to a friend who runs a large beeper company, the authorities can, with a warrant, legally obtain duplicate beeper numbers. Any access to the monitored number also beeps the duplicate number in the police station.
>
> BOB FROM LOS ANGELES

How clever. So now we have beeper tapping. But will the beeper companies be as cooperative with the authorities as the phone companies?

1988

Dear *2600:*

> The very day that I received your Spring issue, I also got my Sprint bill. I read your issue first, of course, and I didn't touch my bill until I read your little blurb about Sprint's billing system in your "Happenings" column. And was I in for a surprise.

My bill was a total mess! Sprint had done two things to my bill as far as I could fathom from the mess printed on those pages. 1) They had charged me for busy signal calls. 2) They had chopped up large calls into four or five smaller calls.

I called Sprint right away and had it out with the billing person. He gave me credit for all of the one minute busy calls (about 40 altogether). As for why they did this in the first place, I don't know. Is their billing computer really that messed up that they can't keep track of the status of a call? They must have a lot of this happening, because he gave me credit without too much of a problem.

As for the chopped up calls, that's a different matter altogether. He refused to change my billing to make the series of smaller calls into one big call. I'll have to write the company about that one.

Here is what I would like you guys to think about: We all know about those thieves who reprogram a bank's computer to shave off .00001 percent of all the accounts in the bank and drop it into another account for themselves. The small amount taken from the individual accounts will be insignificant for anyone to notice, but the total amount can be quite large. Well, here we have a long distance company that is cutting up callers' long calls into smaller calls and then charging the callers more for the first minute on all of the small calls. This amount is small and I don't really care about it. But if they're doing this to all callers—how much are they actually making per month?

Cray-Z Phreaker
Skunk Works

What you're implying here is a very serious matter. If Sprint is in fact doing this, they could be facing an awful lot of trouble (something a lot of phone phreaks would no doubt relish). Let's find out for sure. Let's all put them to the test and keep logs. In fact, why not do it for all of the companies?

1989 _____

Dear *2600:*

> *US Sprint issues a complete rundown of who called an 800 number.*
> *We got our 800 bill and, surprisingly, it showed every number that*
> *called us.*
>
> THE RENEGADE OF PITTSBURGH
SYSOP OF CHARLOTTE

The copy of the bill you sent us looks exactly like a regular Sprint bill, except the numbers on it are the numbers that called you. Something to think about, especially those of you who like to call 800 numbers. Look in our Spring 1989 issue to find out which 800 exchanges are owned by Sprint. We'd like to know if the other companies provide such detailed billing.

By the way, Sprint's FONLine 800 service isn't a bad deal. There's currently no startup fee to obtain an 800 number and you can attach it to any existing phone number. Your 800 number will work all over the country and the monthly fee is only $10. The per-call fee is rather steep, though. It averages about 22 cents a minute. But it's one way to virtually guarantee not getting ripped off by an AOS somewhere. Of course, you can only dial one number.

Dear *2600:*

> *I'm the kind of guy that likes to just try things for the hell of it (what's*
> *this button for??). You know, to see what happens or just for the sake*
> *of knowing something new, even if it's "useless." Anyway, that's how*
> *I stumbled upon this little telephone episode.*
>
> *I live in the "south bay" region of Los Angeles and my phone company*
> *is the infamous GTE. Just recently, I had the "Smart Pack" features*
> *(call forward, call waiting, call conferencing, and speed calling) added*
> *to my service. Anyway, I dialed my own number, for whatever reason,*
> *and, much to my surprise, I did not get a busy signal. What I got*
> *instead were four short beeps (sounding just like "conversation being*
> *recorded" beeps) spaced apart about a half second each. Then I'm*
> *disconnected and just dead silence. I waited a few seconds, pushed*

assorted buttons, nothing. Then a nice steady tone like one would get calling a long distance 800 number. Not knowing why, how, or what to do, I just pushed more tones. Nothing. Then the nasty "line off the hook" tone comes blasting through, so I hung up.

Are you familiar with an incident such as this? Is this related to the Smart Package? GTE? Freak of nature? Sorry I can't tell you what ESS is in use here. If you haven't already guessed, I am a novice at phone hacking.

By the way, I love your publication, filled with neat stuff I may never use but still fun to read.

Some thank you info: 114 in my GTE area gets the computer voice readout of the number you're calling on, and I've been told 1223 does likewise for PacTel.

H.

Manhattan Beach, CA

It sounds like you came in on your own call waiting. That could explain the four beeps. We don't know why you were disconnected, however. GTE has a lot of oddities and we'd love to hear about some more of them. For instance, what "nice steady tone like one would get calling a long distance 800 number?" We in non-GTE land have never heard of such a thing, which you probably take for granted.

Dear *2600:*

I thought the following might be interesting to you. I recently attended a state fair. At one of the booths at the fair, there was a group of Sprint representatives asking people to sign up for a free FON card. All the person had to do was sign a slip of paper. However, by signing that slip of paper, the person also agreed to make Sprint their primary long distance carrier. The representatives really downplayed that fact; they highlighted with a pen all the phrases that contained "FON card," but the part which stated that Sprint would be made the long distance carrier was not highlighted, and in smaller print. I asked if I could have a FON card without making Sprint my primary long distance carrier, and they said that I would need a credit card for that. Well, I wasn't about to let these bums see it, so I declined on the deal. I wrote a letter to the BBB complaining about their tactics. My complaint was forwarded to Network 2000 Communications Corporation, an independent marketing company that is authorized to sell US Sprint services to residential and small business customers. Here is part of their reply:

> "A large majority of customers that Network 2000 Independent Marketing Representatives obtain for US Sprint are acquired at fairs, flea markets, malls, etc. Network 2000 representatives are required to attend a thorough training program to learn proper, professional steps to obtaining customers for US Sprint before beginning their Network 2000 business. The method of obtaining customers used by a probable Network 2000 IMR which you described in your letter is totally against Network 2000 policy. Once we determine the name of the IMR, if we determine he acted unprofessionally, we will take swift action in terminating the individual's status as a Network 2000 IMR."

Dr. Williams
Washington State

If more people did what you did, this kind of rip-off would soon disappear. Unfortunately, you can find these con artists almost everywhere you look today. While Network 2000's response seems to indicate that they're concerned, the fact remains that they're blaming one person for this violation. But you said it was a group of representatives which would seem to indicate that what they were doing was company policy. It's also hard to believe that one person is responsible for reducing the size of the print on a key part of the advertisement.

Anyone involved in similar escapades? Let's hear about them.

1990

Dear *2600:*

> I, too, had a similar experience with Network 2000 and the Sprint card last summer in a mall in Nashua, New Hampshire.

The advertising at the Sprint booth mentioned only the FON card, and said nothing about changing long distance carriers. When I asked the woman about getting the FON card, she gave me an application to fill out. But before I signed it, I noticed in the fine print that I was agreeing to change my long distance carrier to Sprint.

I asked the woman if I had read the application right. She at first said no, I was applying for the FON card only. When pressed, however, she finally admitted it, saying, "Well, wouldn't you rather have Sprint?" Only when I declined did she turn the form over, where there was another application for the FON card only.

Needless to say, you know which form was face up on the table, and which form you were told to fill out when you asked for the FON card. It's impossible to tell who the perpetrators were: Network 2000 or their reps.

THE IRON WARRIOR
NO FIXED ADDRESS

Dear *2600:*

I think you might find this interesting. It was extracted from the RISKS Digest *on Usenet.*

> *"The Prodigy Services publication* Prodigy Star *(Volume 3, Number 1) recently showcased a 'major benefit.' The Prodigy system accesses remote subscribers' disks to check the Prodigy software version used and, when necessary, downloads the latest programs. This process is automatic when subscribers link to the network.*

> *"I asked Prodigy how they protect against the possibility of altering subscribers' non-Prodigy programs, or reading their personal data. Prodigy's less-than-reassuring response was essentially (1) we don't look at other programs, and (2) you can boot from a floppy disk. According to Prodigy, the feature cannot be disabled."*

I think it is obvious how to make use of this "feature" for other purposes. Let us hope that this "feature" is removed from one of the newly downloaded versions....

FIN

Dear *2600*:

You've been duped! Your article in your Summer 1990 issue entitled "An Introduction to COCOTs" was either (a) written by a representative of one of the local exchange carriers or (b) your writer (The Plague) has been receiving some awfully poor information regarding the pay telephone industry.

The real pay telephone rip-offs are not the independent pay telephone companies, most of which are small, independent businesspeople such as ourselves. The real rip-offs are the major local exchange carriers who subsidize their pay telephone operations with regular telephone revenues. Every one of us pays extra in the form of higher local telephone bills to support the LEC's inefficient, unresponsive pay telephone bureaucracy. Why should your home and business telephone charges support your LEC's operations?

This is not to say that there haven't been abuses in our industry. But the vast majority of us deserve better than you've shown us. Your article plays right into the monopolistic LEC's hands, who would like nothing better than to eliminate all competition and return to the days of total uncontrolled monopoly.

R.S. Grucz
Executive Vice President
American Public Telephone Corporation

It only takes a few rip-off COCOTs to give the entire industry a bad name. We think it's important to clearly label those companies that are engaged in ripping off the public. You should do the same and disavow yourself of those companies. There need to be some basic standards introduced (equal access, 950 access, clear rate structure, etc.). We hope to hear more from your perspective and we encourage our readers to tell us if they've had any positive experiences with COCOTs and AOS companies.

1991

Dear *2600:*

> While I agree with you that most of the services Allnet offers are outrageously overpriced, I do have to disagree with you about call delivery. Being the sort of person who travels and likes to call in when passing coin phones at rest stops (cellular is OK but too expensive for routine stuff), the Allnet basic 950 or 1-800 rates are somewhat better (for the most part) than the other providers.

> The call delivery option is very handy when the other line is busy, or if I'm checking in at an ungodly hour. At $1.75 to leave a message, it seems reasonably fair and legit. Also, of course, sending a one-way message means you don't get stuck actually talking to the person.

> On another topic, many of the alternative common carriers will, in fact, give you remote (as opposed to 1+) access if you tell them you're part of a big PBX or Centrex which has been committed to one of their competitors. No guarantees that any specific company will provide you with such an account, but it's definitely worth a try.

> Finally, I noticed an interesting feature of my recently upgraded central office. If I call a number, the ring or busy signal will cut out after about 1.5 minutes. After a bit of kerchunking, I get kicked back to a dial tone. If other COs and PBXs do this sort of thing, it just might be a way to get second, unrestricted, dial tones.

> DANNY
HARLEM, NY

Dear *2600:*

> Thought you might be interested in the enclosed item that came with my latest Pa Bell bill. Note that while they are cutting $1.20 off most bills for touch tone service (not mine, I ordered rotary dial service when I moved in), they are also cutting back on a negative surcharge so as not to lose any revenue (so my bill goes up).

> Note that if you have custom features (Pa Bell calls it "COMSTAR," the touch tone service is bundled in with it and since there is no extra charge for touch tone, no price reduction.

As an aside, several years ago, Pa Bell sent me a letter saying they had detected touch tones on my line and I wasn't paying the surcharge for touch tones, so I had to either start paying the surcharge (since it was "their mistake" that allowed my use of touch tones, they offered to waive back payments if I agreed to start paying now), or they would remove the touch tone service. I called and told the belldroid to remove the touch tone service. She said fine. I never heard anything further, and my touch tone phones still work to this day.

RG
LOS ANGELES

Dear *2600:*

I received one of AT&T's "Tele-Gram" letters requesting that I switch to AT&T for my long distance calling.

If you call the number listed on the letter, you can request to be deleted from AT&T's mailing list. You may also give a reason for your request.

I encourage people to call and request to be deleted. Also, request that they take down the reason and inform them of your concern with AT&T's public deception with respect to the Craig Neidorf case and their attempt to make an example of an innocent person.

DARK OVERLORD

Dear *2600:*

MCI is here to save you money. A new service introduced by MCI allows you to have MCI bill you for "regional" calls, i.e., calls within your area code. The benefit is that your volume discount would be combined for the regional and long distance and 800 calls. The reality of the matter is interesting, however. For example, a call from Antioch, Illinois to Libertyville, Illinois for 11.8 minutes at 9:23 pm is billed $1.42 by MCI and $.17 by Illinois Bell. The volume discount would reduce the MCI charge by about 14 cents. The MCI way of doing business is a net loss of over 650 percent.

Somewhere, MCI's concept of saving money with this program is lost in the reality of their rates.

GR
LIBERTYVILLE, IL

Dear *2600:*

I'd agree that Prodigy is a real turkey, if only for its on-screen adver-
tisements, censorship of users' mail, and remarkably slow response.
(Oh, yeah, and its demands for a loaded PC or Mac that few home
users can afford.) But STAGE.DAT really is the last straw.

Contrary to the bull given out by them when caught, it is clear that
IBM and Sears did intend to read home computers.

I'm aware of two horror stories, firsthand in my role as a computer
and private phone system technician, that prove this trick was done
for and actually used for marketing purposes.

1. *The STAGE.DAT file of one user was found to contain a whole group*
    of mail addresses and telephone numbers when examined. Some of
    these did correspond to names and numbers in other modem programs
    the person used, and, since these were in the same sub-directory path
    as Prodigy, there was a possible legitimate explanation.

    The source of other names and numbers was a mystery as they
    didn't correspond to names and numbers in any modem dialing list.
    The user soon found that they were in word processing files, that is to
    say, in individually addressed letters. (The version of Wordstar used
    didn't have a telecom module.) Prodigy had read word processing files
    in a different sub-directory!

    As a test, to rule out an accidental reading of files that were once
    physically stored where Prodigy is now, Wordstar was booted and a let-
    ter written to a dummy name with a phone number. Then Prodigy was
    contacted. After this, STAGE.DAT was looked at again. The new name
    and number was found within it. This proves that Prodigy deliberately
    incorporates this information every time it's run!

2. *In a place where I do wiring work, LANs are used within departments*
    to link PCs. If contact has to be made with another work group (whose
    LAN isn't gatewayed), it is done through modems, dialing through
    Centrex.

    Now, due to the software involved, these other locations are given
    proper mailing addresses, numbers, and, since the software demands
    names, dummy names consisting of a name of the location as family
    and alpha mnemonics as given names are created. To wit: names like

ABLE LEGAL, BAKER LEGAL, CHARLEY LEGAL, DELTA LEGAL, ABLE SALES, BAKER SALES, CHARLEY SALES, DELTA SALES, ABLE SHIPPING, etc. are given to each computer.

Furthermore, these arbitrary computer "names" are never used outside the company. Also, in the company, a person sending a document to a certain computer in the legal department would know that it was in the legal department, but would never know the arbitrary first name given to that computer.

In short, there is no way, apart from reading the program, to know what arbitrary first names were given for system maintenance. And only management can read this password protected file.

Yet, shortly after installing Prodigy on several computers, junk mail from Prodigy arrived at the company address to such "people" as "ABLE SHIPPING," "ABLE LEGAL," etc. showing that these names are captured and actually used for marketing purposes!

While MS-DOS has a well-known flaw that allows data to exist after it's been deleted, these two horror stories prove that it isn't an accident. It really was a deliberate process. They just got caught.

Big Al
Brooklyn

A most interesting account. We think you should demand an explanation from the Prodigy people. If the company can show that this information was not released in any way and can come up with the proof that such letters were received, it should get some attention. We've always found it disturbing that so many were so quick to excuse what was happening here without doing a thorough investigation. We hope more people continue to look into this and all future services that may do even worse things.

Dear *2600:*

Unfortunately, in his letter on Prodigy in the Autumn 1991 issue, Big Al proves nothing other than his ignorance of how MS-DOS allocates disk space to files. That disk space was once used for a file in subdirectory A, which was deleted and has no bearing whatsoever on whether that disk space can later be used for a file in subdirectory B. It would be proof of strange behavior only if data was migrating across disks, either logical or physical.

I don't know enough about Wordstar to know how it manages temporary files, but assuming that it behaves normally for a word processor, the most likely scenario for Big Al's test goes something like: a) While creating a dummy document with a dummy name in it, Wordstar creates a temporary file, which ends up containing most or all of the document being worked on; b) Wordstar is halted, and while cleaning up, it deletes the temporary file; c) Prodigy is started and when it asks MS-DOS for disk space for STAGE.DAT, it gets that disk area that was most recently freed up (this step can vary depending on MS-DOS version and whether the hard disk has had all of its area used since it was last formatted), which naturally contains all the junk from the Wordstar session. I consider this a much more plausible scenario than Big Al's assertion that this proves that Prodigy is reading data out of Wordstar document files.

If Big Al wants to prove anything here, he should use Norton Utilities or the equivalent to overwrite all unused disk sectors and then see if Prodigy puts anything into STAGE.DAT. Or he should check the sectors that will be allocated for the next file opened both before and after Prodigy is started, to see what Prodigy changes.

As for the names of computers such as ABLE LEGAL and BAKER LEGAL showing up on a Prodigy mailing list, is he absolutely certain, cross-his-heart-and-hope-to-die, that no one registered some of the software associated with the network using the machine names?

So while I agree that the Prodigy affair may have been glossed over mighty quick, there are limits to paranoia on the topic before it gets really silly.

If you do want a scandal, start thinking about how many computer technicians don't realize that using Norton's WIPEFILE on your word processor file isn't enough unless you hunt down and wipe out all the temporary files your word processor used, too.

JON RADEL
RESTON, VA

It's been our position that even if Prodigy was doing nothing wrong, unsuspecting users are opening up their personal systems to outside entities (not hackers) that could one day do quite horrible things. We hope this realization is enough to wake most people up.

1992

Dear *2600:*

> *I know I'm treading on thin ice voicing a corporate viewpoint in 2600. But I think it's important to clear the air regarding Prodigy.*
>
> *There have been a lot of rumors about Prodigy and STAGE.DAT, and what we're doing—and not doing—with our members' data and computers. Prodigy doesn't read, upload, or interact in any way with a member's file on their computer. The sole exception is Prodigy files. There's no way we could or would do the kind of things Big Al alleged in your Autumn 1991 issue, and that were discussed in the letters column in the Winter 1991-92 issue.*
>
> *The confusion and false claims arose because non-Prodigy data found its way incidentally into Prodigy files. When people saw this, they incorrectly assumed Prodigy had deliberately sought this information and uploaded it. In fact, any non-Prodigy data found in Prodigy files was incorporated randomly because of two programming shortcuts that have since been eliminated. None of it was ever looked at, manipulated, or uploaded by Prodigy.*
>
> *The two Prodigy files in question are STAGE.DAT and CACHE.DAT. STAGE.DAT stores Prodigy programs and graphics between sessions. Without STAGE.DAT, all of this data would have to be transmitted every time the member moves from place to place within the service or "turns a page."*
>
> *CACHE.DAT stores Prodigy content for reuse within a session so that the member can move from feature to feature without retransmission of content already sent. CACHE.DAT is overwritten during each session.*

During the offline process of installing the Prodigy software, STAGE. DAT is created as a file either 0.25 or 1 megabytes in size, whichever the member chooses. As with any new file, when it is created, DOS allocates disk sectors to it. It is well known that these sectors may include the contents of previously erased files, since DOS doesn't actually erase information contained in erased files, but simply recycles the space for use in new files.

Earlier versions of the Prodigy software did not zero out the file space allocated to STAGE.DAT. The result was that if you used XTree or DEBUG you might have noticed that, prior to being filled with Prodigy data, STAGE.DAT disk space contained information from erased files. A similar effect occurs with the smaller file, CACHE.DAT.

After the STAGE.DAT file is created, the installation program builds a table of the entries in it. This table allows the STAGE.DAT to keep track of the programs and graphics stored there. The software creates this table in RAM (memory) and then moves it to the STAGE.DAT on the disk. As a backup, we even write two copies of the table to the STAGE.DAT, so there are two places where a member might see this information. We move the whole portion of RAM used for the table, even though it may be only partially filled with entries. Again, we didn't zero the RAM space used to build the table, so any memory that wasn't written over—and its contents—was swept into STAGE.DAT.

Our programmers originally wanted to make installation as fast as possible, and so they did not want to take the additional time to zero out disk sectors or memory involved in the installation.

During a Prodigy session, calls on RAM buffers are used to write new graphics and program data to the STAGE.DAT file. In the earlier versions of the software, the buffers were not zeroed, and the amount of Prodigy data stored in them may not have completely displaced data already in the buffer memory area from earlier programs. Then, when the Prodigy data is written to STAGE.DAT, the other information would also be transferred to the disk. That is the reason Big Al saw fragments from his Wordstar files in STAGE.DAT.

The personal information was of no interest to Prodigy and, in any case, over time, this information is overwritten as programs and graphics are added to the STAGE.DAT file during use. We have since learned of our members' sensitivity on this issue, and have modified our software accordingly. For people with older Prodigy software, we provide a free utility program that zeroes out all non-Prodigy information for existing STAGE.DAT and CACHE.DAT files. To order it, JUMP TECH TALK on Prodigy.

We never looked at or used any non-Prodigy information in STAGE. DAT or CACHE.DAT. There is, in fact, no mechanism that would allow the Prodigy software to pass any information (Prodigy or non-Prodigy) contained in the STAGE.DAT or CACHE.DAT files up to the host.

To help put the rumors to rest, we asked the national accounting firm, Coopers and Lybrand, to audit our operations. They examined Prodigy's computers and files and interviewed our employees for six weeks and found that we did not upload any non-Prodigy data.

As far as Big Al's allegation that he received Prodigy direct mail solicitations sent to dummy names from a LAN he uses, I don't believe it. The names on mailing lists Prodigy uses for direct mail come from lists supplied by magazine subscriptions, computer catalogers, and so on. If Big Al thinks he's got grounds for complaint, we'd be happy to look at the direct mail pieces he got from Prodigy and see where the names came from.

One final point. Big Al mentioned in his letter that Prodigy requires a "loaded" PC or Mac. The truth is just the opposite. Prodigy has taken care to ensure that the service will run on very basic DOS or Mac machines, such as an XT with an 8088 and 540 Kbytes. After all, our service is aimed at the home market. That's why we've designed it to run on the kind of machines people have at home—as well as the ones they might use in the office.

If Big Al or any other readers want to call and discuss this, my number is 914-993-8789. Or send me a message on Prodigy at PGPJ97a.

STEVE HEIN
THE PRODIGY SERVICE
WHITE PLAINS, NY

Going under the assumption that everything you say is true, there are still two disturbing facts that we have maintained from the beginning. First, if Prodigy did not *respect the privacy of its users, it would not be too difficult to do everything that has been suggested. Perhaps other companies will do this in the future. Perhaps some already have. It's a possibility that cannot be ignored and we're glad the issue has come up, regardless of Prodigy's actual involvement. The other fact is that Prodigy was given a fair chance to express its side of the story from the beginning. Nobody seized all of your equipment to investigate the matter. The media didn't label you as potential terrorists. You were never threatened with decades of prison time for a crime nobody really understands. We find it sad that individuals automatically mean so much less than large corporations when their integrity comes into question.*

1993

Dear *2600:*

> *Apparently someone has been applying their knowledge of Simplex locks, especially on FedEx lockboxes, in the Boston area. Apparently FedEx is less than happy about this, and has taken measures to put an end to the robberies. If it were me, I'd do something about the locks. But it's not, and FedEx disagrees with me. They've gone to the police, and gotten them to "stake out" a number of FedEx lockboxes (the ones being robbed, I guess). But they have not (yet) changed any of the combos on their lockboxes (I checked—still the same). I don't know if UPS has done the same, or whether the thief has even bothered to take from them. I personally have seen no instances of stakeouts on UPS. Their boxes continue to use the same combination.*

> A FLY ON THE WALL

It's incredible how stubbornly some companies will cling to their ignorance.

Dear *2600:*

> *I have noticed an annoying and disturbing trend in my local C&P Bell payphones. They have started to act like COCOTs. I first noticed*

it about six months ago, when a new legion of C&P phones with gray (rather than black) handsets started appearing. I placed a local call on one of them, using a quarter, and I could hear this little click a few seconds after the call went through that sounded as if they had just un-muted the speaker (it turned out this was true). Odd, I thought. Then, after three rings, this computerized voice came on and said something like, "Your called party does not seem to be answering. Please hang up and try again later." I was very irritated at first, because I thought it had disconnected me and would not even let me leave a message, but it in fact did not disconnect me. Nevertheless, this genuine C&P Bell phone acted exactly like a COCOT. Is it possible C&P is buying up COCOTs and converting them to C&P phones? The phone looked exactly like a standard C&P payphone, except that the familiar black handset was conspicuously gray. As you can probably guess, red boxing off of these new phones is as difficult or impossible as it is off of a COCOT.

I called C&P to ask them about this, but the woman I talked to knew nothing about any new C&P payphones. She thought it might have been related to their new Send-A-Call feature, which they apparently have been having a lot of problems with. But that didn't make any sense. This particular phone did have a plate below the instructional plate describing the Send-A-Call feature, which I hadn't heard of before, in place of the usual plate that says "Out of Change? Place a collect call, etc."

INHUMAN
ARLINGTON, VA

Nothing is impossible when it comes to phone company sleaze. The best example of this is AT&T warning people not to use weird looking payphones because they'll rip you off. Of course, in more than a few instances, if you take a good look at these weird looking payphones, particularly the ones that try to look like "real" ones, you'll find that they're made by AT&T.

1994

Dear *2600:*

> I've stumbled across a fairly amazing phone scam perpetrated by none other than AT&T! In late 1993 they began using a new automated collect call service which uses voice recognition to complete calls. Allegedly, the system recognizes the words "yes" and "no" when it asks the party who answers the phone if they will accept the charges. However, it also seems to like my answering machine and voicemail—no matter what my message says, AT&T takes it as a yes much of the time, resulting in whopping collect call charges when I haven't even been home or at work! (And AT&T isn't even my long distance company!)
>
> When I complained to AT&T, eventually finding my way to the Vice President of Call Servicing, I was assured that they would "look into it." Weeks later, it still doesn't work and I'm still getting bogus charges. How do I stop this fiasco? AT&T refuses to put a block on the line and the local phone company will only block all collect calls for a stiff fee, not just AT&T's. AT&T is making a fortune on this from bill payers who don't closely scrutinize their bills and I am spending hours every month pleading with AT&T for credit due. Any suggestions?
>
> LN
MINNEAPOLIS, MN

Your first step is to find out where these calls are coming from. Perhaps that will provide a clue. Next, ring your own line when you're away and see if anybody answers. This kind of thing happens all the time. If you can prove that your answering machine is "accepting" these calls, do it and tell the Vice President of Call Servicing that you have evidence of wrongdoing on their part.

1995

Dear *2600:*

> Our basic service where we live consists of call waiting, three-way calling, and flat rate. Last month, we subscribed to call forwarding

with a free connection charge. Then, we called up the business office to cancel an extra listing we had put in the phone book and didn't want anymore. Fine. Last, we ordered a new "free" white pages directory. All's well until the bill comes.

We get the bill, and what do you know, it's $130! Wow! There's no way. So we take a look at it and find this. We were charged $16 for a "free" installation charge for call forwarding. We were charged $23 for a yellow pages directory when it was supposed to be a white pages and was supposed to be free. We were charged for two custom calling packages (i.e., call forwarding, call waiting, three-way calling) when we only had one (a package is any two or more of them) and then charged for a non-published number. What had NYNEX done? They lied about the free installation. They charged me for a free phone book (and sent me the wrong one as well), and, best of all, when we asked to get rid of our directory listing, the operator at the business office thought we meant to get a non-published number and when she realized that's not what we meant, she took it out so a non-published order and then a non-published credit showed up on our bill, which is fine, except along with that is a $9 service charge to change the number at directory assistance! So basically, we were overcharged nearly $50, and more to come.

Our lines were crossed with a radio station's recently. Well, NYNEX decided they would send a repairman over to our house without even calling to tell us, put a recording on our phone line saying "the number you have reached is being checked for trouble" and then charge us for the visit which we didn't request in the first place (and the problem wasn't even in our house)! Think that's it? Nope. Last month we were charged with calls to a certain number that we had never made, $40 worth of them.

What the hell is going on?

Scammed in NY

You've entered the world of *NYNEX*. Better get used to it.

Dear *2600:*

NYNEX has done it again!

If you are a NYNEX customer, here is another thing you should know about your favorite company. Anybody can now know how much your phone bill is. All it takes is having a touch tone phone. No secret code or black magic is needed. It's not a back door. It's an option on an 800 number which will gladly disclose your last phone bill. This option will also inform you, and anybody else, if you have already paid the bill or not.

To test this out: Call the NYNEX account information line, which is listed in your phone book, at 1-800-698-3545.

TTJ

This indeed caused us much concern when we first learned about it a couple of months ago. No PIN at all was required to find out your balance, information which certainly isn't considered public by most people. We broadcast this live on WBAI's Off The Hook program and entered phone numbers for all of the major TV networks. (CBS was overdue by several thousand dollars.) It was fixed within two days. Apparently, invading corporate privacy is the quickest way to get large corporations to notice privacy issues.

1996

Dear *2600:*

Perhaps "all brawn, no brains" is a fitting description for IBM's idea of security.

When a customer receives a new IBM Aptiva, they also receive the Product Recovery CD ROM. On this CD resides all the necessary files to install Windows 95 and supporting Aptiva software. All the files on the CD happen to be zipped with a password. That password happens to be "magic". With such a simple-to-guess password and easily cracked encryption such as what pkzip uses, why would IBM even bother to put one on in the first place?

The consumer has no way of finding out the password without cracking it, debugging the binary recovery program, or calling tech support and outright asking for it. Personally, I got them to tell me what to type by asking for the command to unzip by hand... not the recovery program method. I haven't tried to see if they'd raise a stink if I asked "what's the zip file password?" Anyway, all systems apparently have the same "magic" password.

The consumer has outright paid for the computer and accompanying software, and IBM has simply presented the consumer with a large pain-in-the-ass. I'd just like to say "good going" to the many men and women at IBM who so successfully have kept up the IBM tradition of retarded attempts to control the masses.

STARZ N STRIFEZ

Tradition is the word and it will eventually be IBM's downfall.

1997

Dear *2600:*

In response to SW's letter (Spring 97 issue) I would like to say that in those AOL chat rooms, you will find nothing but idiots with programs used to screw around with AOL. Plus, sometimes (very often) a CatBot enters the room. Perhaps someone knows what I am talking about? CatBots boot you offline if you are in any coldice room (coldice2, coldice3) and you get a message that says something like "You have been booted offline: Illegal Activity." Better yet, you get a TOS point on your account! Unless you are running on a fake AOL account, I would advise not going into these rooms for any reason.

JEDIHAMSTER

So where do you go on a hot day when you want to talk about cold ice? This word control game AOL plays is one of the main reasons they're looked down upon by so many.

1998 _____

Dear *2600:*

> *So I was fired from my job today. I was working at this Place called Consumer Card Services. It's based in Oklahoma, but I was working out of the satellite office in Phoenix.*
>
> *Anyhow, what we sold was financial backing on credit cards. We had a list of rebuttals and if the people were to ask "how would people get my account information?" the response I was supposed to give was, "Well, Mr/s (blank), maybe you've seen this on the news lately, but there are malicious computer criminals called hackers who will stop at nothing to get your account information so that they can make charges on your credit cards." I refused to say this. I explained to them many times that this is not correct and the media is not correct.*
>
> *Because it was only my third week, I was supposed to still be following my script verbatim. But doing it my way, I was making five to seven sales a day, even though the quota is three a day (the service is $200). So the boss was monitoring when I did it my way. The boss called me into his office and said he was letting me go. I went back to my cubicle to get my briefcase and my two supervisors were going through my briefcase. They said it was because they wanted to make sure I didn't steal anything. I happened to have the latest issue of 2600 in there (they published one of my letters!), so one of my supervisors held it up and said, "What the f__k is this? You stealing credit card info?" I was so pissed off that I grabbed my briefcase, stuck my mag back in, and walked out the door. To think that just because I read 2600, just because I defended hackers, I must be a thief.*
>
> *I feel saddened and hurt that that is the view the public has of us.*
>
> TUXEDO MASK

More importantly, you should be proud that you stood up for your convictions. It may feel like shit but what you did took courage and you'll feel better in the end. Hopefully you'll inspire others to do the same and then we may actually get through to some of these thickheads.

2000 _____

Dear *2600:*

> I work for a marketing research company. What we do is call you at work and ask you to do surveys. We don't call people at home on purpose. Occasionally we will have a home number listed. I apologize and terminate when that happens. I get people who say "please take me off your list" and hang up. The funny thing about this is that we can't really take you off the list. We mark "RF" and continue calling other people. The reason we don't take you off the list is, well, we don't have access to the list. The lists are usually obtained from the company that is having us do the survey. My point is if you want your name permanently taken off the "list," you have to find out what company the survey is for. Usually you can ask what company the survey is for, but sometimes we can't reveal that information. But if you take about three minutes, you can easily find out. There is always at least one question that reveals the company, always. You can give bull answers until you get that one vital piece of information, then just say "thank you, good-bye" and hang up. Or you can continue to screw with the person giving the survey. After you get the company name, you can call them and yell at them and have your name taken off. If you refuse to give information, we can always get what we need, so you might as well give it. The only thing that we would have a hard time getting is employee number and total revenues if it is company policy not to give that out. There is always someone who will slip. And not giving your business address is pointless. I have fun getting those and all other information that was refused if it is needed to be able to turn the survey in. And remember to be nice. We know your name and address, you don't know who we are. One other thing: those stupid registration forms people fill out... that's just asking to be called.
>
> CGK

We trust you realize that you're the scum of the earth and we're glad you took the time to write with this info. Perhaps some of our readers can help us compile our own list of these survey companies. Make sure your phone has a ringer on it.

Dear *2600:*

> *In 16:3, page 51, you respond to SpeedDRaven about removal of ban-*
> *ner ads from various free web page provider services. I think you're*
> *wrong in saying that it's not stealing because removal of the messages*
> *is the same as fast forwarding over commercials. Rather, in placing a*
> *web page with one of these services, you're entering into a contract that*
> *is more similar to the TV station that sells advertising. In order to pay*
> *for their costs (and make money, of course), they sell advertising time.*
> *The TV station doesn't ensure that everyone watching their programs*
> *will see the advertisements, but they do faithfully broadcast them.*
> *Removing Geocities banner ads, no matter how detestable you find*
> *them, is the same as if the TV station decided not to play a commercial*
> *that an advertiser had paid for—it's a breach of contract.*
>
> *On the other hand, there's great software packages like junkbuster*
> *(*www.junkbuster.org*) that will remove ads from the client before*
> *your browser ever fetches them. This is the proper action to take if*
> *you don't like seeing the ads. If you don't like that ads will be on your*
> *site, then you should put your web pages at an address that doesn't*
> *require this as part of the contract.*
>
> *Normally I find 2600 to be morally correct, even when the screwiness*
> *of the legal system says that the actions they are endorsing are illegal.*
> *I hope that this was an oversight—it's a big world out there.*
>
> ORN

This is another instance of corporate logic trying to gain a foothold on individuals. We are not advertising vessels. While they have the right to remove the pages of those who don't follow their rules, it goes against human nature to expect people not to try and get around them. It should be noted that many people would have stopped going to Geocities pages altogether were it not for the people who man-aged to keep their annoying ads from popping up.

Dear *2600:*

> *This can't be happening. Eight corporations have united to shut down*
> *2600 once and for all. We have no rights anymore, so you will probably*

lose as the judges are on the side of the big guys, but be assured that hackers everywhere will keep up the fight. What's next? Will there be a list of government (i.e., corporate) approved websites that we have to look at? If you look at a nonapproved website, will the FBI drag you away and have you executed? Will we only be able to perform government approved actions with computers? It's getting apparent that the big guys want total power, nothing less. They want to control your lives like Pol Pot controlled the lives of Cambodians. The only consolation is that America will probably have a civil war, break up, and become about as stable as Russia. Starving to death amid ruins is not an enticing idea, but we can laugh at the corporations who will have to lie in the bed they made. How can I help before I too "disappear" one day and am never seen again? Oh yeah, I've decided it's too dangerous to use my old handle and real email address, so I set up this one.

Mr. Roboto

The best way to help is to get the word out to the many millions who only know what they've seen in the mass media. That means virtually anyone you talk to will learn something from you.

Dear *2600:*

What exactly is the argument? When you buy a DVD (or anything else for that matter), it's yours. Therefore, you should be able to do whatever you please with it. You should be able to watch it on a computer or see a European DVD on an American player. Why is it that you are being sued for helping people do this?

STEVE N AZ
(HERETIC/POGO)

It's a very good question. The short answer is that they're trying to change the rules. When you buy something, they want you to be merely buying a license to use it as they decree you should. That means you would have to accept all kinds of conditions, like not having the ability to skip over commercials. (If you figured out a way to do this, you would be in violation of the contract and subject to what we're facing.) What's interesting is that the MPAA and the film studios had to deceive the courts and the public by claiming this was about piracy when that was not the issue at all. Either they don't understand their own case or they realized just how far they would get by telling the truth.

Dear *2600:*

> I used to work for one of the "major" Hollywood studios. Let me say this. Illegal distribution of copyrighted material is rampant within these companies. Distribution also occurs between companies of films in media formats different than their current release.
>
> I wish you well on 2600.com's fight against the MPAA. The guidance of this organization is very much blinded. A hard look at the internal policy and procedures of each studio should be conducted before attacking outside sources for providing these materials.
>
> I do not deny that piracy occurs outside of the studios by third parties. However, two of the recent major occurrences of films being available for distribution on the Internet were the result of internal control weakness within the "studio system." The first was a copy of The World Is Not Enough *becoming available because a film critic released a screening copy. The second was when an Academy screening copy of a particular film (I do not remember the title) in VHS format was available on eBay. For years now, being able to find an Academy-only screening copy on VHS has been extremely easy. It is because these copies are mailed to Academy members during the Oscar voting period so they can be viewed at home. To easily avoid illegal distribution the Academy should change the policy to force member to visit movie theaters to analyze Oscar nominated films. It is that simple. However, "simple" is not in their vocabulary.*
>
> MATT

Dear *2600:*

> You know, ever since these whole CorporateConglomorateSucks.com *parody sites got to be such a big deal (thanks to corporate America's lack of a sense of humor), I've begun thinking about the overbearing, buy 'em all out and make 'em part of us, Monopoly Inc. corporation*

known as Time Warner (or, as I like to call them, Slime Warner). It
wasn't until the whole ABC vs. Time Warner dispute that I started
thinking about just how much TW owns. Internet: AOL; Television:
TBS, CNN, TNT, Turner Classic Movies, Cartoon Network, HBO,
Cinemax, the WB Network; Sports: all of Atlanta's sports teams;
Stores: Warner Bros. Studios stores; etc. It wouldn't shock me if I were
to hear that TW's next move was to buy Micro$oft. Where does the
greed (and the insanity) end? And these greedy, power hungry, megacorp giants actually wonder why people would want to start up sites
claiming they suck? Not to mention the BS they claim about copyright
and trademark infringement when they're seeking to shut down all
"offending sites." Personally, I call all sites of this nature "defending
sites." You know, as in defending the right of free speech. When will
these parasites learn that until they clean up their acts when it comes
to all this crap, they'll always have a hard time making friends with
those of us who know about their slimy tactics and greedy, overbear-
ing ways? Keep up the good work at trying to provide something of a
wake-up call to these leeches.

7H3 31337 pHr34k4z01d

*Thanks, except it's not them we're trying to wake up. As long as individuals get the
wake-up call and are willing to stand up to these giants, there is hope. Incidentally,
as of right now the Time Warner/AOL deal has not been finalized.*

Dear *2600:*

I have listened to your radio program for years now on the net. I have
downloaded the entire archive at this point. The reason I'm writing
you today is pretty simple: to give you a good example.

On April 16 of this year, my home burned to the ground. With no
insurance, I was left to pick up the pieces as best I could. I've had the
help of many friends and my family. And so far, I've pulled through
reasonably well. But, the fire took most of what I owned. Thank god
for mp3s! My music collection was hanging in racks with my software
on one wall by my computer desk. The racks and jewel cases melted
in the heat. Did that mean I was no longer allowed to hear the music

I'd paid for the right to listen to? Not a chance. As soon as I could get a computer running again, I began downloading the titles I lost in the fire. I still have a good ways to go but I'm putting a big dent in the task. Nearly 150 albums had to be thrown away as they were nearly transparent from heat damage. I kept as many of the jewel case inserts as I was able to. And as the mp3s are burnt to new discs, the inserts are being matched to the albums. If it weren't for an outlet like Napster, I'd be spending thousands of dollars to replace my music.

BRAD BROWN

This also brings up an interesting point insofar as licensing. The MPAA and RIAA would like us to believe that we are simply buying a license to view or listen when we buy movies or music. Using that logic, we should still own the license when the physical disks are destroyed.

Dear *2600:*

I'm not a hacker. I can barely boot up and set the margins on Corel 8. I read your magazine to stay informed about the politics of technology. And those letters and their accompanying answers: they're all gems. Now it's my turn. For the last two weeks some wingnut has been calling me at exactly 9:30 every morning. When I answer, there's no one on the line. I called Bell-slash-Verizon regarding annoyance calls. We ruled out an unauthorized wake-up service. These were my options: Star 69, Star 57 (a police phone trace), get a new phone number ($42.05), or Caller ID with Anonymous Blocker ($7.99 a month). Star 69 and 57 didn't work. I don't feel like shelling out bucks to corporate shareholders just yet. Any suggestions would be much appreciated.

SILVERSPARTAN

Note how every solution Verizon came up with involved you giving them money. This is completely unethical. You do not have to pay a penny to stop this from happening. Don't let Verizon tell you otherwise. Contact their Annoyance Call Bureau (the number is in the front of the phone book) and give them the details you gave us. The fact that it happens every day at the same time will make it easy to track.

They will contact whomever is doing this and make them stop. However, they won't tell you who's doing it.

Dear *2600:*

> *I work in the financial services industry and it strikes me as amazing that so much private information is held by the credit bureaus and financial institutions. Privacy is the responsibility and should be the concern of every individual citizen, but let me tell your readers right now that your consumer credit report contains way more information (correct and incorrect) than you would ever want an anonymous person to know. For the most part, there is little that can be done to protect this information from prying eyes. Financial institutions nationwide have ready access to your entire financial, employment, criminal, driving, and spending records without your knowledge or consent. There is some recourse that has been built as a protection against the information being reported incorrectly or falling into the wrong hands, but it does little to preserve your privacy.*

> *As a part of the internal workings of this industry, I have more access to your data than you do, a lot more. As an example, I can pull a credit report on anyone in the country with little more than their name and a made up address. No social? No problem. When I pull up your info, it will politely inform me that the social security number I have entered was incorrect and that the correct one is XXX-XX-XXXX. By the way, when I pull up a credit report I am* prohibited by law *from giving the customer a copy, and the copy you can request from them (it is your right to get one for free) is* not even close *to as complete as what I see. Experian, CBI, Trans Union, and Equifax have the goods on you right now. They know where you work, how much you make, how much available credit you have on your cards, who your cell carrier is and how much you use it, whether or not you have been or still are married, where you have applied for credit, and also where and at what rate you spend your money and a plethora of other tidbits. Credit is extremely necessary for most of us and also extremely valuable but is based largely on arbitrary formulas. This is a system that needs to*

be hacked and understood. I encourage those of you who are curious, careful, and adept to start snooping (and believe me, there are a lot of back doors). What you find will shock and amaze you.

LoAN RAnGER
COLORADO

2001

Dear *2600:*

Why does 2600 have a problem with the MPAA? They didn't make the DMCA. How come more pressure isn't being put on politicians?

KEYSER SOZE

There's this little lawsuit the MPAA filed against us that has probably swayed us away from their position. And they might just as well have written the DMCA themselves since they are among the DC special interest groups who are directly served by it. How much pressure is put on the politicians is completely up to individuals.

Dear *2600:*

The new movie Swordfish *is about a CIA operative who gets a hacker to transfer money out of a slush fund. Why is it that Hollywood always associates all hackers as "black hats?" Not all of us have a destructive intent. I personally see it as an insult to think that all hackers of the world should be put down like that.*

PSYCHO-MANTIS

They do it for the same reason they make so many lousy movies with the same basic plot devices and overused formulas. It's easy and it sells. They couldn't care less about accuracy. There are and will be exceptions and they need to be her-alded whenever possible. In the meantime, don't buy into the mythology that is built up by the entertainment industry, the mass media, and those who benefit by hyping hackers as evil and scary. You can start by refraining from using terminology such as "black hat" or "cracker." They perpetuate a stereotype that only benefits those with an agenda of greed or power.

Dear *2600:*

> *I was looking over the board members of the MPAA when a thought hit me. Why isn't there a board member for the consumer? Isn't the end idea in business to make the consumer happy with the product and want to purchase more? It also seemed that the MPAA had a real legit reason to be established to begin with but seems to have become a stagnant relic that stands for a corporate feudalistic agenda.*

> QUATRE

You answered your own question.

Dear *2600:*

> *I've recently read that Despair, Inc. has registered the frowny emoticon ":-(", copyrighted it, and is planning to sue "anyone and everyone who uses the so-called 'frowny' emoticon, or our trademarked logo, in their written email correspondence. Ever."*

> *Oops. Looks like I might get a little corporate letterhead soon. This is the lowest of the low for corporate America.*

> SHADOW FREQ

Please tell us you were aware that this is a joke. Despair, Inc. (www.despair.com) defines its origins as "a company that would create dissatisfied customers in the process of exploiting demoralized employees while selling overpriced and ineffective products to remediate the problems caused by the very process itself." That's kinda the tipoff.

Dear *2600:*

> *Ever since I started seeing all those TV ads for Cingular talking about the importance of self-expression and asking people the question, "What do you have to say?" I began thinking about what a bunch of corporate brainwashing BS it all sounded like. After all, corporate America and the federal government both seem to use much the same tactics. Do whatever it takes to get people on your side. Tell them whatever they want to hear if it'll help boost profits any. God knows you can never have too many millions of dollars or too much power, right? Not like it's anything so new. We've already seen it with Verizon and their '60s throwback that co-opted the peace sign. Just further proof that nothing is sacred, and all's fair in love and profit margins. But, getting to the point, if Cingular really wants to claim they care about what you have to say, there's one very simple way to test the convictions they claim to have. Yep, you probably guessed. Someone registering* www.cingularsucks.com *or maybe* www.cingularlovesmoneymorethanfreespeech.com *would not only test how much their thinking is like their corporate ads, but would let them know that there are some of us who don't buy into every last corporate motto we hear or read. And, if it turns out that they end up going to extreme lengths to stifle expression, I wouldn't be the least bit surprised.*

> 7H3 31337 pHR34K4Z0ID

Dear *2600:*

> *Here is a message I got when I went (on the net) to one of my favorite radio stations—KSJO—to listen to some live audio streaming: "Due to continuing uncertainty over rights issues related to the streaming of radio broadcast programming over the Internet, including issues regarding demands for additional fees for the streaming of recorded music and radio commercials, we and our advertisers are forced to temporarily disable our streaming. We apologize for the inconvenience of this interruption. We are working with both our advertisers and the Recording Industry Association of America to find a solution to those problems as quickly as possible so that we can resume our streaming." KSJO has to be one of the wildest radio stations in California (that's a good thing). It's hard for me to believe this sort of thing could happen at such a "liberal" radio station!*

> TONY

Regardless, it's a commercial station and they are subject to the greed and stupidity of the marketplace. In this case, their misfortune represents an opportunity for more alternative forms of Internet broadcasting to become known. While the commercial stations are bickering over who gets more money, noncommercial broadcasters can make their presence felt with the kind of programming these same commercial entities have managed to stifle over the public airwaves.

Dear *2600:*

> I don't know if you heard but Qwest Communications raised their payphone charge from a high 35 cents to 50 cents. Do you guys know why?
>
> NIIHON

Because they can. And if you think that's crazy, check out how much it costs to call a different state from a payphone when using cash. Close to ten times the normal rate! When you consider that the people most likely to use cash for such a call may not have their own phone, credit card, or even a place to live, it's appalling. And Bell South has recently announced that it will soon be disconnecting all of its payphones because they're just not profitable. That's right—the entire Bell South region will be COCOTs! Hell is in sight.

Dear *2600:*

> When you piss against Corporate America, you get smacked and it seems you've been targeted. I read your briefs on the Ford case. Not bad, make it as expensive for them as possible! I don't buy Ford anyway (note to Ford lawyers: due to crappy product, not 2600). In fact, just thinking about it, how about a defamation/libel countersuit? How about reclaiming some of those defense dollars the EFF pitched in for the DeCSS suit?
>
> LITZE

We'd like nothing better.

2002

Dear *2600:*

> I'm really pleased to see you boosting your coverage of recent incursions by corporate America into consumers' privacy/property rights. While such issues might not be the central mission of 2600, this issue is going to become one of the most important and explosive ones in American culture in the past 50 years.
>
> STRUPP

We agree. But it's hardly a recent phenomena.

Dear *2600:*

> I just found out something quite disturbing at my workplace. I'm an analyst for a major ISP in Canada and I had an interesting conversation with my friend at the abuse department. It seems that the RIAA is pressuring us to shut down customers who have been involved in file sharing, especially on the Kazaa network. Apparently, the volume of threats by the RIAA, Sony, and other organizations is around 1000+ emails per month. They are receiving detailed logs with IP addresses and the names of the files that have been traded (even though everyone knows it's no proof). They've installed a new script on the Radius server to break down logs in smaller chunks so they can be searched faster. Needless to say, that is quite disturbing. So far, they have not shut down anyone, only sent warnings by email to the "offenders." They're in the process of deciding what to do next. I'll keep you posted. I thought you would find this interesting.
>
> QUEBEC

It might be interesting to find out exactly how they're getting these logs in the first place. Are they perhaps running some sites of their own? Or is your ISP monitoring what their users do?

2003

Dear *2600:*

> Recently, I bought the Sony MZ-N505 Minidisc recorder. I wanted
> to use it to make high quality recordings of my band and my friends'
> bands in live situations. I had no intention of clandestinely "bootleg-
> ging" the copyrighted material of paranoid mega-acts like Metallica
> or Linkin Park, due to my lack of interest in their lousy, overproduced,
> overprotected, irrelevant garbage.
>
> A few weeks ago, I decided to try to get a good live recording of a
> friend's band at a club. The result sounded excellent and when I got
> home, of course I wanted to put it on my hard drive to edit, EQ, and
> burn copies of it (with the full knowledge of the band—they even
> requested a copy). It was to my surprise when, after installing Sony's
> bundled Open MG Jukebox and NetMD software, that there was no
> feature to transfer (or "check-in" as they call it) data from the MD to
> the computer using the supplied USB/MD cable.
>
> I learned that the USB interface was only to be used to "check-out"
> purchased music from the hard drive to the MD unit. The only per-
> mitted function of "checking-in" is to return previously "checked-out"
> music from the MD back to the hard drive, a function that I cannot
> imagine ever having a use for. Apparently, Sony did not include a truly
> digital USB/MD option in order to discourage piracy (Sony is, after
> all, a major publisher of music content as well as audio hardware).
>
> So what are underground music enthusiasts and "tapers" like myself
> supposed to do to transfer uncopyrighted music to their computers?
> Here's the only answer I have come up with: We must play the MD,
> in real time, into the analog line-in in the computer's sound card, and
> then edit it using a sound-editing program (I use ProTools Free).
>
> This outrageous example of prohibitive software is infuriating to
> people like me, whose main purpose in getting an MD recorder was
> for the perceived ability to record high quality music and transfer it
> digitally to the computer. I've searched the net for shareware or free-
> ware programs that enable high speed USB/MD interface, but have
> come up empty. Mostly, I just find entries on bulletin boards full of

complaints just like mine. At least one petition has been started, but I doubt Sony will alter or update their software.

If anyone has any alternatives or answers, I would love to hear about them. I just hope I don't hear, "You shouldn't have gotten a Sony." It's a shame that such amazing technology should be so incredibly limited because of baseless corporate fear.

Thank you for your great magazine.

SEMICEREBRAL

This is a brilliant example of corporate stupidity shooting itself in the foot. Instead of encouraging people to use technology to be innovative, thereby creating all sorts of new markets they could capitalize on, they choose instead to stifle such innovation due to fears of losing money. We wish these dinosaurs would simply go back to the analog world and leave the digital technology for those who truly want to work with it. We're confident more companies will come along who don't cripple the technology, especially when more people like yourself make their presence known.

Dear *2600:*

As recently as a year ago I had about the same opinion on piracy as revanant in his letter in 20:2; piracy is fine if it is just to "test out" a product. However, I've reached a stage now in my life that I am designing software and I finally understand why that idea is wrong. When you pour your heart and soul into something like a big project, the finished product is a part of you. It is something you created and therefore own. If I want my work to be freely available, it is; if I want my product to cost $1,000,000 per license, it will because it is mine and I get to decide if/how anyone else gets to use it. It is wrong for someone to take what is mine under their own terms. I think that our freedom to create and to decide how our ideas are shared is fundamental, and software piracy deprives us of this right.

EIGENVALUE

Of course it's wrong for someone to take your hard work and leave you with nothing—or at least substantially less than you deserve. But you have to balance this with a dose of reality. If we were to decide that each of our issues should cost $1,000,000, does that mean that anyone who obtains it for less or, heaven forbid, steals it outright, is guilty of stealing a million dollars? Maybe in our opinion, but nobody else would go along with it. And by pricing something so high above the reach of individuals, we'd be setting it up so that people would have to find some nefarious way of obtaining it. In other words, we'd be fools to be surprised and we'd have nobody to blame but ourselves when people don't play by these rules. Of course, there's no way we could ever get a magazine into a store with that kind of price. Software companies manage to come up with incredible markups as do record companies and that's a significant reason why so many people are not only reluctant to pay their prices but also completely unable to. It doesn't make it right but nobody should be surprised when it goes this predictable route.

Recently, a filmmaker friend of ours wanted to buy the new version of FinalCut Pro to edit his movie. He went to the Apple store prepared to shell out the $1000 it cost. But he wanted a guarantee that it would work on the MacIntosh he owned before he paid for something that couldn't be returned. They told him that if it worked on a Titanium (the most advanced and expensive machine they sold), that they wouldn't be liable for any problems he encountered on a cheaper machine. In their words, it was his decision not to upgrade and buy a new machine. The decision he wound up making instead was to buy the program off the street for $50 and never use Macs again after this project. (And yes, the program wound up working on his machine which meant that Apple would have made the sale if they had shown some support of their customers.) Now there's no question that he ripped them off since he didn't pay them for the program and in fact wound up paying someone else for it. But who set this situation up? Has Apple earned any-one's sympathy with this kind of behavior?

There are ways of keeping customers and ways of losing them. And that, despite everything else that's going on, is the real bottom line.

Dear 2600:

> The RIAA's opinions on file sharing are so over exaggerated. Who are we feeling sorry for here? The people whining about piracy are some of the richest people in the world. I'd bet if this was some poor starving artist finding their music online, they'd probably take it as

a compliment, not a threat. There is so much more than just music and movies out there on the Internet, yet all you ever hear about is the media. I think this is partially because the production companies seem to be the most threatened by all of this. If people can go straight to the artist, who's going to need a production company to take 90 percent of the profit?

What's the difference between downloading music and recording something off the radio or TV? If they're going to make file sharing illegal, they should make tape recorders, DVD/CD burners, PC sound cards, VCRs, and basically anything else with recording capabilities, illegal too. The industries seem to be more afraid of change than anything else. What they should be doing is figuring out how to use this technology for their own benefit, not trying to destroy it. Imagine what would have happened had the movie industry gotten their way and destroyed VCR technology.

It's almost as if the RIAA is begging for a rebellion. Their actions of "let's sue everyone and maybe we'll get lucky" seems to have just encouraged people's downloading because it certainly hasn't stopped it. And no matter what they do to try and stop this, the technology will eventually get cracked and people will be free to trade once again. Look what shutting down Napster did. It didn't stop anything and the file trading spread all over the Internet and nearly everything is now being shared. With most of these files being shared on peer-to-peer sites that have no central location, they're basically impossible to shut down.

The RIAA's current actions are basically a present day witch hunt. It's funny, they're always talking about these evil teenagers that have no respect for copyright and other people's work. Yet a good percentage of people sharing these files are adults. I wonder what people would think if someone's 90-year-old grandmother was busted for file trading. Because you know she's out there somewhere, waiting to get caught. Maybe we need something like that to happen, just to prove how ridiculous all of this really is.

Jeff

It's already happened to senior citizens as well as to a 12-year-old. Considering the RIAA is involved in marketing some of the biggest performers in the history of mankind, they certainly should be doing a better job marketing themselves.

2004

Dear *2600:*

> *Can you guarantee the anonymity of submitters of articles? I have an article that may make a large corporation very angry.*
>
> Anon Ymous

Our publication keeps a significant percentage of the corporate world in a perpetual state of anger so your article would be right at home here. If you take sufficient precautions, such as not using a byline that can be traced back to you, being specific as to which name we should use, and not having anything that could identify you in the actual text of the article, you should be OK. Also, be sure not to email us from an account others might monitor, especially one from the large corporation itself. We can't discount the possibility that email traffic could be monitored somewhere along the line so in real sensitive situations, drop it in the U.S. mail with no return address. Wear gloves.

Dear *2600:*

> *I'm a preschool teacher and today, during afternoon snack time, one of my students told me about a bad dream she had had the night before. It involved a character named Hacker from the children's television program* Cyberchase. *The dream was apparently very scary to this four-year-old girl who was starting kindergarten in September. I know people in the past have written about how awful this show is and how it is probably affecting children. I am telling you that all these people were right. I asked her and the other children in the room what a hacker was. Most had just an opinion on the character Hacker and*

didn't know what a hacker in general was. They all agreed he was a very bad person who wanted to rob and defraud you.

I asked if any of their parents copied their DVDs so they could have their own copy to put in the DVD player themselves. Indeed, a couple did. At a three- to five-year-old level, I explained fair use and DeCSS.

"Why don't they want me to have a copy of Finding Nemo *to put in when I want?"*

"Because they want your daddy to buy two so they can have more money."

"That's silly, they should share."

The kids learned a valuable lesson: that their parents and they were in a hacker conspiracy to independently watch movies that they legally own. They learned that people who do bad things are bad people whether they do them on a computer or in the physical world. You should always treat others the way you would like to be treated.

Mark

It may seem thoroughly appalling to manipulate the minds of toddlers until you realize that it's already being done every day through television and other less subtle forms of propaganda. A little debriefing is definitely in order.

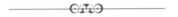

Dear *2600:*

Why is it that evil can only be replaced by those more evil? Jack Valenti was bad enough but now Dan Glickman, the new MPAA head, wants to impose RIAA-style subpoenas. The new Corporate America we see today is no longer based on what the general public wants, but rather what is in the interests of big business! The people who really run the country are the directors of national security, big tobacco, pharmaceutical companies, but most of all mass media! The mass media spreads its propaganda like it was true. Now the only place you can go for non American-biased news is the BBC or maybe PBS! If the MPAA and the RIAA can throw their weight around in the legislature and the courtroom, how is that different than al Qaeda in Afghanistan? They

are panicking because people have another choice rather than to pay
outrageous fees for entertainment. Damned be the DMCA!

MONKEY MINISTER

The whole corporate/media thing really isn't all that new. You shouldn't be sur-
prised when these entities act like this. That's what they're there for. Instead, viable
alternatives need to be encouraged wherever possible. You can't stop P2P tech-
nology nor prevent the spread of alternative media—unless people allow it to hap-
pen. Also, comparing the MPAA/RIAA to al Qaeda probably won't wind up being
the most convincing method of getting people to see the wisdom of your opinion.

2005

Dear *2600:*

> *I work for the telephone company here in British Columbia. Telus has*
> *put GPS units on most of the trucks used for installation and repair.*
> *Telus apparently bought the Geomatics company that manufactures*
> *these devices which are supposed to be able to show in real time where*
> *a vehicle is. These devices are mounted on the driver's fender of the*
> *vehicles we drive with other electronics boxed under the dashboard in-*
> *side the vehicle. The satellite antenna is a hockey puck size and shaped*
> *device with a cell antenna molded into it which sticks up about three*
> *inches. A couple of small wires feed down from the hockey puck and*
> *enter the engine compartment and feed through the firewall to a black*
> *box about the size of a cigar box. I can see lights on this box through*
> *the cracks where the molded pieces of the dashboard fit together. This*
> *is what I know and understand. All our managers have the ability to*
> *access the GPS program from their computer. They can tell when we*
> *start our trucks in the morning, when we drive away (and there is a*
> *detailed map associated with this that shows our route), our speed,*
> *and idle time. This information is sent via cell or 1X data transmis-*
> *sion. If we get out of cell range the GPS information is compiled and*
> *sent out when we do reach cell communication. Telus has only stated*
> *that this is used in case our trucks are stolen. However, an upper*

*manager mistakenly sent an email which we all saw, stating he wanted
the managers to use this to keep track of our productivity and I'm sure
to be used as a reprimand tool. I don't know how to fool or thwart this
action other than putting a pie plate over the antenna, which could
alert management that we were fooling around with this device. Is
there any way we could create a jamming signal from within the cab
that could screw with the communication of either the satellite or the
cell transmission? Does anyone have more technical information about
how these devices work?*

TIRED OF BEING FOLLOWED
PLEASE DON'T USE MY NAME

Comfort yourself with the knowledge that there are people all over the place figuring out ways to subvert these things. We'll publish the results when we get them.

Dear *2600:*

*I work for a very large telecom whose name I won't divulge for obvi-
ous purposes. It all began with the implementation of cameras in our
workspace, then with the implementation of "vericept," and now the
proverbial straw. I work as a network security analyst monitoring
several large networks investigating possible compromises and infec-
tions. We all know how the pay never fits the job. So they have hired
a lot of people I wouldn't have watching over a TI calculator. I get
frustrated because nobody has a clue about signatures or even hacker
methodology or can even fathom the mindset. So I decided to be a
nice guy and put up a bulletin board on my machine at home regarding security, exploits, new code, and several other general categories.
Well, the "telecom" caught wind of this and tried to force me to shut
it down, saying it was a breach of company policy because of the fact
I have a security bulletin board and it pertains to my position because
I work in security. They even went to the extreme of saying if anyone
from work posted on it, I would be the one paying the ultimate price.
A little background information on me and why they feel threatened.
I have been working with exploit code since I was about 15 and spent
some time as a contractor for the DoD working as a security engineer*

and even spent some time in the military as a cryptologist. So every move I make they watch me. Where does it say in the Constitution that you give up your rights when you walk into a place of employment? I have sought employment elsewhere and want everyone to know that telecoms, especially the large and seemingly powerful ones, have no idea what they are doing.

STING3R, CEH

This kind of thing is unfortunately spreading. There are many corporations and institutions that think they can control their employees 24 hours a day. Worse, there are so many people who just blindly buy into this, especially if the paycheck is large enough. We need more people like you to keep this from becoming the norm.

2006

Dear *2600:*

I am a sysadmin at one of the larger school corporations in a Midwestern state. I run security, run the firewall software, do backups, investigate intrusions, give advice, etc., etc. Typical sysadmin stuff. I keep a subscription to your magazine. I find little resistance from peers or administration about keeping a copy around.

I am sometimes confronted with students who are considered hackers. A few years ago, I was introduced to a young man (we'll call him Tom). Tom was a real loner of a kid and seemed kind of down. He had been caught "hacking" some years before. As we all know, these types of evil "hackers" are often just misunderstood. After his hacking incident his punishment was to not use a computer for two years.

The entire school corporation, from the elementary schools to the vocational education department, knew about this kid. He had a "superhacker" reputation. He started hanging around my office and talking with me. I work in an environment that would allow him to have access to some big holes. I had administrators call me and warn me that it might not be safe to have this kid hanging around consoles and logged in machines. They were scared.

When I was told what this "hacker" had done, I proceeded to laugh hysterically until tears were pouring out of my eyes—all to the blank and expressionless stares of the people who told me about it. What a bunch. You want to know what he did? He reset the proxy settings in Netscape so it didn't go through the filter system I was testing. Yeah! What a hack! This kid got punished and derided for changing the proxy in Netscape! What a bunch of morons.

I have found school corporations so totally inept at understanding anything to do with curiosity or discovery. It's a sad thing when a kid like this has the biggest reputation of hacking of anyone in the student body. I have continually been disgusted with their treatment of students that "hack." They just want to enforce their petty little rules so they will seem validated by their subsequent authority.

Shouldn't educators understand the thirst for knowledge? Believe me, they don't! Their definition of obtaining knowledge is so narrow that it only covers going to class. God forbid we could learn anything on our own! Do that and you're a hacker!

I have mentioned to my superiors that I would like to take the kids that get caught hacking and interview them, then put them to work. Their answer: That would be rewarding misbehavior. Instead they run a rod up their butt and hang them like a trophy for the rest of the student body to see.

Hey, teachers, get a clue! If you don't like computers and are scared by the kids who know 10k times more than you, retire now! You'll be lengthening your life and making life better for teenagers who actually need to learn.

G MAN IN THE HOLE

The biggest defense against this kind of stupidity is to simply get the details out to the public. By doing that and by reaching out to this kid, you've helped out on many levels. We can only wonder how many people have wound up taking a bad road in life because so many morons have told them they were guilty of something. Idiots in authority must be challenged at every opportunity.

Dear *2600:*

> *The letter in 22:4 from Ben, a high school student in the Atlanta area, stated that he was surfing from the school's computer lab and was prevented from accessing* 2600.com *because it was blocked as "Criminal Skills."*
>
> *I work for a company that makes a web filtering product for schools and businesses. I had personally categorized* 2600.com *as "Computer/ Internet" several years ago. When I saw that letter, I thought, "Oh, I hope that's not our product." I checked today and one of the other technicians had changed the category to "Hacking." That maps back in older versions of the product to "Criminal Skills." I changed it back to "Computer/ Internet," but there's no telling how long that will last.*
>
> *So in this case, it's not the school that is at fault. It was our product and I'm sorry about that. Of course, Ben's school could be using one of the other filtering products, so this might not help him. But I'm glad he gave me a reason to check and fix it in ours.*
>
> TOOTS

We're fortunate to have people like you in these companies who can do something about such injustices. Let's hope it makes a difference.

Dear *2600:*

> *I just received a letter from H&R Block that says the following:*
>
> > *"Recently we mailed you a free copy of our TaxCut Software. We believe that this complimentary software will meet your 2006 tax preparation needs based on our prior experience with you as an H&R Block client. We hope that you will try TaxCut and find it to be a great solution for filing your next tax return.*
> >
> > *"However, since we sent you this CD, we have become aware of a mail production situation that has affected a small percentage of recipients, including you. Due to human error in developing the mailing list, the digits of your social security number (SSN) were used as part of your mailing label's source code, a string of more than 40 numbers and characters. Fortunately, these digits were*

embedded in the middle of the string, and they were not format-
ted in any manner that would identify them as an SSN.

"Nevertheless, we sincerely apologize for this inadvertent error,
which is completely inconsistent with our strict policies to pro-
tect our clients' privacy. Our internal policies limit the use of cli-
ent SSNs for purposes other than tax preparation. Furthermore,
our internal procedures require that mailing source codes are
formulated in a manner that excludes use of any sensitive or
confidential information. Please know that we have conducted
a thorough internal review of this matter, and are taking actions
to ensure that this does not reoccur."

So, not only are they sending me junk mail... they are sending me junk
mail that exposes sensitive personal information.

DRLECTER

This is probably a lot more common than even the most paranoid among us fear.
While these guys at least owned up to their huge mistake, one has to wonder why
they would use that number in any way outside of having to report it to the tax
people. It makes about as much sense as sticking your total income into a mailing
label code. Such information has no business being used for other purposes. And
yet it is—everywhere we look. We invite our readers to let us know whenever they
see an SSN someplace where it shouldn't be.

Dear *2600:*

I was browsing the Internet at work and I wanted to check out some
guitar tabs. I visited a site that usually offers tablature online. This
is what I saw:

"Due to actions threatened by the National Music Publishers
Association and the Music Publishers Association of America
under the Digital Millennium Copyright Act, `GuitarTabs.com`
is not offering guitar tablature at this time. We are currently
evaluating our legal rights and options at this time, but unfor-
tunately cannot offer tablature in the meantime. More infor-
mation and updates on the situation can be found here. Check
back frequently for updates."

Because of the money hungry corporations who would snatch candy from a baby, this is how we have to suffer. We will have to have pirated music tabs. Scanned PDF docs online. I guess it is illegal to have a copy of a music sheet now. Come on. It's like Metallica and these other bands aren't rich enough that they have to punish people for sharing their music.

KINGPIN

It's funny how this wasn't even an issue years ago. Nobody in their wildest imagination would have thought sharing guitar tabs could somehow be a problem for anyone. We suspect that it's not really a problem but instead is now being seen as another potential source of income.

2007

Dear *2600:*

I work for a small computer support company in the southeast United States. The job consists mostly of field calls that require almost no knowledge whatsoever—broken CD-ROM trays, unplugged network cables, etc. On occasion I receive work orders to repair issues at a local hospital. The hospital is one of the largest in the region with almost 100 independent practices partnered with the 500+ bed facility. I received a work order in January to "revamp" the network for a practice. The networking closets for these independent practices are still controlled by the hospital's management company.

I called the phone number located on a sign that was attached to the locked closet door. A young lady answered the phone and explained that I would have to come to their office and get the key. I ran across the street to their office and talked to the receptionist whom I had just called. She gave me a puzzled look and asked if I wanted a maintenance key or a telecom key. I told her telecom followed by which building the closet was located in. She opened a wall locker and pulled out a key with a tag attached to it. She asked for my name, company, and cell phone number. I pulled out my wallet as I answered the *questions and before I could pull out my ID she dropped the key on the counter. I guessed because of my business attire that she just assumed I was okay. As I walked back to the practice I looked at the tag on the key and noticed that it had two building numbers on it. Sure enough, it opened all closets I passed in both buildings! After the call was finished, I brought the key back. She didn't check my name off in her book. She just took the key back to the locker. I put it behind me thinking that she may have been in a bad mood or something (common at this hospital).*

In March, I had a similar call at another practice. The same exact thing happened! No ID check. No check off in the "log book." And absolutely no signatures! It was a different girl that was working the counter. I don't know about anyone else, but it scares me to think that the proper safeguards aren't being taken with the networking closets at this hospital. Both of my coworkers reported that they have never been prompted for any form of ID or proof of work. I can just imagine the wealth of knowledge a person could obtain by monitoring a network from the closet: SSNs, DOBs, addresses, and medical information! I have sent an anonymous tip to the management company to hopefully resolve this. I guess I will find out the next time I have network work to do!

INF3KT1D

Don't hold your breath. Stupidity and bad security practices have an amazing resiliency.

Dear *2600:*

I've been a reader of 2600 since about 1998, so first let me say thanks for giving me something to look forward to every three months. I also catch Off The Hook and Off The Wall, although mostly webcasts these days as sadly I've moved off Long Island.

Anyway, I just thought you might get a kick out of this website— in particular, the user agreement which can be found here: http://www.cybertriallawyer.com/user-agreement.

> *Toward the middle you will find my personal favorite snippet: "We also own all of the code, including the HTML code, and all content. As you may know, you can view the HTML code with a standard browser. We do not permit you to view such code since we consider it to be our intellectual property protected by the copyright laws. You are therefore not authorized to do so."*
>
> *I am just curious to see your opinion of it, as well as the opinion of the listeners and viewers. Keep up the great work and rest assured you have a loyal reader/listener for life.*
>
> SPEEDKORE

This is just so typical of the corporate world and how their little fantasyland becomes reality on so many levels. We live in a land where filmmakers have to cover up ads in public places or blot out the names of products or logos on t-shirts because they haven't gotten "permission" to use these images. Groups of people who sing "Happy Birthday" face prosecution if they don't pay for the rights. There are even those who believe you can be prosecuted for taking a picture of a building without getting the permission of the people who "own" the rights to its image. And now a website that tells you that you are not authorized to read its contents. Since we have now printed their words without getting specific permission from them, we can only cower in fear in anticipation of the action that will undoubtedly be taken against us. What a screwed up planet we have become.

2009 _____

Dear *2600:*

> *I was not really sure which email address to send this to, but I wanted to get some information on submitting photos to the magazine.*
>
> *I work for the Evil Empire (AT&T) and have access to pretty much all the systems, plant, MDF, switches, DSLAMs, etc. I get to see this stuff every day. I might just be a phreak, but I believe some other people would like to see everything from the ancient equipment to the latest and greatest.*

I would be more then happy to write up a small article on the piece of equipment that is in the photo as well. Thanks for your time and consideration and, as always, I will do it for just the gratification of helping others.

BRAD

We look forward to receiving your submissions. This is a great example of how people within certain organizations—who have access to things we can only dream about—can make our world so much more interesting simply by sharing information. Thanks for helping to preserve the hacker spirit.

Our Biggest Fans

I'd have to say, far and away my favorite part of the letters column—in fact, my favorite part of the entire magazine—is answering the nasty mail. That's why this is the biggest chapter in this collection.

Let's not give the wrong impression. We don't get more hate mail than anything else; these are just so much fun to read that I had to include a lot more of them proportionally. And I'm not even being fair here—most of this is not hate mail at all. It's simply...critical mail of a sort, mail that calls into question stuff we've printed, stuff we've said, just stuff in general....

Some of our earliest critiques centered around our format change. For the first three years of our existence (1984–1986), we had a very simple newsletter format. In 1987 we changed our size, added pages and binding, and started having covers. In 1988 we enlarged our size and changed to the current quarterly schedule. But even in the hacker world, any sort of a change brings resistance, and we had quite a bit of that at first. And we did wind up making changes when we realized we were wrong, such as when we were sending out the magazines without envelopes for a brief period. It was a learning experience for us too, after all.

As we grew and became more well known, the inevitable disenchantment was voiced by a number of readers in their letters. Some of these were nothing more than gentle admonitions. Others were...well, you'll see. I'd hate to ruin the surprise.

There's really an awful lot of history contained in this section. In one of the angry letters accusing us of selling out to the mainstream, mention is made of "flare gun assaults" on phone companies and somehow *2600* was associated with this (only in this reader's imagination, fortunately). The fact is, there actually *was* such an incident involving some people we knew, but nobody who was on the staff of the magazine. It was right around this time that the guy writing *Hackers* was hanging around at the New York City *2600* meetings looking for material. And if you watch that movie, you'll see a flare gun scene. And this is how movies are made. (You'll also see a couple of letters making reference to a writer of ours named The Plague who claimed to have absolutely no morals whatsoever. Well, that character also made it into the film. So there's a little history within history.)

There's nothing we weren't accused of at one point or another: being too left-wing, being too right-wing, selling out, acting like hypocrites, rejecting the commercial world, acting as puppets for the Chinese, insulting communism, helping criminals, helping corporations, supporting totalitarianism, talking too much about politics, avoiding politics, engaging in censorship, insulting Libertarians and gun owners... you name it, we eventually would be accused of it by somebody. And we thoroughly enjoyed it. I think my favorite was being called "snot-nose-right-wing-conservative-ditto-head-Republican vandals." That just doesn't happen every day.

Of course, writing the replies here was a great deal of fun and people always tell us how much they enjoy reading them, especially when they got somewhat contentious. I've always believed the best way to deal with issues is to confront them head-on and some of these collisions were pretty spectacular.

By far the biggest issue, where we were raked over the coals the most, was the whole Kevin Mitnick case. To sum it up in one sentence, we stood up for a hacker who had been imprisoned for many years without a trial, and led a campaign to get him released and to expose the facts of the case. The number of people who took great offense at this was a real eye-opener. I always wondered what it was they ultimately wanted. Five years in prison wasn't enough? What would have satisfied them for this crime nobody was able to even clearly define? So many would keep falling back onto the mantra of "he *broke the law!*" as if that was somehow a license to take away someone's freedom forever. Seeing that simplistic and rather ugly way of thinking did a lot toward strengthening my resolve. Of course, what really made me want to move ahead with this were the thousands of people showing their support in one way or another—so many more than the naysayers, in the end. But I'm happy to have been able to engage them, since being challenged is the best way of examining one's true feelings and motivations.

Also in this chapter you'll see system administrators angry at us for printing information that could be helpful to hackers. You'll see hackers angry at us for printing information that could be helpful to system administrators. One reader was convinced that our long answering machine message was some sort of a plot to keep people on the phone longer. Various people got a lot more upset than anyone ever should at something that happened to them on our IRC channel. You'll see some complaints about our customer service, back in the days before we actually got a system that worked. A company wrote to threaten us with legal action for printing their phone number—even though we never did. At least one person even objected to our using our own name. And of course, there were those people who just didn't understand that certain bits of information could be used for something other than bad and nefarious purposes.

Sometimes the best thing to do was simply to let the more outrageous ones keep talking and eventually hang themselves with their own logic. Other times, a spirited debate was in order. And there were even those occasions where we wound up agreeing. Those were nice, but not nearly as much fun.

Whichever way it winds up going, these are some of the most entertaining letters we've printed in our quarter century of publishing.

1987

Dear *2600:*

I have a few comments on your new format. First, I miss the large format. Its large pages were easier to read, and the page numbering made referencing simple. I also miss the loose-leaf holes. As stated in your first issue (I have them all), 2600 should be filed for reference purposes. The new format makes this very difficult.

I think I see your intentions: you want 2600 to become a widely distributed and accepted magazine, maybe even sold at newsstands or bookstores (where a flashy cover is important for impulse sales). I myself, as a subscriber and supporter of 2600, would not like this method of distribution to be undertaken. For one, it's expensive. A fancy three-color cover does nothing for me except use up my subscription dollars which could be better spent printing more information. I just don't feel 2600 has mass-market appeal.

To sum up my opinions, bring back the old format! *Just add new pages and columns as necessary, and keep the halftones.*

P.S. You wasted four valuable pages by printing cellular telephone frequencies that can be derived from this simple formula:

```
FREQUENCY=869.97+ (CHANNEL*.03) where:CHANNEL=1 TO 666
CHANNEL=(FREQUENCY-869.97)/.03
FREQUENCY=870 to 889.95 MHz
```

BERNIE S.

Correction: we only wasted three valuable pages. And, while some considered that a waste, others were happy with it because, for the first time, they could actually see what the frequencies were instead of having to calculate them. After all, what would they do with the calculation? Probably print out a list. Seems like we've saved them a couple of steps, doesn't it?

As far as distribution at newsstands is concerned, 2600 does have a future here. We have experimented with a few and had positive results. We find this to be a great way to attract new readers who would otherwise never know of our existence. We in turn will provide them with knowledge that they never thought was obtainable. This does not mean we're "selling out" or trying to get mass-market appeal. If you go to a halfway decent newsstand, you'll see quite a few other magazines reaching out in the same way.

Dear *2600:*

> *If I were to search my memory, I would undoubtedly find an appropriate story, anecdote, or analogy which would "make my point" better than this narrative. But I don't feel up to the challenge.*

> *In the January 1987 issue of 2600, you have announced two changes. The first deals with mailing your publication without an envelope, and the second hints at the possibility of newsstand distribution.*

> *As a former TAP subscriber with an alias and an out-of-town post office box address, I was living with a bit more paranoia in my day-to-day living style then versus now, since I receive your magazine under my own name at my residence. I am certain that you may view my conservative approach with a bit of skepticism since this is the land of the free and all of that type of thing.*

> *Nonetheless, I am reasonably well read and carefully monitor the trends in our society, especially those which deal with governmental intervention, and those issues which I call "perceived threats" to the average man. You, my dear friends, are, in my opinion, just such a source of perceived threat to many because of the contents of your publication. Our society remains computer illiterate with much fear about the black boxes that are taking over our way of life. You dare to*

publish mildly technical information dealing with the operations of the system—not for the intelligentsia of computer circles, i.e., scholars, computer literate, or business user—those who may have a need or right to know about such things, but for people who want to know more about what makes things work.

Your magazine contains articles and letters from those underground anarchists who would overthrow our system of checks and balances— knowledge is power, but don't spread it around to the masses since they would then demystify the matters of which you write, and thereby upset the system.

Look at previous issues envisioning a contents page such as the "Contents" page of the January issue, and imagine the implications of having these "threatening" manuscripts delivered to your home or office in full view of the Postal Service and its employees, your corporate mailroom personnel, office staff, family, ad infinitum. Makes no difference, you may say. I say, it damn well does make a difference.

It is not a matter of personal freedom, which should guarantee that I may read anything and everything I wish, that govern in this instance. Why are most copies of men's magazines sold at newsstands rather than by subscription? It is a part of our heritage—do it, but don't offend by blatantly publishing your taste in reading material by letting anyone know that you have such interests. Maybe you wish to help challenge this inconsistency by circulating 2600 in the mails and newsstands. Such is your right, but don't do it at my expense nor others who feel as I do.

Expanding your subscription base is something that drives any publishing entity; you wish to provide more people with the information that is contained in your magazine with a better return on your investment in time and energy. However, there is a cost that I hope you will weigh in making your decisions. Yes, I know that Mother Earth, Mother Jones, Playboy, *and a host of other magazines started their publishing existence in controversial and threatening manner to the then prevailing societal norms; they have gained legitimacy.*

However, please reconsider your actions in light of the comments which I have made in this letter. We are free, and yet we are not. Don't

*jeopardize my right of privacy without at least being aware of what
I and others view as adverse consequences which may occur because
of your actions. Thanks.*

A READER

Contest time: Name us one group of people in any moment of history that has achieved justice through hiding.

Dear *2600:*

> *I am convinced that as a result of your mailing 2600 without enve-
> lopes, many innocent people will be arrested and charged with crimes
> that they have not committed. Your statement that 2600 is not illegal,
> etc. is only true on the part of 2600 publishers but you want to imply
> that no envelopes will not harm your subscribers. This is not true.
> Let me remind you how the criminal justice system works: "You are
> innocent until proven guilty." But even if you are innocent, if some
> creep suspects that you are not innocent, it could cost you $100,000
> to prove in court that you are indeed innocent.*

NEWARK, NJ

We respect your opinion. But why did you have to send us those comments on a postcard so that the whole post office could read it?

Dear *2600:*

> *I was very upset with the misinformation you printed in your
> September issue. In an answer to a letter, you said that pen registers
> can be bypassed by using cordless phones. Nothing could be further
> from the truth! Pen registers record the number you're dialing no
> matter what kind of a phone you're using. And your suggestion of
> dialing on a cordless phone to avoid the pen register and then hopping
> back onto a regular phone to avoid being monitored on the radio is
> ridiculous, to say the least. I just hope nobody gets in trouble believing
> that this technique is safe.*

WORRIED AND UPSET IN ARIZONA

There seems to have been some misunderstanding on this topic, judging from the way 2600 has been blasted by some readers in the last couple of weeks. A reader wrote in last month to tell us that his Radio Shack pen register didn't record numbers he dialed when he used a cordless phone. We found this to be true with this model of pen register and with certain cordless phones. We don't know if that is true of other "real" pen registers and that is what we said. If someone wants to give us access to a genuine law enforcement-type pen register, we'll be happy to tell our readers everything it does and doesn't do. Until then, we have to be honest: we're not entirely sure. We'd appreciate hearing from people who have actual hands-on experience in this field.

1988

Dear *2600:*

> Hi. I am one of your numerous subscribers and interested readers who has a few gripes with the Spring 1988 issue of 2600.
>
> Although I don't mind the new format and appreciate its larger size, I think it could stand somewhat better editing.
>
> "The Threat of Computer Hackers." One or two nice anecdotes but the rest should have gone into Byte or Compute! I mean, you can assume that you have more enlightened readers on that subject that don't need a "HCK-100 BBS & Systems Intro."
>
> "ROLM Phone System." You could have cut this to one or two pages. About 50 percent of the article is fluff, like the complaints that people can't use the new phone with those weird buttons. Times change faster than humans and some of the complaints are hardly worthy of the reader's time. So what if the info number changes from 246-3636 to 632-6830?
>
> Given a larger magazine, this wouldn't be so bad, but 2600 is relatively small and so I'd prefer more and shorter articles (if they exist).
>
> OK. What I liked: "Monitoring TVRO." Although I am no phreak, I love to read stuff like that just to keep informed.

"VM/CMS." Although I hope I will never be on a system like that, it might come in handy sometime.

"Weathertrak." Not my real interest, but interesting nevertheless.

"From the 2600 Files." Fun and informative.

"Happenings" and "Letters." These are my favorites.

I hope you don't mind a little feedback from a reader.

Best of luck to you and your mag.

NATUERLICH!

We never mind getting comments and criticism. It shows that our subscribers are reading the magazine. What more could we ask for?

We presented Captain Zap's article ("Threat of Computer Hackers") not as a revelation but as an example of what is being said by some. We did this with the intention of opening up a dialogue which, judging from the response in this issue and on the boards, is precisely what happened.

The ROLM article was meant to illustrate more than the simple inconvenience of having to adjust to something new. We were attempting to point out how it's becoming increasingly common for the installers of such systems to blatantly disregard the needs of the users and just assume everyone will figure it out in the end. Being denied the freedom to select an easy-to-remember phone number seemed particularly ironic, considering user flexibility was one of the "advantages" of this new phone system.

By the way, another page that we got lots of comment on was the reprint of our six-cent RCI phone bill that's been showing up faithfully here every month for nearly two years. Well, guess what? RCI must be reading these pages because we suddenly stopped getting them. (Maybe we should reprint our $200 MCI bill and hope that goes away!)

Dear *2600:*

Just a note to say thanks for keeping a level head in a warped world. Your publication is well worth waiting three months for. Unfortunately, I am a rather impatient sort and also a recent subscriber so I am enclosing a request for the back issues from the past three years. That should keep this inquiring mind busy for some time to come.

Also, I want to offer my applause regarding the article "The Dark Side of Viruses." Having read too many articles concerning how awful viruses are, yours was such a breath of fresh air. It was a repugnant, putrid blast of air, to be sure, but it came from an angle that was so different from the masses that it was indeed refreshing. I suspect that T. Plague was rather brutally mistreated as a child. I cannot imagine complete amorality such as his without some form of trauma. I do agree on certain aspects of his dissertation such as the need for frequent backups and his lack of respect for program pirates. He is a bit of a hypocrite though (to go along with the rest of his conditions); after all, his program does its best to circumvent even the safety of frequent backups. I also don't think it is quite his place to judge program pirates. Quite frankly, he is not balanced enough to weigh properly anybody's guilt or innocence. It's too bad since he is obviously not an idiot or a fool. Nor do I feel that he should be pitied. He does not deserve my or anybody's pity. Nonetheless, though I obviously do not agree with Mr. Plague's article, I did learn a lot from it. It showed a rare insight into the mind of the virus generator, the serial killer, the child molester, or the arsonist. Take your pick. The lack of remorse or simple morals and the feelings of validity of their actions seem to be prevalent in all these people. I would like to feel that Mr. Plague would resent being equated to a child molester, but he probably doesn't. Most of his prey is just as innocent and helpless as a child. He is just as guilty of taking advantage of these same attributes existent in a novice computer user.

In any case, I am looking forward to reading three years' worth of wonderful, controversial, and informative articles. Keep up the good work.

Jonathan Porath

Dear *2600:*

This letter won't do any good, but I will write it anyway.

I called several of the BBSes you have listed. After a while, I hung up. I don't have time to screw with them. What is the point? Are the users frustrated hackers?

I call a lot of BBSes and they are easy to use. My time is too valuable to waste, and even more so when it is long distance to learn some stupid system just to use a silly BBS.

Too bad, you lose. I am a telecom tech at a large Centrex customer of Pac Bell (actually, a management position). We are such a good customer that I can call the CO and get them to do anything. They do it because we are such a good customer. Not because I lie and tell stories like some do.

I had hoped to share some of this information and my 40+ years of experience with others, but I am not going to waste my time to learn your BBS.

I was a writer for TAP and know the whole story of what happened. Would like to share this also—but your damn BBS pisses me off!

I also have a patent in telephony and a manufacturing company that makes telephone stuff under the patent.

Whenever you get a normal BBS, let me know and maybe I will change my mind.

Boy, it sure feels good to write this letter.

Am in San Francisco today to tour Pacific Bell's San Ramon complex. I am their guest. They pick me up at my hotel and give me lunch and a tour. This is because I am a good customer of theirs and I am designing the telecommunications facilities for a $44 million building going up in the next two years.

See what you missed!

Boy, it even feels better now.

Change those BBSes!

Sorry, I can't leave you my name. I am somewhat well known in the field and information I provide must not have my name on it.

UNSIGNED

We enjoyed your letter very much. We can certainly see how you managed to become so well known. And, no doubt, using your name would not be a good idea, in this or any circumstance. But we do want to thank you for finding time in your busy schedule to convey your concerns.

Unfortunately, no one here has any idea on what you could be talking about. We operate four BBSes, each running on completely different software. You seem to have had a run-in with one of them. Why don't you tell us exactly what happened so we can do something about it?

1989

Dear *2600:*

> Thank you for publishing such an informative well-written magazine.
>
> I only have one complaint. Please try to deal more with phone phreaking than hacking. Anyone can get access to a phone, but not all of us have computers and modems to participate in computer hacking.
>
> Thank you.

GRAND RAPIDS, MI

1990

Dear *2600:*

> Through the years, 2600 has received from its readers much praise for its efforts to make available a certain amount of information to the computer/telecommunications hobbyist that can be found nowhere else. But I think that 2600's actions of late are nothing less than reprehensible and are detrimental to the very same community it tries so hard to defend. It is my hope that you will print this letter in full, as lengthy as it may be, to allow the members of the hacker community outside of the New York City area to understand the recent turn of events you alluded to on pages 38-39 of the Spring 1990 issue.

"We do not believe in cover-ups. By not printing that bit of ugliness, we would have been doing just that."—2600 Magazine, *Autumn 1988, page 46.*

This brings me to the main thrust of my letter: Lately, in the New York City area, hackers have been receiving quite a bit of media attention, probably more than ever before. This has ranged from newspaper and magazine articles to local NBC news coverage of the UAPC hacking ordeal. In each instance, 2600 Magazine *has been prominently mentioned, and your editor has appeared in both televised and printed interviews. Due to these appearances, it is becoming readily apparent to the society outside of our "subculture" that* 2600 Magazine *is a "spokesperson" for the hacker community.*

I have nothing against that. In fact, the hacker community needs a unifying force or even a tangible home base where hackers of different backgrounds and computers can interface. The presence of 2600 *itself, as a public voice for hackers, may also prove to be a medium through which we can help expose inequities in the system itself, in this world of Secret Service confiscations and arrests, biased trials, and unjust sentences.*

What I am protesting, however, is the image 2600 Magazine *is projecting of the "American Hacker" to the outside world. Since its beginning,* 2600 *has coveted its beloved disclaimer of how the hacker is born out of the desire for intellectual stimulation, which can be satiated via the use of a computer and the exploration of it and others with it.* 2600 *feels this is how the world should view us. I quote from Spring 1988, page 8: "...hacking involves so much more than electronic bandits. It's a symbol of our times and one of the hopes of the future." This may be a rosy-eyed, naive view, but it is, however, accurate.*

But lately, 2600 Magazine *has drifted from this ideology, and the hacker is gaining a reputation as a criminal with destructive intent, as the editors and writers of this magazine are getting caught up in the sensationalism of it all. The pictures of several members of the close-knit group of friends (I will call the "2600 Gang") appeared on the front cover of the* Village Voice *the week of July 24, 1990, and Eric Corley himself has appeared on both an NBC prime-time television newscast and in the cover story of* Newsday Magazine, *July 8, 1990, page 12. This simply supports my argument that* 2600 Magazine *is compromising the security of its subscribers, as well as that of fellow members of the hacking community, to gain a spot in the limelight.*

Perhaps it is 2600's *belief that society should be made aware of our "habits," to "show how the machine really works." Does this include the public announcement of the "Flare Gun Assaults" that* 2600 Magazine *has conducted against several telco installations? Or does it include televised admissions that the* 2600 *staff has penetrated the New York City Board of Education's computer system? Does it also include concessions that close affiliates of* 2600 Magazine *are reprogramming ESS switches?*

Do you realize the repercussions of your bragging and arrogance? 2600 Magazine *is the* only *place where such material can or should be discussed, where it will gain worldwide acceptance. The outside world will condemn* 2600 Magazine *for its actions and all hackers along with it. If the "spokesperson" of the hacker community itself is tied to such activities, then hackers will be depicted to the world as perpetrators of crimes far worse than those mentioned above and will be considered detrimental and a threat to society as a whole.*

Your magazine speaks of ignorance of "the system" and the resultant fear of it. In fact, 2600 Magazine *was created in an effort to enlighten people and dispel this fear. But of late,* 2600's *activities and their glorification by the media, are generating a fear of hackers themselves, which is already developing into a hatred. In the public's eye, the hacker has degenerated from the forgotten* War Games *character, an inquisitive and smarter-than-average teenager with a gift for computers, to a malicious cyberpunk that is a threat to society and cannot be trusted in it. This computer whiz kid that was once greatly desired in the work force for his knowledge and ingenuity is now banned from employment in the computer science field as a security threat, and is being viewed as a criminal and the keyboard his weapon.*

I am not claiming innocence. Far from it. No "true" hacker can. But certainly your recent activities and efforts to gain some fame are sacrificing everything for us, since you are being viewed as the representative of our entire community. When 2600 Magazine *was founded in 1984, I don't think this was what you set out to achieve.*

The recent trend of events at your monthly meetings is further evidence of this. The meetings have deteriorated from an informative assemblage of hackers to a chaotic throng of teenagers who are being viewed by the media and authorities as a menace. Within this mob is hidden the "2600 Gang," a very elitist group of close-knit friends who associate with Eric Corley and refuse to share information or communicate with anyone outside of it. This is just another example of the hypocrisy of this magazine and its staff, which has thus far claimed to encourage the free exchange of information to promote awareness.

In light of this, I urge the staff of 2600 Magazine to reevaluate its ideals and actions and to come to grips with the responsibility it has to take on if it wishes to deal with the media in any way. At this time, it might be best to discontinue all media contact and relocate the 2600 meeting place to a more discreet location. If anyone wishes to take on the media individually, he should not implicate 2600 Magazine, as it will simply associate the magazine with illicit activities, which will result in further arrests, confiscations, and eventually the closing down of 2600 Magazine as well as the compromise of its subscribers' list in a big FBI cover-up a la TAP Magazine. I know that the majority of the "2600 Gang" who are less mature than the editors will dismiss this letter as a sign of paranoia and foolishness, but it is not. This is very serious.

DISGUSTED HACKER

It's interesting that you accuse us of "refus[ing] to share information or communicate with anyone outside of [our group]." Yet your solution is to "discontinue all media contact and relocate the 2600 meeting place to a more discreet location," which no doubt would have less "chaotic teenagers." Sounds like you just want more of a grip on the situation.

Our meetings are chaotic, no question there. We see them as a parallel to what hacking is all about. We trade information, talk with lots of people, make a bit of noise, and move forward without any formal agenda. We're careful not to cause damage, but sometimes people get offended. It's not for everyone.

In such a community, there can be no one unifying voice that speaks for everyone. And 2600 does not speak for all hackers. Nevertheless, the media has called upon us to participate in and help investigate particular hacker stories. This has resulted in, despite your claims, some of the best hacker press in years. We fail to see how this could compromise the security of our readers or of anybody else for that matter. Recent articles in The New York Times, The Village Voice, and Harpers have shown hackers in a more realistic light (the Voice piece in particular being one of the best articles ever to have appeared on hacking). A National Public Radio program in August pitted hackers against Arizona prosecutor Gail Thackeray in a lively debate. Even television is starting to show potential, but that's going to take some doing. Sure, there's still a lot of mudslinging going on. But most of this is the result of events, such as the massive raids by the authorities over the past few months. Were it not for the better stories that could not have been written without our participation, the American public would have gotten only one side. Is this what you want?

You refer to another article that accuses hackers of reprogramming switches and shooting flare guns. But you're the only one who says 2600 is in any way connected with these alleged incidents. Why? You're also the only one who says 2600 broke into the UAPC system ("Grade 'A' Hacking," Autumn 1989 issue). It was very clear in every account we saw that the UAPC information was given to us and that we turned it over to the media. Since you're obviously capable of getting our quotes from past issues of 2600 right, why can't you get the basic facts right on such important stories? It reminds us of a recent case where a hacker from New York was reported to have had access to telephone switches. The New York Post took that to mean that he opened manhole covers in the street to access the phone lines—and that's what they printed. Needless to say, we had nothing to do with that story.

We're not saying that your concerns are not valid. The image of the hacker is constantly being tarnished by people who either don't understand or who want to see hackers cast in a bad light. But your facts just don't hold up. Our public stands have had an effect. Journalists must prove their integrity before we give them a good story. And when a good story comes out, the average reader has the chance to see hackers as we see ourselves. With that comes the hope that they will understand.

Dear *2600:*

I was disappointed to see that you published the credit card algorithm in your Fall 1990 issue.

Although I know it was well within your First Amendment rights to publish it, I think that it serves no purpose by being published except to leave innocent credit card holders open to abuse by individuals who just wish to call a phone sex line or place a long distance call over an AOS. And although I know that the algorithm was already well known within the hacker world, I don't believe that your magazine should have spread it further.

In previous issues of 2600, you stated that credit card fraud and long distance code abuse are tantamount to stealing and have nothing to do with the hacker ethic of learning and exploring systems. Therefore, I see no reason to publish the credit card algorithm if your magazine truly believes in the above. The only uses of the credit card algorithm by your readers would be to generate numbers to be used to place calls over an AOS, access to phone sex lines or 800 chat lines which use credit card numbers for billing, or to obtain actual merchandise as the authors of your article state that often credit card numbers are often checked only against the algorithm and then billed later.

Please stick to your ideals. If you believe that credit card fraud and code abuse are stealing and not hacking, then please do not publish any information that would be used to those ends. And please try not to publish materials from authors who call themselves names such as "K00l/RaDAlliance!". Your mag will end up looking like a "s00per-elYte c0dez phile!"

Questmaster
Santa Barbara, CA

You raise good points, but you've missed the point of 2600. We published that information so people would understand how the technology worked. What they do with that information is not our business. Read on for another opinion.

Dear *2600:*

> Thank you for publishing "An Algorithm for Credit Cards." We have need-
> ed something to keep people from "fumble-fingering" on card entries.
>
> KENTON A. HOOVER
CHIEF ENGINEER
WHOLE EARTH LECTRONIC LINK

1991

Dear *2600:*

> Several months back, I wrote to you informing you that I did not
> receive an issue of *2600*. No one answered me nor was the issue ever
> sent to me. I have borrowed that issue from a friend.
>
> I have been a subscriber since just about when you started this pub-
> lication. The copies that I missed I got by ordering the back issues. I
> still have all of your issues but one.
>
> As a matter of fact, I've written several letters. Never a reply was
> sent. I am writing this time hoping that you will respond. If not, I'll
> never write or call again because it's a waste of time. Perhaps you
> will answer two questions for me. I've enclosed a SASE. It won't cost
> you nothing.
>
> 1. On page 11 of Volume 7, Number 4, Winter 1990: what is the com-
>   plete name and address of Telecom?
> 2. On page 26 of Volume 7, Number 4, Winter 1990: what is the com-
>   plete name and address of URR Newsletter?
>
> What gives with the ad on page 41 ("Controversial DTMF Decoder")?
> They use two names same address?
>
> TG
MT. VERNON, NY

*We printed the full address of Telecom Digest in that issue. It's published elec-
tronically so there isn't a U.S. Mail address. The address again is: eecs.new.
edu!telecom. We don't have the address of URR Newsletter but we'll print it if we
get it. We don't understand your final question at all.*

We absolutely cannot reply personally to subscribers (unless it involves a subscription matter). We are deluged with all kinds of personal requests through the mail and over the phone that we just don't have time for. People want us to tell them what kind of computer to buy. They want access codes. They want to talk to a "real hacker." Our favorites are the people who call our machine, listen to the long detailed message about subscription rates, then leave us a message to call them and tell them how to subscribe!

We don't mean anything personal by this. But we just can't reply to each and every question we get. Questions like yours are best answered through the letters section. Regarding your missing issue, let us know which issue you're missing and we'll send it again.

Dear *2600:*

> *I would consider myself a mid-level hacker, now post-adolescence. I remember the "old days" well, especially when manuals of any sort were impossible to obtain. I remember the good ol' days of RipCo (best in the Midwest), and miss it terribly. I have a little experience hacking into Milnet (from an Internet dialup, or local dialup to Milnet), more experience messing with Internet (about two to three years hard hacking), and various UNIX systems.*
>
> *I've been a subscriber to TAP for a while, and even though the newsletter is disjunctional (at best), it has the true flavor of an underground publication. Please treat them with a little more respect; they're really good kids. After reading your publication (on and off) for a number of years, I am disturbed by the administrative trend you seem to be taking. Please, hire more people, and get more personal.*
>
> RN
> LAKE FOREST, IL

We agree about TAP. But where the hell are they?! We haven't seen an issue in months! Being administrative is something we're not often accused of. We'll have to have a committee look into it.

1993 _____

Dear *2600:*

You guys really pissed me off with your Telco News Winter 92-93.

What a stupid thing to put in your mag! It's been well known among the hackers for years that most security is overlooked and in some areas blatantly ignored. Writing about one particular company's security weaknesses is a direct slap in the face. As a result, that company will be highly pissed and most likely take procedures to tighten up security. But you're defeating the whole purpose of hacking: learning! How much information could have been learned from that one particular system? It's hard to say. What do you do though instead? "Oh, hey, let's put it in 2600 so we will show them how stupid they are." Did you ever think that you might be ruining it for the other hackers out there that are trying to learn about the phone company's computers? Nah, I don't suppose that even crossed your mind. The article was lame anyway to those of us who know what's going on. Most of that bull was information found on the Bell newsletters. Of course the phone company is gonna say that hackers cost them money. They want the general public to keep believing in the same "Hacker Hood" image that Forbes Magazine proudly wrote about. It should be obvious to you that after the 911 incident with Neidorf, the embellishment of things damaged or costing money was pure BS made up to make the hacker look bad, malicious, or anything but the truth. I just lost a lot of respect for 2600 when you printed that. Heh! Not that that matters much anyway. I don't think you guys ever did any real serious hacking. Otherwise you would be working on some decent projects instead of publishing a magazine that keeps all the security people up to date on what we are doing or things we have uncovered. My main point is: a hacker would never tell an admin what holes to patch if he wanted to continue hacking the system!

So why are you?

LAYDEN02

First off, we print information that we feel deserves to be shared. We don't agonize over what the enemy will do with it, whoever that may happen to be. If we did, *we'd probably never be able to print anything. As far as your "concerns," let's get a little real. We're talking about a major computer system that has a wide open front door into root! Who would we be serving by keeping that to ourselves? Something along these lines is way too bizarre for our tastes. And, sure enough, at least one of our readers was able to provide some valuable insight into this. Had we done it your way and kept it to ourselves and all of the people like you "who know what's going on," this nationwide hacker trap would never have been discovered.*

1994

Dear *2600:*

> *I read your publication for only one reason—to try to keep up with the enemy. I am responsible for a number of large PBXs, many with voicemail systems. One of my biggest problems is keeping irresponsible hackers and thieves out of my business. You publish on the premise that those who want to know have a right to know. I don't dispute that until they start poking around in my voicemail system (or anyone else's) often with less than honorable intentions and do damage or steal from me. They may have a right to know, but they have no right to explore my system or use it for anything other than what I want it used for.*

> *We spend time and money securing our systems. Features we would like to use are turned off because a thief might discover them and could potentially steal from us at the rate of thousands of dollars an hour. I would rather have my technicians doing productive work.*

> *In your last issue, you put the naive kid from Puerto Rico in his place because it is obvious he only had larceny on his mind. Unfortunately, this same kid is going to be educated in how to achieve his objective by your publication. You reinforce (and implicitly encourage) his notion that it can be done and gotten away with. Many of the articles you publish are reports of crimes committed and how it was done by the perpetrators in enough detail to repeat the act, not simply information about how to get behind the locked door. Often you cross over the line to the side of irresponsibility.*

Thanks for listening. I am sure if you publish this letter, thieves and hackers everywhere will discover they offend me (and others) and stop doing what they do. I won't have to waste time securing my systems. The world will be saved.

PISSED OFF IN HOUSTON

While we understand your frustration, we feel compelled to suggest that you seek another line of work. If securing your systems is a waste of time to you, you're not doing anybody any favors. The reason you can't use those features you want to use is because they're lousy features with gaping holes you could drive a bus through. Be glad you haven't fallen victim to them and the outrageous billing schemes the phone companies slap on their customers.

We print facts on weaknesses and vulnerabilities. It's what we've been doing from the start and we're not about to cut off the information flow because information can be misused. It would be a very scary precedent to set. The information we print can be used by smart people to prevent their becoming victims. Unfortunately, too many think that ignoring what we say or keeping us from saying it will make everything unpleasant go away.

Dear *2600:*

A pattern of events has occurred that I feel has continued for too long. I would like to mention at the outset that while I agree in principle with some of your beliefs, I disagree with the methodology in which you carry out most of these beliefs. Normally, it is not my concern how others run their lives but when their actions have an impact on my life I must take corrective action.

Over a year ago I was reminded that you were still publishing 2600 when I caught a broadcast of WBAI. On that show you mentioned a computerized CNA telephone number. You said on the air that the telephone number would appear in the next issue of 2600. I sent 2600 a U.S. postal money order, my return address, and a note printed on my laser printer in which I requested that my subscription begin with the above mentioned issue. I used a laser printer and a very legible font to avoid confusion from my handwriting. The issue with the

CNA information in it never arrived *and my subscription started* several months later *with naturally a different issue. After several more months, I wrote to you at* 2600 *on* two separate occasions *to request your help. I* never *received so much as a postcard, much less any help or the missing issue. I did, however, receive three of the four issues of* 2600 *where the last two issues reminded me to pay up for next year. Of the three issues that did arrive, two were so badly* mangled *that they were almost unreadable. While I am aware that the responsibility for this mutilation can be attributed to our* wonderful *postal service, I want to point out that other magazines replace mutilated issues when notified.* 2600 never did. *The fourth issue never arrived. I tried calling your offices. While I am not satisfied with the exorbitant rates NYNEX charges, I am even less pleased by the devious manipulation by* 2600. *I refer to* 2600 *leaving a very lengthy outgoing message on its answering machine. Ostensibly, this was done to be informative and helpful to the caller while in reality encouraging the caller to become a party in your scheme to defraud the telephone company in not paying for the incurred overtime charges. All the while maintaining its "plausible deniability". (I wonder how many pay telephones have been removed from service and lives made more difficult because of such behaviors?) I know the alternatives are to: 1) pay NYNEX its outrageous rates (which I'm also opposed to) or 2) attempt the impossible and try to leave a coherent yet highly compact message in the microscopic time you have left available before the NYNEX overtime message activates. Writing to you is pointless and only serves to litter the streets after you have discarded this letter. No mention or provision is ever made on the* 2600 *outgoing message about when an actual human being is present and your answering machine is not screening your calls.*

The final action that repulsed me was that subscription money was used to essentially pay for the editor's personal *vacation to Holland thinly disguised as a reporter on a fact-finding trip. This is as shady an action as those you describe on the radio. But this last part is all a matter of deniability and perspective. I offer the following illustration. If the point of view is first taken from that of a taxpayer, then illegal payoffs from that tax revenue are reprehensible. If the point of view is then taken from the recipient of the same payoffs, then it's a job "perk". The usual argument made to defend such a theft is that the "perk" is being taken "for the greater good." What's next, getting Ed McMahon's picture on a 2600 subscription gimmick?*

In short, 2600 has taken on the tactics of the corporations it professes *to fight. Ultimately, I have decided to fight fire with fire and take up your tactics. I've decided to vote with my dollars and: 1) not renew my subscription to 2600 (yes, I know you are disappointed); 2) listen to you on my Walkman whenever I can free of charge on WBAI and not subscribe to them either. A copy of this letter will end up there; after all, there's nothing like using a little pressure from both ends as you know; 3) encourage others to follow my example; 4) tell them of my experiences. In case you decide to read this on your show or to publish it in 2600, I suggest you do so* in its entirety *and comment if you feel so moved after you have presented the facts as fairly as you are able.*

Please note that I am purposely omitting my return address to avoid any further complications.

ONE VERY DISPLEASED FORMER SUBSCRIBER

Let's start by addressing your subscription problems. Since the issue you wanted to start your subscription with never arrived, your "first" issue showed up several months later, and you only got three issues in total, it stands to reason that the issue you wanted was in reality your first issue and, for one reason or another, it never made it to you. By your own admission, you didn't notify us until several months after you received your first issue, which in turn was several months from when you ordered a subscription. So how many months passed before we could find out there was a problem? Six? There's no way we could have solved your problem if we weren't even aware of it. When you did notify us (not knowing who you are, there's no way we can verify any of this), we probably sent you a replacement copy. Again, it apparently didn't arrive. This, coupled with the poor condition of the copies you did receive, leads us to believe your post office is extremely incompetent or malicious. We do replace mangled copies but we have to be told about them. A complaint of this magnitude would have been remembered and there is no recollection here of such a thing. And, for the record, our labels don't tell people to pay up—each label contains the date of the last issue of the subscription, so that people know when their subscriptions end. The label of your last issue will say "Renew!" Nobody has ever taken offense at this before.

We will readily admit that our "customer service department" sucks. We're not Time Magazine. But we never ignore complaints and, while we may be a bit slow sometimes, everybody gets what they order. We just cannot answer every individual question we get and we certainly can't return every non-problem-related phone call that comes in. Getting the magazine out and making sure people get it are our highest priorities. So if somebody leaves a message on our answering machine asking how to subscribe, they probably won't get a call back because all they have to do is listen to the answering machine! We're not trying to be nasty—we just don't have the time.

Now to address the irrational hysterics that constitute much of the second part of your letter: do you honestly believe that our answering machine message is part of a conspiracy? As we mentioned above, we provide information to people who call. The idea is to be helpful. And we don't make a secret of the fact that you can hit a star to skip the message entirely. Of course, encouraging people to use touch tones probably implicates us in yet another conspiracy.

As for your concluding accusations, we'd be insulted if we weren't so confused. What exactly are you accusing us of? Paying people? Well, we kind of have to do that sometimes. 2600 is a business, after all, even though you seem to prefer that it not be. Where do you get the impression that subscribers are subsidizing these luxurious lifestyles you've conjured up? Or is it just wishful thinking?

Dear *2600:*

> *It has come to our attention that you have published one of our business marketing 800 numbers in your quarterly and also in a hacker's bulletin board. The number you published is 1-800-775-55XX.*
>
> *Our service is a commercial caller identification that operates throughout North America and provides needed information to law enforcement agencies and major businesses.*
>
> *By publishing one of our lines as a novelty number to call for "fun," your disclosure is causing wasted time by our staff and costing not only their time, but also the long distance fees we pay while our lines are in use during your subscribers' games.*
>
> *You are hereby given notice to* cease *and* desist *the publication of our business number, immediately remove it from bulletin board postings,*

and, in the bulletin board, publish the posting that an 800 number had been published by your service which demonstrates commercial caller identification service and is not to be called for entertainment or curiosity purposes and that such calls may create civil and/or criminal prosecution for interference with interstate telecommunications.

You are also hereby notified that all calls to this number are being identified and callers will be contacted regarding their abuse of this number, and your company will be invoiced for the call activity at a rate of $1.00 per call.

We hope in the future you will take more precautions when encouraging your readers to entertain themselves by disrupting business services.

JAMES E. WALKER
PRESIDENT
TEL-SCAN
2641 N. TAFT
LOVELAND, CO 80538
(303) 663-1703
FAX (303) 663-1708

If this isn't the height of arrogance and condescension, we may never know what is. First off, guess what? We didn't even publish your stupid 800 number! In fact, we just protected your valuable seven-digit goldmine by blocking out part of it. We'll await your letter of thanks. Next, what appears on our voicemail system, which we assume to be the hacker bulletin board you mention, is entirely legal. If somebody posts an 800 number there, we are under no obligation whatsoever to erase it. We don't allow codes or credit card numbers because they can be used to commit fraud. Calling an 800 number is not, by any stretch of the imagination, an instance of fraud. However, if you try to bill someone for calling your 800 number, you will be the one guilty of fraud. If a person repeatedly calls your number after being asked not to, it's a clear case of harassment. But that's not what you're talking about here. You've got one hell of a nerve assuming that our readers do nothing but make frivolous calls and disrupt communications. Our readers have designed systems like the one you use and, if you weren't so stuck up, you might have actually gotten some real, legitimate customers out of this unique group of people. Since you've made your feelings about them so clear, we fervently urge our readership to never do business with this company. That should make us all happy.

1995

Dear *2600:*

> *I first want to say I love your magazine. Here is what happened. I was sitting in the airport waiting for my flight. I was reading your magazine, and then I looked up. This women was pointing me out to her husband. Next thing I knew, the husband is getting up and walking over to me. He stands over me and says, "All you little hackers should be dragged out into the street and shot." Well, I did not feel like starting anything with the man, so I just sat there and continued to read 2600. I just wanted to tell you about my little experience.*

> FAST LOVER
> HOUSTON, TX

At least they recognized the magazine. We must be doing better marketing than we thought!

1996

Dear *2600:*

> *I've been reading your magazine for five years, and the information in it has always been at the very least interesting. It's taken me until now to figure out the true purpose of the magazine, or what I believe is its goal. If you take everything written in the magazine at face value, then it would seem that it is against the type of world that was described in 1984. From what I have deduced, 2600 Magazine is not for free speech, is not pro-hacker, and it supports the creation of a totalitarian regime. The magazine's justification for printing information about various holes in different systems is that they should be fixed and can no longer be exploited. For instance, if the different Bells redesigned their payphone system every time someone found a way to make free calls, it would eventually get to the point where an operator would have to come onto the line to verify that the call was legal. However, operators, being human, would not be perfect (2600 would probably*

publish an article on how to manipulate the operators into giving you free calls) and the cycle would continue until it would be impossible to make a phone call without a camera behind you making sure that you were paying for it. So therefore, does 2600 strive for a world that is like that of 1984? Emmanuel Goldstein in the end was created by Big Brother, and is probably its greatest asset.

THE PROPAGANDIST

Well, it only took twelve years for someone to figure it out.

Dear *2600:*

I have been reading 2600 for some time and I find it to be a forum for snot-nose-right-wing-conservative-ditto-head-Republican vandals. I think it's time that you put the tape on your Coke bottle glasses and reinsert your pocket protectors and slither back into your closets. You call yourselves freedom fighters? Freedom from what? Civilization? Law and order? Why are hackers portrayed as vandals and not Thomas Jefferson or George Washington? America is a great place to live and provides freedoms to all its citizens including neo-Nazis, the KKK, hackers, Rush Limbaugh, and close-minded Republicans. Somewhere along the way, a few boneheads started a rumor that certain rights and freedoms should not apply to anyone but them. Wrong again! The "right" to vandalize other people's property is not found in the Bill of Rights. The "right" to steal from someone is not found in the Bill of Rights. Need I go on or do you get the idea, bonehead!

I will continue to read your magazine and watch how far your select group of self righteous gang of vandals will go to prove that Forrest Gump is real and alive in cyberspace. If I may diverge from a civil tone to the type of vocabulary I see in the Letters to the Editor, I will tell you that your f**kin rag is the kind of sh*t that Hitler puked at his sh*ttheads and look at the f*ckin mess he got into. Get a damn life, dick face and stop all this f*ckin around. I hope you are enjoying the abuse... because I enjoy giving it. This is not hate mail nor a threat. It is my opinion and I am exercising my right to express myself. All seriousness aside, who would you get to investigate me? The FBI?

The CIA? Would you call the police? *I think you would use your own thugs. Put the computer away and haul out the spray paint, guns, and crack. Be a real gang.*

I.M. FREE
MILWAUKEE

Our thugs are on it.

Dear *2600:*

While I am a staunch advocate of freedom to speak and freedom on the Internet, it is the antics of people like you that are going to screw it up for everyone. I am referring to your dissemination of the method to cause "denial of service" by flooding ISPs. This technique has no redeeming virtue and can only be used to disrupt and destroy. Ironically, the target of an attack by the method you distributed, Panix, is an ISP that has generously provided free resources to groups that advocate freedom for the Internet. Are you now happy with the results of your thoughtless abuse of freedom? The government is itching to control and censor the Internet and while freedom on the Internet enjoys wide support, a few more incidents like the ones you made possible can sour public support and invite the crackdown we all dread. Do you really want to aid every nutcase with a keyboard and a lust for power to work their will on the Internet community? This is not computer science and lore; it is vandalism. Think about what you have done. If you disagree with me, I would be interested in your rational.

GEORGE

The people at panix.com seem to understand why the article was published as well as the need to do something about the problem. We agree it was most unfortunate that this of all systems was targeted but we feel the greater good was ultimately served by revealing the flaws. And we don't see this as a reason for more control and censorship; if anything, the quick and professional way this was dealt with on such systems shows us that we can take care of ourselves on the net without outside interference.

Dear *2600:*

I read the article on Ed Cummings with great interest (even went to your website to get more information) and would like to put my two cents worth in.

In your preface to the article (in the mag) you use a fairly strong tone to suggest that the whole incident is a fallacy of justice and should never have happened. I disagree with some of the rationale used in justifying your position on the situation. Reading your magazine and the information in it is not just for informational purposes. It is highly improbable that such innocence exists. Instead, it has to be assumed that someone will use the information for some purpose, criminal or otherwise. This is true for Ed and his red boxes. I am not saying that Ed or anyone else is doing this for criminal reasons. But why develop these devices if there is no satisfaction in trying them? After all, would hacking be so much fun if you didn't do it?

I do think, though, that the added misperception of hackers, crackers, and the like as being malicious and criminal is far from true. I also believe that though there are people within our government and law enforcement who want Big Brother watching, that there are equally others who like yourselves are against those concepts and believe strongly in freedom.

Freedom, though, is not without bounds. After all, freedom is merely a concept of our mind that has no tangible presence. It is the same theory behind currency. Our currency is no longer backed by some precious metal. Its strength lies solely in our belief that it has value. It is this concept that defines freedom. And though each person is allowed to interpret that freedom, we have to consider the whole and not the individual when trying to deal in Truth and Justice.

I capitalize Truth and Justice because in philosophy there is talk of the absolute truth and justice by which all events can be viewed. This does not define good and bad, but allows for a method by which we can determine the rightness of an issue.

This is where Ed was wronged. Law enforcement chose to view him with bias and therefore titled the scales. This in turn brought about the problem. Lastly, I hope Ed realizes that driving on suspension is bad

*and he should not do it. And that all your readers exercise discretion
and not forget that reality is very harsh and that true justice doesn't
exist. I send my deepest condolences to Ed and hope his situation is
resolved and that he can lead a regular life.*

KEVIN

*The very concept that someone can be imprisoned for possessing information or
technology should be enough to demonstrate that there are severe problems with
our justice system and ultimately with our so-called democratic society. Do you
propose to judge the intent of everyone's words and possessions? Who will you
trust to make this judgment? It's a very dangerous step that you seem willing to
take. Everything from song lyrics to motion pictures to personal diaries to technological toys can be seen as having only one evil purpose in the eyes of someone
somewhere. You may think it's easy to judge intent as if it were an action but, in
reality, such judgments are extremely difficult and dangerous.*

1997

Dear *2600:*

> *In your latest issue (Autumn 96), you pointed out, in a response to
> a letter, that 2600 was your name. This made me extremely angry.
> It looks like you thought this name to be of your own creation and
> original. The 2600 hertz tone that your magazine is named after was
> never yours to be owned.*
>
> *Second, you point out that #2600 on IRC was started by you. That's
> why you've always resided in #hack, right? That's why you leave #2600
> after a five-minute wait time of not getting opped? That's why I've
> never seen one person associated with 2600 in #2600? I laugh at the
> fact that "the channel exists so 2600 types can communicate with
> other 2600 types in a fairly open environment." If these "2600 types"
> were to communicate freely on the channel, it would be an equivalent
> to #teen and a hint of #warez.*
>
> *I think it would be safe to agree maybe the only thing mentioned that
> you "own" would be alt.2600 (which is garbage anyway).*

MR. KIDDIE PRON

You are an example of someone who needs to get out more. Chat areas like IRC are not meant to be taken this seriously. What was stated here was a fact, that the 2600 channel was started by 2600. You can dispute this all you please but it won't change what everybody already knows. You seem to have personal problems with certain people in the channel which really doesn't concern anyone here. We don't have people stationed in the channel around the clock but people affiliated with 2600 are always popping in and out. That's as official as it will ever get. And, no, we don't "own" the alt.2600 newsgroup any more than we own an IRC channel. It's sort of strange how you have no problem envisioning ownership of things you don't like.

Dear *2600:*

> *I just wanted to drop a line to you on notice of your publication. Two days ago, the company I provide my services to was hacked. I have seen this several times in the past since I am a professional switch tech trained in several PBX and voicemail applications. I just wonder if you people realize the damage you cause or if you even care. You can't even use your real name while you're stealing. You punks aren't just crooks, you're cowards too. But I would imagine upbringing probably has something to do with it. Maybe it's just little sissy-boy compu-dork who never had a daddy or never worked a day in his life or both. But realize this! Hack me and I'll bust your balls! You're not that smart or even close to being good. We professionals laugh at punks like you.*
>
> *Later Scumballs.*
>
> (UNREADABLE SIGNATURE ON A FAX)

You professionals can be so articulate.

Dear *2600:*

> *Just one question: Why do you disrespect the very government agencies that keep every citizen safe? Why do you support criminal activities*

that disrupt the activities of government? And why do you relate the U.S. Secret Service to the Nazi SS? You are simply a menace to society. The "hackers" who like to flatter themselves by replacing government pages with repulsive pieces of crap! You all deserved to be arrested and imprisoned for treason.

FRAAS

First off, that wasn't one question, it was three. Maybe your definition of safe is closer to our definition of brain dead. If so, you're certainly safe from anything we can say to you. The people like you who are in power now and solve every issue by imprisoning people are a far greater menace than any hacker ever could be.

Dear *2600:*

I bought my first issue of 2600 a year plus ago and was quite impressed with the variety and detailed information it held. Over the last several issues I have witnessed something strange, uncanny even. 2600 has not just changed, but it's had its own revolution. Not only have the articles become soporific but many of the authors have become somewhat indolent in their writing, writing articles that lack charisma, detailed info, and that 2600 quality. But what has caused this change? Is it because 2600 has become the trendy thing for teenage hackers to idolize? That every kid using a computer has now got his 2600 stuffed in his backpack, just waiting for the moment to pull it out and show his leet-o mag to his friends? Or, in all our wildest dreams, has something more occurred, something no one would even dream of? Has 2600 become... censored?

A friend pointed out to me that if I am that dissatisfied with 2600's quality, then I shouldn't support their cause and buy it. There's a reason behind every action and, to tell you the truth, who am I to judge 2600? I'll probably get some wisecrack answer to this anyway, but hey, you're a publication. When people "suggest" something is wrong, that they are dissatisfied with the quality, it's your job to fix it. Not mine.

POKIS

There are all kinds of possibilities here. But one thing that's not uncommon among magazines, music, and nearly all other artistic/consumer items: Someone discovers something, it becomes more popular, the earlier people resent all the newcomers, and they redefine the item or the culture itself as "just not the same." We've seen this happen so many times over the last 14 years that there has to be some truth to it. Either that or we've been on the decline since day one. Whether or not this is the case, you seem to have some misconceptions about a few things. First, what appears on our pages comes from the hacker community. We don't write every-thing "in-house" like bigger publications. If the hacker community falls apart, then we fall apart. If it flourishes, then so do we. You also seem to think that because something isn't what you want, that censorship must be taking place. Censorship is something that is imposed upon people by powerful entities. If we don't print an article you wrote, it's an editorial decision, not censorship. If we are prohibited by law from printing your article, then that is censorship. The seriousness of this issue is undermined when the word is misused in this way.

Dear *2600:*

> *I am an avid reader of your zine. But I have noticed that most of your letters and articles seem to take a predominantly liberal/leftist approach. This both confuses and disturbs me. While it is true that the government as a whole does often try to suppress free speech, it is mostly its more liberal elements. It was the liberals who pushed the Clipper Chip and who f*cked up at Waco. It would, in my opinion, be more beneficial to the hacker cause to give less lip-service to the socialists. They won't repay the favor.*
>
> RHYME-CHAI

And the conservative/rightists try to ban flag burning, eliminate gay rights, and force "family values" down our throats. We can go around in circles forever. We don't think about what political slant we take when we spread information. We just spread information and try to wake people up. If that seems leftist to you, you're probably standing so far to the right that everything else does, too.

Dear *2600:*

In the letters to the editor section of the Summer 1997 issue, readers called into question your judgment on a couple of things that make me believe 2600 does not hold itself to a standard as high as I thought.

First, your response to a reader questioning your printing of "Credit Card Numbers via Calculators" as a show of support for credit card fraud. Your defense that it is only an exercise in algorithms and calculator programming is bull. This sounds like something a lawyer would say. I suppose you believe head shops sell pipes that are not intended to be used in any illegal activities. Printing information for knowledge is quite different that printing information that could be used in the commission of a crime against innocent people. I sense you are losing the ability to tell the difference.

Second, the Mitnick thing. What is wrong with you people? You act like Mitnick is some kind of God and that he is being persecuted by the powers that be. The truth is Mitnick is a punk. If he shouldn't be in jail because "there are a great number of holes in the accusations hurled at Kevin," then he should be in jail because he is stupid. Anyone who continues to do what he did after being in trouble for the same thing needs to be punished. What does it take to get through Mitnick's head to stop hacking? If he is such a genius, why doesn't he realize this? He's lucky he never broke into anything of mine. I wouldn't have been as merciful as Shimomura. Instead of spending the last two and a half years in jail, the SOB would have spent the last two and a half years recovering at a local hospital.

Technically, Mitnick is not great at all. After all, he did get caught. And most of the techniques he used were obtained from more clever and skillful hackers. Anybody can use the social engineering techniques used by Mitnick. You just have to be willing to lie like a dog (which I'm sure is OK by 2600 standards). His greatest social engineering feat has been convincing 2600 that he is a victim.

Has Mitnick ever contributed anything to society? Isn't it about time for him to grow up and get a job and go on with life contributing something of value to society?

ORION

You obviously can think of only one use for studying credit card algorithms, which makes you just as pathetic as the idiots who commit credit card fraud. That's your problem.

But your views on Mitnick are truly disturbing. In the interests of space, we'll skip over the childish posturing and focus on your apparent belief that his imprisonment is justified. How can you honestly say that so many years in prison (his trial at press time is being scheduled for April 1998, more than three years after his imprisonment) is a suitable punishment for someone who has never committed a violent crime or profited in any way from his actions? Just how much vengeance do you want and exactly what is it that you think you're avenging? Your loss of privacy and security? You lost that a long time ago. And the people who've locked Mitnick away have no interest in giving it back to you. Mitnick didn't expose your life for all to see. It's the fact that he could have or really that anybody could have that has you so bent out of shape.

Who is the real victim here? You? Us? Corporate America? Not at all. The real suffering has been going on behind bars the whole time. And the real problem is simplistic idiots who go around thinking that violence and imprisonment are the only ways of dealing with things. This method of thinking has transformed our society into the shortsighted reactionary wasteland of paranoia that plagues us daily. And that will make victims of every last one of us. We'll see you there.

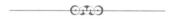

1998

Dear *2600:*

> I am very disappointed. The hacking/phreaking community promised to be the most intense and influential counterculture faction since the punk rockers of the late '70s and early '80s. Alas, you have sold out, and I blame 2600—the largest and perhaps most respected icon in the whole hacker world—for much of it.
>
> In numerous editorials you have cited this fact: Hackers aren't criminals. I disagree. Discarding all "wordy" definitions of just what a hacker is and all romanticisms, we find what hacker really means, from the real hackers. Your magazine, hundreds of web pages, programs

and text files, as well as the majority of actual documented hacker endeavors, all seem to be about infiltrating or abusing a computer network or another electronic system. Phreaking the phone, remotely hacking UNIX systems, and Internet mischief seem to be your specific concerns. Even when programming and other "good" hacker activities are used, they seem to merely facilitate these goals, and are not of any focal interest.

Hacking a system is the equivalent of breaking into someone's house or (in the case of the phone company) office building. If the government allows the production of computers, the right to privately operate one without fear of tampering, destruction, or unreliability should come directly after. It only makes sense. By breaking into a system, you are taking up resources and violating privacy. You tiptoe around it—calling this activity "non-destructive hacking." So you break in, but just hang out and have a look around, as opposed to smashing things? Hacking by its very nature is intrusive and forces the individual computer user to seek the aid of computer-manufacturing corporations for education or tools to counter the attack. It is not a liberation or freedom of information. Hacking as you know it is a repeated victimization of the common (uninformed) people. While breaking into a system rarely effects people harmfully, it is the easiest point at which we can deter destruction of or tampering with computer resources remotely. You say people shouldn't go to jail for guessing passwords— and they shouldn't. However, it is indicative of a potential crime. No one cares that the drunk driver has had alcohol and is behind the wheel for that reason alone—we arrest him because drunk drivers often kill people. That is why hacking, in basically all forms, is a crime. Because, regardless of what you at 2600 do, your readers and everyone associated do not stop at a sensible point. Hackers spread virii, change passwords, cause confusion and frustration in the lives of many total strangers, tarnishing companies' and organizations' reputations, all at their leisure, just for fun.

By distributing your magazine, arguing that hacking isn't a criminal activity, and making your efforts well known to the rest of the world, you have put hackers everywhere under immense pressure. You have turned a once underground activity into a household word, cultivating thousands and teaching them to hack—there were even movies! You have taken something underground, and turned it into "underground" pop culture! In doing so, you sell out so completely that the FBI need only subscribe to enter into your world. You say this is a good thing, the "free flow of information" and all. Well, what are you? The hacker missionaries? The "free flow of information" won't be so cool when the increased hacker populace and computer crime rate demands legislative attention. When the government passes laws and writes network software making hacking almost impossible, you won't be so glad you taught a generation to hack. They won't be so glad either.

ERIC B.
AKA FLYABLE GEORGE

Well, gee. You give us credit for an awful lot. Let's look at what you apparently think we should have done. We should have kept quiet so that our little movement would remain "underground." Funny, that's just what the people in those agencies that keep busting in our doors seem to think as well. See, had we only kept quiet, we would have stayed small, and it would have been so much easier to squash us entirely. But now... yeah, we're everywhere. Kinda scary, isn't it? The authorities will one day realize that they're no longer able to manipulate us into extinction. And you have already realized that hacking isn't ever going to be the elitist social club of part-time rebels you want so desperately to be a part of. We're not sure who to feel more sorry for. What we're certain of is that we have nothing to apologize for. We're proud of who we are and where we've gone in the 14 years we've been publishing. We don't support criminal activity but at the same time we don't feel that using a computer system without authorization is remotely similar to breaking into someone's house. But this isn't about us. It's about the many thousands of people out there who are waking up and exploring, learning, and teaching—moving our technology in the direction they want it to go, rather than marching to a predetermined tune. While we're flattered that you think this is all because of us, we cannot take the credit. But we appreciate your obsession.

Dear *2600:*

> *I have been reading and enjoying 2600 for a number of years and I have to say you're starting to sound an awful lot like the governments you're so afraid of. I keep hearing a lot of "poor us, that bad 'ol media jus' unfairly*

*pickin' on us poor innocent hackers. Don't day know we's the good guys?"
Give me a break! I've been hacking since before there was a distinction
between hackers and crackers and yes, the stupid media, with the help
of the stupid crackers, have lost the distinction between the two.*

*But not even you can deny that hackers (meant in the media sense)
pose a serious and dangerous risk to business, government, and yes
individuals. Your magazine is becoming more a political agenda than
a "free speech, free flow of information magazine." While we're touching on this (the political aspects of the mag), the information you're
spewing about "poor innocent" Kevin Mitnick is just as distorted as
anyone else's. I notice you seem to almost always overlook the fact
that he had all that credit card information, uh, I know, he's a good
guy, he'd never use it for evil purposes. Unfairly imprisoned, no trial,
um, can you say* pleaded guilty, *boys and girls? Or is that not being
mentioned for a reason?*

*The fact of the matter is, Kevin sucked as a hacker. He got lucky and
he was stupid and he got caught (that's how the game is played, if you
don't like the rules, don't play). The good hackers are the ones you never
hear about.*

*Finally, do we really care what the media or general public thinks?
Your attempts to "educate" people about the righteous cause of the
hacking community is going to be real successful as long as there are
Kevin Mitnicks out there. Do you not see where people might get confused when on one page your now "rag" mag is saying, don't fear us,
embrace us, we're the good guys, etc. And on the next page you're saying "How to Hack Your ISP" and "Tips On Generating Fake ID," both
clearly the reading choice of your average law-abiding citizen.*

*This magazine, our magazine, is supposed to be about the free, open,
and honest exchange of information and ideas, not a political soapbox.
Let's get back to what you do best and inform, educate, and entertain your readers. If we wanted sermons on the good works of Kevin
Mitnick, we'd go to church.*

Malkor
(I suspect you've never heard of me)

No, we never heard of you so that must mean you're one of the "good hackers." And we're not even going to get into the whole "cracker" fantasy this time around. Let's start by going over the things you missed while in a coma or orbiting Neptune or whatever caused these wide gaps in logic. We've mentioned the credit card file repeatedly. It was used to vilify Kevin in a most unfair way. The file itself had been floating around the net for ages, yet Netcom had refused to even acknowledge this fact. We reported on its existence a full six months before a copy was found in Kevin's directory. It was easy to get. Hundreds, perhaps thousands, of people wound up with copies. We don't know anybody who wouldn't want to see if such a thing really existed. That is why Kevin had a copy and further proof of this is the fact that not one of those numbers was ever used by him, even though it would have been an easy way to get free stuff. Kevin is not a thief. But by mentioning this in the first paragraph of the story on his capture, The New York Times made him look like a common criminal.

As for pleading guilty, you've got your facts confused. Kevin plead guilty in North Carolina to possession of cellular MINs that were used to make unauthorized phone calls. (This allowed him to be extradited to his home state of California and he long ago finished serving that sentence.) You may consider this to be the same as stealing something tangible but all that accomplishes is to make real theft more excusable. This was literally the only way Kevin could communicate safely (or, so he thought) with half the FBI chasing him around the country. Taking out phone service in his own name may have satisfied your moral standards but it wouldn't have done very much for Kevin's freedom. So the question remains, why was Kevin running in the first place? For associating with a known felon who later turned out not to be a felon at all? For not reporting to his parole officer when phone records have proven the opposite? It doesn't take much investigation to see that Kevin was targeted—why, we can only speculate—and that all of the ensuing charges against him are for absurdities like copying worthless files and making a few free phone calls. For this he deserves more prison time than people who steal cars and large amounts of money or who hurt and/or kill people? What possible agenda do you subscribe to that mandates this?

And just what "government" are you trying to imitate in your second sentence?

Dear *2600:*

> *Those of us at the Chicago area 2600 meeting have reached an un-*
> *derstanding: Kevin Mitnick is guilty, throw his ass in jail. While he*
> *may not be treated fairly, he is still a criminal. He got caught doing*
> *something illegal, albeit a white collar crime. If it was homicide, or*
> *grand theft auto, should you still "Free Kevin" because he isn't being*
> *treated fairly? How "fair" should someone be treated if they have: 1.*
> *violated parole. 2. resisted arrest. and 3. committed crime after crime,*
> *never wising up enough to stop breaking the law? Kevin Mitnick must*
> *really enjoy jail, seeing as he keeps doing things to get more time.*
> *While the conditions of his release may not be so nice, he might have*
> *thought about that when he was committing 25 counts of computer*
> *and wire fraud. While I agree, you should not be in prison for three*
> *years without trial, they have a reason not to grant him bail. Bottom*
> *line: Kevin Mitnick is a felon who ran from the law, and he is getting*
> *what he asked for. If you commit a crime, you do it with the knowledge*
> *that there is a harsh penalty for it.*
>
> D-Recz

*Let's make one thing clear. You're entitled to whatever stupid opinion you come
up with but you're not entitled to go around saying it represents an entire group of
people. We organize the meetings and we don't even do that! Our meetings are
comprised of different people with all kinds of backgrounds who hold all kinds of
opinions. The one thing we all have in common is the desire to share information in
an open environment.*

*With that out of the way, take a good look at what you're saying. You've already
saved us the time and trouble of a trial by finding Kevin guilty. Great. Now you wish
to pass sentence. So how much time do you want Kevin to be imprisoned for? Four
years apparently isn't enough for you. So what will it be, ten years? Twenty? Life?
You seem to equate the rather trivial charges against Kevin (and they are trivial
when you consider how worthless the information he was accused of possessing really is and how no damage was caused except for some bruised egos) with
real crimes that deserve real penalties. His violation of supervised release was
extremely debatable and/or minor yet he received a 14-month sentence on that
charge alone. That time has long since been served as has the time sentenced
for possessing cellular MINs back in 1995 (eight additional months). (Agreeing to*

plead to these charges was the only way he could be sent back to his home state of California and by the time he finally got sentenced he had already served the sentence.) So we have incredibly long sentences for rather minor violations. He was never charged with, as you say, resisting arrest. As for "committing crime after crime," that is a very misleading and simplistic way of looking at it. When you're a fugitive, every day you remain free is a crime. What you view as a crime wave was simply one person trying to stay free and managing to do it by leading a relatively honest life, working real jobs, not stealing when he certainly could have, and simply trying to satisfy his curiosity about technology he was told he wasn't allowed to know about. You seem to believe that every crime should carry not a penalty, but a "harsh" penalty. Every instance of red boxing, every instance of computer hacking. Maybe even every jaywalker. But what is the point? Do you somehow profit from all of the new prisons that are being built? Have you stopped to think where this attitude will get us in another ten years?

Dear *2600:*

> *I came to* www.2600.com *and enjoyed looking at all of the hacked pages that you have listed, for I, myself, am a hacker. But upon going into your hacked page, International Church of Christ, I was quite upset at what I found. I am a believer and follower of God and when I saw what you did to the page, I was angered deeply. In no way do you have the right to do such a thing to a group of religious people trying to make the world a better place. I have a riddle for you. See if you or your "little hackers" can figure it out: There once was a man, or woman at that... who decided stupidly to do himself a little hack. And what he hacked was something of good nature... and what happened to the man is that he was put at low stature. There was after this, a certain web page forged by the tedious mind of a certain webmaster and, upon doing so, formed himself so much rage put upon a hurtin pastor. Now... who is the webmaster, and what is the web page that the Riddler is referring to? Oh, and send your comments, if you're a real man, to my email address.*

> RIDDLER

We have a riddle for you: Who cares?! Get with it, please. For some reason, none of the people complaining about this page seem capable of grasping the fact that we had nothing to do with hacking it. We just reported it. You were looking at other hacked pages and enjoying them so obviously you have some sense as to how the collection is set up. Or do you believe different rules should apply when a religious site gets hacked?

Dear *2600:*

> *I was thinking about subscribing, but I won't because: 1) Why should I have to pay a premium to subscribe? (It's $4.50 an issue, which works out to $18 per year at the bookstore.) 2) You get all of my money up front when I subscribe—you can never be sure that I will buy all four issues so that should be worth something to you in the form of a discount. 3) How do I know that you will be around for the next four issues? You can do better.*

> SANDY

You must be a real fun person to hang around with.

1999

Dear *2600:*

> *The computer underground should not be self regulating. The recent joint statement by various groups, including 2600, condemning the Legion of the Underground's actions sickened me. LoU's members should be applauded for the personal risks they took to highlight an issue that they felt strongly about. Instead, they have been met with derision. Putting your name to that statement was a disservice to the hacking community matched only by your publishing of Justin Peterson's article. How you can claim the moral high ground in Kevin's campaign and then give credibility to somebody who assisted the FBI in putting him in prison is beyond me.*

> RUE-THE-DAY

The sad fact is that if we don't watch over ourselves, somebody else will do it for us. It would have been irresponsible to remain silent while people did something destructive in the name of hackers. The members of LoU themselves realized this and acted responsibly to repair the damage. We have no regrets at all on how this came about. As for printing Agent Steal's article, we've printed pieces from the other side of the fence before and we most likely will again. It is not up to us to judge the moral character of our writers before we print their material. But we certainly didn't try to hide it. As it happens, that article proved to be very informative and useful. We should point out, though, that your logic is colliding with itself. You don't want us to condemn things in the community that we feel are wrong but you don't want us to print things from people who you've already condemned as wrong. That is a Class A fallacy.

Dear *2600:*

> *I've been viewing your site and your mag for quite some time now, and something is troubling me. You often claim, rightly so, that the media has mangled the word hacker to mean a criminal who operates with technology. The correct term for this is "cracked." Yet you refer to the cracked pages on your website as "hacked." What's with this? Are you along the same lines as the media and need the yellow journalistic values to attract viewers, or what?*

> MATT LESKO

We knew this was going to come up eventually. Over the years, there has been a movement to create a new word that basically means "evil hacker." This was a misguided effort on the part of some early hackers who resented the categorization with current day hackers, whose rebellious attitude and agenda sometimes rubbed them the wrong way. (The parallels of early and current hackers are all too often lost on both groups.) The word they came up with, after much debate, was "cracker." Brilliant. (Previous attempts at this same thing included such words as "worm," "phracker," and "hackerphreak.") The main problem with creating such a word is that it basically transfers whatever problems existed with the first word over to the second one. But it's worse because now all of a sudden you have a word that only has negative connotations without a clear-cut definition of what the negative connotations are. This is easily provable by talking to people who define someone like Kevin Mitnick as a "cracker." Almost without exception, these same people will say that Mitnick belongs in prison. No further discussion. All details of the case are simply skipped over. "Cracker" denotes a criminal without defining the crime. Conversely, describing someone as a hacker opens up the door to all kinds of questions about what was really going on. We already have plenty of words that can aptly describe a computer criminal—thief, vandal, extortionist, the list goes on and on. Such people are clearly not hackers and the way we describe them tells us something about the crime. The word "hacker" has most certainly been misused by the media—anyone who says they are a hacker is reported by the media to be one without any confirmation. That laziness is what must be changed, not the words. Manipulation of the language is a very insidious way of controlling the masses. We must be wary of this.

Dear *2600:*

> *Some people, well... myself do not agree with this whole Free Kevin thing. He is guilty, he got caught. Now he has admitted to several of the crimes (plea bargain) and paid/is paying the penalty. The only thing I agree on is the ridiculous amount of time he had to spend "paying for his crime." We are all aware of what he was doing, and looking back in hindsight, he deserved to get caught and pay a price. I think 4+ years is too much, but that's not for me to decide. While Kevin was not actually going to use the credit cards (I believe), he did wreak a lot of havoc and taunted people into taking action. That's where his guilt is. I believe this magazine should point out this fact instead of praising what he did and making him out to be a martyr. Let's find a new cause to fight for, instead of this old bag.*
>
> DAVID

Let's not even get into the guilt/innocence thing here and assume that Kevin is guilty of everything. So what are we talking about? More than four years in a prison with murderers and kidnappers because he looked at software and lied about his identity on the phone? (The credit card file and Shimomura's computer were apparently only hooks to get the public's interest—it seems to have worked very well. But Kevin was never charged with any wrongdoing in those matters.) Ask yourself how you know the things you think you know. Who told you he was taunting people?

Probably the same newspaper accounts that failed to mention that the taunting was proven to have come from another source, especially when it continued after his arrest. But again, let's avoid the guilt/innocence thing—is Kevin's sentence at all in proportion to the crime? You say it's "ridiculous" which is exactly what we're saying. That's all the common ground we need. There will be plenty of time to debate the rest. What's hard for us to understand is why you don't think you have any right to challenge this kind of injustice. You cannot just defer away your ability to speak up when something is wrong. If you don't care, that's one thing. But if you claim to have an opinion on an issue, that opinion should be expressed, not kept quiet because "it's not for you to decide." And finally, we will be moving on to new causes as we always are. But we will not leave this one unfinished.

Dear *2600:*

First off, let me just get off of my chest how I feel about hacking and all that. While I am not a hacker, nor a lawyer, I can honestly say that any figures short of infinity used to express the amount of time and money spent protecting private company, personal, and governmental data is surely an understatement. You bitch and complain about unjustified quotes of measly amounts by prosecutors of your lamer hacker friends when those amounts don't even come close to the total damage that has been done by you and people like you.

I am constantly fixing problems with my customers that were brought about by security issues, and in my opinion these issues shouldn't even exist. I feel that if a person is a gravedigger, and is caught abusing his position for personal, financial, or sexual gain, then not only should he lose his job and never be allowed to work in that position again, but he should be beat over the head with the very shovel he used to dig them up.

So, no, I don't feel one bit sorry for the miserable prick who you claim needs his computer access to build a case against his oppressors. He screwed that up when he took advantage of his ability to gain access to them to begin with. I feel that he's made his bed, and he should lie in it.

I also consider it a blatant monstrosity that you should be allowed to actually publicly display sites that have spent many, many man hours and dollars to protect themselves against people like you, and you somehow invade their privacy anyway, costing them even more money as well as embarrassment. These things cause businesses to close, and the ones that don't close their doors are almost shut down because they are irreversibly damaged due to customer loss because of your intentional actions against them.

So aren't you basically doing the same thing to people who have done nothing to you as the federal government is doing to your friend? You say that they have "boxed him in" by not allowing him to be near computers and the poor fool "can't even work at McDonald's." Aren't you doing that very same thing to small companies that are having a hard enough time keeping their head above water as it is? Do we really need your kind in front of a computer? No, I think not.

If it were up to me, I wouldn't have even wasted the tax dollars it took to provide room and board to the sorry son of a bitch. We should have just shot him to begin with. Of course, then we'd hear whining from you about how a person just isn't "free" anymore in this great land, "...cause we can't hack other people and screw them up now either!"

Why don't you people get a life, and quit bothering others? Did anyone ever ask you to "test their security systems?" Well, did they?

And you can't really be speaking seriously when you say you want me to feel sorry for him and do something for him. He broke the law. Intentionally. He sat up late at night, and knowingly did wrong. And the things he did had repercussions, and anything short of a cruel, deadly, or near-death beating is unacceptable to me. So, instead of complaining about what the outcome was, you should be damn glad I wasn't the judge in the case, because there would have never been any deals. I would have let him rot there.

It's because of people like you that I pay so much more than necessary for things I need to survive.

NONE OF YOUR DAMN BUSINESS

Another shining example of how just letting people talk can save you a lot of time trying to prove your point. When you calm down enough to read this, consider what kind of a world it would be if security issues didn't even exist. You need to research the case and see what it was Mitnick was charged with and analyze the true nature of most hacking crimes. The people in charge of security who get so bent out of shape when security holes are discovered should maybe be doing something else.

Dear *2600:*

> *There's nothing I hate more than hypocrisy. The contradiction I speak of comes when* 2600, *a prominent voice of the hacker community (like it or not), cries out against destructive behavior—attacking websites (government or otherwise), destroying data, unleashing viruses upon the world—and then turns around and defends those people when "hackers" are verbally or legally attacked by the public at large. The distinction needs to be made between those of us who promote peace, good behavior, and intellectual curiosity and those who are simply trying to cause mischief or get themselves put into jail. Perhaps we need a new term—the original meaning of "hacker" has become so perverted by the media that it now bears no relevance whatsoever to the ideal it was created to embody. What we need is a new term—and a hacker manifesto. A document that says, in plain layman's terms, what we as "good" hackers believe in, what we do, and why. A document meant for circulation to the general public—through other magazines or newspapers. A document that distinguishes us from the malicious mob of angst-ridden fools who call themselves hackers because they want to belong to a bigger movement.*

> ENTROPIC
> DALLAS, TEXAS

Well, that may be so but it's doubtful all of us are going to rally behind any one ideal or document. There is always going to be some level of dissent in any group of individualistic people. As for our alleged hypocrisy, consider this. We encourage responsible behavior but acknowledge that people don't always act in the most responsible manner. However, there is a level of degree and a minor offense is simply not the same as a major one. We defend people who create a little mischief with no ulterior motive or whose actions have hurt no one. We don't defend criminals as we define them—but that doesn't mean that we want all criminals to rot in prison. Everything has an order of magnitude and the mere fact that we have to even talk in terms of imprisonment and criminal records for harmless trespassing and minor pranks is incredibly disturbing and indicative of a society heading in a bad direction.

Dear *2600:*

> Goldstein, let me start by saying what you've done with 2600 is honorable. It must have taken a lot of work and dedication to get this far. Now that you're here and seemingly alive, I must express my views in hope of making a difference for the better.
>
> Your content is biased, you want all of us to think just as you do, when in fact your views and opinions should be just that, your *views and opinions.*
>
> Allow me to make an observation if I may. While reporting the Mitnick case, you never once looked at it from the point of the prosecution. The case most likely has been corrupted by media and opposing powers. You've told us as much. But do you really think your loyal readers are going to feel as committed and genuine about the whole thing if the "answer" is so obvious? No, we won't. And if you can't get us (the very foundation of the publication) to feel strongly about the Mitnick case, what chance do you have with the rest of society? You can't be biased towards the judicial system just because you think they are being biased towards Mitnick. That will get us nowhere. In fact, it is counterproductive.
>
> You've got the power, you have the readers, eyes are on you, now make the most efficient use of it. Print more manuscripts, more cold hard facts, and let us do the math. You're bastardizing our cause when you allow us to only see things from your view. Instead of instilling your mindset, instill the facts and let us come to our own conclusions. Isn't that the very essence of hacking anyway? We all learned to tie our shoes. Surely we can connect the dots.
>
> COOKIESNATCHER

Unless you're speaking to us from a meeting of all 2600 readers, what you say here represents your opinion and not necessarily that of anyone else. Presume the same thing about us when you read one of our editorials and presume the same when you read an editorial in a newspaper. Everything is colored by opinion and if we don't present our opinion in our own pages, where else will it appear? If we're not presenting specific facts fairly, we'd like to hear about it, but with regard to the Mitnick case, we believe we show the opposing side quite clearly. That, in fact, seems to be the strongest point in our favor.

Dear *2600:*

> *I purchased one of your issues a while back out of idle curiosity. I found it to be quite dumb. It was oozing with sarcasm and gave way to a very condescending tone toward most of your readers who had taken the time to submit you letters. A word of advice if you would like to keep subscribers: if you think what they wrote you is foolish or idiotic, then don't print it in your magazine. Pissing people off, ignorant or not, does not win you any awards.*
>
> *As for this Kevin Mitnick trash, I don't believe he should have received such a harsh sentence either, but that is an issue to deal with the justice system in general and not just one foolish person who thought crashing computers would be entertaining. I believe our justice system is screwed up for the most part, but this Mitnick fellow's actions were only meant to hurt others. He did it for fun, too. I have nothing against throwing malevolent people such as Mitnick in jail and I don't see why any other respectful citizen of this country would either.*
>
> *Here is a simple ideology for you: respect others and just maybe they will respect you. Now doesn't that sound almost like the golden rule your grandmother taught you? Maybe she really did know a thing or two.*
>
> JOE BLOW

It doesn't surprise us that someone who doesn't get sarcasm would have trouble with the concept of justice as well. Please analyze the facts before you spout off—there was no crashing of machines and no actions "meant to hurt others." Don't believe us—look at the court records and see what he was actually charged with.

Dear *2600:*

*I read the informative article in the CNN Internet section (cnn.com/
TECH/specials/hackers/qandas). I believe it was your editor who responded to the questions by CNN. I really do appreciate your honesty
and candid response. I am a person who believes that the government
and the corporations have been misleading us for decades. There is
much evidence that this is true. I do not believe that everything I
read or see on a website is accurate. On the contrary, being a thinking
person, I take everything that I hear or read with a grain of salt. Being
a thinking person, I feel I should respond to your response. First off, I
believe your logic is quite flawed. Pagers, cell phones, and computers
are primarily communication devices. They are not toys. According
to your mentality, it is okay to steal something if others leave it out
in the open. Your philosophy leaves much room for the justification
of breaking and entering, and copying web pages that don't belong to
you. One could perceive your actions and the actions of all of your
group as the selfish behavior of individuals who have very little respect
for the privacy of other individuals. In response to your opinion that
hackers should not be prosecuted and put in prison, it's not surprising
considering that most criminals do not understand why they are in
jail. We, as a society, cannot let our private belongings and documents
be subject to the criminal class. As long as your organization believes
it has the right to steal from others (just because you can) and take
advantage of new technology to the detriment of your fellow brothers
and sisters, I will never support hackers or their belief systems. It is
interesting that you feel you are doing this country a great service by
being the first to break in and rearrange legitimate websites, believing
that if your organization did not do it first that international terrorists would get around to it. But that is not the way it happened, is it?
Unfortunately, your organization has become the terrorists you say
you so adamantly oppose.*

JEFFREY SEELMAN
MILWAUKEE

*There's nothing like a letter that starts off really nice and then plummets into name-
calling and foolish simplicity. Now, let's try to stay civil. We do not condone theft.
However, your definition of theft is so incredibly broad as to include things like*

copying web pages! You need to realize what theft really is—taking something away that isn't yours to take. Simple enough? When you take something, it's not there anymore. Copying a file isn't the same as taking it. Now you can argue that this doesn't make it right and maybe that's true. But it doesn't make it equivalent to whatever crime you want to punish people for. As for your little rant on our inability to respect privacy, perhaps you should look at who is invading yours. How much junk mail do you get from hackers? How many times have we entered your name into a database and shared it with several thousand of our friends? How many times have we left your private info lying around for anyone to stumble across? Hackers have learned these things through exploring and refusing to believe everything they're told. Hackers encourage the use of encryption in order to further protect one's privacy. Take a good look at who opposes strong encryption and direct your anger that way. We're sorry you don't think of pagers, cell phones, and computers as toys but we always will and it's from that enthusiasm that we will design applications that you would never dream of. That is entirely your loss. You may think it's appropriate to imprison people who don't buy into your values and occasionally embarrass powerful entities. We don't.

2000

Dear *2600:*

> *Don't you guys think that the Kevin Mitnick deal has been blown a little bit out of whack? There are so many other hackers doing just as big stuff and not getting any credit whatsoever whereas Kevin Mitnick is five years ago and still famous! What about Zyklon from gH (Global Hell) or Cruzzed from LoC (Legends of Chaos)?*
>
> KuNg

You miss the point. It's not about getting credit, it's about recognizing injustice. No case that we know of came close to this in the hacker world. We will continue to report on any similar cases as we hear of them—in fact, we reported on the Zyklon story in our last issue.

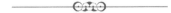

Dear *2600:*

> *I really respect what you guys do and the rights of hackers that you stand up for. I do believe that you have a bad view on what a hacker is. I hate to break it to you, but a cracker is a hacker. These recent attacks were hackers. I bet you're shaking your head right now but it is true. Every group of people has its bad people. There are bad priests, doctors, and lawyers so why can't you guys just agree with that instead of trying to make two separate groups, hackers and crackers? We all do the same thing: mess with computers and the like. If you call Jack Kevorkian a doctor, the other doctors don't get mad and say "He's not a doctor, he is a murderer." Some may say that but the majority still believes that he is a doctor. I do understand that you would like people to stop viewing all hackers as bad, but in the age of morons, that is impossible.*

KEVIN V
TRENTON, OH

We don't know where you got the idea that we want to perpetuate this "cracker" nonsense. We believe the word does a great disservice to hackers everywhere as it criminalizes without explaining the crime and the end result is that the uninformed get a mostly negative view of the hacker culture. We also don't know how you're so certain that these recent attacks were the work of hackers. It's been widely reported that anyone with the right script could have done this. Is anyone who can type a command to be considered a hacker? We recognize the possibility that it could have been a hacker but it's really irrelevant as it's as much an act of hacking as cow tipping.

Dear *2600:*

> *I am terribly sorry about the irrationality of the MPAA. However, I can't quite figure out why you would print articles dealing with United States government security. I am referring to two articles in the latest issue. I mean, the last thing you need is the federal government on your trail. And there is an ad stating that someone will fax secrets of the White House Communications Agency. Why would you print such*

a thing? And don't tell me it's because he's a subscriber. I am so proud to read your magazine but would hate for you to go down in flames over something so stupid.

CRYPTOFREQ

We talk about government security because it's of interest. If we were to self-censor our material because we were worried about what someone might think, we wouldn't be able to print much of anything. Concerning the ad, it's interesting that you inserted the word "secrets" into it. The original ad never said that—it simply offered "documents" that are most likely public but not easily found. This is exactly our point—if we followed your advice, we would have turned the reference material into a secret and not printed the ad even though we had no evidence. Our fear would have silenced us long before any action from a third party. We can't go down that road. Comfort yourself by knowing that anyone foolish enough to trade classified info through our Marketplace will certainly get an unwanted taker very quickly.

Dear *2600:*

I thought IRC was for chat, 2600 for learning, but I guess I was wrong there. Repeatedly on IRC, I have been flamed by people saying I wasn't "cool" or "l33t" because I was using Windows and mIRC (an IRC client that is considered lame by the "elitists" on #2600). My Windows computer has DSL, and my FreeBSD and Linux computers don't have Ethernet cards or internal DSL modems. I do not want to go out and buy these because I simply do not have enough money and time to configure them. So I choose to use Windows. (All this to explain to you why I don't use Linux or FreeBSD with the Internet, just so you don't think I'm a lamer.) Another thing, I have found it is now trendy to use a type of UNIX over Windows so you can flame those who don't. My friend told me he was sitting in #linux one day and he saw someone coming in. The person had a question because he was new to Linux. The question was "how do I set up PPP outside of X Windows on Linux?" He was flamed repeatedly and then when my friend tried to tell him the answer, he was kicked and, I found out afterwards, the person with the question was kicked and banned. That made me mad so I asked the person who did it why he did it. So then he came into my channel that I created, #bacon-humpers (excuse the name, it's an inside joke), and started yelling at everyone because they were in Windows and using mIRC, and because we, heh, used linkers in Windows instead of compilers in UNIX to do our coding. We later found out he was on a shell account in Windows. These two incidents are not isolated. This has happened to me millions of times after I was searching through my logs. This is what the 2600net IRC server has degraded into, and because of that we've moved to a small, privately owned server. Now we have registered our own domain name and are starting our own IRC server because yours has degraded into a point where everyone, even the real hackers, are snobby people who think they are better than everyone else because they know more.

                                                              FLAMEcow

To achieve the kind of atmosphere you want, we would have to monitor and control all dialogue on our IRC server. This just isn't how IRC works. Users define how the conversations go. It makes no more sense to condemn us for immature users than it does to criticize Linux because you got kicked off a #linux channel somewhere.

Dear *2600:*

Kevin Mitnick used to make threats and say, "I'm going to kill you, I know who you are and where you live" before he got busted five years ago. If he were really smart, he would know cell phones are traceable. How would you feel if someone hacked into your 2600 website and changed your index.hml file to something you totally disagreed about? And every time you asked or emailed the person who hacked you, they just said you suck and you're lame? And if you have to stop what you're doing and fix the website or hire someone to fix it, that costs money.

This is like if a Lock Master constantly breaks into your house and keeps putting up messages that said your door sucks and your lock is a bubble gum.

The law is the law *and if you got busted by what you're doing, then you're not the best.*

ILLII

Every now and then, we get anti-Mitnick letters that are somewhat rational but wind up blowing it with some inane or hysterical ranting. You, however, managed to skip the rational part altogether. You also managed not to include any facts at all so we can't even refute them. "Your lock is a bubble gum"?

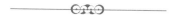

Dear *2600:*

> *It is my humble opinion that pointing out weaknesses (in anything) is wrong if, by doing so, damages could result. The effects of this on the Internet are almost always bad, most especially with security. By pointing out a security flaw in an operating system and making it public in a magazine or an article online, you are helping and you are hurting at the same time. You and I both know there are good and bad people—the ones who use information to help and the ones who use information to hurt. By revealing sensitive material like the ever present security flaws and exploits that float around the Internet, you are destroying the goal of making good by allowing others to make bad based on your noteworthy finds.*
>
> *What if I found a way to steal money from 2600? Maybe it involved a very complicated procedure that was limited by a number of variables, so as to keep your losses at a relative low. In other words, not everyone could take advantage of this, but some could and would. What if a devoted 2600 fan learned about it and informed you by publishing the security flaw online? In detail. To the world.*
>
> *Similar horror stories occur when you post articles such as "Taking Advantage of All Advantage," and dozens of other articles that you are more familiar with than I am. How do you explain this? Don't you think you're damaging as opposed to helping? I am genuinely interested in your response to this.*

MANNEQUIN

You would actually have us believe that it's best to remain silent when confronting security problems? There is no such thing as security through lack of information. All that accomplishes is the creation of a false perception. Any bit of information can be used for nefarious purposes. In fact, in this issue we're running an article on security issues for a particular store chain's cash registers. We have little doubt that many will see this as an endorsement of theft, which it clearly is not. People are curious. They want to know how things work and how systems can be defeated. We exist as a forum for theoretical and specific examples of this. If we start agonizing over what people might do with the information we print, we will very quickly run out of topics that won't have some potentially adverse affect somewhere. And as for your example involving someone figuring out a way to steal from us, we would much prefer seeing it published than to have it go on in secret among a select few individuals. At least we would have a chance to pay attention.

Dear *2600:*

> *I find the letter you received from Microsoft (17:3) regarding your alleged software piracy interesting, but I find your response incomprehensible. In fact, your response seems to have nothing to do with the actual content of the letter. For example, you say that Microsoft accuses you of software piracy "out of the blue," but the letter says that they "received a report that you may have distributed illegal and/or unlicensed Microsoft software products." Given their well-publicized anti-piracy campaign, they undoubtedly get an enormous number of these reports, legitimate and otherwise. This letter is obviously a standard boilerplate response to such a report and not an accusation of any kind. Reading it as such is like believing a letter addressed to "occupant" is meant specifically for you. If Microsoft really thought you were pirating, it would have taken the form of a subpoena, cease-and-desist order, or a horde of FBI agents breaking down your door, all of which are pretty unmistakable.*
>
> *As for the "evidence" you want to see, in this case it would amount to the identity of the person who filed the report and what he claimed. Since the average complaint of this type comes from disgruntled*

employees, there's a good place for you to start looking. And of course you're right, the idea that a company that receives a report that you may be stealing their property would tell you about it, and provide both a simple description of the applicable laws and an easy way to contact them for more information, well that's absolutely unfair and a totally bizarre business practice. It's a wonder they can stay open.

I'm certain this propaganda plays well with the hordes of people who will believe anything bad about Microsoft, but to anyone else it just makes you look foolish.

HERMIT

We don't know what planet you're orbiting, but down here on Earth we don't just accept these things without question. And we question the legitimacy of a company that would send out such a letter without making any effort to verify the claims. It seems that anyone anywhere can simply drop a name to Microsoft and have a threatening letter sent to that name. Imagine the fear you can spread inside an organization that actually takes this kind of crap seriously. Microsoft owes us and everyone else they've tried to intimidate a big apology. And it's a pity you're not capable of seeing that.

2001

Dear *2600:*

I can't for the life of me understand why your magazine endorsed Green Ralph Nader over Libertarian Harry Browne. While I agree that Nader is a sincere man and infinitely preferable to Gush and Bore, a simple look at the respective party platforms will show that the Green Party is all about bigger, more intrusive government, and the Libertarian Party is all about freedom, no questions asked. In the crucial area of privacy rights, the Green platform is vague and poorly written: the bottom line is that neither free speech nor the rights of the individual are listed in "The Ten Key Values of the Greens" (www .greens.org/values/). On the other hand, the Libertarian platform (http://www.lp.org/platform) *is crystal clear and leaves absolutely no doubt as to where they stand.*

Ask yourself: do you want real freedom or don't you? The choice is clear.

LISA J.

You've overanalyzed our message. If we wanted to endorse a candidate, we would have done so in a more obvious way. The cover of 17:3 was a collection of images that summed up the events of the previous months: H2K, the RNC, the treatment of the demonstrators, the rise of the Green movement and the questions they raised, the "threat" of a cell phone, etc. We don't care who you vote for and, as events have shown, it doesn't really matter anyway. And that is what you should be focusing your anger toward.

Dear *2600:*

I have noticed as a reader on and off over the last few years that 2600 has become more of a political and social platform, in certain aspects, than a technical forum. The Fall 2000 issue was good, more techie articles, I felt. Don't get me wrong, I know what the magazine has been through of late, but it is hard to get my new issues every few months and find it filled with articles about what court cases you are going through and reading about kids in high school who are getting busted by cranky old English teachers and such when I am expecting information for these kids and myself about computer and phone systems. I guess my question is: Where do you see the magazine going? 2600 is the place I go to get new ideas about tech issues that are more edgy as well as new ways of looking at them. I hope that isn't lost in these philosophical and boringly accusational arguments. I really want to impress that I do want to support 2600 in the court cases, etc., but I want a tech magazine as well.

C....

We'll make you a deal then. We will continue to try and print edgy technical info that others are afraid to touch if you help us fight for a society that will see this as a good thing. We would like nothing better than to be able to print articles without having to worry about which megacorp will come after us next. But as long as that keeps happening and as long as freedom of speech and association are punished instead of embraced, we're going to have to fight back, in these pages and in other forums. If we lose, you likely won't have anything at all to read.

Dear *2600:*

> *Everyone has responsibilities in life, like it or not. First, let me tell you about mine. I work for one of the largest consulting firms in the world. When first hired, I had very little job security due to the fact that I was well known as a hacker. Over the period of two years, that has changed. Most of the people I work with are now extremely interested in non-malicious unauthorized security audits. 2600 articles are now everyday conversation material. I feel I have done my part, relative to my responsibility, to clarify to the people in my scope what the word "hacker" really means. You, however have a much larger scope and have voluntarily assumed the responsibility of being the voice of the hacker community. Why then is it that all you can do is piss and moan about the bad connotation the word "hacker" has received? We are hackers, not criminals. It is your responsibility to make this known on the global level. I therefore respectfully request that you stop pissing, moaning, and trying to play martyr, and voice to the world what a true hacker is. We will be extinct sooner than anyone realizes if we don't take our name back from the irresponsible, adolescent, power-tripper wannabes who just want power and a free ride on our coattails 'cause they literally can't hack it.*
>
> *(The information in this email is confidential and may be legally privileged. It is intended solely for the addressee. Access to this email by anyone else is unauthorized.)*
>
> TRIGGA BISTRO

Well, you've got us thoroughly confused. You want us to fight for the word "hacker" but not complain when it's misused? We'd sure like some specifics on how such a thing can be done. And keep in mind that we have access to, at most, four dimensions.

Dear *2600:*

> Let me start off by saying that I understand that the extent of your
> involvement in so much legal controversy must require an immense
> amount of money. Of course, the EFF cannot cover everything, but I
> am sure that by lowering the price of 2600 you would get a lot more
> readers. $7.15 CAN is far too expensive, and everyone with at least a
> little common sense knows very well that your production and distri-
> bution costs are not that high.

HEMLOCK

First off, we're not jacking up our newsstand rates to raise funds for the lawsuit.
Our price has been the same for two years and our subscription rate is the same
as it was all the way back in 1989! As for the Canadian dollar, it converts to less
than 65 cents of a U.S. dollar. That means you're actually paying less than people
in the States. For a long time we were selling 2600 at the wrong exchange rate
and we actually wound up owing our distributor money for sales. You're welcome
to use this common sense of yours and try to do what we do for less money without any advertising. We think you'll find that talk is about the only thing that's still
cheap.

Dear *2600:*

> Personally, I think the FBI or CIA is tracing what IP addresses log on
> to your website, and what emails come through your servers. Have a
> nice day thinking about that!

GINO

It's good to know that if we ever run out of things to worry about, we can call on
you to replenish the supply.

Dear *2600:*

> "The greatest injustice in the prosecution of Kevin Mitnick is
> revealed when one examines the actual harm to society (or lack
> thereof) that resulted from Kevin's actions."

A drunk driver doesn't "intend" to kill, and may not on most nights. But when your little girl is killed by a drunk driver, you want them put away. "Intent"? He broke the law. If he was only "curious" and came into my home to look around, or hack into my PC to "look around" that would be a legal and moral *violation of my right to privacy! If it were my business, he'd be violating the trust and privacy of all my clients. So, f*ck you! You're criminals who only justify your own self centered actions. Which one of you has ever "stopped" a hacker from ripping off the public? Assholes.*

BEN

We get so many letters like this and they almost always go down the same road of self-righteous indignation terminating in pure unadulterated ignorance. Nothing convinces us more that we're on the right side.

Dear *2600:*

I think it's great what you guys are doing... causing the youth of America to lose morale for this great country. Honestly, do you actually believe you're doing good for the world? If you don't like America, move to another country but don't brainwash the teens here with your ideas of hatred toward authority. You only fuel the already rebellious fire within them that causes nothing but trouble for the whole country. Please, you only make things worse.

JOHNG54429

Exactly the kind of pep talk we need to make us try twice as hard.

Dear *2600:*

I have been reading your magazine for several years now and find it to be generally informative and useful to my profession. But I have become increasingly disturbed by your apparent politics. I fully expect you to excoriate me in the same smug, condescending manner you take with all other writers who disagree with you, but I simply must

comment on some of the positions you have advocated over the past
months.

I first became really bothered at what appeared to be your defense of
the WTO rioters and demonstrators in Seattle. I have followed some
of the figures involved in organizing these demonstrations for a while
and find them to be nothing more than professional anarchists and
modern-day Bolsheviks. Apart from advocating socialist revolution,
they are in it only to cause violence and disruption and have nothing
constructive to offer politically. I would wager that most of the mob
accompanying them are entirely ignorant of the actual political motives of their "leaders," and are just looking to fulfill an adrenaline
rush. Fortunately, what views this lot does manage to articulate are so
radical and fringe, it is unlikely they ever will gain a wide following.

I also want to address some of your comments in response to letters in
the 18:3 issue. Your attacks on gun ownership utilize some of the same
distorted, one-sided statistics used by gun control advocates for years.
The 75 percent reduction in gun-related deaths in Canada compared
to the United States includes police shootings and instances of self
defense in this country. Citizens in the United States use firearms in
self-defense against crime more that 6,000 times per day, and less than
five percent of those instances require the pulling of a trigger.

The way we do things here in the United States is not now, has never
been, and never will be perfect. Yet many voices such as yours advocate
tearing it all down because of that lack of perfection. As long as human
nature remains as it is, your utopian pursuits will remain a fairy tale
quest. The fact is that, like it or not, we live in the best system in the
world. It should continue to be criticized and improved, and we all
need to be alert to those who try to twist the rules for their own benefit
and the detriment of others. That is something often done well by
2600 by pointing out the danger and folly inherent in things like the
DMCA or MPAA. You have it partially right in your belief that less
government is better, but you also need to realize that corporations
are not all evil. Naturally they are very self-interested and often they
do stupid things, but by trying to punish a couple of dozen people in
a board room, you also end up seriously harming hundreds, if not

thousands, of employees who are just trying to make a living and take care of their families.

So, as you get busy painting me as a Nazi kook or some such thing, I will take my leave of you secure in the knowledge that, like the WTO demonstrators in Seattle, your views will no doubt be regarded as so radically fringe that you won't gain much of a following either.

G. CONTERIO

Calling us names and then virtually daring us to call you names in return says more about you than any name ever could. That said, let's quickly dismantle your logic so we can move on with more technical matters. The WTO protesters, particularly in Seattle, enveloped a wide range of political beliefs, left, right, and center. Even the mass media occasionally got this right. The revisionism that has turned these peaceful protests into riots is very self serving to those who want to demonize the entire anti-globalization movement. But the firsthand accounts and unedited footage tell a very different story. Listen to our own coverage from November and December of 1999 on our website in the "Off The Hook" section where we tracked down dozens of these firsthand accounts. This is not to say there weren't a few idiots who tried to cause problems by destroying property. But these people hardly defined the mood of the rest and even their actions paled in comparison to the actual violence perpetrated by the police, which to this day remains completely unpunished. Talk to people who were actually there and come up with some unedited footage that backs up your conclusions before you condemn an entire group of people. And if you can find any way that what we're saying here differs from the things we've been saying since our first issue, please let us know.

It's wonderful to know that citizens in the U.S. are constantly using guns to prevent crime (although it's a bit puzzling to figure out where such statistics are kept). But in other parts of the world, they somehow manage to prevent a whole lot more crime without using guns at all! And of course, there's the matter of all the gun-related crimes that we fail to prevent, which was sort of the whole point. The simple fact is that we have a major problem and getting more guns is certainly not the answer. And our statistics come from such biased organizations as hospitals, police departments, the Centers for Disease Control, and the United Nations. And they all seem to correlate quite nicely.

To continue the refrain that we have the best system in the world invariably leads to a lack of urgency in getting problems fixed or even in seeing them. And when *people say that in fact we don't have the best system in the world, as we do, they are branded as traitors, utopian dreamers, and people who want to tear everything down, among other things. They are often told to leave if they don't like it rather than stay and fight to make things better. The end result is that the things that really need to change continue not to change. And it's that failure which will ultimately prove to be our downfall.*

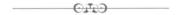

Dear *2600:*

> *I've been reading 2600 for quite some time now and I love the magazine. It kicks ass, but I think you may be glorifying the hacker a little too much. If someone gains access to a computer and takes valuable data, that is a crime. Hackers go into things they shouldn't using exploits/tools much like a criminal opens a safe containing thousands of dollars worth of information. Information should be available to the public, but if people don't want others to know about their works, then you should respect that. Instead, hackers are glorified by the mag for doing sh*t they shouldn't be doing while spouting constitutional rights and liberalism. You're right on many things, but saying that a hacker is not a criminal is the stupidest thing I've ever heard.*

> CHRIS S

It's hard to imagine what exactly you find appealing about our magazine if you bear such animosity toward hackers. We will continue to say that hackers are not criminals because we happen to believe that—quite strongly, in fact. We would never deny that someone who invades privacy, trespasses, or intentionally causes damage is committing a crime. This would apply to anyone including system administrators and corporate executives. But to assume that all hackers engage in illegal activity is naive at best. Those who do, however, should be judged by the actual severity of the crime, not by the fear of those who think that hackers are capable of all kinds of evil.

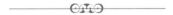

Dear *2600:*

> *It's only right that you lost the case. You publicized, you campaigned for, and you advertised how to "pick" a DVD lock. If you know how to defeat a DVD lock, you go ahead and do that for yourself if you own DVDs. Don't brag about it in school because, if you do, that would reveal your motivation: malice. Publicizing DVD circumvention does not benefit you. It only harms someone else. That's why you lost and that's why you won't win on appeal. It's your doggone motivation. And our laws deal with nuances of motivation. For example, our laws distinguish between murder and involuntary manslaughter.*

> *I see two themes in letters about your case: "free speech" and "educational" reasons for having an intense interest in unlocking DVDs. I don't believe either is at work among your readers. Your readers just want the goods behind other people's Kwikset locks. That's called "thievery."*

> *You wanted to screw the international DVD conglomerate bastards. You wanted to kick them in the nuts for charging so much and for being a dumb ass. So that's great. But you got a bit surprised when the big dumb ass organization turned around and knocked a tooth out of your mouth. Next time, duck.*

> ANONYMOUS READER

Well, that's one perspective. It's hard to imagine how you know all these things, such as the motivation of our readers and what the true effects of publishing something are. It's simplistic logic at best and we don't intend to let the occasional naysayer steer us off course. We're a magazine; we look for things, we uncover things, and we publicize things. Information is our blood. And we're not in the habit of ducking. If you don't like that, you might feel safer watching television.

Dear *2600:*

> *Tell me where* www.2600reallysucksass.com *sends you. It's my site.*

> NEO

We'll see you in hell.

Dear 2600:

I have one question. When will 2600 go back to being a magazine/
organization about technology? Ever since the Kevin thing, your magazine has been nothing but a legal magazine. I will be the first to say
that the legal issues are important, but it seems to me we have lost
track on the real content of the magazine. Why can't 2600 maintain
the level of technology information and add the legal news to their
website? I personally think that 2600 can make more money to support the fight if the magazine was to increase sales by adding more
technology-based content. I personally do not purchase the magazine
anymore because over half the magazine is on the legal issues which
I can read at www.2600.com.

STEVE

*It's a shame you won't see your letter then. We've always focused on the issues
that are of importance to the hacker community and we've done it from a hacker
perspective. The price of not doing this is ignorance. And we cannot afford to be
ignorant on such important issues. While we publish some material on the legal
happenings, we don't believe it's changed the overall tone of the zine. The vast
majority of our pages still deal with very specific technology. If they didn't, corporate America wouldn't be so pissed off at us.*

2002

Dear 2600:

I may excuse you because of the September 11th terrorist attacks, but I
sent you four photographs of payphones (by mail) and I don't have my
free subscription. I also sent an email to letters@2600.com and the
only thing I got was an automated answer: "Thank you blablabla...."
Maybe sending to all of your addresses may work. Thank you for being so communicative.

JOHNNY

*First off, we have always been way too busy to respond to each and every piece
of mail we get. Most people and certainly most magazines simply cannot do this.
Second, we're quite clear on our web page that you will get a free subscription
if your payphone photos are printed. You seem to think that just by sending us
photos you qualify. That's not how it works. Third, the automated answer you got
from the letters email address explains that personal replies aren't possible. Why
you then chose to enter into an extended dialogue with an automated reply function is something people who do have time on their hands may choose to ponder.
Finally, all you succeed in doing by flooding us with annoying mail is to be labeled
as someone worthy of being ignored altogether.*

Dear *2600:*

> *I'm writing to disagree with your analysis that the government should
> release an original digital version of the bin Laden tape. Apparently,
> all digital video tapes have special "markers" for things like time,
> camera lens settings, etc. It seems silly to think that our government
> is good enough to fake bin Laden's image and voice, but can't fake a
> few digital markers to go along with that. The government didn't have
> to release any evidence at all, so be lucky you got any. If you reject it,
> then reject it, but don't expect them to pander to your whims.*

> DAN

*They didn't have to release any evidence at all? What kind of world do you live in?
It is the obligation of thinking people everywhere to question and analyze without
relying on blind faith. Almost every major conflict in the world can be traced to
people who refuse to even entertain the possibility of seeing something they don't
want to see. As people with a technical knowledge of such things, it was a lot more
than a mere "whim" for us to want to see the timecode of the tape. There were
numerous details attesting to the authenticity that could have been garnered by
seeing these values. While they could have been faked, it would take an extraordi-
nary amount of effort and time to get all of them just right. That's why their release
in a timely manner was so essential. And it's a perfect example of how hackers can
help in these troubled times—by using some technical knowledge to let the world
know if something makes sense or not. Of course, to do this properly you have
to accept the fact that you don't know the answer until you analyze the data. It's*

puzzling and quite disturbing that the United States government wouldn't want this evidence to be known. But what's even worse is when people close their eyes to the mere possibility that the facts don't add up.

Dear *2600:*

> *This article is about what waht kinda peoplw the hackers often are!! Im just ordaniray guy surfing suddeny get a nice little present one of your hackers which you gladly call freedom fighters. Whoops suddenly his present destroy all my music files and pictures!! What a nice guy true liberator! hm and he informs me that in colombia the goverment is cruel hm! Nice kinda fought of him and kinda thought who good theyre cruel to him! i kinda start to like CIA FBI and the colombian for treating the bottom scum succing aude eater of this planet some what productive fair way! MY feeling aBOUT YOU HACKERS IS THAT YOUR BUNCH OF IMATURE BASTARDS TALKING ABOUT RIGHTS WHILE VIOLITING OTHERS RIGHTS ! yOU ARE THE TRUE OPPRESSERES AND ERODING FORCE OF THIS PLANET!! yOUKNOW WHAT I WOLUD FOR cia CAMPAIGN FIND HACKERS PROCECUTE THE M FUCKEM FOR LIFE!"!*
> > sINCERLY THE COMMON SENCE!!

Well you certainly told us.

Dear *2600:*

> *I don't pay money for a magazine when I can get the same info for free online:* http://www.elfqrin.com/hack/index.html. *That appears to be the same article that appeared in the latest (19:1) 2600.*
> > MIKE K

You are living proof that no matter what we do, people will find something to bitch about. When articles aren't available online, people want us to make them available. When we tell people how to find the articles we print online, we get letters like the above. Would you have really found the article in the first place if we hadn't printed the address of that website when we printed the article?

Dear *2600:*

> *It's hardly any wonder the general public doesn't like the hacker community. I mean, yeah, I know most of it comes from mainstream society's overall ignorance about many of the details of what we do and don't do and various other things having to do with the hacker community. But I also know that all one has to do to find so much of the lowlife trash that, unfortunately, seems to wind up more or less representing all of us somehow is to go into any conference bridge, IRC channel, BBS, or basically any place large groups of hackers or phreakers congregate. You're always guaranteed to find at least one or two idiots (if you're lucky). If you're unlucky, the better portion of the people on that given thing will be total assholes. I realize that your average hacker or phreaker isn't particularly old. In fact, most are under 18. But the fact of the matter remains that these wing nuts don't seem to give a rat's ass about treating anyone with common courtesy and respect. Not to mention the fact that they don't seem to know or care anything about how their actions reflect on us all as a culture.*
>
> *These self-righteous, holier than thou, "1337" types are poor representatives of the community and reflect badly on all of us. I only wish there was a way to do something about it once and for all! But, in closing, let me just thank you for doing such a good job of casting us in a bit of a better light than the general public seems to prefer to see us all in.*
>
> CAPTAIN _ B

You touch upon a problem that has plagued the hacker community from the very beginning. Much of it is directly related to the ignorance of the mainstream, particularly the media. Look at it this way: Can you go up to a major network and claim to be a doctor, a lawyer, or a carpenter? Odds are they will want some sort of evidence before they do a story on you, that is, assuming they were interested enough to do a story in the first place. But in the case of hackers, all one has to do is tell the media that they're a hacker and, without any sort of proof or display of skill, they are immediately classified as a hacker! This results in all kinds of people claiming that they're hackers when all they really are are attention-seekers. You will find them everywhere. There's not a whole lot we can do about this, short of closing our doors and only letting people we already know into a particular forum. But that defeats the purpose of the forum. The best way to deal with this is for those really interested in what hacking is all about to recognize the bull for what it is and, as with most any group, look for those who really do get it. Don't let yourself believe that they don't exist—they always do. Just consider getting past the garbage one of the first tasks you must achieve.

Dear *2600:*

> *I've perused your magazine in the past and have been impressed with the technical competence your articles display. I bought issue 18:4 today and was considering subscribing until I read your letters section, where you bash Libertarians and gun rights.*
>
> *So the government is AOK in your book so long as they're only abusing capitalists and gun owners, and leaving us poor little hackers alone? That's some hypocrisy. I'm not going to spend money on people who are going to stab me in the back as soon as they get their own pet cause fulfilled. I'd wish you luck on your lawsuit, but why bother? You wouldn't care if the feds bust down my door for owning a gun or not paying taxes.*
>
> VROMAN

We'd say we'll miss you but it wouldn't be true. We like for our readers to actually be able to read what we say, a skill which obviously has eluded you. We didn't "bash," we questioned logic and conclusions. We do this all the time to anyone and anything we encounter. We consider such questioning to be a good thing. Never before have we been met with such hostility from so many angry people at even the mildest form of questions or criticism aimed at these topics. It only makes us want to question them even more.

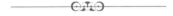

Dear *2600:*

> *I was quite surprised to read that easyEverything, an Internet cafe, would believe they have a right to censor the pages viewed by their paying customers. I will certainly boycott them.*
>
> *I am rather puzzled by your editorial comment, videlicet: "This is what happens when a big company drives all the little companies out of business with artificially low prices. You wind up playing by whatever rules they feel like setting."*
>
> *Could you explain to us, when is a company "big?" Could you please explain to us, when is a price "artificially" low? Could you please mention an example of a business which wanted to have some rules, but wasn't able to because it was "too small?"*
>
> *Under a Libertarian economic regime, corporations won't abuse power, because they will never have accumulated significant amounts of power.*
>
> *There are still a very few examples of unregulated free markets. For example, commercial fishing boats. Under the current free market conditions, no boat owner can hope to fix the wholesale price of fish. Perhaps you would prefer to shut down this dangerous example of freedom.*
>
> *Did you know that Eleanor Roosevelt (yes, the wife of FDR) took out, and renewed several times, a permit to carry a concealed handgun? Yes, handgun permits in New York State are on the public record!*
>
> AMERICAN CITIZEN LIVING ABROAD

We define a "big" company as one which is able to crush its competition because of its bigness and its ability to sell its product for much less than what it actually costs, which is our definition of "artificially low." The easyEverything by us was at one point selling three hours of Internet time for a dollar. In addition, they had hundreds of computers connected to the net and they were right in the middle of Times Square, probably the most expensive area to have a storefront, let alone do what these people were doing. Compare this to an independently run operation which has to charge $10 an hour to recover their costs. Who do you think will go under first? If you don't like the rules that easyEverything imposes on its customers, boycotting them is a good idea. But what happens when there's no competition left *because of the above tactics? You're forced to play by their rules and there's really nothing you can do about it.*

We'd like to know how you plan on getting all of this existing power out of the hands of big corporations without the help of government or some kind of time machine. We suspect, not really knowing much about the subject, that there's more of a level playing field in the fishing business which keeps one entity from gaining an unfair advantage. If easyEverything had fishing boats attached to their current business practices, it would probably be a very different story. (Now we're certain to get all kinds of letters from commercial fisherman on the subject.)

And that's a nice bit of gossip about Eleanor Roosevelt but we're not sure what, if any, point you're trying to make with it.

Dear *2600:*

> In your editorial comments "Time To Care" in the Spring 2002 issue
> you call for your readers to support the ACLU. The ACLU is cur-
> rently defending the North American Man-Boy Love Association
> (NAMBLA) at ACLU expense. I cannot and will not ever support a
> Left Wing Hate Group that is defending a group that openly advo-
> cates the rape of young boys and infants. The ACLU is actively doing
> everything within its power to destroy our country and our freedom
> through the support of groups like NAMBLA.
>
> GREG
> GOLDEN, CO

With the Olympic-style leaps in logic you've demonstrated yourself capable of here, we're probably better off not having you on board. But before adding us to your hate list, consider that you won't have very much worth defending if you only ally yourself with those who agree with everything you believe in. Even convicted criminals and those you consider to be lowlifes have rights, and closing your eyes to this is a sure step toward a world where such rights are selectively granted and arbitrarily refused. It takes a lot of guts for groups like the ACLU to consistently stand up for anyone who is having their rights denied.

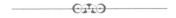

Dear *2600:*

> *Sheesh. I just got done reading one of your mags (most recent), and I am ashamed to even think that I call myself a hacker. From the article on cookies to the article on how someone can post a phone listing, your magazine is full of such crap. You constantly bitch about how the U.S. discriminates against you, and how pathetic and hopeless you are. Why don't you just drop the whole hacker thing and just admit that you are losers? You don't know sh*t about security either. Your web server has netbios ports open on it. I shouldn't have even been able to portscan your server. God, learn ipchains for Christ's sake. And dump FreeBSD get Debian or maybe even Red Hat. Run a server how you are supposed to, with web servers only having 80 open. By the way, your proxy allows me to use it! Also, there was that stupid article on how "stupid" telcos are, just by not listing themselves in the phone book. How retarded is that for an article? That should have been in the letters section, and freed up valuable space. It's a shame that I spent $5 on a piss-poor magazine from a bunch of script kiddies that don't know sh*t about security. Oh yeah, and another thing, your editor Emmanuel was a source on the movie* Hackers? *No wonder it was the worst "hacking" movie that I've ever seen, nothing but a bunch of script kiddies, just like Goldstein. Do yourselves and the rest of the security world a favor and retire. One last thing—you deserved to get your asses handed to you by the MPAA. If I was the judge, I would have also. Maybe you will screw up again (I was hoping that Ford would win and bankrupt you actually), and get bankrupt. Get a life!*

> CHRIS
HNSG LEADER

Are you sure you didn't leave out anything? Well, everyone is entitled to their opinion. You seem to have a number of issues—perhaps an infinite number. As we don't have infinite space, we'll confine our remarks to what we agree with—that it's a shame you call yourself a hacker. One other point—our system administrators are the people to talk to about any perceived security issues on the website. You are welcome to pit your knowledge against theirs by emailing webmaster@2600.com.

Dear *2600:*

> Just wanted to let you know—your bright light is soon to be extin-
> guished. One more major terrorist attack and your (and your type's)
> relevance will cease, your moment will have passed. This is the price
> you will pay for your arrogance and ignorance of human nature and
> history. Thinking any societal structures are infinitely perfectible—
> what dreadful nonsense. Don't blame anyone else (da man) for loss of
> civil liberties—look at da man in da mirror. When security and law
> and order are recklessly neglected and chaos and uncertainty threaten,
> the balance of societal priorities shifts. To quote Aragorn: "Are you
> scared? You're not scared enough." Better get used to your nightmares,
> they ain't going away anytime soon. Enjoy the darkness.
>
> P.S. I hear BuSpar is good.
>
> Kroolee-O

*It may be a paranoid reaction but sometimes we get the distinct feeling that there
are people out there who don't like us.*

2003

Dear *2600:*

> I was browsing the latest mag at Barnes & Noble here in Austin,
> Texas. I noticed some rant about emoticons and stuff. This was total
> rambling, no real meat (where's the beef?). Anyway, I was talking
> to my dad this past summer. He was an Army Intelligence Officer
> in Vietnam. He said they used to use emoticons back in the '60s, on
> teletypes, before the Internet. Can you guys screen these articles a little
> better? This totally turned me off and I didn't buy this issue.
>
> ByteEnable

*You didn't buy the issue solely because you disagreed with the conclusions
reached by one short article? We'd be amazed if you've ever bought anything with
differing opinions. Hopefully, we can get someone in the military to back up your
dad's story or there may be some trouble.*

Dear *2600:*

I've been meaning to mention my thoughts about the magazine's article policy. Personally, I think one part of the article submission policy is unfair. The part saying that all articles submitted to the mag must not have been submitted anywhere else first. Let me give a little analogy here: it would be much like Coca Cola telling all Coke drinkers that they can only drink their product if they haven't drank Pepsi a day or two before drinking Coke. It's unrealistic to think in the span of about three months (actually, over three months for those buying the mag from Barnes and Noble and other stores) that people will always remember they submitted an article to 2600 that they'd really like to submit elsewhere as well, or simply want to be bound by such control freak type policies. As is often said in the mag, in some form or another, the exchange of info is and should be free. Such a policy doesn't exactly encourage such a thing, at least during the excruciatingly long wait to see if an article sent gets printed or is thrown away like so much trash.

One thing I think is pretty much certain. No matter what I or anyone else says, that policy will, of course, not change. That's unfortunate. At least for us article writers it is. And, let's not forget something else here. Every time a copy of the mag is sold or someone subscribes you're making money. Money off of other people's hard work. Therefore, doesn't it stand to reason that with that being the case that it's only fitting and right that you listen a bit if such people voice such opinions as this?

Captain B

Your analogy is a strange one to say the least. But it's flawed for the simple reason that you're conjuring up an absurd restriction placed on consumers and comparing it to the guidelines we ask our writers to abide by. We place absolutely no restriction on who can consume—or read—our magazine. To do so would be insane and self-defeating. But our writers are helping to determine the nature of the magazine and for that we have to insist on a certain level of standards. It's a disservice to our readers to simply reprint information which can be found in other publications or on the Internet. The readers are the people we must ultimately answer to and that is why we make this rather simple stipulation. With relatively few exceptions, the articles we print here have not shown up elsewhere. And after their articles are printed here, writers can do whatever they want with them, unlike most other magazines. Why it's such a big deal that we ask you not give us material that readers may have already seen is difficult to grasp. Since you already seem to have convinced yourself that we're exploiting you, we doubt any answer we give is going to satisfy you. We only hope our readers and future writers see the value of these guidelines.

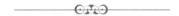

Dear *2600:*

It's funny to see 2600 *complaining about being associated with those who took down* aljazeera.net *on their news page. It seems to me if it talks like a duck, sounds like a duck, feels like a duck, it's probably a duck. In other words, when you host mirrors of hacked webpages, publish articles on how to exploit IIS, and advocate hacking websites as a "form of expression," it shouldn't come as a surprise when you are associated with those who do this sort of thing regularly. How is this not blatant hypocrisy? Either these people who hack sites aren't really hackers, or you're lying. But if they're not hackers, why do you call it "hacking" web pages?*

Another example centers around some of the articles you publish. Articles that come to mind are "Outsmarting Blockbuster," "A Password Grabbing Attempt," etc. What possible relevance does this have to "protecting privacy" and "preserving security?" Teaching readers how to circumvent late fees is nothing short of stealing. Thinly veiling this as a way to get out of a situation similar to arriving 15 minutes late because your car broke down is inexcusable and irresponsible. In "A Password Grabbing Attempt," one is clearly trying to exploit unaccustomed users' ignorance in an attempt to... grab their password. This is not just pointing out a security hole; it's pointing out a security hole and explaining in very close detail how to exploit it for no justifiable purpose. Pointing out a security hole is much more like your article entitled "The Current State of E-Commerce Security."

I suppose this would be a good time to explain that I don't find all your articles immoral and unjustifiable. The "History of 31337 SP34K" was thoroughly entertaining and a lot of your social commentary rings true to me. The article about setting up a home server was informative, and Comcast's Operation TIPS talking points sheet was relieving and yet haunting at the same time.

The bottom line is you can't keep riding the gray area. Either live up to your supposed ethic of protecting privacy, pointing out security holes, and taking necessary steps to assure they're taken care of, or drop the facade. Dogmatically excusing your exploitations as free speech is almost as inane as the government encouraging fellow citizens to look over each other's shoulder for "suspicious activity."

FYRWURXX

We've obviously bothered you a lot for you to write two such letters in the space of a month.

Let's start by getting our facts straight. What happened to aljazeera.net was not something so innocuous as an altered web page that could be fixed with a single command. It was a systematic denial of service attack which had the (in all likelihood intentional) effect of silencing their online presence and cutting off their perspective from the world. It really shouldn't be too difficult (unless you're the mainstream media) to see that such actions have got nothing at all to do with hacking and are, in fact, in direct opposition to the open society and free speech that so many of us value. It's a bit less obvious whether or not those who simply deface web pages should be considered hackers. We think it depends on the motive and the execution. Someone simply running a script written by someone else isn't really doing anything that requires hacker ingenuity. Unfortunately that's how a lot of so-called hacked web pages come to be. With commonly available exploits, it's possible for a site to get hacked without a hacker being directly involved. But that doesn't mean that creative hackers aren't still figuring out ways around security.

You may not recognize the value of some of our articles but be assured that there are many who do. While you may see the intent of publishing a particular security weakness as only serving the purpose of someone who wishes to exploit it, it's not that simple. Showing the end result is an important part of disclosing a security weakness. Seeing that end result is often necessary in order for someone to take action to either fix it or prevent similar occurrences. And learning the methodology is a vital part of any sort of hacking and what better way to do this than to see specific examples with as much detail as possible?

We simply do not believe security through obscurity is an effective approach. We will continue to expose security holes by discussing them and demonstrating them. History has proven that this is often the only way to get them to be taken seriously.

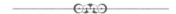

Dear *2600:*

> *We are eighth grade students attending a school in Queens, New York. As a part of the eighth grade curriculum, we must complete a social studies exit project dealing with one of the problems of New York State. We will be based on a high school level, for our school has accelerated programs.*
>
> *The topic we have chosen to study is that of the dangers of chat rooms. We understand that you are affiliated with this topic. As a necessary component of this project, we must write letters and conduct interviews. We would like to know if you might aid us in our mission by contacting either by email, letters, telephone, or in person to give any information regarding the topic. Specifically, we'd like to know why your organization is supporting chat rooms when it is known that they harbor such dangers.*
>
> *It is strange that there are still organizations that promote the use of chat rooms as a communicative device after so many incidents have occurred. Why does your company promote them? Especially your company. You are hacking magazine? A magazine that utilizes such dangers to take advantage of children and honest companies? What is the moral behind this? Our group would like to know why you and your company think it is OK to hack and as a result of this, promote the abduction and abuse of innocent adolescents. It would be extremely helpful if you could answer our questions as we are interested in your organization. If you have further information or brochures of any kind, advertisements, please contact us.*
>
> AMANDA, CAMILLE, MERIAM, CHRISTINA

And who says that schools these days are propaganda mills?

We appreciate the questions and only wish we had received them before the end of the school year. But it sounds as if you've already made your conclusions and are simply looking for us to fill in the parts about the bad guys.

When exactly did we go around promoting chat rooms anyway? What's all this about taking advantage of "children and honest companies?" And we promote abductions and abuse of adolescents?! Your teacher must have worked for a political campaign to successfully get you to believe such crap without any supporting evidence. Your leaps of logic are a whole lot more accelerated than the program you're in.

We don't enjoy insulting a bunch of eighth grade girls. Not a whole lot anyway. But we feel it's only right to also offer you some advice, which is clearly more than you were given in this sorry excuse of a class. When seeking out the facts in a story, seek them before reaching your conclusions. What kind of response do you expect when you make such ridiculous accusations and state them as if they were fact?

Perhaps this was all some subtle way of teaching you of the dangers of prejudging a group of people, in which case your teacher is a genius. We're trying real hard to cling to this possibility.

2004

Dear *2600:*

> *I am writing in response to your article "Paranoia vs. Sanity" in 20:4. In it, you make reference to "innocent people" going to jail for accessing computer systems without authorization or for simply making "free" phone calls....*
>
> *Don't you think that there are certain computer systems out there that need to be, and should be off limits either because of the data that they contain or the systems that they control?*
>
> *When Cliff Stoll was tracking the person(s) who had broken into "his" computer systems, he'd found that this person was shutting down any and all processes that "looked" as if they were put in place to "spy" on his activities. Considering that some of the systems that he had gained unauthorized access to were medical computers, it isn't a very*

big leap to have seen him shut down a process that looked to him as if it were a security program designed to catch him, but was in fact a control program for a piece of medical equipment, thereby killing an innocent bystander. Wouldn't that have had a consequence in the "real world?"

And on those "free" phone calls, granted they might be "free" for the person who made the call. But in the long run, who do you think pays for those "free" phone calls? The legitimate customers with increased fees. Or the innocent third party who has had their phone number co-opted and used to make long distance/international phone calls. I know as I was the victim of such a "free" call.

When I was living down in St. Petersburg, FL shortly after having the phone turned on in my new apartment I received a bill from then GTE for the better part of $1,000 for several international calls. I am a disabled veteran living on a fixed income. At that time, I was collecting just under $1,000 a month in benefits. And I can tell you that I would have never made even enough long distance calls to warrant a bill of over $100, let alone enough international calls to exceed $1,000. Yet when I tried explaining all of this to GTE, I got nowhere, except for being given the "company line" of, "Well Mr. X, because of the hour of day (they chose late at night), and the amount of your bill, we feel as if you did make the calls." I had two choices. Pay a bill I couldn't afford, or not pay and lose my phone service. I choose the latter as I couldn't afford the former.

So here I sit, a black mark on my credit report for failure to pay a phone bill I wasn't responsible for and I cannot get service with GTE/ Verizon because I refuse to pay for calls that I never made. So please explain to me how the calls that had been made by someone "just" looking to make a "free" phone call were "free?"

I'm sorry, but there are some lines that shouldn't be crossed.

DIGITAL _ COWBOY

We definitely believe that certain systems (including medical systems) should be "off limits." But that doesn't mean simply making it a bigger crime to access them and having no actual protection. Such a system has no place on a public network where it will be vulnerable to all kinds of problems and potential breaches.

If, on the other hand, such a system gets broken into on a private network where presumably users have inside knowledge, you actually have some sort of motive attached to an attack, unlike the randomness of the public network.

As for the "free" phone calls, you should never have been put in that position by the phone company. They are obligated to remove any charges from your bill that you did not authorize. This certainly doesn't excuse people who make fraudulent charges but one thing they're not doing is intimidating innocent people. If it's any comfort, only wireless phone accounts can show up on your credit report. But we believe you should pursue this and get your name cleared.

Dear *2600:*

> Mitnick merely played a series of tricks, changed files as he went along, was stupid enough not to change the ones to cover his tracks, and got arrested. I would dearly love to know what could cause people to want to free him. It's idiocy displayed in the greatest manner and respect of all things that should be considered easy as hell. This turkey didn't do anything great. Why the hell would you want to free someone who enjoys destroying things?

> REWT

We get these kinds of letters all the time but it's good to occasionally address the points. Here, however, there are few to find. You contradict yourself by expressing moral indignation at someone who committed a crime and then chastise that same person for not getting away with a crime. Mitnick is the first to admit the wrongness of what he did. But what he didn't do—and what nobody affected has accused him of doing—is intentionally cause damage or harm to anything. It's really quite disturbing to see people who apparently believe five years in prison wasn't enough, regardless of what they believe he actually did.

Dear *2600:*

> In 21:1, you responded to a letter by saying "Hackers who uncover unprotected private information are treated as if they created the weak

security when all they did was figure out a way to defeat it. The media portrays them as the threat to your privacy when in actuality hackers do much more to protect it."

You're wasting your breath. The media's definition of the word "hacker" isn't going to change any time soon. Why don't you just accept their definition and choose a new name for yourselves? Otherwise it seems futile. The energy you spend trying to defend hackers could be used to promote yourselves.

MANNEQUIN

If we did such a thing, do you honestly believe it would end there? Any word used to describe us would wind up being subverted by those who continue not to get it. So it's best to continue fighting to educate people.

Dear *2600:*

Picked up your mag for the first time in a year or so and laughed at the articles written by rich white boys (Hilton hacking, Cruise hacking, Mercedes hacking, Adelphia hacking, etc.). Maybe you should change your mag's name to $2600k. And stealing is still stealing (re article on "bypassing website security"). Those same frustrated white boys taking images belonging to other people. Maybe another cruise will cool them off.

JUAN IN AZTLAN

Let's get this straight. People shouldn't talk about manipulating technology that you consider to be available only to a privileged few? That certainly serves the interest of those companies that would prefer we keep their security holes secret. We won't even address your racial problems as it would be a waste of time. But equating copying an image on a website with theft only minimizes what real thieves do.

Dear *2600:*

> *I've been reading your magazine on and off for a few years now, and I've noticed that you tend to be a little too hard on "big corporations" and a little too easy on "harmless explorers."*

> *The fact of the matter is that if you were ever successful in your attempts to put the RIAA out of business, you'd be putting several thousand families out of business at the same time. While we all agree that the prices for CDs have gotten a little too high in some cases, we need to remember that we live in a capitalist environment in which we have the choice to voice our dissatisfaction by simply not supporting ideas and organizations that we believe to be overcharging or corrupt. This does not mean that we need to hop on the local P2P network and start downloading the newest Jay Z album, but we need to simply not listen to the new Jay Z album.*

> *The MPAA has also come under fire from your organization, and I find it a bit odd that you seem to have trouble seeing past the "outrageous" copyright protection schemes when all you have to do is view the end credits of any film you see in the theaters. Look at the hundreds of names that are attached to these products. Remember those names when Internet piracy seriously endangers the prospects of profitability for future releases.*

> *I understand that you don't advocate stealing movies and music as a way to get back at these corporations, but openly supporting decryption packages and security bypass measures allows people to continue pirating new media. Is that your intention? I don't know, to be honest with you. I know you'll feed me the line about open systems and how people have the right to explore, but far, far more people are stealing as opposed to exploring, and that's the problem. It's unrealistic and unpragmatic to write off the potential for theft and loss when you promote these supposed altruistic efforts and programs.*

> *And on the flip side, maybe I'm ignorant of all the facts, but it seems that you are too willing to forgive and forget when computer hackers are charged with serious crimes. Mitnick was imprisoned for a long time, and there's no doubt that the government should have handled his situation a little bit more efficiently than they did, but don't forget that Mitnick put himself into that situation. If he didn't have stolen*

source code from Sun, credit card numbers of real people, phone cards to call people, and then if he hadn't run from the police for a year, he wouldn't have been sitting in a lonely jail cell with thousands of people chanting "Free Kevin." We all need to take responsibility for our actions, and that includes hackers. It's a nice little utopian idea to think that all information should be free and shared, but it's not realistic. Not in today's world, and especially not in tomorrow's world. Not everyone is as honest as you'd like them to be, and to not take that into account could be disastrous.

HALEON

There are a bunch of misassumptions here that should be addressed. First, we're not attempting to put anyone out of business. The simplistic, old-fashioned, and self-defeating practices engaged in by entities in the music industry will do them in without any help from us. They fail to understand that the world is changing and the advent of technology now makes it possible—and in some cases mandatory—to do things in a different way. Those who don't change with the times will get swept to the side. We don't make these rules.

Not listening to the products of these dinosaurs is certainly an option. But do you really think all of the industry people will be better off if nobody listens to their product? At least if people listen in whatever way they can, the industry still has a chance of figuring out a way to profit from the popularity. Remember, there is still and there always will be an insane amount of money in the music and film industries. The only thing that seems to be changing is that consumers are getting more power over who they want to hear. And that can really scare those who are popular or in power. It can also lead some newer or less popular artists to the conclusion that they're losing money to this sort of thing. But it's much more likely that they would be heard by far less people without P2P technology. And it's a mistake to assume that everyone who listens to something for free is someone who would have rushed out and bought it otherwise.

For those in the business who continue to worry about digital copies of their music being distributed free of charge all around the world, the solution is simple: stop putting out your music in digital form. By going back to vinyl, you can be assured that anyone going through the time and trouble to encode and copy your music will be getting a second generation copy. But those of us who choose to remain in the digital world will continue to use the technology and shape it to fit our needs. This is a natural progression.

We will never hold back on knowledge of a particular subject (such as encryption) merely because its application could annoy or inconvenience some people. That's a road that's very difficult to back out of.

As for your Mitnick assertions, let's make this crystal clear. Mitnick did not "put himself in that situation." "That situation" was unjust and unfair. That is what the focus needs to be on, not the minor transgression that it all began with. Mitnick is the first one to take responsibility for his actions and to admit exactly what he did. But who will take responsibility for the tremendous injustice that took so many years of his life?

Dear *2600:*

I am writing in response to the editorial from 20:4.

Simply amazing. Denial—on all of you. Isn't Denial in your terminology? Or should I simply say "Denial Of Service?"

For starters, you lose all creditably by writing anything anonymously. Your "Paranoia vs. Sanity" wasn't even signed. Hmmm. In fact, everyone in this magazine, anonymous. Why is that, I wonder. Because maybe you don't "catch the security holes?" When in fact, you do commit crimes.

"Your hacker culture," why do you think some of us perceive you as the enemy? All one has to do is to read and listen to the news: New viruses, worms, and Trojan horses, etc. So you can attack whatever website you are attacking. Why don't you simply admit to yourselves you are all a bunch of overgrown snot nosed idiots who simply do not know how to behave?

In fact, there is now a virus going around hitting every web page the innocent people visit. In addition to that, there is a "cell phone" virus. But I do not need to mention these things when you already are aware of what is lurking on the net, and they are probably being sent from your very own computer.

Why are you all set out to destroy modem conveniences? I haven't seen anything "fixed." But I have more or less seen it destroyed, except from the security side of it.

I am certain that most of your readers have more than one computer sitting in their place, constantly running, searching for whatever it is you are searching for—or should I say destroying. What else, that you're a male, single, loner, and don't have a life. That when you were a child, you were neglected somehow from society, and possibly abused.

Yes, you may be "elite" in this "culture" that you weasel around in. But in regular society you are a bunch of morons and losers. Why else would any one of you set out to destroy other people's property?

Why the imbalance, you say? Well, I believe I answered that. And I guess you are correct. It always does come back to ignorance. *It is a complete shame a large group of individuals who are as intelligent as yourselves go out to ruin so many things. So, yes, it does always come back to ignorance.*

I have read many of your magazines. I had become "more educated" in your so called hacker culture. I've come to a conclusion you all are very sick minded individuals who need strong medication, lots of therapy, and prison sentences.

I have not read anything in your magazine saying "Hey, I fixed this and got a job." It's more like, "When you do this... hehe."

So, Paranoia vs. Sanity. Well yes. Us un-elite persons know better. Lots better. That is why you don't see us going to prison. That is why you don't see us setting out to destroy anything.

If I were any one of you, I would look around your place and look at what you are doing with this so called "knowledge of computers." And answer me this: is it legal? And if you cannot honestly say yes, it has proved my point. It proves my point every time I read or hear anything of hackers doing wrong. Your culture is very deranged and in need of therapy while filling out your sentence in prison.

Don't forget, you'll slip. And when you fall, you are on your way to prison. The laws are getting stricter regarding what your so called culture is doing. That is when the Nation sits back and laughs at all you "elite" netizens.

So which is more elite? A law abiding citizen or the "elite" jerk hacker committing crime. It doesn't take a rocket scientist to figure out the answer.

STEVEN JACKSON
JOLIET, ILLINOIS

You really need to turn off the TV and take a little trip into reality. Anyone can send a virus or be destructive. It's even easier than spouting mistruths. Hackers are blamed because the simpletons in mass media refer to anyone doing anything they don't understand with a computer as a hacker. Most people see through this. Some don't.

If you were to take away this one major factual fiction, you would see all of your other points collapsing onto themselves. And then maybe you would be able to understand that aliases and anonymity are not in themselves a bad thing. Why are they even needed? Read your own letter to answer that one. You're not the only person intent on sending anyone they feel to be a threat straight to prison. With this kind of attitude out there, it's no wonder we see students being suspended for reading our magazine, employees being threatened with dismissal for having a copy at their desk, bookstore clerks making snide remarks to people who dare to support us, and all the other little things that serve to make people afraid.

Dear *2600:*

> *Your recent cover for 21:3 highly offends me. While I can't tell if the soldier is from the People's Liberation Army from Mao's era or a soldier of the Democratic People's Republic of Korea, seeing how their poster drawing style is very similar, nonetheless it is certainly meant to defame the accomplishments of Chinese and/or Korean socialism. I've always enjoyed reading 2600 Magazine and agreed with your fight against the DMCA. However, it seems like you have overstepped your boundaries of knowledge politically. This cover is an insult to progressive forces around the world. All that you know about the accomplishments of Chinese and Korean socialism is what you might see on NBC or CNN. You Liberals can hardly understand what "Totalitarianism" and "Dictatorship" really means, but that's besides the point. It is simply unfair to insult the history of an entire country which has struggled against U.S. and Japanese imperialism, provided free health care, housing, food, and education under capitalist encirclement and threat of capitalist restoration. As a Venezuelan citizen, a revolutionary participating in the Bolivarian Revolution, we recognize that solidarity is key to implementing our socialist reforms, reaching out to fraternal*

socialist states in the world system, and embracing the accomplish-
ments of Revolution wherever it is. I always read your magazine for
the technical information and depth of knowledge authors show, but
I am now dismayed at the overtly counterrevolutionary and insult-
ing image on the cover, which diminishes the struggle of millions to
overthrow bureaucrat-capitalism, Japanese imperialism, and establish
a socialist state.

Evan

This is how you build solidarity? By looking for things to get offended by? If we
want to insult "Chinese and/or Korean socialism," we'll do it in a much more direct
fashion. Until then, we suggest becoming acquainted with the concepts of parody
and anachronism. Incidentally, we're pleased as punch that after 20 years we've
finally been hit with the label of counterrevolutionary. We've pretty much been
accused of everything now.

2005

Dear *2600:*

I have been a long time fan of your magazine. However, I believe that
politics needs to be left out. I like to read and be informed of technical
issues and I know people from New York loathe Bush because, let's
face it, he is a Republican. New York is not known for their support of
Republicans and I understand you are pissed off that he won and need
to vent. But please do not do it in this magazine. I know you think it is
cute to put Bush on the cover and whatever but I cannot go anywhere
without hearing about politics. It is over and I suggest the people get
over it. Yes, I agree with rights, I am an anti-federalist, and I believe in
state rights. I do not believe Bush is a warmonger and I do not believe
that terrorists should be sent into a court like we should.

With that said, I agree that U.S. citizens should not be subjected
to random searches of their houses without their knowledge and
Americans should not be held without trial, lawyer, and so forth.
You have my support 100 percent on that. However, if we capture

terrorists or someone who we suspect is a terrorist (who is not an American), then I don't care if they don't have rights, because they don't! The Geneva Convention does not grant them this right at all. As far as torturing them, if it saves our troops' lives, go for it. We did not start this war and our soldiers should not die because we are too afraid to let them go without sleep because a bunch of left wing nut jobs are protesting them to regain their lost power.

I know most "hackers" are really left wing and are almost communist. Granted, I cannot group all of them in the same category since I believe my stance is right wing even though Bush is the first Republican president I have voted for. Making people aware of their rights is one thing, telling them they are losing them is OK, but to blame it on one man is a joke. It is both parties' fault that we have our rights degraded as far as they are now (Lincoln started this with the backing of a strong federal government). But it's even more the fault of the American people because they have let it slip this far. If you ever watch Jay Leno's jay-walking or Sean Hannity's man on the street quiz, the majority of people my age and younger (23) have no clue who the vice president is or what the amendments are. Let alone the Bill of Rights! I know I have turned this into a political rambling and I am sorry but I beg of you, please, no more. Talk about rights, talk about how they are being taken away, but be as partial as you can. I cannot take anymore "Left hates America, Right are fascists taking our rights away" propaganda.

RAGE1605

Nice job keeping politics out. Or did you mean for us to stop talking about these issues after you talked about them? First off, we discuss a lot of things and the space taken up by this kind of a topic has always been fairly minimal. Second, if it's something that's on people's minds, then why should we deny them the right to express themselves? Like anything else, hackers have interesting perspectives on these issues. Plus, it's generally a good thing to express yourself and expose yourself to other opinions.

Having been exposed to your opinions, we cannot react with silence. You believe it's acceptable to abduct people from foreign countries and torture them? We hope you realize that there are many people throughout the world who have the desire and would have the right to do the same to you under your own logic. If that's the world you want to live in, you're well on the way toward getting there. You say we didn't start this war? We invaded a country that never attacked us and had neither plans nor ability to do so. Regardless of what kind of society we manage to create over there, you can never escape that fact. You obviously have all kinds of problems with what you imagine to be the "left wing." But these issues are of concern for people of all political bents. Hackers come from all kinds of different political backgrounds and ideologies so please don't assume that they all believe the same thing. One thing that most would probably agree upon is that expressing something that's on your mind is a good thing. We're glad you took the opportunity and hope you understand why we'll continue to give others the chance.

Dear *2600:*

> On your website in the foreign payphone section, I am very shocked that you incorrectly put my country Taiwan as "Taiwan, province of China." I hope you would understand that such mistake hurts all Taiwanese. Taiwan is an independent country, not a province of any other country. Please correct that mistake immediately to show your respect for all Taiwanese. Otherwise we will take more actions to protest against such humiliation! Thank you!
>
> Hsiao-Ling Liao
Taiwan

OK, let's all calm down here a moment. We're not in any way responsible for how your country (see, we used the word) is officially designated. That's the name according to the United Nations and subsequently the ISO 3166-1 standard. Those are the people to threaten.

Dear *2600:*

> For some reason, I have been "uninvited" from my local 2600 group. This was rather surprising. I simply received an email asking that I no longer come to the meetings.
>
> Your meeting guidelines say that "nobody is excluded." I have attended other 2600 meetings without problems, as well as other technical

groups in the area. In fact, one IEEE group is even having me speak to them later this week.

Incidentally, the person who sent the email did not identify himself. It appears to have been sent from some anonymous account. Considering that my business cards were stolen the previous week, I really don't consider being "uninvited" to be any great loss.

CHRIS

And just why do you assume that this "uninvitation" carries any validity whatsoever? You correctly interpret our guidelines as meaning nobody can be kept away from the meetings, so why not apply them to the situation and realize that this anonymous person has absolutely no authority to enforce such a thing? By setting yourself apart from the group in this way, you're doing exactly what this person wants.

Dear *2600:*

I am very disappointed by your response to Hsiao-Ling Liao (22:2). What happened to your rhetoric? "...we have a history of not blindly accepting what we're told" (page 5, line 12, 20:4) Do you believe that ISO 3166-1 has "Taiwan, province of China" for scientific reasons? I can assure you that it is from political pressure from the Chinese government. Isn't it ironic that we hackers use extra effort to filter what the U.S. government tells us, but take in what the government of China says without thinking?

Yes, we Taiwanese, fighting against China imperialism (they claim to be socialism but behave more like imperialism), understand that ISO 3166-1 is the source of misinformation and we are fighting on that front, too. Taiwan is not so stupid as to call itself a province of another country.

You are fully responsible for the content on your website, even though you are not exactly responsible for how Taiwan is officially designated. I checked it just now (http://www.2600.com/phones/newindex .khtml?region=asia) and you are still using that insulting suffix despite your lip service in 22:2.

Label Taiwan as "Taiwan." Do not act like the coward Google: they removed the insulting suffix when facing massive protest from Taiwanese netizens but reverted after pressure from the Chinese government who threatened to block Google from the search engine market in China. Sadly, Google is not the only one. Many U.S. corporations do the same when facing threats from China.

Keep up the good work and use your independent thinking—not only independent from the U.S. government, but from other governments as well!

(Google has changed their map.google.com *and removed the offending suffix when searching for "Taiwan," so I will no longer call them coward.)*

Tim Taiwanese Liim
New Jersey

We all knew it was inevitable that 2600 would wind up in the middle of this conflict. But let's get a few things straight from the outset. We are not referring to Taiwan as "Taiwan, province of China." We are merely accessing an official list of countries and that list happens to be worded in this manner. The mere fact that Taiwan is represented at all on the list has annoyed mainland China, so it's a bit of a two-edged sword. It would solve nothing if we went in and changed our copy of the list and it would open us up to having to change all of the other names that people have a problem with. Then there would be people who have a problem with us changing the list. We would then become mired in the world of international conflict where we wouldn't stand a chance of addressing those issues that really matter to us—like fixing the definition of the word "hacker." The solution to the Taiwan issue is to fix the list and if voicing opposition in this forum helps achieve that end, then we're happy to be of service.

There are those in Taiwan, incidentally, who believe that mainland China will eventually be reunited under the Taiwanese flag. They consider all of the provinces of mainland China to belong to the Taiwanese regime. That, coupled with the fact that Taiwan calls itself the Republic of China, gives a much more positive spin to the whole "province of China" moniker. It all depends on how you define China. But seriously, the one sure way to solve this problem is, rather than start a fight with us, to declare independence from the mainland. It may take a civil war and several million lives but ISO 3166-1 will be changed.

2006 ⎯⎯⎯⎯⎯⎯⎯⎯⎯⎯⎯⎯⎯⎯⎯⎯⎯

Dear *2600:*

> *I subscribe to a computer security forum and have met a person who knew Kevin "back in the day." And I have recently learned a little more about "poor, misunderstood" Kevin Mitnick. Did you know:*

a) *That he'd been arrested as a juvenile? And that by continuing to engage in the kind of behavior that had gotten him arrested as a juvenile got into trouble (again) with the law?*

b) *That he and/or his friends did in fact change the class of service on home phones to payphones? So that whenever they picked up the receiver a recorded voice asked them to deposit twenty cents?*

c) *That he and his friends redirected operator assistance calls, answering them themselves?*

d) *That in 1981 he physically broke into a Pac-Bell office stealing a list of Bell's COSMOS accounts? For which he got three months in juvenile hall?*

e) *That they also did a lot of dumpster diving, etc.? Not a lot of hacking, but social engineering and theft?*

f) *That in the '90s when he was on the run he sold home addresses etc. of the agents who chased him, posted a few stories about how they were convicted child molesters, and other "non-malicious" acts? Did you also know that he was placed into "solitary confinement" not for what "the powers that be" were afraid that he would/could do, but rather for his protection as the other "older" cons would not have looked too favorably on him and would have probably killed him? And that like the LOD (which I got the impression that he was a member of) are/were racists? And that the blacks would have likely wanted to kill him as well?*

> *I'm sorry, but that hardly sounds like someone who is a "scapegoat/ whipping boy" for "the powers that be." And it sounds more like he got exactly what he deserved.*

> *I'm not saying that exploration and learning are wrong or anything. Just that there are some systems that should not under any circumstance be entered by those who do not have the legal right to access those systems.*

And I am sorry if you cannot understand that, or that breaking into a computer that one does not have the legal right to access should carry the same criminal penalty as if they physically broke into someone's home or office.

Also, if you'd stop and think about it, you'd realize that every time someone breaks into a computer system/network that they do not have the legal right to access that they undermine/chip away at the trust that the legitimate users have/had in that system, as well as cast doubt on the integrity of their data and/or any experiments that they may be running at the time of the break-in. I remind you again of the cybercriminal that Clifford Stoll was tracking who was breaking into "his" computer system—a person who was indiscriminately shutting down any and all processes that looked as if they might have been "spying" on him.

So for all the comments on how hacking is different and not like "real" crime, at the end of the day it would appear that Kevin Mitnick was just another thief and con man. If you don't believe it, ask him to have his juvenile record. I'm betting as is my friend that he won't do so because he knows that it'll speak volumes about the type of person he is/was.

DIGIAL _ COWBOY

It's really rather funny that we're still running into this kind of attitude so many years later. And also pretty sad when you consider that this is the mentality of a lot of people who can control the fate of those in trouble. Let's be clear. Even if someone were to do all of the things you mentioned above, it absolutely would not justify the kind of treatment Mitnick received. There is a rather barbaric attitude in our country that justifies everything from torture to lengthy prison stays simply because someone "broke the law." Here's a newsflash: everyone breaks laws in some way. Much of it is very minor but if we follow the simpletons, every transgression defines us as criminals. And nobody cares what happens to criminals, right?

Now, as to this specific case, you quote a lot of "facts" without any kind of documentation other than meeting someone online who claims to have known Mitnick back in the day. Did you really think that would somehow be enough to sway anyone? You heard what you wanted to hear but there's simply no substance here. And that seems to have been the theme of the prosecution throughout the history of this case. We're not going to get into the whole house analogy thing yet again except to say that accessing a computer without authorization just isn't the same thing as breaking into someone's house. But if it were, as you seem to think it should be, then the penalty should logically be the same. If someone is "just another thief and con man," then why treat them as if they were a true criminal mastermind? You simply can't have it both ways.

Thanks for the entertaining allegations. They provided us with much amusement. And, for the record, that glaring typo in your name didn't come from us.

Dear *2600:*

> *I'm a fairly new subscriber to your glorious magazine and I've loved every issue. One thing I've noticed though is that every time I receive a new magazine in the mail it looks like someone has opened/torn the envelope and then taped it back up. Seems a little suspicious to me. I mean, it has happened to every single issue! Am I on a watch list now? If so, cool—I'm finally on a watch list. Or is it because the children in your basement are too shaky and malnourished to correctly stuff envelopes without mutilating them? If so, give 'em a freaking Happy Meal so I don't have to feel so paranoid.*
>
> C

The children would have no reason to reopen the envelopes after sealing them. And the penalties for this have been made extremely clear to them. What we suspect is happening in your case is that someone in your post office is overly curious and can't contain themselves. As there is no specific information about you inside the envelope, the various people keeping you on a watch list would have no reason to open it. With regard to them, we suggest you turn your attention to the van across the street.

2007

Dear *2600:*

> First, let me get my nose brown here by saying your magazine is excellent.
>
> Now that that's out of the way, I'm a 44-year-old male who did phreak back in the 1980s (using 950 numbers to call long distance BBSes) so I'm not squeaky clean here, but that was a youthful digression.
>
> Having said that, I feel you are hypocrites. I'll explain: You say that hacking (or using vulnerabilities) in the system shouldn't be for gain. But in 23:2, you printed a letter from Zenmaster who wanted to know how to "hack into 'Fastpass' machines" at Disney World. Yet, two pages before, you had a letter from Jeff who was replying to an earlier letter to Jack whose father wouldn't let him subscribe to 2600 because of the word "hacking." Jeff said to let Jack's father read the magazine. If I was Jack's father and saw the letter from Zenmaster, that would reinforce my beliefs about hacking, thereby perpetuating the myth about hackers being bad people. There are a lot of closed minds out there. We need to open them, not add dead bolts.
>
> Computer Bandit

You generally don't open closed minds by keeping your mouth shut. And it would be wrong for us to restrict knowledge and tell people not to ask certain questions because there was no seemingly legitimate reason for asking. As far as we're concerned, there is always a legitimate reason: curiosity. And while we're not kidding ourselves into believing that there aren't lots of people with ulterior motives who could also benefit from such knowledge, if we help others learn how things work, we're doing what we set out to do. Some parents get that. Many, sadly, don't. But we can't change who we are in order to appeal to people who don't like who we are. There's too much of that in our culture already.

Dear *2600:*

> This is just a friendly reminder to please print the full portion of people's letters to you. An editor's job is to edit, not to slice people's letters in half.

> I could be selfish and just ask that you extend me this favor for my
> own letters, however I must speak up for everyone else who I know has
> written you letters which you decided are unworthy to print.
>
> Censorship sucks, and yes, 2600 has even censored. Please stop, or at
> least separate your mail into "moderated" and "unmoderated."
>
> ANONYMOUS

*Perhaps you're unfamiliar with how magazines operate. Let us enlighten you. Editors
edit things. That means trimming extraneous bits, cutting repetitive or irrelevant
sections, fixing grammar and spelling, and otherwise making the submission fit
for printing—assuming it's even selected for printing at all. And all of this is at the
hands of an editor.*

*The "moderated" and "unmoderated" divisions you wish for can be found on
something called Usenet, as well as countless blogs and forums throughout the
Internet. That's not what we are and it never will be.*

*And as for the censorship allegation, please. If you were forbidden from expressing
certain opinions by a government, that would be censorship. If a magazine doesn't
print your letter, that's their decision and their right. You are still free to express
yourself on your own.*

2008

Dear *2600:*

> I am a Sergeant currently supporting the National Security Agency
> and I thought I'd let you know: Big Brother is watching you. Also, we
> think you guys look like dorks!
>
> Hooah.
>
> DAVE

Nothing like establishing an intelligent dialogue with intelligence forces.

Dear *2600:*

> *The article entitled "Pirates on the Internet" was absolutely terrible. Did anyone bother to proofread it? Running it through spell check doesn't count.*
>
> *The information presented was inaccurate and incomplete. About a quarter of a page was devoted to a rant about a message board that used to be good. I could list specifics, but it hurts my eyes to read the article again. I actually passed the article around to my coworkers because it was so terrible. I understand that you may have felt the need to fill some more space in the magazine, but a blank page would have been better and left your reputation in a better condition. I would gladly rewrite this article with more useful information for the next issue, however, it doesn't seem like the right article for the magazine.*
>
> *Keep in mind, I used to love reading 2600 about ten years ago and would like to see it get back to what it was back then—informative and useful hacks.*
>
> DAVID BARRIOS

We love getting criticism and letters that point out when we've done something bad or stupid. But this little diatribe doesn't qualify. Here's why. You don't ever get to the point of why the article was bad. You pull the old trick of conjuring up phantom people who all agree with your assessment, thereby justifying it without producing anything of substance. You decline to list any specifics because "it hurts my eyes to read the article again"? Please. If it had so much of an effect on you that you felt compelled to write this letter, surely you can remember more about it than a little rant about a board which took far less space than you claim. Finally, the proverbial dig at us for "the need to fill some more space in the magazine." If we had that need, why would we have added additional pages in the last year? We know that nobody is going to like every article that gets printed here. But just because you come across something that differs with your perspective, there's no reason to conclude that we've become desperate for material and will print anything. The only thing those kinds of accusations do is piss us off and detract from the point of your letter, which in this case never was made in the first place.

We appreciate anyone who truly does want to help out and make the magazine better. But simply bemoaning the fact that things aren't as good as they used to be isn't constructive. We've been hearing that critique since our second issue.

Dear *2600:*

> *Who pays for these? Seriously, do you actually make money off your quarterlies? I just sit in Barnes and Noble and read them there. That's just me.*

> ANDREW
> SENT FROM MY iPHONE

While that's your right, we're fortunate that not everyone does that. If they did, then we wouldn't be around for very long. Unlike other magazines, we rely solely on our readers to keep us going. Other publications simply rely on advertisements. They can actually not sell a single issue and still convince their advertisers that people are being exposed to the ads, perhaps in scenarios such as yours. We don't have that luxury, nor do we want it. You're obviously reading us for a reason so we hope you'll see the connection between supporting us and having the material continue to flow.

2009

Dear *2600:*

> *Recently, a couple of contributing editors from 2600 the magazine have been hacking my computer. I don't like it. I already have proof that one member has already hacked my computer. If people from your magazine continue to illegally hack my computer, I'll call the police. Please remove whatever backdoor your members have put on my computer.*

> *I have hard evidence that I was hacked. I won't say who did it because I need this evidence for a courtroom so I can have an advantage as the prosecutor.*

> ANONYMOUS

We think involving the cops is the best course of action at this point. We have an unmanageable staff and this is really the only way to get through to them. When the officers arrive, we'll be sure to have all of our staffpeople help them figure out what's really going on.

Best of luck in your career as a prosecutor.

Dear *2600:*

> *I don't think it's a writer of the magazine anymore that hacked me... however, the person is a member of 2600 in some way. I'd really prefer to avoid the police or a confrontation in that way. I did a whois on the domain and couldn't get an abuse email so I sent it here. It's that someone is hacking me and opening many windows on my machine and I want it to stop. They found out I had Knoppix on my computer....*
>
> ANONYMOUS (AGAIN)

No, it's OK really. Sometimes a head-on confrontation is the only way to deal with such matters. These people need to be taught a lesson, after all. Leaving windows open on a machine is an invitation to burglary and there's nothing funny about that. So we'll await the authorities and then lead them to the "member of 2600" that is making your life so miserable. Considering we don't actually have members, it shouldn't take long at all to get this resolved.

Dear *2600:*

> *I was reading my recent copy of 2600 and I noticed the article about hacking your hospital bed. I took a deep breath and thought "OK, just learn to try something new, it might be worth it." Before I got past the first paragraph, I wound up banging my head on the wall so hard I started to draw blood and fainted. Wouldn't you know it, I wound up in the exact same hospital bed that was in the article. I was wondering if you could re-send me a copy of 2600 so I could learn how to hack this thing.*
>
> *Actually, that was sarcasm. The real reason I write this letter is to tell you to stop whining about the media's portrayal of hackers being an unknown widespread group of powerful rogue users able to globally bring down communications, banking, warfare, and governmental agencies just with a simple double-click. If they found out that you are a bunch of nerds writing articles about hacking hospital beds and heating control panels, well, it probably would not be good.*
>
> ERIK S.

With your powers of sarcasm on our side, we have nothing to fear.

Dear *2600:*

> The reason I'm writing this letter is because what was once a well renowned hacker organization, an organization once respected and even feared, is now, to many in the black hat and security world, a joke. I'm writing this not to offend or "hate on" 2600. I am writing a truth. A reason and a need to truly change.

> I'm a person who lives in silence. A person who watches. For the past year I have held back from buying a 2600 magazine. Walking through Borders last week, I had to give in to my temptation and purchase the magazine. When buying a magazine, always use precaution. Call me paranoid, but my own situation is not one to be trifled with. To tell you the truth, writing this letter is taking a risk on my part. I'm too close to joining Club Fed. Anyway, the risk is nothing for what I'm about to share with you. This message, this distress call, is to all who read this.

> Upon reading the 2600 winter edition, I grew excited just holding it in my hands. It smelled fresh from the printers. The ink gave a new shine and the paper felt brand new. When I started to read the first pages, I always try to comprehend the way others think when describing their point of view of the world. Their perspective. "Finally!" I said to myself. "The information!"

> There was something different this time. Something odd. I found myself already knowing the information. As I kept reading, I became humored with the objectives of hacking; what they were hacking. "Hacking Beer" and "Hacking Thy Self"? I had a good laugh for a moment. Then I realized something. This isn't the same 2600 I once knew. Like pages gathered in a book, I realized what the black hat hackers and the respected security professionals told me was slowly becoming truth. 2600 is not the respected and feared organization anymore. There was a time when, upon mentioning 2600, curious people asked what it was. Now, when talking about 2600, there is always a chuckle at the end of the sentence. Reading the magazine disappointed me. Not much for me to glean from.

> Who I am? What gives me a right to say such things? I will educate you a bit of who I am so much so as not to overeducate you to the point of exploitation. I know what a real 2600 magazine looks like. I know

what a real 2600 meeting is. I attended 2600 meetings at their source, New York City. First time attending the meetings, I knew I found a place that flowed with never-ending fountains of information. I met friends that till this day I trust my life with. The attendance at the meetings easily made 50 to 90 people. I remembered being invited to dumpster diving, after hacker parties, and late night hacks. This place was Hackerdom to me.

Of course, I moved and could not attend my 2600 meetings. The day came when I returned to visit my oasis. I found something I did not expect: solitude. Ten people attended, maybe less. What happened? What happened to the hacker haven everyone in the world runs to? The 2600 meetings were a place where I, and many others, found their niche in life. It was our home. Today, 2600 is barren. Not taken seriously by the electronic community, not taken serious by its own attendees. "Why?" I kept asking myself. "Why is 2600 so deserted?" My answer is they tore each other apart. Their own drama. Their own cliques.

Today, I'm a respected black hat hacker. I find myself setting up servers with three operating systems, creating electronic devices from scratch. I understand technology and programming fully now. All this wouldn't have been possible without 2600. If it weren't for my friends that I had met at 2600, I wouldn't be here among the living. No, we wouldn't be a lot of things if it weren't for 2600. That is why today I write this letter to the readers of 2600. I am writing to you, a loyal hacker to 2600, to make a change. 2600 isn't what it once was. This organization helped me beyond what I deserved. This organization changed my life.

Attending HOPE was an eye-opener. I accomplished my goal to attend and I accomplished my goal to learn more about computers and systems before attending HOPE. I enjoyed the information, but still it wasn't enough to satisfy me. Hacking is an art. It's a gift. It's to be enjoyed and taken seriously. I relate hacking to fire. It's a gift to possess fire, it's a gift to know how to wield it, and fire is even to be enjoyed. Fire also needs to be taken seriously. Hacking needs to be taken seriously. We need to take it seriously. Too many people call 2600 and HOPE conventions a group of script kiddies, cyberpunks, and n00bs. If you didn't notice, Wired made its own joke of 2600 in the April

2008 edition (page 42), saying: "2600 has gotten too commercial."
Yes, I know there will always be such comments and jokes, but what
are we doing about it?

ANONYMOUS

First off, there's no reason for all the cloak and dagger techniques to keep your identity from us. We can take (and we welcome) criticism such as this.

What we find more often than not is that the real change takes place in people who read the magazine. People turn from rebellious kids to people with jobs and then to parents of their own rebellious kids. Readers gain more technical knowledge as they grow. All of this changes perspectives. What seemed totally amazing to you five years ago is nothing new today. However, for someone else just coming into the scene today, this kind of knowledge is just as exciting. And their fresh perspective of it is what makes more of the magic happen, something the rest of us may have forgotten. Our first letter accusing us of losing our way came in 1985, one year after we started. We've heard that the hacker world isn't what it used to be since well before then. This is nothing new, not in this community nor any other.

Things have certainly changed on every level imaginable. What used to be the domain of relatively few people has turned into the playground for millions. Yes, millions. It freaks us out too. The very nature of what we talk about here is a deep connection to the kind of change that makes the technology we used a decade ago an antique today. There is so much more to play with now than there was in the past and it's no longer essential for hackers to break the rules just to get access. So all of that changes the dynamic without a doubt. But does it change our spirit? That spirit of inquisitiveness, rebellion, and creativity, all wrapped up in openness—that is what defines the hacker world for us. One sure way to lose touch with this would be to close the door on the inexperienced and get caught up in a world of jargon and name dropping as we make more and more connections. This is the path that lots of people go down because it's a progression from one part of life to another. As a magazine, though, we have to keep our focus on our unique type of audience. It's possible to remain a part of this audience while also changing who you are. But it's also possible for interests to change. It's all a part of life.

We would love for our readers to always be with us. But we know that isn't always possible. A more realistic hope is that whatever period of time people do spend with us is remembered as constructive and perhaps even formative.

We do need to set you straight on a couple of things. We don't know what meeting you attended in New York City that had less than ten people but we can tell you it most certainly wasn't one of ours. We also don't recall ever having as many as 90 people show up. You seem to be exaggerating on both ends to suit your disenchantment. The people you once knew are likely not there as they've moved on to other things. But the people who are there now are every bit as enthusiastic about what they're into—again, maybe things you're not interested in. Similarly, our conferences are anything but "script kiddies, cyberpunks, and n00bs." The diversity in our attendees and speakers is nothing short of staggering, as is the range of technical and non-technical knowledge. The conferences bring these people from different backgrounds together and this is one of the achievements we didn't have in our early years. Finally, we're supposed to be upset that Wired *thinks we're too commercial? We can only assume that was an exercise in sarcasm.*

We appreciate your writing and believe it's good to always do some self-examination. We exist as a voice for many parts of the hacker community and, as such, the potential is always there for people to change the focus and steer the discussion— just by speaking up.

Behind the Walls

The group of people that surprised us the most, both with their numbers and their contributions, were prisoners.

When you think about it, there really shouldn't be *that* much of a shock. After all, what is there to do when you're in confinement but to try and use your brain as much as possible? I guess what got to me the most was realizing how hard these people were willing to work to stay sane and not fade into the background.

The hacker mindset is an amazing thing in and of itself. You put that in a place like prison and fascinating interactions start to occur. First off, they're two diametrically opposed forces: the pinnacle of conformity and rule-following matched with a curious, observant, and rebellious individual. To say that this created problems would be a vast understatement.

We devoted many pages of the magazine to the prisoners most of us have heard of: Kevin Mitnick, Phiber Optik, Bernie S. These were icons in the hacker world, and their tales of injustice infuriated and motivated so many of us. But there were a vast number of others, some imprisoned because of their hacker activities, some for completely different reasons. The common thread that links *all* of these people held behind bars is the fact that they never gave up their unique perspective and humanity, despite so much pressure to do so by the powerful entities in charge. In accomplishing this, they managed to inspire those of us lucky enough to avoid such a fate.

Getting *2600* into all of the prisons, halfway houses, and other places of detention was always a challenge. We tried to find humor in the cluelessness that we encountered along the way from authorities who had no idea what this little magazine was all about or why it was so sought after by the inmates. There was also a bit of a Catch-22 involved in talking about this process in the letters page, as that discourse would often lead to the publication getting banned for being a threat to the continued order of the institution involved. Some people had their collection of magazines confiscated, some wound up facing severe discipline for daring to read such material, and others managed to actually open some minds inside the system. No matter the outcome, those on the inside with the hacker mindset never stopped writing to us and sharing their experiences. It would be impossible to gauge how much we learned from them, but it's irrefutable that we could never have heard of their experiences from any other source.

There's a real frustration involved in seeing so much mail of this sort coming in. Unlike the vast majority of our current letter submissions, all mail from prisons is analog, either in the form of a typewritten page or a handwritten letter. For most of us, attempting either of these would be a real challenge. So right away, it's somewhat sad seeing communications from people who seem to be so detached from the rest of us. That's merely an illusion, though, as oftentimes the thoughts and theories presented in their mail is more cogent than any other we receive. There's also a surprising lack of bitterness in their communications and nothing short of pure joy in simply being acknowledged or included in some way. The frustration, then, is that of not being able to do more and of seeing so many worthy cases fall by the wayside because there simply wasn't enough time to follow up on all of them. I know there's little more we could have done, and I only hope what we did do managed to make some difference.

You'll find in this section that most of the people here were trying to figure out ways around various systems. We felt it was important to foster such curiosity because it kept their brains working and also was a potential victory for an individual against the most oppressive of environments. So we felt no guilt if we managed to help defeat a phone system that was charging an unforgivable amount to a prisoner's family whenever they called collect. The phone companies did this because they could, and they knew nobody of note would speak up for these people. *That* was the real crime. I think by giving a voice to this issue, we helped get word out to the mainstream about these injustices and eventually helped push for changes in a horribly unfair system. The sad fact is that most of us write these people off because we simplistically condemn all criminals as not deserving of any consideration. That opinion tends to change rather quickly when you realize how easily fate could land you in a very similar situation.

These are letters from people who were imprisoned for everything from hacking a web page to committing murder. In the eyes of society, they were all just condemned people to be swept under the rug. Here, they have a voice and a lot of interesting things to say.

In this collection, we haven't printed any of their addresses (as we do in the magazine) because these change over the years. Also, many of these letter writers have since been released — some to successful careers, others, regrettably, to a repeat engagement in the slammer.

If there's anything that we at the magazine learned from these correspondences, it's that communication is truly the key. In current issues, we continue to print such letters along with the addresses where the writers can be reached — and many of our readers send them news from the outside world. This is quite literally a lifeline, and oftentimes this contact makes all the difference. I hope our non-imprisoned readers continue to realize this and help those on the inside hold onto some sanity, either through personal letters or by writing articles for *2600* that help to feed their brains.

As one of our more prolific contributors from prison said, "Our only access to technology is by what we read through the mail." That was from a hacker known as Stormbringer, as said in one of his many incredibly detailed letters on technology — technology that he's often never even seen in person. There are so many others, including some high-profile cases that you may have read about in the papers, and kids who wound up in "juvy" for one offense or another.

Each of the letters contained here focuses on some aspect of the prison experience — nearly all of them were sent to us directly from an institution. The prison culture is far more prevalent than most of us know, and this is but a small sampling from a few very unique spirits.

1984

Dear *2600:*

> I'm working on a book that gives the hackers' viewpoint and explains why he/she penetrates computer systems. I believe that even though I'm currently incarcerated, I could get a publisher to publish such a book.

> To get this viewpoint, I need help. I need the input of people who are active — the more the better. I also need the views of people who trash systems, too. All I've ever seen is the viewpoint of the law enforcement agencies, media, business, and hackers that are caught, etc., etc., etc. It's time your views were heard.

> What I would do is just edit letters, etc. sent to me and use these as the basis for the book. By edit, I mean pick the ones to be used in their entirety.

People interested in helping me with this can write to me under handles or pen names. Do not use your real name or address as my mail is censored by officials here.

JOHN GREGG
MARION, IL

1987

Dear *2600:*

Got a couple of newspaper clippings for you. What I'd like to know is how the county jail inmates got hold of all those long-distance codes. I just can't picture an Apple II with autodial modem attacking a dial-up node from a jail cell.

THE HOODED CLAW

They didn't need one. All they need is human contact with the outside world. Guards can prevent visitors from bringing in knives and guns, but so far they've been unable to keep people from reciting numbers. Someone could also easily set up a voice mailbox to read out this month's Sprint codes. All an inmate has to do is call that number and write down the codes. But isn't it true that all calls from a prison have to be collect? That's no problem — simply make the first part of the voice message say "Sure, I'll accept" or something similar.

1989

Dear *2600:*

In the Spring '89 edition, I read your article on "How Payphones Really Work" and enjoyed it immensely. I thought that it was a very accurate and informative piece. Continue the excellent work.

Now that I have given your ego a boost, I will ask for a favor. Could you please include in one of the next articles a piece on "collect only

phones" as I am incarcerated at the present time and all that is avail-
able to use from this crowbar hotel are those damnable gadgets. They
are the most exasperating items ever invented; you are unable to call
800 numbers or to bill to a third party or even be able to use a tele-
phone credit card with them. The party you are calling must pay the
exorbitant prices which they charge for collect calls, and who the hell
wants to try to persuade individuals to accept collect calls? There has
to be a way around these mechanized monsters, and any info that you
could possibly print about them would be greatly appreciated.

INCARCERATED

It's hard to experiment with something without having access to it. That's why people
who find themselves locked up with these hell-phones have to try everything possible.
It is entirely possible there are no holes, considering what the purpose of these
phones is. In that case, there are still options. For instance, just suppose you called
a voicemail system or an answering machine that answers the phone with the
message: "Hello? (pause) Why of course I'll accept charges." If you're lucky enough
to gain access to a voicemail system that allows you to dial out, you'll be able to
make phone calls (and rack up two bills at the same time). Unless your DTMF pad
gets cut off after a connection is made, in which case you'll need a white box (por-
table DTMF generator) to hold up to the mouthpiece. And that's probably illegal to
possess in prison. Readers, any ways out?

1990

Dear *2600:*

As far as phreaking from inside prison, it can be done but only on
non-AT&T phones. We have collect-only here, but I got around them
as follows. Ours has a recording that asks you your name. When the
party you are calling answers, it plays the recording and tells you to
press three to accept the call. To start with, I dialed a number to a
recorded message like the one at our helpful AT&T office (ha). The
recording triggers the phone to accept the call. You don't state your
name when asked, but bypass it by pressing a number on the keypad

until the call is placed. As the call is accepted, you'll hear the recording say "Thank you for using XXX." As soon as you hear the click that kicks in the recording, you press the receiver level down for about 30 to 50 milliseconds to hang up the switching network. You'll hear the unrestricted dial tone under the finish of the "thank you" message. You quickly hit the 0 once for local and twice for long distance. When talking to either operator, you simply ask to be connected to a particular number because your call is not going through. Keep it simple to avoid suspicion.

C. REBEL

We left out your location because we assume you want to continue using this.

1992

Dear *2600:*

Many greetings from the gulag. In recent months, I've noticed more and more letters and such from imprisoned hackers. Another prisoner and I edit and publish a monthly newsletter called Prisoners' Legal News.

Apart from organizing against the state parole board, we have been lobbying hard for the state to allow prisoners to have PCs in their cells. For three years, prisoners at a state prison had PCs in their cells. All PC owners who got released have gotten jobs and none have returned to prison. There were no security or other problems but, in an arbitrary decision, prison officials made prisoners send the PCs out.

PAUL WRIGHT
WASHINGTON

What you witnessed was the typical panic reaction that authority figures have shown toward technology. Their ignorance frightens them and annoys the rest of us. We wish you luck and hope you keep us updated.

1993

Dear *2600:*

> *I have an unusual question about my phone system. I'm one of your few subscribers who is currently held in prison (I hope), and the phones I have access to seem to be restricted lines, allowing only collect calls. I have been unsuccessful in placing toll-free calls (1-800) or getting another carrier (10288).*

> *Since there are many phones in this same institution, I assume they are all a part of a PBX or similar system. My question is this: how can I determine what system they are using, and once I do, what sort of vulnerabilities do you think it might have? I estimate about 50 of these collect-only phones in the institution. Some have numbers, but they don't accept calls.*

> *Do you have any info on typical prison systems, or what one can do on a "restricted line" that only allows collect calls?*

> M

Our Winter 1992-93 issue had some info on prison phones. It's not likely that your system is part of a PBX because phone companies have a class of service for prison phones. That is, while there may be a PBX in the prison, it's not typical for payphones to be hooked into them. It would be nice, but it's not very probable.

1994

Dear *2600:*

> *I know some ingenious person has the answer to these problems:*

1. *Our phones in the prison system here in Michigan are quite weird. They are payphone-like in appearance but have no change slot or information printed on the outside of the metal housing. In effect, they are those crippled calling-card-only types that you see in the airport. The problem is that they are connected to some weird pulse system that MCI is running just for our incarcerated friends. The system does not require you*

to dial a zero before your number but an automatic computer generated voice comes on and asks whether you'd like your collect call to be person to person or a plain old garden variety one. It then prompts for your name and tells you to wait while it connects. It then asks the person who picks up the phone on the other end if he or she will accept a collect call from (inserts your recorded voice) and if the answering person pushes 1 in tone mode, you get connected. If you listen carefully after you've given your name, you can hear other people's pulse numbers as they dial their family or whomever. Is it possible that this system is some combination of tone and pulse generated switching? When they first installed this system I found that all I had to do was cover the mouthpiece when it asked me for my name. It would stall for a few seconds and then put me through to the correct party, but not as a collect call! For some reason, doing this allowed you to call anywhere in the world free of charge, but not the 313 area code where the prison is located. They've since updated the system so that this little trick won't work.

2. The county jail's phone system is a little different. I'm going to go down there in a little while so I'm hoping someone can figure this out for me. The jail's phones are regular payphones that accept money but don't allow you to use your calling card. I haven't tried dialing 10288 for an AT&T operator, but I do know that trying to get an operator the old-fashioned way (0) won't work. You also can't call outside the 313 area code. Weird, huh? Any ideas, people?

WOG

The phone system uses pulse dialing to get to the MCI automated operator. Perhaps some paranoid prison official thought inmates could hit touch tones and accept their own collect calls, so they disabled the touch tones. In any event, the pulse system has got nothing to do with MCI — it's simply how your call gets placed by the local company. There are an almost unlimited number of possibilities with your county system — 800s, 950s, carrier access codes, collect calls, green box tones from the called party, maybe even black boxes if you're in a primitive area. If you do manage to get an operator, the trick is to make sure she doesn't see the class of service, which is undoubtedly showing up as a prison phone. It's not easy and it's different in every area.

Dear *2600:*

> *I was at one point an avid reader but now I am in prison for about $753,000 in computer-related theft. I just wanted to ask if there's anyone out there who would accept payment in the form of a money order or (preferably) stamps for single sheet printed (readable laser or equal preferred) for some of the Internet or hacker-related conferences, just one or two. Twenty-five to 40 pages at a time would be about the max. I'm willing to cover postage, paper, and toner costs and would be eternally pleased. I am in need of some food for the gray matter, that's a definite. Please, no sample books, magazines, or anything that could be "considered" of that nature because it will get refused without a permit which are all currently used on my part.*

> ES
> LANCASTER CORRECTIONAL
> TRENTON, FL

1995

Dear *2600:*

> *I have been in federal prison for twenty months since I was arrested by the Secret Service for placing a phony ATM in a Connecticut shopping mall. Actually, the ATM was real — I just forgot to connect it to a bank — the Secret Service has no sense of humor.*

> *I never knew your magazine was available before coming to jail. Maybe it was for the best — I probably would have gotten myself in more trouble. You have great articles. It takes me back to my high school and college days 15 years ago when I lived to hack the DEC-10 and DEC-20.*

> *As you have stated in several articles, the Bureau of Prisons (BOP) are major jerks. They do everything they can to keep me from your publication. I finally had a friend photocopy some old issues and staple a few pages of religious material on top and send the disguised copies in. This seems to get past the mail room hacks every time.*

A word of advice to your readers: If you ever come face to face with the Secret Service, keep your mouth shut. Nothing you say will help you. They feed on intimidation and threats and can make an arrest a horror scene. They will then try the smooth and friendly approach to get what they want. They will promise you the world if you will just cooperate before it is too late. (It will not be too late — no matter what they say.) They will start with only wanting your help with your software or your little tricks of the trade. Don't do it! They lie! Someone will always have a superior who will overrule them when they are done with you. The government will screw you over. *Keep your mouth shut and never, never say anything without a lawyer.*

The Secret Service promised everything they could to get all the copies of my ATM software, along with the message protocols and technical manuals on the ATMs. They didn't want that crap on the streets. When they thought they had everything they wanted, the U.S. Attorney's Office proceeded with the screwing over and their lies came out. Don't trust — don't believe. *You'll regret it — I do.*

ATM Bandit

This is a valuable lesson a lot of people have learned and one that even more will still have to experience. Many of us read about your ATM "hack" in the papers — while the idea was quite clever, setting it up and taking people's money was pure theft. Not bowing to this kind of temptation is one of the hardest challenges hackers face.

1996

Dear *2600:*

My handle is Alphabits and I've been in the H/P scene for over nine years. I'm currently in federal custody in New Jersey waiting to go to trial for cellular phone fraud, mainly "trafficking in counterfeit access devices" in violation of title 18, section 1029(a)(2) of the U.S. code. In September of 1995, I was indicted by the U.S. government, and then shortly thereafter I was arrested by Secret Service agents on a freeway in southern California. I was one of the key figures busted in the "Celco 51" incident. The U.S. Secret Service, Cellular One, and an informant operated an H/P BBS in New Jersey for about two years. To my knowledge, there were a total of 15 other people arrested across the country during September. Since Cellular One was a key partner in the operation, they were mainly targeting cellular fraud. On September 3rd, I was extradited from Los Angeles to New Jersey to stand trial. During my two-week journey, I was incarcerated with a few hackers including Agent Steal and Kevin Mitnick. Although I cannot talk specifically about my case now, I can say it is amazing how small the government's knowledge is regarding computers and hacking. One example is that on one of the computers they found a text file of FTP sites. They are trying to figure a loss value of $500 per site, $73,000 for the file. Excuse me, loss value of what? Did ftp.cso. uiuc.edu (exec-pc) lose money somehow? In any case, hopefully I will be free sometime around January of 1997.

I'm currently being held in a 100+-year-old jail (similar to Alcatraz), which is a total intellectual wasteland. I would appreciate it if you could post my address or forward it to someone who could. Any letters, printouts, etc. would be greatly appreciated!

JEREMY G. CUSHING #63366
UNION COUNTY JAIL
ELIZABETH, NJ 07207

We wish you luck and encourage people to send mail because prison can be a very lonely and mentally crippling environment. While we don't know particulars about your specific case, we do know that many questions are being raised about the Celco 51 sting operation of 1995. In particular, we have heard numerous reports of the informant you mentioned appearing at 2600 meetings trying to get people to commit crimes. We know this is accurate because we'd been getting complaints about this individual back in 1994. Tainted though this case may be, it's quite likely these questions won't change a thing. But we can learn something important. Odds are that if someone approaches you and tries to get you to turn your knowledge and interests toward the world of crime, they are either trying to trap you or they are trying to con you. If you feel nice and secure because the person you want to commit crimes with is a trusted friend, be aware that nothing tears apart a friendship more quickly than a federal indictment. There is absolutely no way of knowing how someone will react to that kind of pressure until the time comes when they are confronted by it. Take heart in the fact that these days you can still wind up in prison and be considered a major threat to society without committing crimes. When people recognize this, we have a chance of winning some important battles.

1997

Dear *2600:*

> On May 5, 1995 I was sentenced to 70 months in federal prison. The judge ordered that upon my release I shall not use the "Internet or any other computer network." I became the first person to be banned from the Internet. Additionally, the judge prohibited me from getting a job as a computer programmer (my hobby since age nine, and my career throughout high school and college). If I violate these conditions, I could be sent back to prison.

> Although hacking was a "hobby" of mine for several years, I have never had a hacking-related criminal charge, and my current crime has nothing to do with computer programming or the Internet. I admit that I have committed undisputed crimes involving theft and sale of telephone equipment (stolen from Southwestern Bell Telephone). And for this I will spend five years in prison as punishment. But banning me from the Internet and from programming computers when I am out of prison is unjust and will not help foster my rehabilitation into society.

> So on April 22, 1997, I filed a Federal habeas corpus petition challenging my Internet ban on First Amendment (and other) grounds. I claimed that banning me from the Internet is a free speech violation in light of recent cases, like ACLU vs. Reno *recently in the Supreme Court. The government has been ordered to respond to my petition by July 11, 1997. If I do not win in the district court, I will appeal to the U.S. Court of Appeals and, if necessary, to the United States Supreme Court.*

> I am writing this letter for two reasons: (1) I need to find an interested lawyer to help me fight my computer restrictions pro bono; and (2)

I want to publicize what the government is doing with this absurd "Internet ban" restriction as a Free Speech violation.

While I may be the first person banned from the Net, I won't be the last. Recently, I learned through the Freedom of Information Act that the Departments of Justice and the Parole Commission plan to add restrictions to ban parolees from the Internet and to prohibit parolees from using or possessing encryption software (like PGP, or even PKZIP since it has an encryption option).

If you are interested in helping, or want more information, please visit my page on the Web.

MINOR THREAT

1998

Dear *2600:*

I'm new to computers and the Internet. I was reading the news when I saw an article about The New York Times. *Then I read why it was "hacked" — because a man named Mitnick is being held prisoner wrongfully. So I put his name in the search thing and then I came to your page and read a bit. How can the government hold a person for over three years if they didn't bring him to trial? What is he supposed to have done and do they have any evidence of whatever? I totally don't get it. Go ahead, call me backward. I don't even know what hackers do! All I know is to beware of viruses and I'm still paranoid about that! (People always say hackers give you viruses.)*

EXHALIBUT

Your questions get to the very core of the issues we're involved in every day. Answering them in this small space isn't possible but if you continue to read the facts as reported on our website and in these pages, you will at least get another perspective on these things. In the end, you will have to decide for yourself who's right.

2001

Dear *2600:*

> *I'm always reading your articles about how atrocious the public school system can get so I thought I'd try to give you an accurate portrayal of the Federal Bureau of Prisons. I am currently serving 18 months for a non-computer-related conspiracy conviction, a charge where no evidence is necessary to convict, only testimony, and it is my first offense. When I arrived, I was not provided with a copy of any rules and regulations, nor was I given my customary phone call. I picked up one of the inmate phones and dialed 1-800-COLLECT to get a message through to my family and a voice came on and said "You have dialed an unauthorized number" and the line went dead. A week later I was called up front and informed that a report had been run that identified me, through the use of my PIN, as a violator of Program Statement 53264.06, page 12: "Consistent with the Bureau's correctional management objectives and except as noted in this program statement, an inmate may not place calls to telephone numbers for which all the actual expenses for the call cannot be directly and immediately deducted from the inmate's account." This was a 200 series offense. Other 200 series offenses include extortion and assault.*

// BUDDHA

Dear *2600:*

> *Hi! With only seven or so hours of incarceration left, I thought I'd write and thank you for all you have done for me, and for spreading information to the public to help fight the good fight. It was a good experience seeing our country, our society, and our government in action, and I have come to see what 2600 really stands for.*

> *I wish you luck with all your troubles, current and future, and hope for all our sakes that reason and freedom will prevail.*

ERIC BURNS

Welcome back. Putting someone in prison for simply hacking a web page still seems unbelievable to us. But we're glad you're out and keeping a positive outlook on the whole thing. Further proof of a non-criminal mind.

2004

Dear *2600*:

> *I am incarcerated at an "unnamed" facility in the Indiana Department of Corrections. The phone system has recently been taken over by AT&T and now, after five to ten collect calls to my family or friends, the phone company puts a restricted block on the frequently called numbers. Then it requires the owner of each number to prepay an account. When the prepay balance is diminished, the restriction kicks in again without notice to the number's owner. Does anyone know any tips or tricks about this system that may be of assistance to me? The phone setup is like this. Once the receiver is lifted, you are prompted with the following: "Press one for collect call. Press two for a prepaid collect call." Once I press one or two, I am prompted to dial my phone number, then my six-digit DOC number and four-digit PIN. The call then either goes through or the restricted calls message comes on.*
>
> SYSTEMX

Dear *2600*:

> *I felt you should be informed about what is happening here at the Colorado Department of Corrections. I have been a long-time reader of your magazine and decided to start subscribing back in 2000. You have always provided interesting information and commentary.*
>
> *As a hacker, I believe as many do that information should be free, and that there is no such thing as good information and evil information. People make their own choice on how they use information. Nonetheless I'm faced with a wall of ignorance. I have worked as a*

computer technician, programmer, and network administrator here at the prison for many years. With this job come many responsibilities, not all of which are technical. My job provides me with many opportunities and benefits that I would not want to have taken away from me. This being the case, I have to keep myself out of trouble and keep a low profile.

When the fall issue came out in November, I was taken by surprise. Instead of getting the issue, I got a contraband slip! The issue was then sent to the reading committee. I don't have to tell you how pissed I was. As usual, I kept my mouth shut and put my mind in gear. I took the wait-and-see approach to see what would happen. A few weeks went by and I got my answer. No way! Now I got to thinking. I could start filing grievances and start a lawsuit, at the same time putting myself on Front Street with a big sign saying, "I'm a Hacker," "I'm a Cyber Criminal," "I'm a Terrorist." Or I can keep quiet and not put my job and what little freedom I have left in jeopardy. I want to fight this ignorance and injustice. But the thing is I can yell at the top of my lungs and demand my right to read whatever I want, but I can also be easily dismissed and locked up and lose the one thing that has made my life in here bearable. Because I'm a prisoner, I'm no longer an American deserving of the rights most Americans take for granted.

I know that the DOC is supposed to inform the publisher of its decision to censor your magazine. I'm betting they haven't and this is the first you've heard of it?

I would really be fascinated in hearing your position is on this matter.

ZUCCHINI

It's a bit of a "Catch 22" for us because the more we talk about this, the more prisons reject our publication. But as it's clearly an issue for a number of people, the facts deserve to be spread.

We did receive a rejection notice from your institution along with a number of others. The official reason given was "entire publication depicts illegal activities contrary to security interests of the facility." (Substitute the word "country" for "facility" and you may be looking at the future.)

Some of the more specific descriptions include the following: "Contains threats or plans of criminal activity; Violates or concerns plans for activities in violation of the Code of Penal Discipline; Is in code and/or not understood by the reader; Contains information that constitutes a potential danger to a human being or threat to the security and order of the facility. This includes gang related activity, gang signs, or gang related activity; Contains material that could create racial tension within the facility."

We've been accused of lots of things over the years but some of these are new even for us. It's not surprising that they think we're talking in code; some of our concepts of free thought would certainly appear alien to prison guards.

In the end, there isn't much we can do other than publicize their actions. American prisons are horrible places to be stuck in and the authorities there are able to get away with a huge amount of rights abuses. We wish you luck even though you most likely won't be allowed to read these words.

2005

Dear *2600:*

This letter is in response to SystemX's letter in 21:3. I am also incarcerated, albeit in a federal prison, so I may have some useful information for SystemX and others in the same unfortunate predicament.

I was in the Warsaw ("Northern Neck") County jail in Virginia. You are allowed to make three calls to a number and then a prepaid account must be established. Well, I was in transit and only in Warsaw for seven days. I made my three calls, which are free by the way, to my loved one. Then we thought that maybe I could call the second line of my loved one's house for free also. It worked! Six calls times fifteen minutes was a whole hour and a half! This worked even though I had to enter my Warsaw jail-issued inmate number. I guess that they will let you call any number three times in the hope that you might have to set up a prepaid account with each number (mother, girlfriend, lawyer, friends, etc.).

So you can take advantage of this system by calling any number three times. Let's see: two house phones, work phone plus extensions, pay-phone outside of work, cell phone, friends' phones, etc.

Of course SystemX, I believe, must make collect calls, not three free calls to any number. Depending on the cost of calls made via a pre-paid account, it may be cheaper to pay for the most basic service for a telephone line, accept all of the collect calls you can, and repeat. This isn't very nice or honest, but neither are the outrageous prices that inmates and their families pay to communicate by phone. Here, and in all federal prisons nationwide, inmates prepay 23 cents per minute for long distance in the U.S. The money comes right out of our accounts. If we call collect, the rate increases by four times! That's 92 cents per minute!

To SystemX and all of the rest of us who are down: I understand your plight and hope that you can find a way to stay in contact with your family and friends. Shout out to Stormbringer!

TONY SPARX

Speaking of whom....

Dear *2600:*

Stormbringer can open mouth and insert foot. Acidus' article in 20:1 was pretty close to output power on XM Satellite, which in 20:2 I said was incorrect. I read recently that XM Satellite puts out about 18kw worth of power into the antenna for an effective radiated power (ERP) of 10 megawatts or so. Sweet! I was wrong.

I have been locked up awhile so have not played with WiFi or read much about it. From previous experiences on hacking hardware, I know a lot of products can be hacked to do things the manufacturer never intended, including being on other frequencies.

As for WiFi cards, making your own channels above or below the standard ones would allow one to put up a fairly secured WLAN since script kiddies and most professional software probably won't be looking for these channels. This could be a big problem for someone who has a LAN with a rogue wireless hub on nonstandard frequencies.

I'm assuming all of the frequency channelization is done on the ROM, controlled by firmware on the WiFi card. Pretty easy to pull the ROM and blow your own and put it back in the WiFi card, the very same thing you would do with an OKI 900 cell phone or Motorola radio to make it do special things. If the card is controlled by a software driver, it would be much easier to do.

Now I have seen some block diagrams (very basic) of a WiFi card and noticed it contains everything needed to decode just about anything you could throw at it, provided you can control the frequency and deal with the bits coming out of the I/Q decoder.

The I/Q decoder is much more versatile than the 2- or 4-level decoders I've mentioned in the past. The I/Q decoder is limited to what you program to decode, and the sampling of the DSP chips on board. Right now I'm aware of projects, including GNU radio, that use an I/Q decoder to do AM, FM, SSB, and some digital modulation schems such as WiFi and modes used on data over radio. Theoretically, one should be able to decode FLEX/Golay/POCSAG pagers, digital cell phones, HDTV, satellite radio, or satellite TV via an I/Q decoder.

In the 2.4GHz frequency range, the WiFi card uses there are cordless phones, ham radio, and other things to potentially decode. Those would be the very basic things to try out if the ROM or driver can be hacked. I do not know how far out of spec the WiFi cards can go before performance rolls off. Down at 2.3GHz we have satellite radio: XM and Sirius. A really good antenna or LNA might have a WiFi card doing satellite radio if the performance does not degrade too far dropping that low in frequency.

If a WiFi card can in fact be controlled to camp out on frequencies you want, and the I/Q decoders can decode what you want via roll-your-own software, there are some tricks to get other frequencies of interest converted up to 2.4GHz where we can deal with them assuming the frequencies are below 2.4GHz. For those above 2.4GHz, we would have to down convert them. That would make GSM/PCS phones, satellite TV, satellite radio, pagers, ham radio, and spread spectrum signals all potentially decodable via WiFi card.

If the WiFi card can't be hacked, all is not lost. The I/Q decoder chips are available for pretty cheap, easily interfaceable to the computer. The

I/Q decoder input would have to be put on a receiver, scanner, satellite radio, etc. device so you can tinker with the data being spit out.

Either way the wind blows, I'm willing to work with people on hardware issues and designing some circuits for use, which means I'll have to order some books.

In 21:4, jjr wrote in concerning more info needing to be written concerning RFID. I agree. RFID is trampling into a territory that most in the community have not explored: RF (Radio Frequencies). Some have dabbled in cellular technology, pagers, and WiFi, which are all RF-based. Learning the basics of RF is not hard. Many websites explaining radio theory will get one schooled in the foundations of RF.

RFID is pretty simple technology that is radio-based. At a simplistic level, RFID is just a very simple radio transmitter and receiver (transceiver) with a memory chip. When it receives a signal from a transmitter with proper query sequence, the RFID will spit back an ID code or other info with its transmitter. It has no internal power and thus must take a little bit of the querying transmitter power and convert it to usable power to transmit its information. This part is pretty much basic electronics.

RFID in a product is pretty easy to kill. Tossing it in the microwave should either kill the silicon chip by plasma arc or overwhelm the circuits and burn them out. Of course, there is a potential fire hazard. Static electricity is also another potential killer of RFID. As computer guys, we all know the potential problems with zapping our boxes. Those old static guns to remove static from records may generate enough to kill an RFID chip. Doubtful, but a cell phone up at full power with the tip of the antenna against the chip may kill it. A ham radio walkie talkie at full power may also kill it. A high powered ham transmitter will definitely do it, but not something you carry around. A stun gun will definitely do the job, as will taking a hammer to it.

Exploits? I'm not sure if RFID uses spread spectrum or not. If it does not, a DoS attack is very plausible. If memory serves, some of the frequencies I've seen are 13.56MHz, 403MHz, 915MHz, and the 2.4GHz band. The latter would be interesting if WiFi cards could be tricked to operate on the same frequency as RFID. Then you'd be able to query RFID chips and spoof your own queries if you were close enough.

Some of the ham radio transceivers can be easily modified to operate on frequencies outside of the ham radio bands. Of course, transmitting inside or outside of the ham radio frequencies without an FCC license is a federal offense.

There may be other frequencies in use by RFID. You can find these by surfing the manufacturers' websites. Out in the field tinkering, you'll need a decent frequency counter. OptoElectronics makes a handheld frequency counter (The Digital Scout) that should be fast enough to capture the frequencies in use by RFID. They make another version (The Scout), but I don't think it has a fast enough "lookup" time to accurately capture the frequency in use by RFID. Anyhow, simply holding the frequency counter next to an RFID scanner while it is scanning an item should give you the frequency of the device.

Digging around the cell, I found specs on the Em Electronics (www .emelectronics.co.uk) EM4223 RFID chip. It is in compliance with the ISO IEC 18000-6. It carries a 128 bit ROM user memory, operates in the 862-870MHz, 902-950MHz, and 2.45GHz bands, and has no apparent security. Of similar spec is the EM4222 which uses 64 bits of ROM. One version of it has an additional 1024 bits of read/write memory.

In the 13.56MHz frequency range, the EM4006 has 64 bits of ROM while the EM4035 and EM4135 have 64 bits of ROM, and have 3200 bits and 2304 bits of read/write memory respectively. Security is done via lock bits or mutual authentication.

Most of the Loompanics products appear to be a series of RFID chips in the 125kHz range, with 48-128 bits of ROM and 256-2048 bits of read/ write memory. Some of these follow ISO 11784 or 11785 standard, and use lock bits and password, password, or mutual authentication security. Some versions have no security at all in the read only versions.

Being that I'm in a prison cell, I'm taking a stab at the data encoding method over RF, and will say it is simply FSK (Frequency Shift Keying) to query and parrot back information. For costs and simplicity, I doubt they are using any more exotic modulation schems to transmit the data.

FSK is easily decoded on a scanner with slight modifications and an external interface which connects to the serial port to get the FSK *data received to the computer. The Pd102.exe or Hamcomm interfaces available on the Internet are perfect for use in experimentation and easy to build. The cost is about $10 in Radio Shack parts.*

Your receiver will have to cover the appropriate frequency ranges, although I prefer using commercial radio equipment by Motorola. The Motorola 800 Spectra and MaxTrac will cover the 800MHz frequency RFIDs without modification for transmit or receive. There is a pinout on the accessory jack in the back for transmit and receive data. For transmit, you'll have to build an appropriate interface to take data out of the computer and transmit it. Data received via these radios will work with the above mentioned interfaces.

The 900MHz Motorola Spectra and MaxTrac radios will receive frequencies 928MHz and above without modification. The Pd102.exe or 4 level decoders work very well for decoding pagers. Below 928MHz, these radios need modification to the VCO circuit to work. The modifications are available on www.batlabs.com. In the 902-925MHz band, there are cordless phones, RFID, video links, wireless mics, and other FCC Part 15 devices, as well as ham radio communications.

Motorola does have some data modems that connect to the Spectra or MaxTrac radios that will do most FSK data modes and transmit and receive up to 19.2kbps. The RDM-600 will do many modes as far as encoding if you set up the programming software right.

Hopefully, some of this information will be useful to someone. I'd like to correspond with some people "in the know," and newbies to radio tinkering as well. I do respond to all people.

Stormbringer
Cumberland, MD

2006

Dear *2600:*

Hello my brothers and sisters of the digital underground. I am writing this in response to a previous article or letter which I read in another *issue, but unfortunately that issue is floating around my personal library somewhere and cannot be found. The article I'm referring to actually talked about using 711 or relay calling to make collect calls from prison. I thought this was interesting because it's kind of crazy what they charge the families and friends of the incarcerated. I hear that prisoners sometimes have access to computers that have active Internet connections. If this is true, they could easily create an AIM (AOL Instant Messenger) screen name and add the screen name MYIPRELAY to their buddy list and use the relay service to make calls to whomever they needed to. This not only allows you to make calls at times you might not normally be able to, but it avoids incurring any collect call fees. After adding the MYIPRELAY to your list you can type in the following: **dial xxxxxxxxx**. Replace the x's with the telephone number you're calling and the operator on the other end will make the call for you to the desired party. Now if the facility the prisoner is in blocks the AIM Express website, it's time to use an old workaround, a proxy server such as* www.proxify.com *or* www.thecloak.com. *Because these prison systems may not allow users to install* .exe *files, I would suggest using the AIM Express website to login. Plus, there is a hack to add AIM contacts to your Gmail Gtalk list since they both use Jabber logins. This is just a random thought from someone who works tech support for a living and is unhappy with the current political condition and hopes that it will save some people some money from the very greedy phone companies. The Gtalk hack can be found in a book entitled* Googlepedia: The Ultimate Google Resource. *Enjoy and happy relaying!*

SOURSOLES

While we think it's a great idea, we know of no prison that actually allows its inmates this kind of access on the Net. It would certainly make the Internet a much more interesting place if they did. Regardless, something needs to be done about the horrible rip-offs prisoners' friends and families must endure at the hands of those phone companies that charge exorbitant collect call surcharges. Communications costs have gone way down across the board. It's unconscionable that rates many times higher are being charged to those who have very little choice in the matter.

Dear *2600:*

> *First, I need to thank you. I have thoroughly enjoyed your magazine for a few years now. I've learned a ton and it's been very useful in conveying the mentality that so many of us share to the outside world. Many times, I've answered questions by simply presenting your magazine to the curiosity seekers.*

> *Second, I was 17 when the FBI first raided my home. I was 19 the second time around. I was 21 when I was sentenced in 2005 to 17.5 years in federal prison. And because of my charges and what I had admitted to doing and what I was told to expect, that sentence was quite a shock. No, not pedophilia or even sex-related. Not drug-related. A minor role in a credit card fraud scheme. The judge apparently was none too happy with me, giving me the statutory maximum.*

> *I would love to write an article for you describing what exactly it's like to go from bad to worse to worst. A report from the front lines, if you will. My hope is that in the "unlikely" event that any 2600 readers are ever charged by the feds, they won't receive five to six times the sentence they expect, as did I. I would most like to spread the word about how dirty feds can, and will, play. And a few points to watch out for.*

> *Let me know if you might like me to write you a little article. And thanks again guys.*

> Jason C.

By all means, write the article. Your story serves as a reminder to those who may not yet know it that the prosecution will do anything — including lying to you —to secure a conviction. Putting people away is their business. While there are many overly expensive, incompetent, and dishonest lawyers out there, you are still far better off getting one rather than trying to work things out with the authorities on your own. We've heard so many horror stories of people getting screwed at sentencing and with today's prosecutorial climate, it's bound to get even worse. And, needless to say, this sort of thing does nothing for rehabilitation.

Dear *2600:*

> *I am a 16-year-old male, currently incarcerated in an all-male juvenile treatment facility. As you can imagine, being here is quite boring and I still have four to six months ahead of me. Most of the people here are the "cool" kids. You know, the ones that listen to rap music and smoke weed. The ones who think we're "losers" because we sit in front of our monitors whenever possible. Well, turns out quite a few of them respect me. I was quite surprised to see that a few people picked up my issue (22:1) and read it. When I got 22:2, people were fighting over who got to read it first after me. Pretty crazy, right? A few people actually approached me and asked if I'd teach them about computers and stuff. So I started with basic hardware, basic TCP/IP stuff, etc. The thing about it is I'm just so shocked that the people we'd expect to not accept us actually do. Hopefully, this trend keeps up and we start becoming more generally accepted. Just thought it would be nice to share my experiences.*

UNDEFINED32

It's not really a trend, just that part of humanity that allows us to accept people for who they are and for what we can learn from them. It probably wasn't the lesson you were sent there to learn but it's a good thing nonetheless.

2007

Dear *2600:*

> *I'm currently at a halfway house in Oklahoma. I figured out a trick with the phones here and now everyone calls long distance for free. But what I'd like to know is what kind of system are these phones based on that would allow us all to make free calls? Here's what we do: we pick up the handset and dial 18, count to three slowly or wait for a tiny click from inside the phone (I have to count because I'm hard of hearing), then press 00 and quickly press one or two numbers eight times. (I like pressing 7 and 8 back and forth... makes a cute jingle.) An operator will say "thank you" and if you did it right it will say*

"thank you" again and give you a dial tone. You can then call wherever except for international for some reason. I can call Canada, though. Sometimes it makes a loud whistling feedback noise and sometimes it gives you a dial tone but the keys don't work. Could you clarify what's occurring for this to happen?

I love your mag and still get it even though I'm incarcerated.

NOAH

It's hard to say exactly what's happening, but there's surely some sort of a drop down to a dial tone at some point, which might be the tiny click you hear. Or it could be the dial tone you get after the "thank you" that is bypassing the normal restriction. Then again, dialing 18 could be connecting you to a distant line somewhere. The important thing is that you're continuing to use your mind and figure things out while incarcerated which is always a good thing to do. These days, getting around dialing restrictions is less about the cost and more about just bypassing whatever controls are being placed on you. In a world where you can have unlimited long distance for next to nothing, these kinds of controls shouldn't even be around much longer. At least not for reasons of cost.

Dear *2600*:

Please stop all subscriptions addressed to the facility listed above. This is a state hospital for civilly committed sexually psychopathic personalities and sexually dangerous persons. It is inappropriate for them to receive this subscription. Your publication jeopardizes the security of our facility and places a risk to patients, staff, and the public.

OFFICE OF SPECIAL INVESTIGATIONS

We've been accused of a lot of things, but jeopardizing the security of a civilly committed sexually psychopathic personality is a first. We're also not sure how such a person reading our magazine puts the public at risk but we'll defer to your judgment on that. However, as the person(s) who subscribed to us at this institution paid us for it, we must notify them and issue refunds for the unreceived issues. Hopefully, that won't cause more grief.

Dear *2600:*

I am a new subscriber to your magnificent magazine, enjoying the extended access to new technologies through you and Maximum PC, *and a resident of Pennsylvania's D.O.C. I'm writing in response to soursoles' letter concerning AIM relay for prisoners.*

The rumor of Internet access in prisons, Pennsylvania's at least, is just that. A rumor. Unless an educational course requires it, inmates aren't permitted to see a computer, let alone touch one. What little access I have had has shown a basic network with no Internet access. Security is surprisingly lax, but I attribute this to the basic inmate population being your usual Layer 8 idiots. Should I come across something with potential, I'll be sure to share.

The phone system itself was upgraded to an automated system some time back. Since the upgrade, all phone numbers are pre-approved before calls are permitted. Even then calls are limited to one or two a day, depending on your custody level. Calling cards are an option. This is just a credit to your account with the phone company, not an actual card. Unfortunately, the cheapest card for us is the equivalent of a minimum-wage employee on the street paying $375 for a 40-minute card. That is a whole other can of worms though.

I appreciate your efforts in trying to aid family/friends of the incarcerated. It almost reminds me of what it's like to be amongst people again.

Thank you, 2600, for your notice of the need for change. Most people would sooner forget about us and our friends and families than help speak out about injustices we endure.

SN

In recent months there has finally been attention given to the horribly unfair telephone rates forced on prisoners and their families. We have a very unhealthy attitude of forgetting about our incarcerated citizens and, in fact, treating them as if they were subhuman, regardless of the actual circumstances behind their imprisonment. As more and more of us are found guilty of one thing or another, this mentality is really going to wind up biting us in the ass.

2008

Dear *2600:*

> Over the years I've read many letters in your magazine about how numerous individuals have been singled out unfairly by either viewing your website or by being in possession of the 2600 publication itself.
>
> I now am one of those proud martyrs. I'm finishing out the last year and a half of a six-year prison sentence at Delaware Correctional Center. On February 8, my cell was shook down while I was at a typing class. When I returned to my building, a lieutenant pulled me aside and informed me that I was being written up for possession of non-dangerous contraband.
>
> When I asked what this contraband was, he told me it was two issues each of 2600 and Make Magazine. Confused, I asked how they could be considered contraband when the prison mailroom here has been allowing me to receive these mags for the past three years and anything the mailroom here considers a security threat they would not allow the inmate to have.
>
> The lieutenant, looking equally confused (or maybe it was just the blank stare of a man waiting out the workday clock), gave me the "I'm just the middleman here" speech and told me I'd be moved to a higher security area to await my hearing. Now I'm on a near 24/7 lockdown.
>
> My point to all out there reading this is simple. Don't wallow in self pity if you're ever singled out by fear peddlers. Use whatever skills you have to show those ignorant of your passions that you're driven by a healthy curiosity, not a malicious nature. Don't waste time arguing with middlemen, go to the source. If you're barred from doing it in person, don't underestimate the powerful proxy of presence using repeated correspondence. Keep up the good work, 2600; your pages truly are the few remaining bastions of originality and free thought left.
>
> MAX RIDER
> SMYRNA, DE

Dear *2600:*

> Every federal prison has a networked LexisNexis database computer intended for legal research by inmates. But it's connected to the same network that the Bureau of Prisons officers' computers are connected to. It's not a closed terminal. So it is possible to get in. I did it when I was at the Terre Haute penitentiary.
>
> In addition, when I was in county jail in Portland, Oregon, I figured out that you can access different extensions that allow free court calls. If you connect to a voicemail, you can enter a different extension and get pretty much any extension in the building. One guy did it from an inmate payphone and called up the kitchen and ordered extra trays for himself.
>
> VERY ANONYMOUS

Probably not the wisest use of that little security hole. But it does show that where there's a will, there's almost always a way.

Dear *2600:*

> At this point you are like an old friend, although we have never spoken. I have felt compelled to write for some time and, finally getting around to it, decided to go all out: this letter, a personal letter, and an article submission. (Yes, this is my first attempt at getting published. What other publication matters?)
>
> But what catalyst led to the break in my, ahem, lazy spell? A "little" book about a hacker's odyssey.
>
> I knew nothing of 2600 coming to prison — hell, I didn't know much of anything arriving at the age of 17. A year into my sentence, as the reality of prison life came into focus and my paradigm shifted to study, a Jersey kid came along and altered my path forever. Over the next six months, I picked his brain for every box plan, phreaker tale, and piece of hacker lore he could remember. With zero technology access, I can remember handwriting DOS commands and being very frustrated by all his damn error messages.

*It was a year after he and I parted that I got my first copy of 2600 —
which you sent me for free. In a word, I felt empowered. In the prison
information void, I encountered the summum bonum of information.
Much of my education in the tech sector was reverse engineered around
topics and leads in 2600.*

*Fast forward to this July — my 25th birthday. I got a copy of 2600:
A Hacker Odyssey. I read all 871 pages before 50,000 volts of macro-
cosmic lightning struck my brain.*

*Hacking is more a philosophy and approach to life than a means to
an end. It is reason by default in an age now rampant with Orwellian
nightmare. Sure, we could happily spend our days dissecting some
new technology, but how often are we pulled into pointing out, and
oft times defending the conscious from ludicrous invasions of rights
and privacy? Or how about poking holes in all the faux security that
never cease popping up?*

*Simply put, thanks. You carved a niche for our culture, spearheaded op-
pression with an illuminated voice, and always remained a lighthouse
for stragglers trying to navigate a sometimes foggy hackerdom.*

JOSEPH

Dear *2600:*

*I'm presently serving time in the federal prison system, but, seeing the
news on TV regarding wiretapping and the carte-blanche freedom to
do so provided by the U.S. government to their new allies the telecoms,
there is no freedom left. The Electronic Communications Privacy Act
of 1986, a law I believe that was created in reaction to Mr. Mitnick's
research, is now void. No warrant is needed, no fines are given to the
telecoms for any breach into what was once considered private: our
emails and phone conversations.*

*To quote loosely the elderly Biff Tannen from Back to the Future, "Get
a safe system!" Encrypt your whole system, keep your passwords secret
when asked for by the "authorities" (Fifth Amendment privilege),
whether it's in their Waco-like raids or at the airports and borders.*

Even do Freedom of Information Act requests if you feel the need to know what the Injustice Department is up to.

My mail is checked, my phone calls are monitored, but I'm in prison, a so-called "security risk." Ask yourself then: if you are so free, why are your communications, your downloads, your uploads, your snail mail, and your movements (through the Real ID chip) kept track of?

To quote Michael Chertoff, in response to a reporter's question about the constitutional right of citizens in regard to Homeland Security and the Patriot Act, "Homeland Security's and the Patriot Act's only purpose is to fight terrorists and terrorism. It does not have any harmful effect on citizens' rights."

Then why, on the warrant used with me did it have above the Treasury Department letterhead "Homeland Security?" Counterfeiting and computer crimes are not the same as striking fear into innocent victims.

DAVID L. WILLIAMSON #22678-057
LORETTO, PA

2009

Dear *2600:*

I'm not sure where to start. I've read your magazine for a long time but never had an urge to write until now. Maybe because I am currently incarcerated in a state prison facility in East Texas and have a lot of free time. I recently requested your magazine from my family to test my limits to see if I could get it in. I would say I was surprised it made it to me, but that would be a lie. What was slightly surprising was that the package it came in was never opened and inspected. They wonder why we have contraband issues in Texas prisons, especially pay-as-you-go cell phones. I'd say the security issues and loopholes are amazing, things you never would imagine in such a so-called secured facility. The door that's supposed to keep me locked in this room can easily be talked open through the intercom. Press the button, the officer says "ID?", you say something like "Chaplain." Click — voila!

Simple as that, opened cell door. But, of course, I have never done it. Attempting to escape is a serious charge.

Anyway, I got to thumbing through my newly received contraband, courtesy of the U.S. Postal Service, the Autumn 2009 issue of 2600 Magazine, and really wish I could take a picture of the payphones in here to submit to you. They are bolted to the wall. The receiver has no cord, but is sticking out of this oddly formed green box and all it has is a touch tone keypad. That's the best I can do because having a camera in here is another charge that carries a lengthy sentence.

My favorite part I love to read is your letters section. So I found it humorous to read a letter from Sc0ut. He asked a question, "When was the last time any of us sent or received a real letter?" I laughed because I can answer honestly and say nearly every day for over a year. If you want to write someone who truly values the timeless form of communication, write someone in prison.

After revealing obvious security flaws from within the system in this letter, I bring my next test. If this letter arrives, it proves yet another flaw. They didn't read it. Or they didn't care.

NICKO

It seems like the facility you describe isn't one of the high or even medium security ones, so it's not so surprising that there's a very slight degree of trust there. We shouldn't be surprised or outraged by this because it's the ultra-security mentality that should be the exception to the rule, even among the incarcerated. We're certain you wouldn't get very far if you opened your door, nor could any real contraband come in through the mail undetected. Receiving our magazine should not be considered a security risk, even though it's often categorized that way by various prison wardens who simply don't get what we're all about. Unfortunately, there are some who will even see this letter as a risk and thus deny the entire publication to an inmate. Knowledge and dialogue are not inherently a bad thing. Education is often considered a true threat, however, to those in charge. In the end, its absence invariably leads to a worse environment for all concerned.

We would have printed your address so you could get some letters, but we're happy to see that your incarceration has come to an end.

Dear *2600:*

Greetings. I wrote with a question a couple of issues ago but never received a response or an answer in vowels and consonants but, because of a very strange happening, I thought I would write about this strange happening and re-ask my original question.

I am a subscriber who is incarcerated and, due to this fact, I have limited abilities at finding things for myself. Because I want to start a business when I get out, I have been making plans and, of course, those plans include a company name. I want to secure my company "domain name" now but cannot seem to find the way to register the name for the Internet. I have written to several places including Verizon and Internic but neither responded. Any help you could provide or that a reader could provide would be greatly appreciated. I have no computer access here.

Now the strange thing that happened: When my hacker quarterly Volume 26, Number 3 arrived, I headed straight to my bunk for hours of great mind stimulating reading. When I opened up the envelope, I noticed a white sheet of paper encircling my issue. Now, because I am incarcerated and have witnessed many things the system will deny ever happened, I became immediately suspicious. Removing the white paper revealed in large *letters:*

PUBLICATION(S)

REVIEWED & APPROVED

BY MSCP

ET/MSCP

All in uppercase letters (like I write in, sorry). Now, nobody here seems to have ever heard of MSCP or ET/MSCP.

But it becomes stranger. As I looked at my copy, I noticed two small light blue plastic streamers sticking out and opening to the pages. They are clear plastic with mild stickiness. These are definitely made for marking pages. The pages, 15 and 19, contained the "Google Calling" and "Free Trials" articles.

Because of where I am, I want to say that the institution did this. But the name of the division that does that here is the Director's Review Committee or DRC. But they do not put papers in with the publications and in 13 years I have never seen those page markers. Also, the envelope that you sent was, as usual, opened and taped back together, but strangely had also been stapled. They never do both of those here at this unit. Strange, strange, strange. Or I really need to go home because I don't have a life.

If you like, you can print my name and address in case someone else would like to write me.

Michael E. Short #774048
Rosharon, TX

Paying attention to such detail is always a good thing. Most people would never have noticed what was right in front of them. What we were able to find out was that the MSCP is the Mail System Coordinators Panel. These are the people who actually review the publications and decide whether to approve or deny them. Perhaps they're supposed to remove their name (as well as any markers like the ones you found, which may point to articles of particular concern) before the inmate gets the publication delivered. The DRC seems to be more of an appeals process. Their responsibilities also extend to removing people from visiting lists. From the Offender Orientation Handbook: *"All publications are subject to inspection by the MSCP and by unit staff. The MSCP has the authority to accept or reject a publication for content, subject to review by the DRC." We imagine that "ET/MSCP" means that someone with the initials E.T. was the person typing the report or the one in charge.*

As for registering your domain name, all it takes is someone with Internet access to grab the name for you. They can find listings of registrars by entering "Internet registrars" on Google and then picking one that's cheap and has a good reputation. They can then hold onto the domain until you're ready to use it. Depending on how long that is, you might want to consider waiting until you get out, unless you really believe something will make someone else take your domain name that, to this day, hasn't already been claimed.

Dear *2600:*

> *So I am sitting in my cell the other day reading the latest issue (26:1) and in walks the unit counselor. He looks at me, smiles, and says "here you go." I look down at the glossy flyer with the corporate logo I faintly recall from all the bulletin boards around the joint. "Serving over one million inmates..." Huh!? More confused or intrigued than sold, I read on. Simple money transfer alternatives, digital same day deposits, just walk in to any participating Wal-Mart (read: Sam Walton Correctional facility grand opening soon!). My cellmate happens to be unintentionally computer illiterate and he asked me, "I wonder if someone could hack in and put money on my account." I wonder.... Anyway, since this is the only company in town, we are rather curious to know more about them. Social or technological vulnerabilities? What are we being exposed to here? Will the Jpay logo one day be the header of my parole papers?* www.jpay.com?*

ANONYMOUS

This is an interesting site that allows you to do all sorts of things from transferring money to making restitution to sending letters to inmates. If there are vulnerabilities, we have yet to hear of them. We'd also like to hear if this site is helping prisoners or taking advantage of them.

Dear *2600:*

> *I am a Temporary Incarcerated Hacker (TIH). I enjoy reading your back issues as well as your quarterly publications and I admire the radio show Off The Hook every Wednesday from 7-8 pm on 99.5FM WBAI. Thank you for making my time worthwhile and educational. I am also prison self-taught in computer technology/repair/troubleshooting/hacking and programming. I am very enthusiastic when it comes to this line of education. The reason for this letter is for the benefit of myself and others in my situation who use snail mail in ordering books and supplies from prison. Where can I send for my copy of The Best of 2600? What is the cost and the shipping? Keep up the good work and future success.*

PH1UK3R _ TIH

Probably the easiest way, since we don't sell the book ourselves, is to have someone on the outside buy it online from a site like `amazon.com`, `borders.com`, *or* `barnesand noble.com` *and have it shipped to your address. You could also buy direct from the publisher at* `www.wiley.com`*. This might be best since some institutions only allow printed matter direct from publishers.*

8 A Culture of Rebels

Rebellion. Individuality. The sharing of information and the quest for knowledge. That's really what the backbone of the hacker world is all about. And it has remained unchanged since the very first letter was printed in *2600*.

Of course, circumstances themselves have changed. You'll note in the early years that people seemed almost obsessed with getting "busted" or "raided." The very basic reason for this is because that's exactly what was happening to an awful lot of us. It was a very different world. You couldn't just easily connect to networks, exchange information, and spend long amounts of time on the phone like you can today. But that didn't mean we didn't *want* to. Those of us infected with the hacker bug *knew* just how cool it all was to communicate and learn all about technology. It simply wasn't all that easy, not without breaking a number of laws.

It wasn't at all uncommon for an innocuous thing like a computer bulletin board system to be seen as a threat by the authorities. This is why there were so many BBS raids back then. Those in charge had no idea what the hackers were up to or what we were talking about. By seizing our equipment, they had the opportunity to learn themselves. Of course, the hackers were also trying to seize equipment that wasn't theirs, mostly in the form of accessing telephone switches and the crude data communication networks of the day. Along the way, we tried to hold onto certain values: information should always be shared freely, systems should never be damaged, privacy should be respected. Of course, that last tenet was almost impossible to hold onto because there was practically *no* privacy online, and also because we were only human. I certainly wasn't immune from that; when I discovered that the electronic mailbox for NASA was protected by a single-letter password, you *know* I took a look at what was inside. I doubt many others could have resisted. (Incidentally, what I saw shocked me to the core, but that's a story for another book.)

We had our share of the criminally-minded who sent us letters, imagining themselves to be hackers. When they wrote to the letters column, we had no problem correcting them in no uncertain terms. I hope we managed to set such people straight or, at the very least, get them to stop thinking of themselves as hackers.

There was also no shortage of childish rants and tales of odd adventures, which we had great fun with and our readers loved. Sure, we were relentless in our mocking at times, but sometimes it was necessary. We never set out to make anyone actually feel bad. Well, not unless they *really* deserved it.

Overall, we felt that people were defined by their intent. Merely breaking a law wasn't enough to brand someone a criminal. Nevertheless, that wasn't the prevailing mood of society, which led to a constant sense of apprehension in the community. We turned into the sounding board for that bit of frustration.

I think the battle was worthwhile because things changed over time, often as a direct result of some of what we were going through. As BBSes were lost to raids, we knew that the only response was to create more BBSes. We started a *2600* BBS network and insisted that software be utilized that kept user email private. This was not only good for the user but also for the owner of the bulletin board. By not being technically capable of reading a user's email, the system operator could not be held accountable for whatever the authorities believed might be going on. We also fervently pushed for the same protections afforded a magazine like *2600* to be extended to the electronic world.

As word of the various injustices was spread via the magazine, we noticed something surprising. Other people were paying attention. Even the mass media occasionally gave us positive press. When a series of particularly unjust raids hit in 1990, we engaged in a massive publicity blitz that wound up getting a lot of attention and led to the founding of the Electronic Frontier Foundation.

Having a voice through the magazine for this rebellious group of individuals was key to becoming more visible and less prone to victimization. In the late '80s, after we started having a monthly *2600* gathering in New York City, a simple remark in one of our replies to a letter ("It would be nice if people all over the world had meetings/get-togethers on the first Friday of the month.") led to a global rush of hacker meetings that continues to grow to this day, and has had such a positive effect on so many lives. There were, however, some setbacks in that arena, specifically a Secret Service–led raid on one of our meetings in a mall in Washington DC in 1992. What's interesting here is that a letter printed in *2600* prior to that incident reveals that they were scoping out the location in the months before this ultimately unsuccessful attempt to shut down our gatherings.

Technology, of course, also changed so dramatically over the decades that a lot of what put hackers in the crosshairs simply became unnecessary. We often pondered in the letters column as to whether or not there would be so much telephone fraud if calls were simply more affordable. As that began to become a reality, our focus shifted away from merely making free phone calls and toward hacking the *functionality* of whatever systems we were using. The tools changed, but the spirit never did.

I think one of the most touching remarks contained here is from one of the letter writers who recognizes how *2600* affected them in their formulative years: "I owe you people more than I can pay. You saved me from a life of mediocrity." Obviously, we can't take the credit for such things. But we can recognize that we're a link in a chain that helps to make us all stronger, so long as we support each other and recognize our collective value. Going through these writings from some of the most spirited individuals around, I believe we lent a hand to precisely the right people.

1984

Dear *2600*:

In reply to October's article "Getting Caught: Hacker's View," I was in the reverse situation. I had turned in a close friend last spring. I was faced with a situation of turning him in or being an accomplice to fraud. Being in a spot like that, no one can make a decision to do that without always doubting yourself. Choosing between being an accomplice or keeping a friendship is a place I wouldn't wish for my worst enemy. In dealing with the feds, you can't take everything as truth — they tell the guy who's busted one story (in hopes of making him crack) and tell the "informer" another story (in hopes of scaring him into saying things he wouldn't normally say). The people who read that in the October issue probably thought the person who turned this guy in was a rat, a fink, or a fed. What they may not realize is the other side of the story, the part where the "informer" gets cornered into telling what he knows, or sacrificing his freedom (ending up in jail) if he doesn't tell. In my case, that's what happened. I was cornered and had to tell and provide evidence to keep my ass clean. The guy I turned in had fouled up the job and would've been caught without my telling, although him and his friends still think I'm a rat. What they may not realize is what they would've done if they were me. Would they have gone to jail to protect a friendship? Or would the friend you're protecting do the same for you if he were faced with turning you in or going to jail? The other point being that since he would've been caught anyway, I would've been subpoenaed to testify against him because he had involved me by using my property for the fraud. To tell a friend you're going to commit some fraud (or whatever) is not a crime, but using that person's property and, by that, making them an accomplice, is.

THE TROJAN HORSE

Thanks for writing and giving us an even more ignored side of the story. You may have opened up some eyes. Try letting your "friend" see this letter and he might realize that he wasn't the only one going through hell on a rubber raft.

1985

Dear *2600:*

Are any of your readers familiar with the International Day of the Phreak? It's an annual event that's been going on for about three years now, with growing support each time. On the first Saturday after tax day (this year that would be Saturday, April 20), phone phreaks all over the world "get together" and do funny things to phone companies all over the world! Two years ago some pholks knocked out a Sprint satellite link by repeatedly calling the same access number with the same code from many different cities at once. It was great phun.

Perhaps your readers can suggest ideas for this year's "holiday." Also, does anyone know of a similar day for computer hackers? I think it takes place in the fall. (Phreaks can outdo hackers any day, by the way!)

FATHER

This is truly horrible. Do keep us informed, though.

Dear *2600:*

The following is a true story.

Monday, 04/01/85 6:08 a.m.

The phone rang. I got up and looked at the desk clock. It was 6:08 am, an hour before I go to school. I picked the receiver up. "Is this John McKee?" asked the caller urgently. "Yes," I replied, half asleep. "You better get rid of your printouts and your stuff on disks. You're gonna get a visit within the next 20 minutes," the kid said. He hung up. I got nervous. The phone rang again. "John, this is Jim. Greg just got busted and his brother has been calling up all of his friends on a sheet Greg had. Did he call you?" "Yes, he did," I said. "You better believe it, because you're gonna get nailed with the rest of us. Get rid of everything, burn it." I thought to myself, "What did I do to make them want me? Codes? No time, have to burn everything pertaining to illegal wrongdoings." I was panic-stricken. I got it together and went outside and burned it, disks, printouts, everything. As I was return- ing to my house, I wondered if they had a tap on my line. The phone rang another time. "Oh no. Who is it now?" I went in and answered it, only to be told "April Fools!" Click.

JOHN

Dear *2600:*

I've been thinking of starting my own bulletin board. But I'm not look- ing forward to the possibility that some jackass will leave a credit card number or other nasty information on my board and that some even bigger jackass will see said message before I can delete it and accuse me of conspiring somehow to defraud or steal or build explosives or whatever else they happen to be afraid of will happen at that moment. The recent raids in New Jersey indicate that even a conscientious sysop (as the fellow who was running The Private Sector *claims to be) can get screwed over by computerphobic police and Federal agents. What preemptive protections are available for a bulletin board operator who plans on staying within the confines of the law and yet does not want to stain her or his board with warnings and continually censor the flow of messages? Freedom of the press is a marvelous concept, and apparently allows folks like* USA Today *to stain every available street corner with their one-legged vending machines. What would one have to do to become a "press"?" You don't have to be made out of paper, since radio and television reporters qualify. Is there a union I can join? A professional society? Maybe we should start one? Can you recommend anyplace where further information on such would be available?*

W.U. Friend

You ask many intriguing questions and we believe that we could devote an entire issue to answering them. In fact, we spent a great deal of the August issue of 2600 *discussing the very things that you brought up. Many of your questions could be answered by allowing yourself to get busted and letting Warren Burger and the rest of the Supreme Court decide. This may be the easiest way because there are few laws, guidelines, or precedents. Right now, we do not know of any "unions,"* but there are hundreds of computer user groups that are actively discussing these problems, and we also foresee groups forming to specifically address the problem. *Especially since those computerphobes you were referring to are trying to get legislation passed to limit BBSes in this country. You must remember that this is a very popular issue, and it will come into play in various elections this fall, including those of the prosecutors who are pressing charges against* The Private Sector's *sysop.*

1986 _____

Dear *2600:*

My high school has a PDP with 48 VT101 terminals. They are very reluctant (probably just ignorant) to give out any sort of information. They feel that the system's use is only for learning BASIC and Pascal — no experimentation. But this should be expected.

I have inquired many times about controlling the cursor and the graphics on VT101 terminals, and they have threatened and warned me not to play with things I don't know. I am requesting information on where I can acquire information on the VT101 terminal (books, companies, etc.). If you could publish this information, I am positive many readers would find it useful.

Artful Dodger

Perhaps one of our erudite readers will send us such a list. In any case, yours is a familiar problem — one that breeds the hacker instinct.

Dear *2600:*

> I have a great idea that seems so simple, but I have never heard anyone mention it. It concerns protecting the userlog of a BBS from the prying eyes of the Gestapo police, or FBI, or whoever.
>
> You see, when they raid your house to take your BBS, they have only a few reasons. It is either to punish you for asking questions or to get a juicy list of people to investigate along with their favorite passwords. Sometimes they will call up other boards using the user names and passwords they just confiscated and try to read personal mail. This strikes me as being both immoral and illegal. But anyway, the trick is to not have the userlog available.
>
> I have solved this problem by putting the user list in memory on a RAM disk. I have a simple program that makes my computer think that part of the memory is really a disk that you can write to or read from. When the cops come racing in and pull the plug in an attempt to confiscate my computer, the information is gone. It just disappears. The only problem is that you need a computer that has more than 64K, like a PC or something, because most programs need 64K of available memory to run.
>
> It is unlikely that they will try to probe your computer before they unplug it and take it from your home "as evidence," because even their technical people are pretty incompetent. And they don't usually send their technical people along anyway. I am pretty sure of that, because they like to take calculators and normal telephones along with the computer, and that shows an extreme lack of knowledge.
>
> Because the BBS is almost always on, the userlog can be backed up on a disk outside of the computer, but encrypted in some way. All you have to do is scramble it, then rename it and put it in the middle of your BASIC programs or wherever. No one but the NSA would find it. And they have better things to do....

MOJAVE DESERT

Dear *2600:*

> *In response to police "sting" BBSes, why not get one of those books that
> list stolen and expired credit cards (they are issued weekly or biweekly).
> Type the contents into a disk and dump 40 megabytes of burned credit
> card numbers into these cop traps to spring them safely. If it comes to
> trial, tell the jury where you got them and watch the DA blush and the
> jury laugh. If the cops had any sense, that is what they would dump
> into any system collecting credit card numbers.*

JN
ILLINOIS

Good idea, but how many of us are willing to go through with the expense and
embarrassment of being hauled into a court of law just to make a DA blush? And
what happens if the jury has no sense of humor? Because we're not especially
fond of credit card fraud, we have no objection to people posting whatever numbers come into their heads or even random computer-generated numbers. That
way, the criminals are confused, the authorities are confused, and democracy is
safe for a little while longer.

1987

Dear 2600:

> *One bright day last March, a week after my 16th birthday, I came
> home to discover that the cops had raided my room and taken every-
> thing — computer, printer, modem, monitor, 350 disks, but left the
> Apple IIc power pack. Among those 300 disks were about 20 phreak/
> hack disks, 300 pirated programs, and a number of personal disks.
> MCI had caught me hacking out codes and put a Dialed Number
> Recorder on my line. They had followed all my calls for a month and
> a half.*
>
> *My first meetings with probation and lawyers scared me to death. I
> was informally threatened with going to juve, having to pay immense
> fines, never getting any of my stuff back, etc. The next two months
> of waiting for my trial were hell. I was originally charged with nine*

counts of various crimes including phone fraud, accessing of MCI's computer, and annoying phone calls (exchange hacking).

As it turned out, I used a county lawyer and ended up paying nothing for his services. I got off on most of the counts and had to pay a fine of $479.32, $29 of which were phone bills and the rest were "service charges" of having to switch the 22 codes I used. I also had to serve 80 hours of community service and remain on probation until these items were done.

I got all of my computer stuff back minus 11 disks of phreak/hack stuff (they missed quite a few). I did pay the fine, which was a hell of a lot less than what it should have been. I actually completed about 15 hours of community service but my probation officer was easily deceived.

I just got off probation last week and all in all I've got to say it was well worth it. I wrote to give you my account of being caught and what the end resolution was (not very harsh). I do hope that none of you have to go through what I did in those first two months.

THE SULTAN

Getting caught at something illegal is never "worth it" unless it's something you really believe in or something you can erase later. And if you brag about this to lots of people, you'll probably find yourself reliving history. Keep us posted. We care.

Dear *2600:*

In the July 1984 issue of *2600,* Quasi Moto, sysop of the late Plover-Net BBS, said he had the "perfect" disclaimer for a BBS. I have some friends who are starting a BBS, and they could really use his "perfect" disclaimer.

MAC???

There is no such thing. Many computer bulletin boards ask the question, "Are you a member of the law enforcement community?" And members of the law enforcement community simply answer in the negative. You won't find many judges who will sympathize with a defendant that was "lied to" by a cop. Other boards claim they're not responsible for anything that's posted by others. Well, that may be so, but if the law this month says sysops are responsible, they will feel the heat, disclaimer or no disclaimer. So what are we saying? Disclaimers are useless and offer a false sense of security. In many cases, they do more harm than good because the very presence of a disclaimer leads some to believe that something illegal is going on. You're better off running a board you can be proud of and whose contents you're prepared to defend. It being the '80s, you may very well have to justify your existence.

Dear *2600:*

> *I would like to comment on your July issue discussion on disclaimers. Your response that there is "no such thing" as a "perfect disclaimer" is not correct! We have yet to be prosecuted or sued over any of our publications. No police entity has even talked to us about them! A Ma Bell security type once came to my home to lecture me on phone color boxes (1981). I threw him out. End of conversation!*
>
> *I'm aware of a number of controversial BBSes run by teenagers with twice my IQ. However, when it comes to effectively disclaiming their user files, their IQs drop to room temperature. The wrong approach is to question users as to police affiliation. The right approach is to present controversial files for educational purposes only — even to state that no illegal use is suggested, implied, or intended. It also helps much to intermix purely illegal applications with those that are legal so it can't be claimed that your files have no reasonable applications except those that are illegal. For example, great sex associated with a plot is "necessary for plot development." Otherwise, it's just pornography.*
>
> John J. Williams
Consumertronics

Unfortunately, a lot of those rules still don't seem to apply to computer bulletin boards, even though they are, in effect, just another form of publication. We feel the key lies in making this connection clear to the people inside and outside the computer world.

Dear *2600:*

> *I don't understand your listing of CNA (Customer Name and Address) numbers. For instance, my area code is 305 in Florida. According to your listing, I have to dial area code 912 to get a customer's name and address. This seems strange because area code 912 is located in the state of Georgia and I have to pay a toll charge if I use this area code.*
>
> *I have Radio Shack's Duophone CPA-1000. If all "pen registers" work the same as this one, they can be easily voided. The pen register will not record the number of an outgoing call if same is made on a cordless telephone. The call is listed as an incoming call without the telephone number.*
>
> *If anyone has a suspicion that spies are registering their outgoing call numbers, they have only to use the cordless phones without worrying that same are being recorded.*
>
> *No mention was made of this in your article "A Pen Register for Phreaks" in your last issue, or didn't you have any knowledge of this?*
>
> SAMUEL RUBIN

If you take a look at our CNA list, you'll see that many area codes have their CNA bureaus located somewhere else, often in other states. It's one of those bitter ironies we hear so much about.

It's quite true that the pen register can be fooled into thinking that a cordless call is really an incoming call. We're not sure if all pen registers can be tricked this easily. However, keep in mind that when you use a cordless phone, you're broadcasting your conversation over the radio, which can be quite damaging. If this works consistently, the best method would be to dial on a cordless phone and then transfer to a regular phone. Unless, of course, you're being tapped. A face to face conversation in the middle of a huge empty parking lot might be the answer. But then there are satellites....

Dear *2600:*

> *About a year and a half ago, I was apprehended for "unauthorized use of phone lines." Here's my experience in a nutshell. Myself and my friend, The Ice Lord, rang up most of about $8000 worth of fraudulent*

calls to a small long distance service that couldn't afford to take the loss. Through carelessness, we were busted by the jerkwater sheriff's department in cooperation with some incompetent PIs and the FBI. They fumbled around with my system and gave away the fact that they had just busted Ice Lord by the way they accessed disk directories before packaging up my computer, notes, and joysticks. I would advise that anyone who gets into a similar situation not talk, as I did, because in my case cooperation didn't make it any easier on me. It just strengthened the plaintiff's case anyway. The judge went pretty easy on us and the insurance company settled the lawsuit, so as soon as I get a new keyboard (the cops managed to waste most of my Comm-64's chips), life will get mostly back to normal. By the way, even though they had evidence, other crimes were overlooked. Just wanted to share my experience — hope it's of some value.

I love your mag but can I anticipate something more in the way of how-to articles and beginning to semi-technical projects? Also, I'm looking forward to hearing about a 2600 meet on the west coast. Any chance of it?

Lastly, can you give me the full story on Bill Landreth's disappearance?

THE SORCERER

We hope when you say "life will get back to normal," you don't mean you'll continue to openly commit fraud on some poor phone company. There is very little of what you told us that sounds like true phreaking or hacking. Anybody can make free phone calls these days but only a few know how to thoroughly explore and discover new tricks.

We're looking for more how-to articles that our readers are encouraged to submit. As far as meeting on the west coast, that depends on how many people seem interested.

We don't know much about Bill Landreth (author of "Out of the Inner Circle"), but word has it that he's reappeared.

Dear *2600:*

> *First off, thanks to you I now have the Radio Shack Duophone Computerized Phone Accountant model 1000. What a nifty little device! I always wondered who the babysitters were calling... and for how long.*
>
> *Secondly, here's some cellular phone information that the dealer gave me after I showed him copies of 2600 and its cellular-related information. He was very happy to swap information.*
>
> *Thirdly, in reply to The Sorcerer's letter, if the police were as inept in their "capture" as he claims they were, it says one of two things: either The Sorcerer wasn't as "discrete" as he should have been, or the rest of the hacking/phreaking community is put on warning when a "Robocop" starts cleaning up.*
>
> *The Sorcerer also requested information regarding Bill Landreth (aka The Cracker), author of "Out of the Inner Circle." Enclosed please find the cover story, September 20, 1987, to the Southern California computer magazine* Byte Buyer, *which I penned. This should give you all the information you may need on Mr. Landreth.*
>
> *Lastly, I run a BBS called* Mainstreet Data. *In it is a section called "TAP Magazine." This section of the board is filled with information gleaned from the AP wire, international, national, and all 50 states individually regarding the keywords: hacking, phreaking, and computer crime. It is an extremely popular section of my large online system. To receive a complimentary account, call, enter 12 for your ID, for your password enter DAKOTA, and at the first command prompt enter PRO (of course, there is no punctuation). You will be given access to the entire system. I would be happy to be one of your west coast BBS envoys.*
>
> *Thanks for being!*
>
> RAINER MUELLER

Thanks for the cellular info. We will try to do something with it for a future issue.

Your article on Landreth was very informative and, while we cannot print it in its entirety, here are the main points for the benefit of our readers. As a result of intruding on GTE Telemail back in 1983, Landreth was sentenced to three years of probation. He then put out a book entitled "Out of the Inner Circle" which sold more than 50,000 copies. Because of this, he became something of a celebrity, a role which he apparently wasn't comfortable with. In the fall of 1986, he vanished entirely. He wasn't seen again until early this summer when he was discovered in a town 40 miles north of Portland, Oregon, "apparently dressed like a bum." He was arrested on a charge of federal probation violation and sentenced to five years in prison. He is due to return to court on October 13. His sentence may be commuted at that point or he may receive a different sentence. Regardless, as of this writing, Landreth was still incarcerated at the Metropolitan Correctional Center in downtown San Diego.

As ones who have seen the results of being thrust into the spotlight unwillingly or half-willingly, we find this whole series of events to be quite sad and unfortunate. Too often the media jumps on individuals for one thing or another, completely forgetting that they are mere human beings, subject to the same fears and insecurities we all have at one time or another. It's happened to rock stars, lottery winners, and crime victims. Now it's happened to a computer hacker.

Clearly, Landreth should not be locked up in jail. His "crimes" have hurt no one more than himself. Imprisonment in this case is barbaric and inhuman. We call on our readers to speak out against this kind of injustice in whatever way they can. And we wish him well.

Readers who want to hear more about this case should call the above-mentioned board. Hopefully, the facts will be passed around on different bulletin board systems as well.

We thank the many readers who have expressed an interest in running bulletin boards for 2600. Last month, we mentioned certain features we would require: full access to all callers, private mail that ensured privacy, and no verification of identity for users. If you want your board to be a 2600 board, it must also have 24-hour access, 300/1200 baud capability, the ability to store at least 100 messages on at least three public boards, the ability to handle at least 100 users, storage capacity for certain text files, and a way of having information uploaded. If you can meet those requirements, then contact us. All kinds of computers are welcome as are all kinds of software, provided they can handle the above.

Dear *2600*:

> *After reading the June issue of* 2600, *I decided to get right into the
> idea of putting up a system that would be either a network or just
> another* Private Sector. *I already have a system up that has the exact
> same sub-boards as the* Private Sector *did. I also have most of your
> old g-file section and almost all of your digests already online. Pretty
> good? My system has been up since the beginning of the year. However,
> I have had numerous hardware problems and the system has been up
> and down. I've raised my memory to two megabytes and now have a
> US Robotics 2400 baud modem. I also have a 20 meg hard drive with
> about 14 megs left.*
>
> *I was very impressed with* The Private Sector *and I have the same
> rules you did. No codes. Just information. Even there I am regulating
> what goes on (credit card fraud).*

LOS ANGELES

*We wish you luck. In the interests of freedom, don't go overboard with "regulating"
discussion. Keep the codes and passwords from being posted, as well as anything
obscene or offensive to users, but be careful with trying to control the flow of conversation too much or you'll be running a dictatorship. And if you have private mail-
boxes, they should remain private. System operators should not read their users'
mail unless that is their stated policy.*

1988 ⎯⎯⎯⎯⎯⎯⎯⎯⎯⎯⎯⎯⎯⎯⎯⎯⎯

Dear *2600*:

> *I have recently subscribed to your magazine because I am starting an
> "on call" personnel business, screening potential employees.*
>
> *Frankly, I am quite new to computers, but am determined to get a
> setup that will enable me to conduct business from my home.*
>
> *I am wondering if there are any people around who could help me in
> this regard by telling me what software to purchase and how to gain
> access to public records in all states, for background check purposes.*

Some of the types of things I want to access are county records, federal court records, worker's comp records, and driver records.

The process through the mail (which most governmental agencies make available) is very slow.

I am also interested in obtaining any other personal background information (credit history, military records, assets).

If there is a publication with access codes, etc., please let me know about it, because I really want to get this business going.

ANONYMOUS

It sounds as if you want to bypass the system and do things efficiently. Often, this means bending or even breaking the laws. You won't get anywhere if you depend on publications that print access codes. You want exclusive access to your sources. If you have to share this access with anyone who can get their hands on a publication, it just won't be effective. We distribute information, but there is a limit to how far we can go. If we were to print passwords or codes (despite the fact that it's illegal), so many people would use them that they would soon get shut off or monitored very closely. For that kind of information and the kind we suspect you're after, you need to make personal contacts — through the mail, on the phone, on bulletin boards, or on the street. You'll have to use your instincts insofar as who you trust and what information appears valid. If we've misread your question and you actually want to do this by the book, we're sure it's possible. Simply go through the agencies involved. But, as you've already noted, that tends to be slow, and, quite often, expensive.

Dear *2600*:

In the October 1987 issue of 2600, you wrote about how people from all over the world wish to run electronic bulletin board systems under the name of 2600 magazine.

Here are my ideas: enlist the aid of hackers and phreaks from all over the world to write a combined version of Diversi-DIAL and Fido for all major brands of personal computers. Second, since this is supposed to be like a global village setting of telecommunications hobbyists for the Communications Revolution, why not subtitle it "Foundation" after Dr. Isaac Asimov's Foundation novel?

Because what you are trying to do is gather people and data together to create a digital sanctuary for ensuring freedom of speech, especially now since advancing technology allows us to use that basic freedom to reach more people than ever before. That is sort of what the Foundation *novel was about.*

I hope the hackers and phreaks of the world are willing to write this much needed BBS software, because too many of us are kept apart by the telephone systems of our countries. For if we really *wish to learn and finally* control, *we need common places where we can go to draw on and then expand our knowledge.*

THE NATO ASSOCIATION

We need as many methods and channels of reaching people around the globe as our imaginations permit. The computer/telecommunications revolution can be mankind's salvation or doom. We're helping to make that decision.

1989

Dear *2600*:

Let this be a warning to those who engage in illegal activity.

On June 27, 1988, I came home from being out with friends at 1:45 in the morning. I parked my car in front of my apartment and got out. I am normally a very security-minded person, always looking over my shoulder, never getting overconfident with my sense of security. Many people know me in the IBM/Apple modem/hacking world, but I never let people know me too well.

Or so I thought.

As I stepped up my walkway to my building, I heard someone call my name. Before I turned around, I knew something was wrong. FBI agents as well as state police and local detectives had been watching and waiting for me all day. In no time, there were police cars everywhere, and I was shoved up against a car and searched and handcuffed, the whole neighborhood ablaze with flashing lights.

Of course I didn't say anything. Of course they played games like "Let's just go inside and talk this all over." I have always known better than to keep anything in my apartment that could incriminate me, but why attempt to make their job any easier?

Well, that was six months ago. I am still in jail.

That night I was driven 250 miles to a small, conservative farm town, a place I had never been to in my life. At my arraignment three days later, I found out that I was being charged with six counts of computer fraud-related charges, and my bond is a hefty $150,000, cash only. My parents live in another part of the country, and I have few connections with them anymore, and, unlike your average juvenile, I can't call mummy and daddy up and expect them to come running, cash in hand.

Now I can handle having to serve time for my own mistakes, but the way I was caught will show you that everybody who does anything illegal better be careful.

In February, 1988, I met with a person who I had known through various bulletin boards. I was going to school in the state he was from, so we decided to meet each other.

I drove and met him, ate dinner, and talked. He and I got along quite well, but at no point did he ever know my "real" name. Of course in the "modem community," relationships like that are common and understood.

That was the last time I saw him.

About a month later, this friend was visited by state police as well as security people from Sprint. Apparently, another "hacker" (I'm using that term loosely) had an argument with said friend, and, as a type of revenge, called Sprint Security and reported that said friend was a habitual code abuser. It took very little time for security people from Sprint and his local telco to put a DNR-type register on his two step-by-step phone lines.

Two months and 30 rolls of DNR paper later, a search warrant was obtained. His residence (he is a juvenile) was searched, and all computer and telephone equipment was taken and brought to a state police post for examination. At this time, said friend was smart enough to not talk without a lawyer present, so the police left, leaving him with his parents, no charges pending at that time.

He was smart to keep quiet. Too bad this trend did not continue.

Many people underestimate police investigators or the FBI. Don't ever let yourself be part of that group.

My friend was questioned several times after that. I now have all transcripts of all conversations. He told various names of people all over the country who had supplied him with codes, passwords, accounts, etc. He also said that he had a friend who was currently living in the state, who was involved with various activities similar to his own. He told the police what he knew of me, which wasn't too much, as well as what he thought my first and last name was.

Some time later, the police returned and asked him if he had any more information, as they had been able to find nothing on this other person he had mentioned. He could think of little else, except that he thought I had lived in a particular place prior to my living in his state.

The police wrote to that place and state, giving a basic age and description, and asked for copies of any mug shots they might have fitting that description.

Many years ago, some friends and I were arrested for trying to purchase alcohol underage. Although the charges were dropped, that picture stayed on file.

The police came back to this individual and presented several dozen photographs of the people who had fit that description.

The police report says that he "without hesitation pointed out photograph #13 as being the individual he knew."

The next day, warrants were issued, and today, here I am in a county jail.

Since that time, I have said absolutely nothing. I did not talk to anyone and try to lie, or offer to turn anyone else in. I simply refused to talk to anybody for any reason. I had to front $5,000 to a lawyer, and because I have not said anything or made any statement, I may be able to walk away from this, uncharged.

But the damage is done. I was in my final year of college and taking summer courses. I had an excellent job with a well known DoD contractor, and my future looked good. I was no longer doing anything illegal, and was keeping quite straight.

All of that is gone now. Even if I come out of this without charges, I have lost an entire semester of school, and have little hope of getting that job back after the FBI came and went through my office. I have lost six months of my life that can never be replaced.

My arrest made every paper in the state, so of course my future in this state looks bleak.

The juvenile is facing possible probation.

My message in this is that if you engage in illegal activities, you must trust nobody. There is not one person you can trust. When more than one person is caught, courts usually offer "plea bargains" or less time to those willing to testify against their friends. I cannot hold a grudge against the person that put me in here. I'd be lying if I said I never did anything wrong, but you can bet that 99 percent of the time, it will be somebody else that gets attention put on you, not yourself. It is terrible that we now live in an age where our friends today are testifying against us tomorrow.

If you ever find yourself in a similar situation, I can never stress to you how important it is to not say anything, not make any type of statement. The police are not here to help you. Do not try to lie or mislead them. They have more resources available than you may think. I hear people say how they would know "exactly what to say and do" if ever arrested, but sadly enough, when leaned on, it is amazing how many people will "break." The police are good at what they do. They know how to scare you. They have told me several times that I am looking at 36 years.

The best and only thing you can do for yourself at that point is to hire a lawyer. They can find out exactly what the police have on you, and what your real position is. If the juvenile had listened to me earlier, neither of us would be in this situation. I only hope I can reach those out there that he has told on before they find themselves in a similar situation.

Every time you leave your phone number on a bulletin board, you expose yourself. You trust that the sysop will not reveal that information to anyone. Frankly, you are risking your freedom every time.

In today's "hacker world", people are going to have to better secure themselves if they want to avoid a situation similar to the one I am in. Wish me luck.

THE DISK JOCKEY

Your letter provides a great deal of sobering insight. We hope this is not wasted on our readers.

While we don't know what, if anything, you did, it sure doesn't sound as if you are being treated fairly. You imply that you've been sitting in jail for six months without being charged with anything. If this is true, get rid of your lawyer and go back to those same newspapers that reported what happened. Go public and get some people behind you.

Naturally, if you feel this may backfire and encourage the authorities to file charges, don't do it. Once you're out, however, let the truth be known. If you think the system is screwing you, speaking out about it may prevent the same thing from happening to others.

If this is nothing more than a case of fraudulent phone calls, sitting in jail for six months is preposterous. Even credit card fraud, which to us is nothing less than stealing, should be dealt with by making the offender compensate the victim for their losses. Apparently, though, not everyone holds this view.

We have some difficulty understanding why you're not answering any questions. If you don't know any names or details, you really can't put the finger on anyone. If you do know names and you're protecting them, then you are indeed being quite noble. But are you sure this is what you want to do? In other words, do you owe these people anything? And are you expecting something in return? Odds are you won't get it.

Regardless of how you choose to handle this, your life is not over. You're having a very unpleasant experience, granted. But you will recover from it and you will benefit from it if you try. Be honest and open and reach out to others as you have in this letter. Don't concentrate on how miserable things are and on what opportunities have been lost. If you acknowledge your mistakes and refuse to let them defeat you, anything is still possible.

Please keep us updated as to your situation.

Dear *2600*:

> *There is good reason to put return addresses on the* back *of mail. While snooping in first class mail goes on all the time, any informa-tion obtained in this manner would be inadmissible in court. There is no restriction on copying the outside of the envelope, however. If the return address is on the back, there is no proof that it was on the same envelope as the "to" address.*
>
> Name Withheld

Not until someone invents a two-sided copying machine....

Dear *2600*:

> *In Austria we have a very sad situation concerning the phone system. Our system uses pulse dialing only and dates back to the '50s. Charging is being done by hand every month! They photograph the charge coun-ters (mechanical, of course) every month and the clerk types them into their 15-year-old computer that prints the phone bills.*
>
> *Collect calls or any of the other features you "enjoy" in the U.S. don't exist in Austria. However, they started introducing an MF-system in some parts of Vienna recently and blue boxing seems to be safe as far as I know. The situation is improving.*
>
> *Hacking in Austria is pretty boring because phone costs are astro-nomically high (one minute local: 50 cents!). Most systems do not use direct-dial but leased lines for communications.*
>
> WM

Dear *2600*:

> *"Any person having the phone number and password of a specific intel-ligent payphone can do such things as program the calling rates, check the amount of coin in the box, or even check to see if the phone has been vandalized. An FCC-approved data access arrangement must be used to connect the system to telephone lines with an automatic ring detect circuit answering incoming calls. Upon receiving an incoming call, the software could be set up such that the payphone issues a false ringback*

tone or busy tone to discourage unauthorized users. Personnel with the password, however, could simply enter DTMF codes over the false call progress tones to gain access. Once the password has been correctly entered (from any DTMF phone), commands can then be entered."

Upon reading this information (from the "California Micro Devices Data Applications for the G8880 DTMF Transceiver"), I promptly went down to the local mall where I knew there would be some "intelligent payphones." For some reason, the numbers of the two payphones I found were printed on the outside of the phone. Armed with this information, I went home and proceeded to dial up the payphones. During the ringback, I tried beeping in a few DTMF tones, but to no avail. But after a few rings, a computerized voice came on which advised the operator that this was a public phone (and therefore collect calls should not be directed to it). When the voice stopped, I tried some DTMF tones once again. The phone beeped some tones back and then eventually hung up. After calling back a few times, I stumbled into something remarkable. I began to hear the sounds of cars starting and people talking. I had somehow caused the payphone to monitor the area near the payphone and transmit these sounds back to me at the other end of the line. Needless to say, I was quite surprised. I began to ponder several questions: is this legal? What legitimate purpose is there for a function like this on a payphone? Should the general public know? It seems to me that we should experiment more with these private payphones and see what other hidden features they may have.

Mr. Upsetter

By all means, experiment. We'd like to know what formats exist for the security phones, i.e., how many digits, when are they entered, etc. In answer to your other question, it's probably legal, although for what purpose it's intended, we're hard pressed to say.

Dear *2600*:

There's a question that every hacker has asked at least once in his life and I am surprised that you have not as yet covered it. When hacking onto a system, everybody always wants to know "Who does the system belong to?" and "Does this system trace?" The answer to the first one should be obvious. CNAs have always proven to be very useful here. But what about the second question? How common is it for a mainframe to have tracing equipment on it, and after hacking it for some time, is it possible, if the company detects you, for them to obtain tracing equipment to catch you, and, if so, how likely do you think it is that they will obtain such facilities? The reason I ask this is that I often scan exchanges looking for computers to hack and I often wonder how "safe" a system that I am playing with is.

THE CPU RAIDER

We've covered this many times. Any system, be it a phone system or a computer system, can install a trace if abuse is suspected. It is not wise to call any system directly from your home for just that reason. Calling an extender to reroute your call to a computer system won't do you much good if the extender people put a trace on their system! But don't let us mislead you. There are always ways to get in and stay in if you're good, determined, and smart.

Dear *2600*:

In your Autumn 1989 edition, you mentioned that you thought the hack/phreak spirit in the USA was dying. I agree, but would there be a way to start an open hack/phreak group similar to Chaos Computer Club? If you want, you could call it "2600" and advertise in the Marketplace for people to start the clubs in their areas. They could have meetings similar to the ones you have once a month on Fridays.

BK
SYRACUSE, NY

We'd like for that to happen, but we can't wave our wands and expect it to occur just because we want it to. There has to be a desire from various people in various places. We can inspire that but we can't control it. It would be nice if people all over the world had meetings/get-togethers on the first Friday of the month. Ours have been going quite well and recently we've been having hackers from Europe call us on the payphones at Citicorp. We invite anyone to do this. We're there on the first Friday of every month between the hours of 5:00 pm and 8:00 pm, Eastern time. A warning: many strange people come to our meetings, so you may get an unpredictable response when you call. You may even get a regular person who knows nothing about 2600. We guarantee nothing.

1990

Dear *2600*:

> *I recently came across a very major security problem when using private phone systems such as in hotels.*

> *Most of these have a Station Message Detail Recorder (SMDR) that keeps track of all digits entered at your extension. At checkout time, these numbers are compared, either electronically or by hand, with a rate chart and the bill gets calculated.*

> *Because I generally use alternative common carriers for long distance calls, I almost always have a local, free (950) access number.*

> *Recently, one institution tried charging me excessive amounts, claiming that I had accessed some of the other, ahem, special exchanges (anything above zero is wrong, but I'll grant them the 25 cents if they insist), so I asked to see the printout.*

> *I discovered, to my very major dismay, that the paper had the 950 calling number and my security code, as well as the final number dialed.*

> *On checking further, I discovered this is not only a common feature of SMDRs, but is also on many private coin phones.*

> *Very curious, and very worrisome.*

> *I found a way to (sometimes) get around this. Most of the listings are limited to 20 or so characters, so I will punch in some random characters, and hit the octothorpe for a new dial tone. That way, the hotel printout merely gets the first, defective, series.*

> *This problem certainly raises some curious questions....*

> DB
> NEW YORK CITY

Why do you think so many phone phreaks work in hotels?

Dear *2600*:

> *In the past, you have printed letters telling tales of woe about flawed college telephone systems. I recently discovered an interesting flaw in the telephone system at my university. All students living in the dorms must dial "8" first to dial out on local and long distance calls. However, if one merely dials "7" instead of "8" before any long distance call, the call doesn't show up on your bill. Now those are the kind of flaws that I like.*

MR. UPSETTER

They're also the kind that don't last very long.

Dear *2600*:

> *I learned of a trick that might be of interest to you. To get someone else to pay for your long distance calls when you're in a payphone, grab the phone book. Dial 0 and the number you want to reach. Then tell the operator, when she comes on, that you want to bill this call to another phone. When they ask if someone is home to verify it, say, "I think so." For selection of the number, there are several methods to use.*

> *(a) The number of someone you know (and presumably hate), using the name of one of their loved ones who might ask them to take the charge.*

> *(b) A number at random from the phone book, using the name of the person who is listed for the number.*

> *(c) A number at random from the phone book, using a bland name like Joe, John, Frank, Bill, Sam, et cetera. (This works more effectively on phones designated "Children's Phone" and phones in rich neighborhoods.)*

> *(d) A person's office. After hours, many people have answering services covering their calls, and every once in a while they might accept charges if you use the name of the person who employs the service.*

> *Warning: be prepared to hang up, especially on (b) and (c). The odds of actually succeeding are low, but not as low as you might think. (The*

person who told me this trick pulled it off the first time he tried it, and has done it twice since. Most of the time, nobody's home.) Also, if you're doing this from a payphone, it's practically impossible to get yourself caught unless you're trying.

There is the difficulty of running into the same operator twice or thrice, but this can be avoided by having two or three people running shifts calling four or five times in a row and then passing it along to the next person. It's easier for the caller to recognize the operator's voice than vice versa, especially since they speak first, but be prepared to pass the phone to another person quickly.

(In case you're wondering, my friend is a bored dorm student who gets desperate to talk to his girlfriend who lives several hundred miles away.)

BIRMINGHAM

We'll be honest. Your methods are as old as the hills. Apart from that, simply billing calls to another person really doesn't have all that much to do with hacking. But continuing to figure out ways around the system does. We hope you know the difference.

Dear 2600:

I am writing to thank you for your excellent article on COCOTs. I am glad that someone finally told how it really is.

Recently, I was a victim of a collect call placed from a COCOT. I was charged close to $30 for a ten-minute call. The offending company was "Operator Assistance Network." I quickly called my local phone company and had the charges deleted. But I'm sure many other people who get victimized by such rip-offs don't do anything about it.

Taking the suggestion from the article's author (The Plague), a group of friends and myself have formed a neighborhood patrol called C.O.P. (COCOT Obliteration Patrol). By the name, I'm sure you can figure out what we do. To date we have eliminated about 65 COCOTs, and only three of those have been repaired. We prefer to "behead" the COCOTs by removing the handset, thus innocent people are not *ripped off by dropping money into an otherwise dead phone. Our neighborhood is now almost free of these evil phones and C.O.P. will not rest until all COCOTs are out of commission.*

DAN
DENVER, CO

This isn't quite the way to go about it. All COCOTs are not necessarily bad. To assume they are is to write off an entire branch of technology because of a few bad experiences. Rip-offs should be eliminated. But COCOTs can actually do some good if they improve upon the service already available. It's up to us to see that they do.

Dear *2600*:

I have recently read the two articles about the E911 case that were published in the Spring 1990 edition of your magazine. First of all, I want to thank you for bringing things like these into the open. The federal government is always trying to keep their misconduct (which occurs all too often) under their hats, and it's great to see that people still have the guts to stand up to it.

I have also been feeling the effects of these "crackdowns" here in the Twin Cities. Many a BBS have disappeared (along with their operators). Many more have been looked into, but allowed to remain. Almost every BBS in the state now posts a warning message about the "privacy" of email. I feel sorry for one BBS in particular: Hotline. It was clearly known to everyone that this BBS was completely legitimate. Yet, recently, they were the subject of a federal investigation. Apparently they had a set of users that were referred to as "privileged users". Someone who was uninformed and didn't take the time to look into things further assumed that the "privileged users" were hackers and received access to some secret part of the BBS. Actually, a "privileged user" is someone who contributes money to the BBS and receives privileges such as more online time, extra downloads, etc. The operators have since changed the status to "contributors" rather than "privileged users" to avoid future confusion. It is hard to believe that this anti-hacker paranoia has grown to such proportions that people even get harassed for merely contributing money to a BBS that they like. In any case, I'm glad to see that this board, as well as many others, has survived the attacks and has the pride, determination, caring, and guts to remain in operation.

Finally, since my interest in cases such as these has grown recently, I would like to know what else is going on. Here in the Twin Cities, I have been waging a battle of my own: against censorship. I am concerned about how successful the PMRC (Parents Music Resource Center) has been in limiting the rights of musicians to say what they feel. Also, I feel that hackers are not doing anything that would cause harm to anyone, and should also be guaranteed the right to the First Amendment. I would like to receive more information about your magazine and how I may subscribe to it. I want to assure you that I am not a federal agent, nor do I have any contacts with the federal government. I am not interested in busting you or your magazine, but simply in learning more about what is going on.

THE SPECTRE
ST. PAUL, MN

It wouldn't matter if you were. We provide the same information to anyone who's interested. We hope to see hacker bulletin boards recover from what has been a crippling blow. There are a great deal that are truly underground now. The need for public hacker boards has never been greater. Anyone who has questions about this should contact us.

Dear *2600*:

I really don't want to write another one of those "Gee, I really, really like your magazine...." letters, but unfortunately that is exactly how I feel. I am in my mid 20s and way, way back in the silicon dark ages (put it this way, I can remember when the IBM PC was thought by some to be a flash in the pan that would never oust the Apple II as the market leader), I discovered computers and modems. I had a secondhand Apple II+ (which I still use with pride and some choice hardware enhancements), a Hayes Micromodem II (since upgraded to a Practical Peripherals 2400 external), some "borrowed" software and a lot of naive curiosity. I was never a "hacker" per se since I have about a third-grade computer literacy level and the extent of my hardware knowledge is knowing what card plugs in where, and I did do some things in that dark time right after the breakup of the phone company that some water under the conscience tells me were not too nice, but I really didn't know any better.

With my little toy I discovered a whole new method of communications, with the immediacy of a telephone call and the depth of a letter to the editor. It also opened up the world of everyday technology: I heard about the rainbow of boxes that certain people use to test the limits of the phone system that 99.9 percent of people (myself sometimes included) take for granted. I heard about different computer systems and how to get into them. Frankly, I've never really wanted to hack myself, but it's always been fun to find out how I could do it, and stories from those who did such things were always fun to read.

In short, I experienced what the framers of the U.S. Constitution had hoped for when they sat down in Philadelphia in 1787: the free and open exchange of ideas (to borrow from WABC's Bob Grant). Even if the information shaded a little to the gray, it was still useful. But, freedom and paranoia go hand in hand: if you are free to do what you wish, eventually the exercise of that freedom may impinge upon the freedom of someone else. That is why we have laws, some fair, some not. Now, I'm not saying that laws cause criminals because there is a certain percentage of humans who will always do things at the expense of other humans, but I do believe that unfair laws will awaken otherwise latent tendencies in people. Since people will increase their "law-breaking" in the face of unfairness, those in power will retaliate with tougher laws, and so it spirals up until it can go no higher and suffocates in the stratosphere of social collapse.

What does this have to do with 2600? Your publication is one way responsible citizens have of combating the unfairness in our post-industrial society. Since information has become power in our society (witness the inordinate influence that CNN has over government policy), those in power, whether they are government or business, find it incumbent upon themselves to control what people know. Fortunately, we live in a more-or-less free society and we can get access to information if we dig for it. *There is enough self-incriminating information spread across all of the U.S. government's own pamphlets and press releases to keep self-appointed "government watchdog groups" in Brooks Brothers suits, but that information is not publicized. So maybe the key to our so-called "Information Economy" is publicity. Sure, IBM gets all the publicity for marketing a bug-ridden, hard-to-use computer, and Apple Computer can "Win the Hearts and Minds" of computer users, but who outside of semi-hardcore computer buffs know about the Amiga, or even Steve Jobs' neXT? They can blow the disk drive doors off even a fully-loaded IBM power user's dream machine, but who's really heard of them?*

So this isn't the "Information Age," it's the "Publicity Age." As Adolf Hitler said, if you must lie, tell the most outrageous lie you can. It's easier to believe that way.

THE DISCO STRANGLER
SOUTH RISER, NJ

1991

Dear *2600*:

After reading your summer 1990 issue, I would like to throw my two cents in. Most of the negative feedback writers compared breaking into a house with "breaking" into a computer. I find this to be an inaccurate comparison.

The reality of the situation is this. The hacker made a phone call. When the computer at the other end answered with a high pitched carrier tone, the hacker's computer made some high pitched whistling sounds back. What are those whistling tones? They are a language, words, a representation of human thought. In America we have an outdated set of laws called the Bill of Rights. perhaps the most radical legal document of all time, but dated, nevertheless. The First Amendment of the Bill of Rights protects a citizen's freedom of speech. A modem and a computer are just as much a tool of language as a typewriter or a printing press, and should be afforded the same protection under the law. If we can agree on that point, let's continue with this stream of logic.

The hacker has called a phone number. The phone is answered and some words are exchanged through the translation of the modems. The computer asks who is this? The hacker replies this is so and so. The computer says how do I know this is so and so. Prove it. Tell me the password we agreed upon when you called before. At this point, the hacker must either guess or have access to a password. The hacker repeats a word he has heard that he has gotten from friends, found on another computer, etc. Hearing this word, the computer says, okay, you must be so and so. Now ask me whatever you want. The hacker now has use of that computer by false pretenses because he has said the right combination of words. At this point, the hacker reads information that is stored on the computer. He decides he wants a copy of a certain document and the computer says okay, since you are so and so, you can have it. The hacker is not stealing it. It is still there on the computer. He has an exact copy made just for him. The hacker is done now. He has what he wants and hangs up the phone.

What has happened? The computer has given the hacker an exact copy of some text the hacker requested over the phone, thinking the caller was someone else. The hacker has lied and said, yes I am so and so, give me a copy of that text. The hacker has misled the computer, but has he broken a law? If so, is the law he has broken legal? That is, does it follow America's fundamental laws laid down in the Bill of Rights?

In my opinion, the hacker hasn't broken the law. What the hacker has done is what collection agencies, private detectives, and market research companies do all day long. They call someone up saying they are someone else and if the person who answers the phone is trusting enough to give out information over the phone, then the caller has achieved his goal and received the information he wanted. This may not be very nice, but it is hardly illegal. People who hook up computers to the phone systems should realize that they are hooking their computers into a public system that anyone in the world with a phone can get at. If security is an issue with your information, you should take precautions to protect it. The world is filled with people who act in a way you may consider to be unethical or not nice but they're not breaking the law. Both sides of the issue should recognize that all laws including the Bill of Rights are just words of men and women who want to make you behave in a certain way. Laws are just a way of exhorting power over people who disagree with the law maker. If you disobey their laws, you shouldn't be surprised if the power behind the law confronts you. It has come down to a power struggle between the two parties. Behind all laws is the threat of violence and imprisonment. In breaking the rules, you run the risk of confronting the beast that hides behind the law.

Computers are amazing devices that are radically shifting the pre-established power structures. Expect a fight for the power.

SCOTT ALEXANDER
SAN FRANCISCO, CA

We've been living that fight for more than seven years now. The more people we drag into it, the better. Above all else, we have to fight the knee-jerk reactions that come from people with a very shallow understanding of the technology. We hope more people think the issues through as you did.

Dear *2600*:

I have bought two issues of your magazine and find it interesting and enlightening. I hope to be able to contribute an article someday. I have only your word that you are not, in fact, some FBI/SS/AT&T front to obtain hackers' names and addresses. You really should print some information on your operation to provide some assurance to your readers that this is not the case. For instance, are our names and addresses kept in a computer database? Printed files? Could the feds be monitoring what checks pass through your bank account? Do you have a bank account? Do you mail 2600 from one central location where packages can be tracked from source to destination? Is there dynamite strapped to your hard drives to be triggered in case of a raid? Inquiring (and paranoid) minds want to know!

Anyway, keep up the good work; it is appreciated nationwide!

QUANTUM
AUSTIN, TX

We're not running a covert operation here. Everything we do is open to public scrutiny. Our mailing list, though, has never been touched by anyone outside of 2600. Of course, the post office could be writing down every name that ever shows up on a copy of 2600. But that would be pointless and extremely time consuming. If, by some bizarre twist of fate, the government were to actually launch investigations into everyone who received interesting mail, the way to fight such oppression would not be by hiding and allowing it to continue. Challenging authority is our obligation, particularly if that authority is being abused.

Dear *2600*:

> This letter is intended for those people who break the first commandment of the Phone Phreaker's Ten Commandments (TAP #86) which is: "Box thou not over thine home telephone wires, for those who doest must surely bring the wrath of the chief special agent down upon thy heads."
>
> Blue boxing is something that is done quite easily here in Ontario and Quebec. All we need to do is dial any phone number (handled by AT&T) that goes to the United States. The two areas in which we can box off of are Springfield, MA (4132T) and Buffalo, NY (7162T). From there you do whatever you want and can with your blue box.
>
> I began blue boxing in 1986 and always boxed from a payphone. In 1988, I began boxing to Compuserve's CB. Since we only have Tymnet and DataPac, which both charge about $10 an hour, it was much cheaper to box to a local CIS number at 30 cents an hour. I was even nice to AT&T by boxing to the local number in Springfield, MA so as not to charge them with an LD call. I did all my computer boxing from a local school to be safe, and still obeying the first commandment.
>
> In 1989, I was subscribed to call forwarding. I noticed that when I forwarded my number to an 800 number in the States, an operator would come on the line to do a number verification. Hmm, this was interesting. Bell Canada didn't know who I was, so I would give them any number except my own. This made me think that I could get away with boxing at home, because AT&T, if they received my number when dialing over there, would have the number I gave to the operator. I

began doing this in November 1989. 1 began using the blue boxing techniques to call anywhere, anytime. It was a lot of fun.

Now I knew that the Bell equipment here (DMS-100) was recording everything I dialed even as an operator with my blue box. I also knew that Bell should be ringing my doorbell soon. But they never came by. I got rid of my call forwarding, but continued calling from home. Every once in a while, I would slow down, because 1 was making just too many calls.

Well, it finally happened. Recently, a friend of mine called me up and said that Bell Canada Security just visited him. They handed him a nice little bill of $3,000. He was dialing 976 services every night for a couple of hours. Then, about an hour later, Bell Security showed up at my door. I was freaked out and panicking as I went to the door with my parents yelling at me. I looked down at the amount they wanted from me and then almost laughed. They only wanted $350! Boy, what a relief. Of course, they took all my spare change, but at least I was able to pay for it. They only had my calls for the previous month. My theory is that the computer erases the dialing info every month when the bill is made.

I found out that for the whole 418 and 819 area codes, there are only three security people from Bell Canada working them. That's the whole province of Quebec excluding Montreal. I guess that's one reason why it took over a year and a half for them to come visiting, but then again maybe not. I have another friend who just started phreaking this month and was caught for $80. And there were quite a few others being caught that day, the security guy told me. I wanted to ask why it took them so long to come and get me, but of course I wasn't going to let them know how long I was doing this for.

Now if you're asking yourselves why I didn't just say that I didn't have a clue as to what they were talking about, you can blame that on my parents' big mouths who started talking way too much.

Anyway, the point of this little story is that if you are boxing from your home line, you should stop while you're ahead. Hoping that Bell won't come by just isn't enough. If you want to take that risk, as I did, then go ahead, but always be prepared to pay the price when security comes by.

The only real bummer in this is that I lost 350 bucks and that I can no longer phreak to bulletin boards. Plus I've gotta start trying to blue box a 2600 over the payphone, which just isn't as easy as it is at home.

T.15
QUEBEC

One wonders if there would be as much boxing if access to bulletin boards was made affordable to everyone.

Dear *2600*:

The "Where Have All The Hackers Gone?" article in the Summer 1991 issue was relevant and personally powerful enough to bring me temporarily out of the "woodwork." I admit I am guilty of the article's charge of hackers "submitting to unacceptable terms and remaining underground like criminals."

Contrary to some of the rumors I have heard over the years, I was never arrested, never had my house searched, nor had anything confiscated. To me, this seems like an absolute miracle due to the many security and law enforcement people who seemed intent on getting that "bastard, Lex Luthor." And no, I have never betrayed the trust of those who were then colleagues to avoid trouble with the law.

Perhaps my belief in freedom of speech and its consequent visibility, and not any alleged illegal acts perpetrated with a computer and modem, was what made me a target. 2600 has published my articles in many issues over the years. There were a number of other articles distributed electronically, which attempted to inform those who wanted to learn about the use and abuse of various technologies. And of course, my affiliation with the Legion of Doom helped to enlarge the bulls eye.

I cannot say that my ego had nothing to do with writing "files," as being recognized for accomplishments, however dubious as they may have been, had some gratification. The drive to "fix the system" by informing people of the insecurity of computer systems was more of a factor in writing files than my ego was however. In retrospect, I realize that I was the one who needed the fixing and not the security.

For two and a half years, I did not use a modem for any purpose, thus succumbing to the same fear that was mentioned in the article. Like Frank Darden, "I am a prisoner of my own hobby" with the obvious difference being that I am a free person. I will always live with the reality that my past transgressions may one day catch up with me. I never gained monetarily and I never acted with malice when I used my computer and modem. Yet I am still fearful. I suppose I am a victim of my own curiosity, the thrill of a challenge, and the enthusiasm of trying to inform others of what was out there. I was no "superhacker" nor "arch criminal."

Today I use computers sparingly. Like most people, my computer use is limited to assisting me with tasks that are too tedious to do "manually." And for the record, any time I touch a computer, it is for strictly legal purposes only. It appears to me that as one gets older, one becomes more ethical. In my opinion, those who hold to the cliche "once a thief, always a thief" are obviously misguided, narrow minded, and distrusting of humanity as a whole including themselves. People can and do change.

The Atlanta hackers — Frank, Rob, and Adam — have been sentenced to a life term of financial imprisonment. How can they pay the enormous fine levied against them plus their own legal fees, which I assume are astronomical, when most employers will not hire them in their field of expertise: computer science, due to their "background?" The punishment does not seem to fit the crime in this case.

It would be interesting to see a bulletin board that discussed hacking topics with some of the "old timers" who have gone underground along with the newly curious, while remaining within the boundaries of the law. But with the current state of eroded civil rights and "shoot first, ask questions later" mentality, only the bravest of people would agree to run it.

I am relieved to see some respectable businesspeople taking a stand for everyone's rights, in the form of the Electronic Frontier Foundation (EFF). Victims like Craig Neidorf graphically depict the unjust state of affairs and the need to protect the Constitution. Perhaps the activities of the EFF and the current awareness of civil rights abuses is the reason I have finally acknowledged that I am indeed alive.

I am still a hacker in its pure sense: being curious, trying new approaches to problems, expanding the envelope, etc. The hacker in the darker sense is dead. Partly due to fear, partly due to necessity, partly due to self preservation, partly due to the realization that the ends do not justify the means.

As for where has this hacker gone, I have a four year engineering degree which took a bit more than four years partly due to all that time spent on computers which should have been spent studying. Today, I spend time hacking engineering design problems. Still fearful of persecution and prosecution, I am prevented from saying anything more. Perhaps I have said too much already.

(I USED TO BE) LEX LUTHOR

1992

Dear *2600*:

In response to the "Why Won't They Listen" article, I have this to offer. I think we all know why the establishment will not listen. We have them scared senseless. Not scared in a physical sense, but a deeper sense. In a way, we should congratulate ourselves. We demand change and people see us as a force with which they should reckon.

Unfortunately, the problem is that the establishment fears we are terrorists out to destroy all their possessions. They all sit around watching Geraldo and think we're launching missiles at the nearest hospital or shopping mall. In reality, the average 16-year-old hacker's main interest is figuring out a way to change his grades and finding 800 back doors to 900 numbers. They think we work for some leader of a third world country or that we're child pornographers. Again, we all know what the reality is. We are interested in technology and would like to remove the greedy people from power who hoard it all.

The fear of the establishment is this (obviously); they are afraid of losing their control. Maybe they are afraid of another revolution. Who better to crush the system than people that understand the ways that the system imposes itself upon us and pries into every nook and cranny of our private lives? We all know that 80 percent of the people don't support George Bush. We can all see the lies the straight corporate media tries to feed us. Things are screwed up right now and people could get irate and change them, if they knew how. Who would be most adept at this? Who has the smarts enough to outsmart the system? Hackers and phreaks!

The other people that fear us are those who refuse to cut the umbilical cord of their MTV long enough to take a look at the world around them and be forced to think for five minutes.

People who are afraid of free speech and free thought like the CIA, and its previous leader George Bush, have learned well from Hitler's reign. They have learned to control what people say in the media and attempt to control what we say to each other. The Dutch resistance knew that in World War II and thus were probably the first "phreaks" by today's standards. They rerouted calls as to avoid being monitored by the Nazis. Do you think the Dutch would have survived if they sat around all day watching soap operas?

Maybe that's not what most of the computer underground is interested in, but it's why the establishment is afraid. Most of us don't like many of the bums that have power over us and they know it. Maybe today is not the day for a sudden change, but when it needs to come, we will have archived a wealth of information when it is needed the most!

DISPATER

And hopefully we'll be able to find it.

Dear *2600*:

To the Fed: I read your article in the Summer 1992 2600 on how you say you work for the federal government (Treasury Department, to be exact) and how you got on hack/phreak boards because you told the truth and the sysops just let you on.

I can tell you this. I run an H/P board here in Maryland (home of the NSA) and can tell you that if I knew that you worked for the feds or even had any contact with them I never would have let you in. I know that there might be the chance that feds are on my board of 140 users, but I sure don't know about it. If I did they'd be Gone like The Wind.

I have nothing against you and I'm sure that you're a pretty cool person. It's just that I'm upset that a person who out and out said that they were a fed is even given the time of day by some dumbass sysop. Maybe one day the 14-year-old sysops might wise up to the facts.

ALBATROSS

Dear *2600*:

I recently came into contact with your magazine for the first time (the Summer 1992 issue). Now, I first started programming in 1977 (which I suppose makes me a hopelessly outdated relic to some people) when the word "hacker" had a very different meaning, and there was no danger in uttering the words, "I am a hacker."

To my shame, my first thought when I saw 2600 was, "It's probably full of adolescent rants denigrating those who don't agree with the authors' particular points of view, and boasts about their "hacking" abilities, peppered with words like "keul" or "awsum."

I was quite pleasantly surprised when I found my initial knee-jerk reaction to be almost completely unfounded. 2600 contains quite a bit of interesting reading, written by articulate, intelligent individuals.

I was so impressed that I intend to subscribe. Keep up the good work!

JL
TAMPA

Lots of people have similar reactions upon meeting their first hacker.

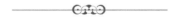

Dear *2600*:

I'm a Japanese student and new subscriber to 2600. Yesterday, I got a bunch of back issues and enjoyed every page. Yours is one of the greatest publications I've ever read.

I'm a fourth grade student, so I had to find a job, and I got it! From next April, I'll work for Institute of Research (one of five large think-tanks in Japan) as a researcher. Maybe I can play with some super-computers and other interesting technologies.

In Japan, there are some public phone phreakers. About ten years ago, NTT (Nippon Telephone and Telegram) introduced telephone cards and new public phones which had the capability of using these new cards. Before this, we had only "coin-op" ones which accepted 10 yen and 100 yen coins. The cards were magnetic and prepaid. There were four types: 500 yen, 1000 yen, 3000 yen (with novelty of 20 units), and 5000 yen (with novelty of 40 units). NTT charges 10 yen for a local three minute call (long distance calls cost more). This is considered a unit. If you have a 3000 card, you can use 320 units; a 5000 card can use 540 units.

Our telephone cards were easily modified by using some magnetic card readers/writers. Some people tried to steal public phones so that they could inspect the structure of them. And some people got arrested. Then many phreakers, poor foreign workers (they used illegal and cheap cards to make phone calls to their home countries), and yakuzas (Japanese mafias) made modifications so that these cards were usable forever (by writing infinite units onto the cards).

About a year ago, NTT decided to stop producing expensive cards (3000 and 5000) due to widespread modified cards and modification methods of the card. Now we have two types only.

JAPANESE SUBSCRIBER

We wonder if the modified cards still work and, if so, will they work forever? That's an interesting concept.

We suspect your definition of fourth grade differs from ours. In fact, we sure hope it does.

Dear *2600*:

> *The [September] DC 2600 meeting wrapped up a couple of days ago. I thought I would share a little visit we had from the Secret Service! We can not confirm that it was the SS, but all evidence leads to that conclusion.*
>
> *It started with some guys in sports jackets who kept walking by and sitting near us. Then, toward the end of the evening, a couple of guys in dark blue-collared t-shirts sat near us and seemed to look at us with a lot of attention. Then they proceeded to move on. A little later, the same two were spotted on the level above us. Two more joined in, all dressed basically the same (dark blue-collared t-shirts). Boy, did they stick out like sore thumbs! We would occasionally stare directly at them, wave, etc. At one point we all stared at them! A couple of us got adventurous and moved to their level and closed in. One of us started chatting and he noticed "Secret Service" in small letters on one of their shirts. Then one of the guys asked if we knew anything about boxes that made beeps to get free calls. The meeting goer said something like "What's a box? Beeps?" Then everyone at the meeting (who was still around) decided to relocate right next to the SS guys. After noticing the 5 to 1 against odds, they deduced that it was better to mosey on, which they did, and that was the last we saw of them!*
>
> TECHNO CASTER

1993

Dear *2600*:

> *At last I've found a niche. After being confused beyond belief by those goons at PC Week and psyched out after thumbing through the pages of Mondo 2000, I've discovered that 2600 is where I belong.*
>
> *I was at a bookstore, looking through gaming mags. Between a seriously misplaced Better Homes and Gardens, and a way outdated Electronic Gaming Monthly, I saw a torn page with the remnants of what looked like the numbers 2600 on it. Underneath this was printed*

"The Hacker Quarterly." My curiosity then got control of my body, and I investigated further. Despite the crappy condition, I paid the four bucks. When I got to the counter, the clerk told me that the store would stop carrying 2600 with the next issue. Looking at my copy, I see that it is the Autumn issue. No doubt, by now the winter issue is out and I have no place to look for it! At any rate, I sat down that night and couldn't believe what I was reading. All this talk of telephone "tricks" with the use of electronic medium made me think to myself, "Self, this is cool stuff and I want more!" I'm now thinking of subscribing. I just have one question. How come a one year subscription costs 21 bucks, when cover price is 16?

Phord Prefect's article on getting started really spurred me on. Being an extreme beginner, I have little or no knowledge of these "boxes" that everyone seems to be referring to. You should make a "guidebook" available for the price of a back issue. This book should explain what all current readers are assumed to know, so that we (new readers and novice phreaks) don't go into this thing blind.

Kudos to Count Zero for his info on COCOTs. With his article, I was able to successfully build a combo box by making enhancements to an existing Radio Shack tone dialer. I had a hell of a time getting the materials, though. It would appear that Radio Shack employees are very reluctant to fork over their warez unless they know what they're going to be used for. When they see a 14-year-old getting a pocket dialer, a mini toggle switch, and a little bit o' wire, something must go off in their heads. My conversation:

Radio Shack Techie: *So you're into phones, huh?*

Me: *Me? No, not really.*

Radio Shack Techie: *Well, why're you getting this?*

Me: *It's (hmm) a Christmas present(!)*

Radio Shack Salesperson: *For who? Your dad?*

Me: *(go to hell) No, my friend wanted me to pick it up for him; I don't know why.*

Radio Shack Techie: *Well, you could do some pretty nasty stuff with this thing if you know how to use it.*

Me: *:)*

Radio Shack Salesperson: *Well, there ya go. Have fun.*

Come on! Is it really necessary to ask all of these questions? I was afraid that if I reminded the man that it was none of his business, he would forget about the sale that was in effect that day.

Please write back your response, because I doubt that I'll be able to read about it in your mag. Under the circumstances, I don't think I'll be able to find 2600 as easily as I did last time.

THE APPLE II EVANGELIST
PALOS VERDES, CA

Your problem is very easily solved. All you have to do is subscribe! It costs a little less to get us on the newsstand but there is that degree of uncertainty that you have to go through. Regarding Radio Shack, we don't know why they have to interrogate all of their customers the way they do. It's extremely annoying and has led many of us to go elsewhere. On those rare occasions when we have no choice, we always feed them bogus info. A little thing like an eight-digit phone number or a zip code with a letter in it can ruin their entire day.

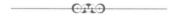

Dear *2600*:

I just received my first copy of your magazine and last year's back issues, and I love them. I don't know if I'll ever have the guts to climb up telephone poles and do late night hacking sessions, but I have been known to poke around a few Internet sites and have a look. Your publication has already given me ideas on some new fun things to try.

I'd like to know two things: 1) Do you or your readers know how I could get into any of the virus BBSes that are out there? Every time I read an article on viruses I keep hearing about the "awful BBSes" that carry virus source. But I'll be damned if I can find one. 2) Are there people in the Rochester, NY area that would be interested in having 2600 meetings? I'd offer to try to set things up myself, but I travel quite a bit and my attendance would be sporadic.

Maybe if I find some European virus BBS numbers I'll have a good reason to build the Radio Shack red box and do my BBSing for free!

YFNH
(YOUR FRIENDLY NEIGHBORHOOD HACKER)

There probably are people in your area interested in having meetings but some-body has to take the initiative. There are BBSes that specialize in viruses but they're kind of funny about giving their numbers out. If you succeed in your quest, you will certainly be a sight: a hacker with a laptop hooked to a payphone using a red box to connect to a European virus BBS. You just can't get more evil than that.

1994

Dear *2600*:

> *Just picked up your Winter 1993-94 issue (I love the looks my local bookstore clerks give me whenever I buy it), and I must commend you upon another first class effort. I first came into contact with it thanks to the meetings in my area, which are always excellent. Of course, since I started going to them, I have become known as a weirdo who goes to hacker meetings by my normal friends. They always say "hacker" as if they are literally spitting out the word. Ah, well, if we were all made to suffer fools gladly, why did they invent mental institutions?*

> *Your journal is one of the magazines I most look forward to and the best thing to ever happen to the H/P community. What annoys me to no end is that most of those who are coming into the fold now are only in it to make free phone calls and get pirated games. There seems to be very little desire to learn any more. That is one of the things that makes your magazine refreshing.*

> SCUDDER

There are lots of us who are in this to learn and spread our knowledge. As we all know, there are kids who just want a free ride, criminals who just want a new scheme, and reporters who just want an easy story. Either we ignore them or attempt to reach them on our terms — anything so long as we don't join them.

Dear *2600*:

I just had an amusing experience that I'd like to share with my fellow 2600 readers.

I had just read the article in the Autumn 1994 issue by Toxic Avenger (which was very good by the way) about using a Hallmark card to build a $10 red box. I figured, 10 bucks, what the hell, and decided to build one. I was in Radio Shack buying a Modular Wall Plate for something else and noticed a Hallmark shop. I decided to get the card while I was there. I brought the card up to the counter to pay for it and put the Radio Shack bag on the counter next to it while I got out my money. The lady at the counter saw the card and the Radio Shack bag and got this sour look on her face. She then proceeded to ask if she could see what was in the bag (like she'd have a clue of what to look for). I asked her why, then it dawned on me what was going on. She mumbled something about store policy and I told her that all I wanted was to buy this card, not to get a critique of my electronics buying habits. She promptly got "The Manager." I asked why there was a problem and his explanation was that some "kids" were using these cards for illegal purposes and they were just acting in the public interest. Since I didn't have all day to waste (and the people waiting behind me were getting restless), I showed him what was in the bag, bought the card, and was on my way. Actually, it was pretty funny because since I wasn't going to mail the card, I almost forgot to grab the envelope that goes with it!

Helpful Hint: Never bring a Radio Shack bag into a Hallmark shop and don't forget the envelope for the card!

> Mr. Hallmark
> Rochester, NY

We suggest that all of our readers bring Radio Shack bags into Hallmark shops and cause a holy scene if anyone pulls that kind of garbage. Last we checked, people still had the right to buy products of their choice without harassment. (Be sure to bring your 2600 shirt to the fun.)

Dear *2600*:

> *My friend told me about you guys and what you do, so I'm taking the time to write you an article about a hacking experience of mine.*
>
> *On May 2, 1992, I was using my modem to transfer files to my work. After I was done, I decided to check out a bulletin board I had heard about a long time ago from a friend.*
>
> *As I dialed the number, I mistakenly mistyped the number. But instead of a NO CARRIER message, I got an answer. It was one of those host programs on a remote computer. I decided to see what I could access, so I looked further into the system.*
>
> *By some accident, I was given access to the system's hard drive. I first erased all contents of the hard drive and then inserted a virus called Mr. X.*
>
> *Mr. X simply formats the hard drive, causing the unit to become useless. After that, I left the system.*
>
> *This story may not be as far out as some others but it's true — that should count for something. I also heard that if you accept this article, I get a free membership to your board.*
>
> JL
Highland, CA

You get a free membership to our list of morons who go around calling themselves hackers. Do you honestly expect us to respect you for destroying a system? What's amazing is that you did this apparently under the assumption that this is what a hacker is supposed to do when he gets into a system. Nobody could be that stupid, so this has to be a joke. Yeah, that's it.

1995

Dear *2600*:

> *I am a white, college graduate, conservative, clean living, law-abiding, God-fearing, married, work 40 hours a week, Republican-voting, citizen.*

The day 2600 is not allowed to be published is the day the revolution has to begin.

JOEL
ORANGE COUNTY, CA

If we wait that long, it may be too late.

1996

Dear *2600*:

Sorta different but at the same time relevant. A local joke around here is to tell someone to call "The Pickle Man." You call 617-PICKLES and ask the guy who answers to tell you a joke about pickles. Well, I did this many years ago while drunk at a party but I never forgot it. The number is the direct line to the Boston FBI. I thought you might get a kick out of the number. Enjoy.

CACHE $$$
BOSTON

Either you were drunker than you thought or the FBI finally lost its patience. Either way, that number is disconnected.

Dear *2600*:

I stumbled across something that I figured might be of interest to other 2600 readers. The other day, at an ATM machine, I happened to see a VISA CheckCard lying on the machine. Being the good person that I am, I called the issuing bank and asked where to send this lost card so it wouldn't fall into the wrong hands. The friendly operator then proceeded to tell me the person's address and phone number, without me asking. I mailed the card to the person, but I can only imagine what kind of trouble could be caused had I been a malicious hacker.

HELL-BOY

Not to nitpick, but "malicious hacker" is a term coined by the media that's designed to strike fear into the hearts of the average American and improve the ratings. There are hackers who turn into malicious people and that's when they move away from hacking and toward crime. It's in the interest of governments and large corporations to blur that distinction so that we equate exploration, curiosity, and rebellion with things that are evil. Your actions reflect exactly what a hacker does: you discovered something, you told everyone about it, and you realized that you found a major privacy violation. We'd like to know the number you called.

Dear *2600*:

> *I have a question regarding frog's article "Imaginary Friends" on scamming Ma Bell with a fake identity. OK, so you provided the phone company with all that fake info. Don't they need your real address to give you phone service?*
>
> THEDESPISED

Yes, but the reason for doing it like this is so that your imaginary friend begins to turn into a real person. He just happens to be living in your house for now. And the flip side is that if the phone service is in his name, it isn't in yours.

1997

Dear *2600*:

> *In Volume 13, Number 3, alien13 writes that his mom found his 2600 between his mattress and she went crazy. Well, me being a kid as well, I know this problem and have solved it with a great hiding place — alien13 wasn't far off when he hid it in his bed. But not the right spot. The best hiding place is inside your box spring (that hollow thing that looks like a second mattress). On the bottom of the box spring is a very flimsy cloth. Poke a large hole in the cloth and place all contraband in there. I keep all my hacking mags as well as other things in there. If you*

don't have a box spring, I guess you could make a small hole in your
mattress but I wouldn't recommend it. I hope I may have helped out.

EDOBAN

It's really heartwarming to know that we're thought of in the same way as drugs
and porno in so many households.

Dear *2600*:

Exactly how safe are your meetings to attend? I've heard of the incident
at the Pentagon Mall, and how cops will sometimes attend meetings.
What is the possibility of a police raid, or of equipment being confis-
cated, or arrests made? What is safe to bring (tone dialers, laptops,
printouts, etc.) and what isn't?

ANONYMOUS, NJ

Authorities of all sorts have a tendency to panic when a group of hackers are
around. Which is exactly why we must continue. They want us to be driven underground and cannot understand why we insist on meeting in public spaces. They
see us as criminals and want us to act that way. When we don't, it throws them off,
they begin to question their beliefs, and fear takes over. That's why it's important
that, no matter what they do, we are completely accountable for everything we
bring and everything we do.

Dear *2600*:

It was 20 years ago today... not really, it was only ten, but one fine day
ten years ago I had the privilege of taking part in an historical event.
On June 5, 1987, I was one of about 30 computer enthusiasts who made
history by attending the first 2600 meeting in New York City. When
I first became a computer enthusiast, the players had names such as
Cheshire Catalyst, Jim Phelps, Fred Steinbeck, and Cap'n Crunch.
2600 was about to become the undisputed champ as the new major
conduit for the flow of data of what used to be called the Computer
Underground. In TAP, I always read about the Friday night meetings

at their favorite watering hole, and how you could stop in the TAP office and help out with the publishing of the paper. I wanted to be at instead of read about the meetings, but with the demise of TAP, I thought that it would never be. Now 2600 gave me a chance.

When the bus pulled out of the station, I had no idea what was in store for me. I knew no one in New York, and had never been there. From the stories I had heard about New York, I didn't know if I was going to make it back alive, but being the steadfast computer enthusiast that I was, I went anyway. I got up that morning at 1:30 a.m. so I could catch the bus from Pittsburgh to New York. I should have known that it would be an interesting day when I stopped for a red light and was passed by a speeding stolen car and about four police cars. The bus pulled into the Port Authority station at about 2:00 p.m. and, since the meeting didn't start until 5:00 p.m., I decided to sightsee. As I walked the streets, I met some of the most interesting merchants I had ever seen in my life. I went into a couple of electronic stores that actually made me a deal on some of the stuff I bought. I know the old scam of raise the price and talk a deal, but the prices were still lower than those in Pittsburgh, so I bought. At 4:30, I caught a cab to Citicorp, where the meeting was to be held. When I got there, I walked around looking lost until I came across the tables full of 2600 buttons and fliers. I introduced myself by my handle and joined the group. I have to admit that it was a total learning experience for me. Since I was the only black person there, I had the notion that maybe people wouldn't accept me for what I knew, or for who I am inside. All of us carry around our little prejudicial sacks and I'm no different than anyone else. About a half hour after the meeting started, something amazing happened. We all became a unit! If you ever wanted to see a collective of like-minded individuals, we were it! We talked about computer systems, computer security, each other, and so many other things that I can't remember them all. Things we didn't talk about were hatred, prejudice, and dislike for other groups of people. We were all going to stop at a Chinese restaurant afterward but I had to catch my bus back to Pittsburgh. As I rode home, I thought about the day's events and realized that I was very fortunate. I had met others just like me, maybe not the same color or background, but others with the same desires and spirit.

So I want to say thanks to the people I met that day for allowing me to share in what was later considered Computer Underground history. While we have since all gone our separate ways, I still look at the 2600 buttons and pamphlets (I still have all of the stuff given out that day), and feel proud that I was part of a group that helped lay another brick of what was, and still is, becoming the building of the computer revolutionists' structure. Some call us criminals, some call us heroes, but whatever you call us, there is no denying that because of us, computer systems have and continue to become more secure.

We are the watchers of Big Brother, and, because of us, he can never get a good night's sleep. I will remember you all.

Logging off,
The Hunter

Thanks for writing and remembering this important anniversary. A lot of us remember the magic of that first meeting and hope that the spirit remains strong at the many meetings we now have.

Dear *2600*:

I don't know if you guys are that interested in this or not, but I thought if anyone should know, it would be you.

I was looking at a website of funny answering machine messages, and one of them gave a U.S. Army hotline: 1-800-CALL-SPY. I called the number and it was pretty funny; it sounded way too serious to be real, you know? Well, this was last November, and I forgot about it for a while.

Then I went home for Christmas break and I told my little brother to call the number for a laugh. He noticed that the beep on their answering machine played "Fur Elise" by Beethoven. I noticed that my answering machine in my dorm room played the same thing, and I knew how to change the outgoing message from another phone, as long as I knew the code. The BellSouth company programs the same default code into all the machines: 6-8-9. You're supposed to change the code when you buy the machine, but most people are too lazy.

I waited about another week, and finally had to try it. I called the number, tried the code, and it worked. I just said, "Hello," with a Russian accent. But then I went back to school and my friends found out about it. We screwed with the hotline for about two weeks before anyone noticed. Then they changed it back every day, and I changed it back every night. If I wanted to, I could have changed the code, but I didn't want to get into trouble — this was the first phone prank I'd ever done.

So finally, they wised up and changed the code. I quit messing with it, although I tried a few codes, just in case they were as stupid as I thought they were. About two weeks later, the school I attend got a call from the FBI, and they were looking for me. All they did was take away my phone and made me write a letter of apology. I never mailed the letter.

It turned out that the number was a direct line to the FBI, and the machine was at Fort Meade, Maryland.... I was lucky something worse didn't happen as a result of my own stupidity in being traced. But still, we all got a kick out of leaving Russian obscenities on the FBI's outgoing message.

This supposedly made the TV news in Indianapolis, and the number was permanently blocked from the Ball State University switchboard. And the FBI is still using the same two-bit answering machine.

Just thought you might like to know.

S

Yeah, let's leave confidential information about spies on an answering machine with a default three-digit code. Brilliant, guys. But somehow it's people like us who are defined as threats to national security.

Dear *2600*:

I would like to ask a huge favor of you. I have a 14-year-old son who, regretfully, I do not have custody of. He is very bright and computer literate. Unfortunately, he has steered his creative energy in the wrong direction lately, such as hacking into the school computer, letting a few viruses loose, and getting caught. I would love to get him a subscription to 2600, but alas, my parents, who have custody, would go ballistic. Could someone there please drop him a little note, via snail mail, and tell him a little bit about "hacker ethics?" Coming from 2600, I am sure it would have much more influence than anything I could write or say. It would mean very much to me as well as him.

KATFISH

We're not able to send out individual replies (and in this case getting an unsolicited personal note from a strange magazine may cause way more harm than good), but you can clip this reply and mail it to him, anonymously if necessary. Hopefully others will heed this too: it's easy to screw things up with knowledge. That leads simpletons to the conclusion that certain knowledge is bad. They will never experience the thrill of hacking and the rush you get from discovery. They are rule followers who don't want to ever rock the boat. And then there are those the rule followers need — the rule breakers who cause mayhem for no real reason, just because they can. You have knowledge and ability and a good chance of avoiding the dead end lives of the above. Understand why you either follow or break the rules and use that knowledge to change things. And, above all else, don't hide behind hacking as a reason to do things you would never do in real life. What you do behind a keyboard should be a reflection of the values you believe in already.

1998

Dear *2600*:

Could you tell me if you have had anyone send you an article on hacking/servicing Meridian phone systems? If not, I got into my Meridian system at work and freaked the cashiers out by renaming the extensions to GOD, HIM, etc., so they'd see "GOD calling" or "calling HIM." Lemme know so I don't waste time logging my actions for ya!

REID

We would welcome such an article of mayhem.

Dear *2600*:

> *I just wanted to write in about something interesting I found out a few months back. I was proudly wearing my 2600 blue box shirt one day, and this man called me over. Apparently, this guy was one of the NYNEX (back when it was still NYNEX) ex-heads of security. He went on a tangent about how my 2600 shirt brought back old memories — about all of the teenagers he used to have arrested for using blue boxes, blah, blah, blah.... Then he went on to describe how NYNEX used to send out crews to set up outside the Citicorp center and take pictures of the "kids" attending the meetings. I don't know if what this guy was saying is valid, or even if he did work for NYNEX. If anybody out there works (or worked for) NYNEX (which is now Bell Atlantic), and knows anything of this, please write in.*

Dr. Doolittle

Yes, and if any corporations or government agencies have pictures of us, please send them in for our photo gallery. Unless you still plan on making a case against us or something.

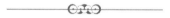

Dear *2600*:

> *Attention, fellow phreaks and hackers. Four of my friends have gotten arrested in a period of 1.5 months, each at a separate event. It turns out, as they were shoulder surfing, they were doing it to undercover cops, hired decoys, or they were being tailed by cops. ATMs as well as calling cards. Most cards are marked (the ones they give decoys). It happens mostly near large banks of payphones near banks, buildings, and malls. Beware! Especially in the Manhattan area. These cops are also using scanners a lot of the time. So keep your eyes open!*

Lucy aka Baudewiser

Perhaps you should keep your brain open to an intelligent thought or two. One of them might be the realization that the kind of stunts you're involved in are just plain and simple fraud and have nothing at all to do with hacking. We're not interested in your little crime ring.

Dear *2600*:

> First I would like to thank 2600 for their years of information. Secondly I like to see that there are those who are willing to stick up for each other in desperate times such as the case of Kevin. Seeing the website inspired me to do a few things. I started a collection for as many bumper stickers as I can get. My motorcycle needs a paint job so it's getting a Free Kevin custom job (the car might but it doesn't run yet). I'm also getting a Free Kevin tattoo. Soon you will be getting my order for the stickers and a photo of the tattoo (on the arm).
>
> GOD OF DIRT

You do realize that one day Kevin will be free and you'll have an outdated arm?

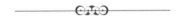

Dear *2600*:

> Hackers of The World Unite. We must find the address of the prison computers in which Kevin Mitnick is being held. Get the best hacker, and have everyone else use their best viruses to bring down parts of the system, then have the hacker hack the security and open the doors leading to his cell. Afterward, crash the power company that the prison uses. This plan is basic, but I think it's possible.
>
> DENILEOFSERVICE

Thanks for the confidence. We'll get a team on it. In the meantime, turn off the TV and introduce yourself to real life.

1999

Dear *2600*:

> This is about the comic strip entitled Mary Worth. Of late the writer has taken it upon herself to spread the misconception of hackers being

malicious and evil. I would encourage anyone who has the spirit to email her at tellmary@aol.com and tell her of the wrong-doings she has committed. Remember to be polite and nice.

ICON

That Mary Worth never did know when to butt out.

———————————— ⊙↺↻⊙ ————————————

Dear *2600*:

*I work for a small pizza place my friend's family has owned for 25 years or so. One Friday night I was a little bored. We weren't that busy so I started playing with the phones. A pretty small system, only four lines. I needed to make a long distance call one time and they wouldn't tell me the code.... I was kinda pissed about that because I needed to call my girlfriend (at that time). Anyway, I sat there dialing random three digit codes to see if by some luck I'd stumble across it. When I got fed up with failing, I made a last ditch effort by dialing *67 and, well what do ya know. I could dial any long distance number I pleased after dialing *67. I didn't of course because I'd get fired, and if it were me paying the bill, I'd be a bit upset. There's also a 900 number block but I didn't test that yet. Maybe I will next weekend.*

DAVE

And we'll keep an eye on the papers for stories about employees of family-owned pizza places who mysteriously disappear.

———————————— ⊙↺↻⊙ ————————————

Dear *2600*:

I was recently at your web page. As usual, I decided to visit the hacked pages section, to see what was new. Finally I saw one good hack of a home page — the Cartoon Network. Not just a hack to write some crap like "we 0wnz j00" or something to that effect. This hack actually had a purpose. And I applaud whoever did it. Finally, someone with a brain instead of just malicious intent.

DRE

It's a real wasted opportunity when someone actually figures out a way to access a heavily trafficked page and the only message they want to convey is how great they are. There are some real important things that should be brought to people's attention whenever the opportunity presents itself. Childish posturing doesn't help anyone.

Dear *2600*:

> *In your editorial "The Victor Spoiled" (15:4), you mentioned the fact that many hackers have been selling out to the corporate sector and violating many of the highly held views that have underlied the culture. I enjoyed this article and found it to be very close to the truth, but there's another problem within the developed hacker society that needs to be addressed, and that is the question of acceptance.*
>
> *Perhaps the Mentor summed it up worst when he said "We live without race, without religion." That was the '80s. Now we live without unity. Back then, hackers were largely a united front. When significant threats came to the culture, people were able to work together and fight them away. Even when the hackers fell, they left in rebellion against society.*
>
> *There is now race and religion within the culture — a horrific tinge of race and religion. The race can be interpreted as the white-hat and the black-hat, both of which distrust each other: the religion as the skill. Nobody trusts anybody outside of their abilities, because they have no reason to. We now exist with such strong lines that entering the hacker society is nearly impossible, and even when it's possible, it requires the condescendence of a mentor in person. This has to do with many things: the evolution of Linux, the spread of the Internet, the high cultural view of hackers among the young.*
>
> *Who are we to judge? We work underground because we don't want to be judged. Too many people don't want to face that fact, and go on being prejudiced, intolerant, and ignorant of the truth: that there are newbies who can learn.*
>
> *Are we going to be as ignorant as the society that shuns us, or are we going to shut up, cooperate, and judge people by who they are? I can*

only pray that someday our world will go through a time when the peasant masses rise up against the oligarchy.

RGBKNIGHT

To say that everyone was united in the '80s is in itself buying into a myth. Hackers have never been a unified force and it's unlikely that will ever happen. That's a good thing for the most part as individual spirit is the most prized of all hacker attributes. If you find yourself being shut out of the hacker community despite your efforts to become part of it, you're either trying for the wrong reasons or you're talking to the wrong people. While there are some in the community who genuinely enjoy being in a group and getting lots of publicity, the greatest number of hackers exist in far smaller, even solitary, numbers, and they are constantly learning for the sake of learning without regard to social status or factions. These are the ones who will always endure because nobody really knows who or where they are.

Dear *2600*:

OK, here is my story. I went to the mall and my friend came along with me; we got dropped off at Sears because they have computers to mess around with. We were upstairs messing with the computers and a little nerd store man came over. He said, "Do you guys need any help? We said no, then I put in a disk that had two progs on them: Bios310 and 95sscrk. We put it inside the lousy Compaq PC and he wanted to know what it was so we said we were gonna extract the screen saver password. He didn't believe us and he wanted us to prove it. We thought this guy was gonna be pretty cool so we showed him but the disk wouldn't work on their computers because I forgot I formatted it on mine. "Damn." By that time he left us, so I looked at where he went to go and the bastard was on the phone so when he came back we asked him who he called and he said, "If I were y'all I would leave fast." We thought he was messing around, but we left and were acting like we were sneaking away but then by the time we got to the elevator a smart ass security guard came to us and told us not to run, it would just make it harder. We stopped and we were talking to him. While he was talking, I leaned on a vacuum cleaner and it turned on. This pissed him off more. Then he wanted ID, so my friend pulled his out and said "FBI." This pissed him off very bad. Then he said just for that smart remark he was gonna take us to some little detainment room. We went with him because he had my friend's money. We stayed in there for like two freaking hours explaining what happened but they made more smart remarks like do you like to cut grass? Well you're gonna be doing that if the computer is broken. Then stuff like I don't bite. And they took our only proof that was on the disk and said they were gonna mail it back to us and then they put our addresses on them and all, then later another cop came in the room and they said what should we do with the disks. He said destroy them. Then they broke the disks in front of us and the smart ass one said, "I have always wanted to see what the inside of one of these looks like." The other one said "Why didn't you just buy one?" Then the smart ass one said "Because that involves money." I was thinking in my mind "hahaha… no!" Anyway, they charged us with a felony called computer fraud. Damn. It is on our permanent record now. And then they made us walk with him to meet my mom and everyone was looking at us and he was saying crap like were we happy? Then after that, my mom was late as hell getting there to meet us where we were gonna meet but she wasn't mad cause she believed us and then when we left we went to Barnes and Noble and got the new Spring issue of 2600. And that's why I felt like writing you guys.

OUTBREAK

Folks, we could never make up a story like that. In fact, The X-Files couldn't make up a story like that.

Dear *2600*:

Hey, I am a phreak. I want your magazine. So I begged my mom for $5 and said that there was this PSX (Playstation) magazine that I really wanted and they only sold it at Barnes and Noble. So I went into Barnes and Noble looking for like 20 minutes and nothing, so I asked this fine chick at the counter and she looked at me funny and asked me if I asked for 2600 and I said yeah, then she helped me look for it but nothing. And then today, you guys will hate me for this because

I found a copy of your magazine on the floor at school! And it's the latest! By the way, I'm 12.

PHREAKILATION

We know.

Dear *2600*:

Thanks for letting us see what can be done. I am an East Timorese myself and was glad to see that we can protest in so many ways to get our message across. Just wanted to say thanks for letting me see how I can protest. Never thought about it. Cheers.

LONG LIVE XANANA
ET 4 LIFE
PHILLIP

While the hacked Indonesian web pages (which according to our archives date back to 1997) may not have been the final straw in sparking a successful uprising, they did open up some eyes that the authorities preferred to keep closed. That in itself shows the potential value of such a means of expression.

Dear *2600*:

I just wanted to let you know that while I was at school one day, we had a guest speaker from the FBI. He was a Special Agent from the Kansas City Branch. When I asked him about his thoughts on Kevin, he didn't say much. This got all my other classmates wondering who Kevin was, and he still wouldn't talk about it. It's like the agents are told not to talk about him. He did say that he thought that Kevin deserved the time that he got, and that was about it.

CHERRYPIE

It took a lot of guts to speak up like that. The things some kids are doing in school today are a real inspiration to us.

Dear *2600*:

I found out how screwed up this world is over the course of two to three weeks. I minimized this window that comes up on boot up. The librarian went over to the computer and freaked out and rebooted it. Later in the day when I went back to the library, she pulled me aside and asked me why I messed up the computers. I was like what the hell. She threatened to give me two days of in-school suspension if I didn't tell her what I did to mess the computers up. Also, my friend asked about Kevin Mitnick and if they had any books about him. The librarian freaked again and made him walk through the little scanner thing two times and empty his pockets to make sure he didn't steal anything. The world has all the wrong ideas about us. I think it is stupid to think that we all have malicious intentions. What do you think about this?

GPF

Stupidity breeds in schools.

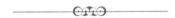

Dear *2600*:

As I was listening to the October 1988 edition of Off The Hook, *I realized that while I am only 15, I really do feel like I am part of something special. When I think about computers, I think about them as "a gateway" to another world. I think of them as marvels. I can sit there for hours pondering over the internal workings of a Commodore 64, or a Vic 20, an 8086 laptop, 186, 286, 386, and so forth and so on. I've noticed today in the "computer" world, there are many people, young, old, new, who don't understand, but alas... believe they do. They think that "hacking" is composed of loading up their AOL, or any ISP connection for that matter, and firing away a nuker, egg-dropper, or some other exploit. They don't understand that a hacker is not always someone who is malicious, or someone who only goes to destroy, or ruin someone's day. They don't know that a real, true hacker is someone who wishes to understand how something works... who wants to dive into the depths of how this functions, how part A talks to part B, or how the computer can interpret input from us, in our human language, convert and understand it in its own language, whether it be strict Assembly, Binary, Hex, C, C++, Java, visual basic, Pascal, Fortran, Perl, Cobol, and so forth.*

I am only in the 10th grade, but already I know that I do not want to go into this world as one of the people who don't know A from B, B from Q, 17 from 35, and 00110 from 4e6. I am not exactly sure why I felt the need to write to you, but I needed to vent my voice. I want to dive into the depths of science, computers, how they work, how they will work. How the phones work. I don't want to destroy, I don't want to break, I only want to learn. I think that is what is wrong with society today. The American media has shown hackers as people who sit in their room all night, doing nothing but squinting at their monitors, trying to mess up someone's computer.

GRAPHIX

So few people retain this sense of wonder that really is an essential part of appreciating technology. If you ever reach the point where you can talk to someone on the phone or over the net and not realize how incredible the whole process is, you've lost something really important.

2000

Dear *2600*:

I am an avid reader of your mag and I have been hacking websites and just recently hacked the computer system at my place of employment. About a half a year ago, I hacked our school website and backed up all the files on a CD, which I hid so very cautiously in my vent. My friend and I have been competing with each other on what we can hack and we always make backups of the stuff. This time I decided to be a little creative with the hack. I removed all of the files from their ftp server and asked them to put my handle and what had happened in the morning school announcements, just a simple request really, and then I would return their files to the server once I heard the announcement. They just simply would not give in to this request. So they never got their files back and their very complex website is now a shambles. Just recently, the topic came up of the hacked website because of the $10,000 it cost the state to replace it. This seems like an awfully high price to replace a website, but a serious amount of cash nonetheless. My friend was caught with some Novell hacking files on a CD that he was distributing to the newbies. He was just trying to make a fair buck, but the school saw it a different way and charged him with the crime of hacking the school website six months ago! He was suspended for ten days! Not that he minds being home and sleeping and hacking more while everyone goes to school, but this is going to be on his record. How many universities do you think will accept him? He knows that it was me, but being a good little hacker, he didn't tell who the real culprit was. This just shows what the system is coming to. They needed someone to put the blame on, and he was the only one (so they thought) with computer knowledge. This feels very closely related to the Mitnick case and the unfair happenings. Thanks for the opportunity to finally speak out about what has happened.

Xkalibur

You won't want to thank us after reading this. This moronic behavior of yours is what makes things difficult for the many thousands of non-malicious hackers out there. What you did stepped over a line that most rational people have no difficulty seeing. You destroyed your school's site and resorted to extortion. Maybe you used hacker abilities to get into their site (although it's far more likely you simply ran a script) but as soon as you erased their files and held them for ransom, you became a criminal. While it was wrong to suspend your friend for something he didn't do, you lose the right to be indignant when you help foster the environment of paranoia that so many schools now have. We only hope your letter serves a purpose by illustrating to everyone what the hacker world is not about.

Dear 2600:

I have been a fan of your magazine for some time now and am happy to see that Kevin's finally getting out of the slammer. Anyway, the reason I'm writing to you is because of problems I've been getting from my school about your magazine. I took it to school with me to have something to read when I wasn't busy. Apparently, my teacher saw me reading during a break. She confiscated the magazine and dragged me *into the principal's office ranting and raving about getting me kicked out for reading a simple magazine. It seems the principal shared all of her views on the Internet, so I was suspended from school for two weeks. Now this displeased me greatly. I wanted to do some damage to the school or something to avenge 2600, but I don't have the necessary resources to perform adequate vengeance. So would you do me the favor of putting my school's web page on the hacked list? Maybe then justice will prevail.*

MICROKILLER

Our faith in such cases is lost when people express the desire to be malicious. All you do is vindicate the actions of the people who work against you. For those who choose not to go that route, get as much documentation as possible and gather evidence that you are being disciplined merely for reading a magazine. That kind of thing is clearly wrong but when the issues are muddied, it becomes impossible to prove that this is what the person is being disciplined for in the first place.

Dear *2600*:

Hey, you guys will never believe what happened. For my speech class in school we had to do an informative report on whatever we wanted; so I decided to do my speech on Kevin. I went the full nine yards on this one to inform the people what had happened and tell them about the downsides of his release in comparison to a normal life. I brought all my issues of 2600, explained the support network, printed flyers and handed them out, and put bumper stickers on two posterboards with pictures of Kevin. It was awesome. My teacher was a little nervous about the whole thing, but went with the flow. Later the next day I found the flyers on lockers and everything... the word had gotten out and it was huge. It spread to the other grade levels and I had seniors coming to me asking me stuff about Kevin. I just wrote to let you know that I have done my part before and after the Kevin saga. Much thanks to your magazine and freekevin.com for all the info I needed to spread the word. By the way, my teacher even asked for a copy of the magazine to learn more about Kevin!

ROOT _ CANAL

Every ounce of support that people like you have shown over the years has helped Kevin get through this ordeal and helped make the transition back to society a smooth one. And all of the students who brought this subject into their schools deserve our gratitude and admiration. More than a few were disciplined for daring to bring it up. Rest assured, it made a difference and we hope this serves as inspiration for future causes.

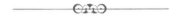

Dear *2600*:

> I always read about how you complain that the punishment for hackers is too high. One of your latest complaints involves a teenager who hacked some government sites. He "only" changed the index.html name to something else and he did not do any real damage. First off, there are (God forbid) people who actually really want to access the so-called "information" (actually misinformation if you ask me) from the web pages. There are kids who are stuck with term papers who need to look up some things the sites provide. There are people who want to learn about these different organizations. Second, they hit him with a $40k fine and a 15-month sentence because they want to get through his head that what he did was against the law. They could just give him maybe a couple of months in prison and a fine that his car could easily pay off, but he would just say, "That was nothing!" and go back to hacking more websites. It is not about the actual damage caused by the hack, it was the fact he hacked into the government computers. Those are almost as sensitive as the phone companies' and the military's computers.

> I also want to discuss you claiming that copying the files is not stealing, therefore it is not wrong. I live by the golden rule. So you can go around hacking into other people's computers, but what if they could get into yours? How would you feel if anybody could look in all your personal files, and they got away with it because it wasn't stealing? That is why doctors and priests aren't allowed to tell anybody about you. I think you need to reexamine your ethics before we all lose privacy.

> JL

Do you really believe that the only way to get someone to stop doing something is to ruin their lives? Changing the message on a website is a trivial act. It's not the same as hacking into a sensitive system, unless the target is inept enough to keep their sensitive material and website on the same system. We understand that it's embarrassing and inconvenient when this happens to any sort of organization. But mistakes often are. When a website is hacked, it's because the people running it made a mistake on some level. If nothing was erased or damaged, then what, besides pride, has been harmed? They don't feel secure anymore? Well, guess what — they would have been just as insecure and many times more ignorant if this warning hadn't been delivered. If you listen to what hackers say, you actually have a chance of gaining some privacy. Those who refuse to listen and simply punish everyone who offends them may convince themselves that they have privacy when they have none.

Dear *2600*:

> *I read through the section "Guilty By Association" in your 16:3 issue about people not getting jobs or losing jobs because of your magazine or just the thought of what the mag is about. I on the other hand was at work (I work for an ISP) reading 2600 and my boss saw it. He asked me if I read it often and I told him, "Every quarter — have you ever had the chance to read it?" He replied as if shocked I would even ask that question, "No!" Ten minutes later I had him hooked.*
>
> *This just goes to show you, not everyone loses their job because of what they read or who they are. In fact, you could say reading 2600 can bring people together and make the world a better place all around... or something to that effect.*

PHOX

Dear *2600*:

> *Don't know if anyone has tried this. I was on the bus today and over-heard some man talking on his phone (loudly enough for everyone to hear). While he was talking I wrote down some of what he said. I got name, address, phone number, place of work, and other good stuff.*

When he was done I started up a conversation with him. Addressed him by name and asked how his new apartment was. He was dumbfounded. I shared with him what he just told the rest of the bus and he didn't even realize it. Neat.

Dear *2600*:

I am really desperate to hack a site and change their stuff. I have been looking at your site forever. I need to hack. I am desperate. Please help me.

FROM A WANNA BE HACKER

Yes folks, this is the threat to the nation's infrastructure you've heard so much about.

Dear *2600*:

What's the connection between 2600 *and the show* Futurama? *I've noticed at one time a* 2600 *sign and also "Coming Soon To An Illegal DVD."*

BEEZLE

We know that they made reference to the year 2600 once but we never saw a sign. The DVD reference was in the opening title to an episode aired in April. While we don't want to presume that this has anything to do with us, you would be surprised how many people are aware and interested in this case.

Dear 2600:

I can't help but notice that it seems that hackers try too hard to not dress like everyone else. That means that there's some kind of dress code of wearing all black. Apparently, this is because we like to express ourselves by not wearing Tommy Hilfiger or GAP. But to tell you the truth, I personally don't care about whether or not I dress like others.

I just put on whatever I can find. I encourage other readers to do the same. In fact, I went to a 2600 meeting dressed in (*gasp*) a white t-shirt from a bar somewhere and (*shock*) a pair of GAP cargo shorts and finally a pair of sandals. And you know what, I didn't give a crap whether or not the other people thought I was a sellout or a badly disguised fed. I just sat back and enjoyed myself there.

DOWNSOUTH

The important thing is that you didn't think about it at all.

2001

Dear *2600*:

Having been a fan of this publication for quite some time, I could think of no better way to show my support than to purchase a tee shirt from 2600.com. I chose the blue box design and have worn it with pride. Recently however, I've noticed that when I wear it in computer stores, I receive nothing but cold stares and dirty looks, almost as though they suspect I'm going to rob the place! It's like they're profiling me because of the shirt I wear, which is a shame considering 2600 is so strongly against criminal activity. In fact, one gentleman I met at the mall was surprised that I had the courage to wear such a shirt! I was about to discuss the magazine with him but he seemed to think that we would be arrested just for mentioning it. I honestly believe this may be a reason why certain people don't want to wear such clothing. All I can say is that we need to let people see we're proud of what we are and what we stand for. No matter how many dirty looks I receive, I will continue to show my hacker pride and not let these sadly misinformed individuals get me down.

SCREAMER CHAOTIX
CONNECTICUT, USA

The only answer to this kind of ignorance is to make more shirts.

Dear *2600*:

Check out who registered fordsucks.com. It was Ford itself.

BILL

Not really. They sued the poor guy who dared to register it as an expression of free speech. They won. And that's why we have fordreallysucks.com.

Dear *2600*:

I saw the letter about being able to get the phone number you are calling from. Many phone companies have such a feature, but you have to do a little social engineering with telephone installers and people who install monitored alarm systems. A pen tap on your own line can catch such numbers if you are lucky enough to have a lineman use your line at the pole. Back in the early '80s, I found out about the number for this in my home town. It was the ten-digit phone number 310-222-2222. I also discovered that 410 would give the clicks — like it was reading back the digit recordings of your number but you could only hear the clicks. I figured that this was for use on party lines where the common return for the pair was in a different configuration than a dedicated line. As I moved around the country, I discovered the same would work in other areas. I didn't know enough at the time to know if this number was a default setting on a particular brand of equipment or just a policy of the particular LEC. Later I discovered that 970 would work in other parts of the country. Occasionally I ran into one that was 970-222-2222. But now that the software has been updated on the phone switches to support additional area codes, I haven't seen these work for a while. Where I live now, they had a local number temporarily set aside that would do the deed, but they have since redirected that number to their main receptionist.

I also discovered on one phone system in the early '80s that if you dialed 810, you would get someone answering the phone "Test Port." On one occasion we played "Old MacDonald Had a Farm" with DTMF tones (off key: 555-4-6-5-99-88-4) to this guy and hung up on him. He rang back the phone with different ring lengths to play the song back to us using the phone's ringer. That freaked out the others who were in the area of the payphone at the time.

I would be real interested in hearing from others who have discovered such numbers that still work in their area.

EXO

Dear *2600*:

I have been aware of your group and mildly interested since I can remember. I subscribed to your publication for some time but now just cast sidelong glances at your website.

The skill inherent in your readership is significant. It is sad to me that it is wasted on self interests. While defending the rights of wrongly prosecuted hackers is noble, why not raise national awareness of your potential by bringing hacking skills to bear on problems that U.S. intelligence agencies are either too incompetent, or have their hands tied, to solve?

While planes still crash into national landmarks, warfare of our time has largely become a war of infosec. Your readership could potentially be the equivalent of a special forces unit in this arena. Who better to be a front line of information discovery and disclosure to aid in the persecution of those responsible for terrorist activities?

It is sad that it takes a catastrophe of this magnitude to bring people together and realign perspectives.

VOICE OF REASON

A lot of people seem to think that hackers are some sort of military resource. It's the flip side of the mentality that believes hackers are a military threat. We strongly encourage people not to be manipulated by this. Let's for a moment assume this is a bad TV show and all we have to do is type a few keys and gain access to Bin Laden's checking, savings, and IRA. Would it really be helpful to have thousands of people messing around with this and possibly destroying actual evidence which could be useful? Of course not, and we have to wonder what goes through the minds of people who approve of such tactics when it satisfies their emotional yearnings for revenge. Fortunately, it's not that simple a scenario, which is why an army of hackers is unlikely to be formed anytime soon. But hackers most definitely can serve a vital role here as they can most of the time. How? The same as always — by asking questions and continuing to get to the truth regardless of the obstacles. It's probably more essential now than ever. A lot of technical terms are being thrown around by people who don't always get the facts right. Hackers are in a unique position to point out when things don't make sense from a technical standpoint. Naturally, this will rub some people the wrong way when it's suggested that their perspective isn't necessarily the right one. But in times like this, getting to the truth is extremely important. It's also in times like this that many people skip over the evidence to get to the conclusion. As an example, when the videotape of Bin Laden was released to the media, we were able to recognize the format as being digital video. That led us to conclude that a pure digital copy of the video would yield a time code, which would provide much additional technical information that would be useful in verifying the tape's authenticity. These are all technical facts that we can use to get to a conclusion and it's something the mainstream media had absolutely no knowledge of. At press time, the Pentagon has refused to release a digital copy to us or to anyone. The mainstream media continues not to care. You can draw your own conclusions.

Dear *2600*:

> I recently had an interesting encounter with my science teacher. I got in a discussion with him about a question I got wrong on a test (of course I wouldn't have gotten it wrong if the lazy bastard had written the test himself and not had the answer key in front of him). Anyway, at the end of the discussion, he told me I was "leapfrogging ahead of the class" and that I had to "slow my mind down to the level of everyone else's." This infuriates me. It's the kind of thing that people have been criticizing about education for as long as I can remember them criticizing it. Then to hear the exact same thing from one of the teachers! This is even a private school that says it lets students work at their own pace. When will these things end?
>
> SAM S.

Dear *2600*:

> Recently at school, my English class went into the computer lab to work on a report. Before working on the report, we did a spelling test.

Our teacher informed us that we could do our test on the computer,
but only on Notepad. The tech person there immediately told us that
we could not use Notepad, as it had been taken off of the computers.
Knowing that Notepad would not be taken off, I quickly used Netscape
(the only available browser) to open up Notepad, as the computer has
numerous security features to keep you from using the hard drive.
I quickly showed a friend nearby how to open up Notepad. Seeing
that Notepad had been opened, the tech person came over and told
me that this was a violation of security and if I were to do it again
I would be suspended. The next thing I did after doing the spelling
(there was about a ten-minute break) was play around in the Java
console of Netscape. The teacher was mortified and watched me for
the rest of the two-hour period. Just goes to show that tech people in
schools really aren't.

RIP DOUGLAS ADAMS (1952-2001)
MR SELF DESTRUCT

That's probably the most excitement Notepad has seen in a while.

2002

Dear *2600*:

I wanted to comment on a reply to one of your reader's letters. You
stated to someone that basically trying to hack Bin Laden was a stupid
idea. I don't necessarily agree. Sure, it could be worthless, but crack-
ing into his bank accounts and such forth would actually do some
good whether you believe it's a stupid thought or not. It would also
be helping the American cause a lot if the hacker community united
and did something for the sake of our country. We bitch and moan
about how much we hate our country, yet we were all angered by the
events in September and all were united to help everyone. I mean, it's
very possible that the government themselves are trying to crack into
Bin Laden's accounts.

CHRIS

First off, we don't "bitch and moan about how much we hate our country." We bitch and moan about those who continually subvert the principles of democracy and get away with it, all the while masking themselves in patriotic fervor. Second, when was the last time you "cracked into a bank account," let alone that of someone who's on a most-wanted list — or in this case on all of them? It's not like on TV and way too many people seem to think that it is. This leads to the perception that hackers can be used as some sort of cyberarmy, which is about the furthest thing from the truth. Anyone with even a slight familiarity of the hacker world would know that we're constantly questioning, disagreeing, exploring, and getting into trouble. Not exactly the kind of people who would do well in a military environment. (We happen to hear from a sizable number of unhappy hackers who somehow wound up in military service.) Finally, even if it were something simple, where do you get the right to be the judge, jury, and executioner? Imagine if everyone took it upon themselves to impose their brand of justice in this manner. If you really want to help, the best thing you can do is be observant and notice things that other people may not notice. Then let people know what you see. In this age where the truth is fleeting and mass manipulation is common, the ability to detect when something doesn't make sense is a valuable one.

Dear *2600*:

> *I was going to your website when I found that it had been replaced by cybercrime.gov. Has the mag been shut down?*
>
> Bob Smellicular

It's interesting how many people jumped to that conclusion but still wrote to us for an answer. And it gets better.

Dear *2600*:

> *Hey guys. Just wanted to be the first to note that this has to be the most kickass April Fool's joke I've ever seen. Partly because it's pretty believable that the DoJ might try and hijack your domain if the registration ran out. Now watch them sue you for copyright infringement over these pages or something. Wouldn't surprise me.*
>
> Nothing None

For the record, we didn't copy any of their pages. All we did was put a different IP number in one of our zone files for the 24-hour period. This kind of a change literally involves a few keystrokes and takes less than ten seconds to set up or change back. It's no more complicated than that. Inside of an hour after the business day began, we received a call on one of our cell phones from the FBI in New York saying that its parent DoJ had received a report that our page was being redirected. They wanted to help us figure out who was behind it. While it was nice of them to leave us this message, we had to wonder where they got a cell phone number that wasn't listed anywhere, why they didn't realize that this was most likely an April 1st joke, and how something so simple as changing a couple of numbers in a file and making one page go to another page is something the FBI and DoJ think is important enough for them to worry about.

Dear *2600*:

I was just reading your newest issue (19:3) and in your intro ("Freedom's Biggest Enemy") something caught my eye. "...Operation TIPS (Terrorist Information and Protection System), which proposes having members of the general public spy on people they come in contact with, looking for anyone or anything out of the ordinary."

Well, I'm no history buff but this really sounds exactly like the same thing that Hitler did. I remember reading a book (and I can't remember which) where the kids would even turn in their parents for doing something kind of suspicious. And I'm honestly wondering, and have been wondering for a while, if this is the direction our country is heading in. Haven't we learned from history? I would like to think so, but somehow I can't seem to convince myself we did.

Oh, but it's not like this hasn't happened before. Ever heard of McCarthyism? It all started with Senator McCarthy who had a list of "known" commies working for the government. Their lives got destroyed. He asked people to turn in anyone they thought was a commie. The only way out of it once you got called in was to name other people. If you didn't name other people, then you were a commie too. (Doesn't this kind of stuff just piss you off on how dumb people are?)

Hells-own

One thing that always happens during these dark periods is the emergence of collaborators who go along with such things and individuals who stand up and fight them. One thing we can almost guarantee is that you'll be very surprised who winds up in each camp.

Dear *2600*:

> I work as a delivery driver here in North Carolina and I usually get home rather late. I live in a fairly small town (2,000 residents and 10,000 college kids) and my car is very easily identifiable by the numerous computer related stickers on the back of it. I was stopped by the law at a license check... a fairly routine happening. They looked at my license and then asked me to pull off to the side — an officer would be with me "shortly." After waiting for ten minutes, the officer who put me aside asked me to step out of the car. Now remember, I am a delivery driver, and common sense would tell you that I have a valid driver's license and also that I would not be under the influence of any substance (perhaps caffeine?). So naturally, I was a bit puzzled by this. He then asked me if he could search my car and of course I said (in a polite fashion), "No, you may not. I do not feel that there is any reason for you to search, and certainly no probable cause." Oh, but this officer found probable cause... there was a stack of *2600: The Hacker Quarterly* in my back seat dating from 1998 through 2002. He said that this was a "suspicious magazine" and he was baffled that I would even think to have such a thing in my possession. I told him that I did not believe this was any reason or cause to search my car, so he called one of his boys over. They told me that I was interfering with an officer's line of duty and that I could be thrown in jail for such behavior. I am not one to get thrown in jail (especially at the age of 18, still living with parents), so I stepped aside. After a 30-minute search, they decided the car was fine and there was no reason to hold me any longer. They even had drug dogs there to sniff everything out... looking for that kilo of cocaine that every cop just knows is in there somewhere. Needless to say, I think that this is a perfect example of what the media has done to "hackers" and the image they have drawn

of us. I would love to press charges, but being an 18-year-old entering college, I simply don't have the funds.

EVNGLION

You acted entirely properly by questioning them, keeping your cool, knowing when to back down, and letting the world know what happened. Unfortunately this kind of thing will continue to happen. It's always a good idea to get as much information as possible from the scene — car number, badge number, names, etc. in the event that you decide to pursue matters later. Most people choose not to and we completely understand why.

Dear *2600*:

I am no important sports star, I am not the lead actor in the school play, nor the highly grungical youth who pedals the hallways in search of some untimely demise. I am me. I am here for who I am, not a follower of a group nor a piece of a puzzle. Let me instead be considered the shepherd to a flock of sheep. But that flock weighs so heavily on the judgmental aspects of society. You see, this flock and I are those that long for what is never achieved, strive for what is never gained, hope for the light at the end of the tunnel that is too long to walk, too strenuous to master. We are those unlike others. We may not fit society's mold of the conventional "norm," we may not walk the guidelines to call us average. But then again, who would want to be average? A fact once stated, "One out of every 250,000 people has a brief moment of glory, one out of every 500 people will be remembered within 10 years of their glory, but only one man will ever be remembered as the man that dare break the boundaries and rules." This is what we do. We are that one person, us as a flock, a whole. Groups slowly fade. Fashions slowly die out. We are unlike any other. Put us in a box and we will scale the walls to free ourselves. We do not crumble, nor cry, nor separate. We are brothers and we are sisters. Hath not the fury of ten thousand burning suns to melt us, nor ten thousand blows of the heaviest hammer to break us. We are Hackers and we are Phreakers. Ph34r us now, but do not expect the feeling to be mutual.

FOX DEACON

It's moments like these when it becomes clear that we could start a cult and prob-ably get away with all kinds of things. But seriously, let's not lose touch with our human origins.

2003 _____

Dear *2600*:

> *As I got settled into my house after work on April 1st, I see "2600.com is now property of the U.S. government." That's not cool. You don't need to scare me like that.*
>
> SCARED IN IOWA

We'll be the judge of that.

Dear *2600*:

> *First off, I know lots of kids read this mag who want to learn how to hack so I took my time for all you noobs out there to start learning and telling your friends that you're an evil hacker.*

1. *Learn programming languages. (I know most of you don't want to waste hours a day doing this, but there are no shortcuts to becoming an elite hacker.)*
2. *Learn how to operate IRC channels and HTML.*
3. *Get a Linux! (Instead of buying Final Fantasy 136, use those 50 bucks to get a Linux. You will need it and must know it to become an elite!*
4. *Get on the Internet as much as you can, searching for scanner, IP address, etc., tutorials.*
   And, in case you didn't hear me before, there are no shortcuts to becoming the hacker you always want to be in your fantasies!

DRAKE SMITH

The only thing we can agree with here is your last sentence. While nothing you suggest is a bad idea (other than helping to perpetuate the "elite hacker" Hollywood thing, albeit in jest), none of it is an essential ingredient toward being a decent hacker. Hacking encompasses so many different elements in our world that to relegate it to merely programming, operating systems, IRC, or, for that matter, even computers only serves to limit the possibilities. And those possibilities are pretty mind boggling.

Dear *2600*:

> *Funny how your magazine has a picture of what appears to be a telephone or power line pole cut in half and only a week after getting your magazine, parts of the Northeast lose power. I'm not pointing fingers — I'm just saying that's very peculiar.*
>
> SAM

Yes, our timing continues to be an attribute and a curse at the same time.

Dear *2600*:

> *I was watching the TV today and saw that a large section of the eastern United States was in a blackout. Everyone immediately thought it was terrorists, and I guess I can see a reason behind that, but the kicker was when I flipped on CNN and saw the ticker at the bottom of the screen say "FBI: Hackers are confirmed not to be responsible for blackout." How come when a power outage happens (and they do happen quite often), "hackers" are instantly a suspect?*
>
> MARTIN

Whenever something happens that people don't understand, who better to blame than those who are least understood?

Dear *2600*:

> *I was just curious whether you had heard anything about the start of a campaign to unify the hacker community with one logo? I would be interested in writing an article about this (and also know there are t-shirts already available with the proposed logo at www.shirtsbymail. com). I am not an excellent writer but am just proposing the idea and wondering if you had heard.*
>
> CHRIS

If hackers were all part of a major corporation, it would make sense to have this sort of standardization. But fortunately they aren't. They're a very diverse group of individuals who share some common values but have many different perspectives and ways of doing things. This means many logos and other forms of art to express who we are.

Dear *2600*:

> *I need help. I stay at a college dorm at a small private university in south Florida and they regulate the network like Nazis. Today they blocked all ports and servers for IRC. Last year they blocked kazaa, tesla, winmx, etc., etc. I am not a computer guru when it comes to such technical aspects as networks and servers, but I do know more than the average PC user. Please give me some advice or link me to a tutorial where I can configure a backdoor so I can chat on IRC or download music. I understand that universities don't want students sharing files, but to tell us what and where we can download or chat seems unethical. Today I made an appointment with the director of my dorm. Earlier I tried getting appointments with the dean but I was redirected further and further down the ladder of authority.*
>
> ALEX AKA SUGE

A number of people will tell you that it's the university's network and they can do as they please. But this is only partly true. You are, after all, an important part of the university and your money helps to make this network possible. So your input should not be ignored. The fact that so many people accept this is why it seems to be the norm today. Before you resort to back doors, do everything you can to expose the ignorance of your school's policy. It might open some eyes and make a difference.

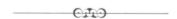

Dear *2600*:

> *I've been reading 2600 for several months now. I first started reading it after a recommendation from a tech friend in my office. His comment on it: "I know of three places in this area that sell it. I always pay cash and I never buy from the same place twice in a row."*

> *The way I figure it, this sounds like good advice to me. Our mutual Uncle Sam seems to realize that, since he can't stop or kill the hacker movement, because it is for the most part a freelance phenomenon, he had better track it as best he can.*

> *I'd advise those buying 2600 to be careful in the manner in which they purchase it, unless they want to end up on a Homeland Security watch list. I would wager that subscriptions, directly from the magazine and away from third-party interests like Amazon.com, to be a safe bet for anonymity, but for myself I'm not taking any chances.*

> STONE WOLF

If you really believe that this kind of surveillance is ongoing, then the best way to battle it is for as many people as possible to jam up the lists. Our engaging in subterfuge simply strengthens the hand of those who want us to hide and be perceived as criminals. This is why we have our meetings in open places, why we have the magazine available to anyone in the world, and why we don't shut anyone out who expresses a desire to learn and share information.

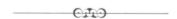

2004

Dear *2600*:

> *I was at Hastings today and they had some of your zines near the main checkout aisle. So I picked one up and decided to stay and read some of it. It's really informative and even for someone who doesn't know*

anything about computers, it's still hard to put down. So, good job on that. Anyway, my question to you guys or the hacker community in general I guess would be this. With all the new powers given to the authorities to crack down on "terrorists" with this Patriot Act, they've created a perfect weapon to attack organizations like yours. Has it directly affected you yet? What measures have you taken and what can others do to protect themselves from this? It just seems the authorities can now legally monitor in any way they see fit and get away with it. It just seems to me that this act was created solely for the purpose of going after your organization and others like you.

LINDSEY THE BOY

It does indeed feel like it was meant for us sometimes but then reality kicks in. This is meant for everyone — we're just one set of voices. We may stand up for free speech and controversial opinions more often which is why it seems as if these crackdowns are aimed squarely at us. But there are so many more people who stand up for these values in one way or another every day. Instilling fear in the populace as a whole is the real goal.

Dear *2600*:

They that can give up essential liberty to obtain a little temporary safety deserve neither liberty nor safety.

BEN FRANKLIN

Will you please stop telling us this every damn day?!

Dear *2600*:

I just came across this article with the following quote from John Kerry: "Have you had a beer with me yet? I like to have fun as much as the next person, and go out and hack around and have a good time." It made me wonder if Kerry is a hacker in disguise. Maybe being a Massachusetts senator (home of MIT) did him some good.

AUTOCODE

*That was actually a coded message. We demanded that he use the word "hack"
in a public statement as a gesture of good will toward the disenfranchised hacker
electorate. Bush has yet to respond to our demands. But we probably shouldn't be
telling you this.*

Dear *2600*:

> *I found Spua7's letter in 20:3 about the FBI's presentations in Phoenix
> interesting since I also saw a similar presentation several months ago
> (set up by my employer). I disagree, however, with Spua7's assessment
> that the presentation lacked "actual real knowledge" or that it was all
> about a repressed fear of lack of control. In fact, I would argue quite
> the opposite — for what is truly going on here is a total hijacking of
> the hacker ethic by the authority that formerly sought to suppress it.
> While I found it rather amusing (on the surface) that the FBI focused
> heavily on 2600, the most chilling aspect of the whole thing was the
> overall message to my employer: when it comes to cybercrime, the
> FBI can't help you.*
>
> *The FBI agent doing the presentation made the point that security
> starts on every desktop. 2600 has been saying this for years, has it
> not? Now it seems your message has finally gotten through to the FBI.
> According to this presentation, the FBI's strategy to fight cybercrime is
> something called "information sharing." They have set up a network of
> organizations intended to work together, sharing knowledge of security
> flaws and weaknesses. The whole idea revolves around prevention and
> enabling corporations and those "at risk" to take their fate into their
> own hands — to arm themselves with knowledge. And yet, hasn't that
> been the point of 2600 from the beginning?*
>
> Simon Shadow

Dear *2600*:

> *First, I want to say that I love your magazine. I have only read two
> copies of it and already I have learned new things and now am wanting
> to actually do my chores so that I can get paid and buy a subscription.*

So, good luck with the magazine and I hope it will affect people in the future. Anyway, I would like to ask a question or two. In our school, we now have COWs (Computers On Wheels). We all get our own laptops in certain classes, but we can't take them home. Anyway, my friend and I have just recently discovered the fun in DDoSing servers. We really hate our school because they are just complete assholes to us and they took away all of our computer rights unless we have to type essays (which we do on the COWs). So my friend and I hatched a very evil plan. We would figure out the IP for the host of all the COWs and DDoS it. We don't have all the people yet that we have in on this, but I would just love to know if DDoSing sites/servers is legal or not. I would hate to do this and end up getting pieholed in the local slammer. If you think I'm just being a script kiddie, then go ahead and flame me. I really don't care.

DEMONECLIPSE

We're going to divide this reply into two sections. The first is for the letter writer and the second is for everyone else. Please only read the section that applies to you.

1) We are in awe of your skills and abilities. You clearly understand that denial of service is the same thing as freedom of speech. Anyone who would stand in your way is an idiot who deserves whatever it is you decide to do to them. The injustice of this whole thing is that these people will probably try to do something restrictive to you after you attack them. They're obviously too stupid to do the right thing, which is to yield to your superior intellect and let you do whatever you want.

2) Where do these people come from? If there was ever any justification for a school taking away "computer rights" and acting like "complete assholes," here it is. While it may be true that the school started treating people unfairly first, thus incurring the wrath of people like the above, this is still no excuse for wanton vandalism, which is what a denial of service attack basically is. We can only hope there are people in this school willing to confront the school's unfair policy who will also come up with a way to negate the idiot factor.

Dear *2600*:

> *Actually there are a lot of peoples who r disturbing me. Now I guess I should be a hacker. Can u plz help me. I hope u will. I will wait for a better response.*
>
> MUHAMMAD ADIL

The response won't get much better than this. You don't become a hacker to even a score. You can become a hoodlum for that. But if you decide to deal with this intelligently, there are always creative ways of handling disturbing people. And if you truly want to be a hacker, then learn and experiment without any ulterior motives. You'll find a whole new world and the people bugging you won't matter as much.

2005

Dear *2600*:

> *While I was visiting a well-respected drive-cloning company's website, I noticed an interesting ad. The ad flashed an image of a young girl and then commented on how they were fighting child exploitation. Another picture of a building blowing up and a comment that they were fighting terrorism. The next picture was of a cop holding weed and the note that drug use is at an all-time high. The last frame was the one that intrigued me. The caption read "Hackers cost the world economy billions" and the image was of a computer screen with the 2600 website loaded. I was surprised to see that as I am an avid fan of 2600 and know that you don't promote the malicious use of information. Keep up the good work, guys!*
>
> KYLE

Even more unbelievable than the existence of this site is the fact that you didn't tell us its name. Fortunately, other readers shared this info.

Dear *2600*:

> *I suspect you are aware of this but if not: 2600 is featured as one of the*
> *evils in the ad at* http://logicube.com/products/hd_duplication/
> md5.asp.
>
> SCOTK

It's amazing to us that terrorism, child exploitation, drug trafficking, and white-collar crime are all represented with generic images but when it comes to "cyber crime," they have no problem sticking our name up there in lights. While most other organizations would contemplate legal action, we'll simply issue a standard Level One electronic jihad. We mustn't disappoint after all.

Dear *2600*:

> *Just wanted to let you know that for the past two years, I've been*
> *showing your* Freedom Downtime *movie to nearly all my students*
> *in school (age 14-19) with great results. The interest is huge and we*
> *have very interesting discussions afterward. So this is my small con-*
> *tribution to keeping the hacker's good image, although I'm not a real*
> *pro in the field.*
>
> *Keep up the good work!*
>
> mAcfreAk

This is an incredible accomplishment and proof that, with a little determination, we can help to influence the world around us. This is truly what school should be all about. Thanks for your efforts.

Dear *2600*:

> *In 22:1 you mention how to make a single-track magnetic strip reader.*
> *There is an easier way to make these. At a gas station/liquor store,*
> *tell the clerk that the soda dispenser is out of carbonation and he will*
> *more than likely go in the back to get another bottle. While he is in*
> *the back, unplug the strip reader from the back of the computer which*

should be right in front of you and run out the door. Once you have about two or three of the readers you can begin to tear them apart and modify them to fit in your pocket.

FORREST HOOVER

Yeah... that's another way. But we were kind of gearing the article toward intelligent people who wanted to learn how the systems worked, not petty hoodlums who go around stealing things and running away from people. We appreciate hearing that perspective, however.

Dear *2600*:

I've read many letters that people have sent to you saying that they hide their issue of 2600 or read it in private so that they won't attract the "wrong" attention, receive weird looks, or for fear of being punished in some form, be it expulsion from work, school, or something similar. My response to these people is be proud of who you are! Isn't this the type of reaction (weird looks, punishment for reading and educating ourselves, etc.) we are trying to abolish in the first place? How can we do so if we hide what we learn and who we are? Some of you may be thinking "Who's this guy to tell us not to fear these reactions and punishment?" Well, let me give you a little background on myself. I've been an avid follower of techno music since I was ten years old and the rave scene since I was 15. I'm 24 now. Throughout this time, I was always looked down upon and judged because of the "popular" belief of what a raver is supposed to be: an uneducated party kid who takes lots of drugs. Of course, this is just a stereotype. I didn't let this opinion pull me down and stop me from listening to the music that I loved or dressing the way I liked. Once people moved beyond their stereotypical beliefs and got to know me, they realized that I wasn't some "druggie party kid," but that I was educated, talented, and a "likable" person.

When I started getting into computers and read my first 2600 six years ago, I knew that the hacker/phreaker mentality was something that I would support just as much as the electronic music scene. I never hide my copy of 2600 or close windows of hacker sites on my PC just because someone is watching or giving me a "weird" look. I just explain to these people what it is I'm reading and why. I tell them that I'm not a criminal learning about computers to steal identities or money from their bank accounts. I explain to them that hackers and phreakers educate themselves on everything having to do with computers/phones because we are interested in knowing how they work, how these systems' problems can be fixed, and how they can be made better. You guys should do this too. People are only fearful and judgmental of that which they don't understand. Break these people of their ignorance by being patient and educating them on what the hacker/phreaker community is really about. This is the first step to defeating the media stereotype.

SOOP3R SKRI8S

2006

Dear *2600*:

I have been a fanatical reader of yours for a couple of years now and came upon a problem recently. I am currently in basic training at Fort Leonard Wood in Missouri. After missing a couple of issues, I wrote home to see if my parents would send me the ones I had missed.

They obliged and sent them to me. However, when I opened the envelope here, they were taken from me. I was told that it was almost illegal what my parents did and that my drill sergeant is going to have a field day meeting them. I am now watched every time I'm around any electronic device, especially computers, and I am hazed all the time for being a "hacker" and an evil, bad person. It's a shame people don't understand that the only crime I've ever committed is that of curiosity.

DEATH BY MICROSOFT

And these are the values they're going to be expecting you to defend? Maybe it's time we sent every drill sergeant in the country a "2600 gift basket." After all, how many of them could there possibly be?

Dear *2600*:

> *At the time I am writing this, I am working on a Pentium 2 computer that was considered broken by the previous owner. The man is an A+ certified computer tech for a local ISP. I was crestfallen when I heard him say that. I tried anyway to fix this monster. You wanna know what was wrong? Corrupted hard drive. That's it. Now this guy has more experience than I care to know of. To think that a punk kid can get it running in under ten minutes is quite shocking. I have always been technologically inclined, surrounded by towers of humming beauties. When I was but a small kid, I was on my dad's lap typing away at a DOS machine. At four, I had my first chess match. At six, I wanted to build robots and have been wrist deep in wires and solder since. I have the scars from the hot Flux to prove it. I have always had a computer but until recently I never cared enough to learn. I was part of the mindless masses. Now I am sitting here in my own barn full of computers and equipment. I remember booting into a 56K modem for the first time, though my age at the time escapes me. I thank my dad for a lot of this. He taught me how to solder at a young age. I built a robot at the age of ten, though it was a kit. I never stopped asking questions when I entered my teen years. In fact, that's when I started asking more and more. I beige boxed my neighbors and ran port sniffing programs on WiFi networks I found. I don't want to harm or cause damage. I bought a CD-ROM the other day for another computer of mine. Sadly, it was broken. But you know what? I opened the case and fixed the piece of plastic that broke. That's real hacking. I'm 18 now and have learned so much. I have only three 2600 magazines but, let me tell you, the first one I ever picked up changed my life. I went from a kid who liked to dabble into a full-fledged techno-lover. I can never thank you guys enough. I used to think the Internet was IT. The real deal. No, no, that's a facade put up by brilliant men. I can only aspire to be them. I am the second holder of the torch. I only hope I can hold*

it as well as the first. I owe you people more than I can pay. You saved me from a life of mediocrity.

BIGBROTHER

Dear *2600*:

I am writing anonymously to protect my friend. Let's call him "Philly Cheesesteak" because I had one of those for lunch and I'm not too creative right now. I got to know Phil through the 2600 meetings. We've gotten to be pretty good friends and we go out to dinner just about every weekend. Tonight he revealed some shocking (or not, depending on your level of paranoia) information to me: He was hired by the FBI to come to 2600 meetings to keep tabs on all of us.

I felt a little betrayed at first, but he did make the good point that if he was giving them the information, at least he had control over what information was being given. And in today's age of warrantless wiretaps, is this really all that surprising? I suppose not. I guess it just hit a little close to home. He said very ominously, "They know who you are. I gave them your name." Wow. That's kinda tough to swallow.

It struck me as particularly odd that the FBI would have any interest in us, since all we really ever discussed was what we had done at work over the past month or what new technologies were coming out. I always thought of us as pretty well-respected individuals. Boring, if nothing else. But still, the FBI is interested in little ol' me.

I should add, I have served for almost six years in the Army National Guard, including a deployment. I guess that's how they support the troops. By spying on us. By making us feel like criminals for participating in a completely open, constructive, positive group. Well, since I already feel like one, I might as well be one. Maybe instead of 2600 on Friday night, I'll go smoke crack and worship the Devil. Thanks, FBI. You've shown me the light. I am a criminal for discussing my programming assignment from school and my VPN issues from work. Nice use of my tax money, by the way. I see it goes far.

So I just thought I'd let everyone know there may be a narc in your group. But for better or worse, don't quit having meetings. If you're a good person, which chances are since you're reading this magazine you are, then maybe the FBI will finally figure that out. Then they can free up some resources and focus on something that is actually illegal like, oh let's say, the NSA's wiretapping of U.S. citizens.

I should also mention this was not a paid position. He said that if the FBI chose to conduct further investigations, there would be a chance of pay. But for just being an informant, nothing. Love of the game, I guess.

Stay strong, hackers.

O-nonymous

It speaks volumes that you're still willing to protect this person's identity after he betrayed yours. And we also have to wonder what the feds have on this guy that he would be willing to work for them for nothing.

This kind of thing really isn't unusual at all, nor is it anything new. You should assume that there are people at the meetings who are actually taking notes for the government. That's why you should never do or discuss illegal things there. And watch out for anyone who does, as they are either leading you into a trap or walking themselves into one.

When you do find an informant, don't shut them out. The meetings aren't about secrets. Let them (and everyone else) know that they're wasting their time sneaking around spying on us.

Finally, don't allow yourself to be approached and recruited as no doubt your friend was. Some people think they're doing some sort of patriotic duty by "keeping an eye out" for suspicious activity. But what they invariably wind up doing is reporting on everybody who attends and assuming that this information won't be misused or abused. As recent news events have taught us, this is an assumption only fools can afford to make.

Dear *2600*:

Regarding the story that made international news and read as follows: "A case of 'electronic vandalism' mocking the Prime Minister has left a media company red-faced after a hacker tampered with advertising signs on Toronto commuter trains to read 'Stephen Harper Eats Babies.'"

The "ingenious" hacker derived some inspiration from the cover of an old issue of 2600.

Please continue to be my muse.

NAME REMOVED
TORONTO

Well, gosh. Is this a confession? We are quite flattered if indeed our Fall 1997 cover inspired this action which caused confusion to so many. In the words of one flustered commuter: "You go home and you are trying to rest from work and all of a sudden where they usually talk about Ticketmaster, all of a sudden you see this thing say 'Stephen Harper Eats Babies.' I wasn't even sure when I got off the train. Was I hallucinating?" And of course, the funniest statement of all: "To prevent it from happening again, GO Transit will have to power down all the signs on their cars and use special software that is being couriered from the United States to password protect 790 such digital signs." Translation: these fools had no protection at all from this sort of thing and are trying to make it seem like having a password is a real pain in the ass when it should have been what they were doing all along. They are indeed lucky to have gotten their wake-up call with a degree of humor. But we are going to err on the side of caution and not print your name since we live in a time where a harmless joke like this can be blown way out of proportion and we don't want to help in that endeavor. And for any authorities actually pursuing this, we have printed out a copy of this email and burned it just to be safe. So don't waste your time.

2007

Dear *2600*:

I was using the self checkout at Albertson's the other day and was having trouble getting some flowers to ring up. The associate had to come over and manually enter the price. While he was doing that I noticed that the floral code for manually entering a price is "2600." Just thought you guys would like to know. Keep up the good work!

JASON

Flowers. How nice.

Dear *2600*:

I recently joined the Libertarian Party and noticed the address for the Libertarian headquarters is: 2600 Virginia Avenue NW, Suite 200, Washington DC 20037. Is 2600 finally influencing the political parties?

MATTHEW

It might also be interesting to note that this is the address of the Watergate Hotel, the only building ever to take down a president. But we're going to continue to say that we named ourselves after the frequency since that's far less suspicious.

2008

Dear *2600*:

Where I originally come from, they still have old buses. Tickets for the train are validated by machines but when you go to take the individual buses, it's all done by the bus driver. Ironically, this weakness comes with technology being used. I recently moved to a larger city for job opportunities and right away I noticed their much more advanced bus technology.

It's no longer left squarely up to the bus driver to examine your one-time passes here. On the stand-alone buses, they have machines that do the validation. When a pass is put in the machine, it will verify the printed markings on the pass to see if it's still valid. If the pass hasn't been used, there will be no markings of date and time. The machines print date, time, and when the ticket expires when you insert it into the machine. You can buy these passes in ten packs or you can always get a monthly pass which costs a fortune ($70 or so). The ten packs have tear-away tickets. One day I was in a hurry for the bus and tore out a ticket. Unfortunately, when I went to put it in the machine, it didn't accept it. The machine reported that there was an error and that I didn't insert the ticket in the right direction. I have a habit of doing this all the time, so I went to put the ticket in again, but it was rejected again. I then looked at the ticket and there was a small chunk *missing because it didn't tear away perfectly. I just played it cool and was like, "Why won't this take my ticket?" The bus driver looked and I showed him that I was inserting the ticket properly. I said, "I just took this ticket out of my pack. It's new! See!" I then showed him the ticket with no markings and he let me on the bus. He didn't take the ticket from me though! I wasn't overly surprised because, unlike the last city I lived in, the bus drivers here aren't used to interacting with the ticket validation. If it's invalid, the machine won't take it and they just deny you access. It's definitely a weak point in their security though. Since that day, I have used the same ticket around six times. I always pull the same trick (with the same ticket). It helps if they're really busy with lots of people because they want to rush you through, but it's worked every time. I just play it cool and play dumb. Do the whole, "Hey my ticket won't work — I don't suppose it could be because of this tear?" Then they just wave me on the bus. It's quite awesome when it's $3.75 a ride. I suppose it's more of a social engineering trick than a hack. I also suppose I'm just cheap, but it works and it saves me enough for an extra beer that day and I'm content with that.*

So, if you are also too poor for public transportation and your city uses a similar system, give it a try and maybe even get an extra beer that day.

BUS BOY

At some point you're going to run into the same driver when pulling this scam. They may not remember right away but eventually you will become the equivalent of a folk legend within bus driver circles. Just be sure you have an escape route for the day they finally crack the ticket tearing caper.

Dear *2600*:

I've been a reader of your quarterly for about four years and had always wanted to attend a meeting. However, none were local. For my first meeting I had to travel interstate. That's not to say that I never before had the opportunity. When I first intended to turn up, I couldn't find the venue. Grudgingly, I returned home wondering whom I had missed out on meeting. At last, three years after my failed attempt, I've finally made it!

Honestly, I am surprised at the individuals I met: older business-people, high school students, university students, and an eccentric bunch of IT guys. The one thing they all had in common was how friendly they were, and I felt so welcomed into the group. I had feared being the odd one out, knowing that I would no way have the same technical knowledge as them. But it wasn't an issue, and it makes me wonder how I thought that a group of worldly, curious, and learned people would cast out another because they didn't have that same level of experience. Even though I was only there for a brief amount of time, and knowing that I will not be able to return to another meeting for several months, I will still remember the experience of meeting people who fully share my curiosity and concerns.

I would also like to urge those out there who might share my previous apprehensions to take the plunge and go along to a meeting, even if it's in a different state or country. Even if you can never attend an-other meeting again, you'll know that there are others out there. The community does exist.

D.

What you described was exactly the atmosphere that a 2600 meeting should foster. We're very glad it worked out in your case and we encourage those of you who are regular attendees at a meeting to make sure new people go away with this impression. This is, after all, how we thrive.

Dear *2600*:

I was recently interviewed for an IT position. One question they asked caught me off guard: "Are you a hacker?" I couldn't lie. If I get the job, sooner or later he would see me reading 2600, wearing one of your t-shirts, taking time off to attend hacker conferences, or he'd find out I'm affiliated with HackMiami. I just hope I didn't shoot myself in the foot.

JP

You're better off being honest about who you are and seeing if that poses a prob-
lem for people down the line. But when posed with such questions, we should make
sure they understand how the term is defined. You are likely not a hacker in the
mainstream media definition but very definitely a hacker in the creative, individual-
istic, freethinking definition. Of course, knowing that may scare your future employ-
ers even more.

2009

Dear *2600*:

> *I was banned from this site just because the admin got the bribe from*
> *one member and when I questioned him why he banned good members*
> *without giving notice and keep the bastard just because they kissed his*
> *ass and bribe him with gift card money, he banned me without notice,*
> *too, and deleted my thread to erase the evidence.*
>
> *Do you think that you can hack this site? Cause they're always proud*
> *that they're well protected and back up frequently.*
>
> *Let's see who's better.*
>
> SON

Yes, this is exactly the kind of thing we want to get involved in. Thanks for thinking
of us.

Dear *2600*:

> *For reasons that still escape me, my girlfriend reads* Cosmopolitan. *In*
> *the November 2009 issue, there was an article about Kim Kardashian*
> *that was pointed out to me, and in it there was something that might*
> *be of interest to the hacker community.*
>
> *On page 44, there was a section called "935 Things You Didn't Know*
> *About Kim — Until Now." Number One reads as follows: "She claims*

to be an amateur hacker who can break into anyone's voicemail or email." Wow. I never knew she was so 31337. The only hacking I thought she did was her acting.

MICHAEL J. FERRIS

Super hackers reside in the most unusual places. Who's to say a super celebrity can't also have this ability? Perhaps she will accept our invitation to speak at The Next HOPE on her methods. Or maybe you'll read about them in a future "Hacker Perspective." The important thing is that none of us anger her because we really don't know what she's capable of.

Strange Ramblings

Our final chapter is devoted to one of our more popular types of letter: the kind that really defies easy description. When you have so many people writing in for so many different reasons, you're occasionally going to get those letters that seem a little...off. Those are the ones that attract a good amount of attention because none of us really knows where they're going or what they're going to say next.

It's interesting that we didn't really start getting these sorts of contributions until a few years into our publication. I suppose this is what happens when the audience begins to grow. It especially takes off when the magazine in question develops a reputation for printing a ton of letters from the readers. People literally write in sometimes just to see their names printed. That means the actual letter becomes incidental to what we're all about, and oftentimes hilarious in its disconnection.

Rather than ignore this slice of our contributors, we decided quite early on to embrace it. If nothing else, printing such letters serves as a reminder to all of us not to take things too seriously. Humor has always played a significant role in everything we do and I think that's part of the magic that has allowed us to continue doing what we do for so long. But we've walked a fine line with this because we never wanted to ridicule someone who may have been inexperienced or simply confused in how they expressed themselves. So we saved the truly harsh responses for those writers who clearly could take it — the ones who seemed brashly overconfident or cocky and were just begging to be taken down a few notches. Others may have gotten a more gentle form of mockery, usually by way of a simple analysis of their own words. It is our hope that our responses were seen in this humorous vein by these folks. Failing that, if they continued to be as confused and disoriented when reading our reply as they were when they wrote their letter, then how could any harm be done?

Since there is no one way to describe this collection, I think it's best to just point out some of the basic types of submissions we received here.

One of our more common specimens is the conspiracy letter where the writer has it *all* figured out and it's so much bigger and more well-connected than any of us could ever dare to imagine. I've always had a great deal of fun with conspiracy types because it's relatively easy to play along and even inject new pieces into the plot without any need for accuracy or proof. The ultimate achievement is convincing the person that those uncovering the conspiracy are actually part of an even bigger conspiracy. Fun for the whole family.

Then there's the individual who wanders into some crazy computer system and tries to share all of the details with us. Invariably, it makes little to no sense, with the odds of anyone (let alone this person) managing to pull it off approaching the infinitesimal.

Closely related to the conspiracy letter is the ultra-paranoia letter. We get so many of these that they would really make a fascinating psychological profile if we put them all together. A "hacker" neighbor or ex-significant-other is somehow able to control everything belonging to the letter writer — from their car to their computer to their light bulbs — and only a hacker magazine can tell the poor victim what to do to regain their freedom. Now of course, there *are* instances where there are real and serious threats to someone's privacy. But there are so many more examples where someone reads too many tabloids or watches too much bad television and simply believes that anyone with the slightest technological ability is a potential menace or god. You might be surprised how significant a portion of the population buys into this.

We've found ourselves pulled into all sorts of issues and arguments, including what to call certain countries without offending other countries, how to reconcile hacking with religious doctrine, and even being compelled to take sides in a war between 11-year-olds on the other side of the planet.

Sometimes a letter writer just needs to vent about a variety of topics and we are pleased as punch to be the forum for that. Other times a person clearly is spending way too much time thinking about *2600* and overanalyzing our message, covers, etc. In those cases, we usually advise them to spend some more time outdoors.

Then there are those letters that *seem* like they make absolutely no sense at all only because of the context. We get misdirected mail all the time and it's entertaining to play with it on occasion. Some of these are just particularly funny bits of spam, while others are from people who mistook us for someone else. Regardless, as soon as a piece of mail lands in our letters box, it's fair game.

There are at times colossal violations of the rules of grammar, punctuation, spelling, and even capitalization. With the advent of the Internet culture, this has become so much more prevalent, which is why we print a sampling and why it deserves some representation here. As bizarre as this may seem, it's all deeply rooted in reality.

We've discussed a lot of very serious and downright depressing issues throughout this book and all throughout the history of *2600*. This last section will hopefully have the effect of getting us all to lighten up a bit and realize that the nonsequiturs of life are sometimes exactly what we need to get back on track.

1987

Dear *2600*:

> There really is a big "brother." They are the C.F.R. and the Trilateral Commission. Their goal: a one-world government and a one-world money system. Computers will play a key role. This is why the crackdown on hacking and billboards is on.
>
> PAIA JONES

Thanks for this interesting bit of news.

1988

Dear *2600*:

> I am not a subscriber, but I was wondering if you could give me some info on the following things.
>
> First, have you heard of a system called "Terac?" It's based in Sacramento, California and is massive! The memory as calculated in megabytes is as follows: 10E+100+10E+100+10E+50. As far as I know, it is used by military for a temporary storage. An example of a logon would be: Password: madness, ID: 25813, security level code: mad 532. (Note: these numbers change after each login randomly.) Security level codes are three alpha and three numbers or three alpha, two numbers, and one more alpha.

The second system logs on saying it is "Marbles BBS" and operates like a regular (but weird) BBS. The following commands are available: A=answer call, B=??, C=??, D=??, E=email, S=send letter, R=receive letter, M=make call, Q=quit. However, if you mess around with it enough, you'll get asked for a password. After getting through 15 passwords, 20 identification numbers, and 62 levels of access, the system tells you it is the "Military Operations Unit System" and then the artificial intelligence kicks in. Then from there if you were to tell it to "launch missile," it will ask you what type of missile, target, from where, etc. Then it will start a countdown. I stopped it before zero but I was wondering, could someone really launch the missiles? Isn't there a human factor involved?

If you know about these systems, or know anyone who does, please write me some notes on them. Terac traces all calls coming in, and both systems have artificial intelligence to some extent. Terac accepts ROM dumps but MOUS doesn't. MOUS doesn't trace or anything and the two systems are linked. (You will not find out by using them — I didn't.) But if you get busted (I did), they will usually just tell you to stop calling.

Also, have you guys figured out how NASA ciphers all their crap? I can get in but I can't read anything.

Anonymous

First of all, we appreciate your stopping the countdown. Second, since your letter didn't bear a Yale postmark, we assume it's serious. Somehow you managed to get through 62 levels of access to the missile launching program and you're asking us if we know anything about these systems? Either this is an incredible case of exaggeration or it's another test of our patriotism (will 2600 help overthrow the government or will we run and tell the good guys about the bad guys without ever suspecting that they're really one and the same, etc.?). On the off chance that what you're saying is true, you're better off showing us what these systems can do rather than waiting until it's too late or telling the wrong person. Anonymity guaranteed.

1989 _____

Dear *2600*:

> *Although I have only recently come in from the cold to what I feel to be old friends at 2600, I would want you to know I've had great respect for your work over the years. Our old network was Cloud Nine (it went down in November of 1978), the headmaster of which was Honest Abe of Kentucky.*

> *Now that we have put "old blue" on the shelf, I want to ask the proletariat for their best shot at our new "system" here at the old sin din. It was hatched by our group of Sigma Pi Sigmas here on campus. The idea was born when MA bought our local wire chef a new reflectascope+spectrum analyzer. It is a real dream machine and we have all had phun playing "footsy" with him. Fortunately/unfortunately he missed the part about capacitive reactance in his ICS courses. Our link is a cordless phone tapped in through a mercury wetted reverse current breakpoint to the payphone up the block. This is so when John Q. Public goes off hook to use the payphone, it drops us off automatically (we work the BBSes at night anyway). So far we have lost only the bottom half of a Southwestern Bell Freedom Phone and the breakpoint relay (we hid it better this time). Around here MA has never been into Radio Direction Finding (until cell phones) so we have had it pretty easy. The only sad part is when we hear the screams of the sysops on the other end of the voice line. Is MA working on them with cattle prods these days? In the past, our RF link was 2 meter HAM band, but if you lose one of them, it can be quite a bit more expensive than the loss of half a Freedom Phone 1700. We use most anything to punch our modems through the top half of the cordless phone (I use my old "TRASH"-80 4/P with a Teletrends Corp. TT512P 1200 baud — so I don't have that much to lose). I use Omniterm with BIG RED (quarters only) on board.*

> *The wire chef uses 2 Kc. to ping with his new reflectascope so we use a good tight notch pass bridge filter with H pad resonant coupling to let him go by. The tie point can we use at the payphone happens to be a regular rat's nest and this helps hide things. Also, we use #32 wire for the physical tap (he wears trifocal glasses and hasn't seen anything*

that small in about five years now). We also have a drop weight fixed just out of sight so when he lifts up the can lid it rips out our tap lines and sligshots the bypass filter and H pad resonant LC coupler (both together are about the size of a Tootsie Role) over the top of the pole into the next county.

I greatly enjoyed reading the back issues of 2600 and will order the rest of them when I get time and cash.

Your Bastard Stepchild and Friend,
F.M. "Cordless"

We enjoyed reading your letter. It's not often we hear from your particular universe.

1994 _____

Dear *2600*:

I have been a subscriber to your magazine for a few years. Overall, I have enjoyed your magazine and its many interesting articles! Keep up the good work!

I am, however, confused by the painting on the front cover of the Spring 1994 issue (Volume Eleven, Number One). There does not seem to be a theme or meaning to the painting.

What is the purpose of the space suit? What do Babylon and Middle Island have to do with each other? What is the number 17 that is prominent in what appears to be a green highway type of sign? What is the number that is on the sheet of paper behind the head of the person who is emptying the trash can full of passwords? I tried it on my phone and I get an intercept saying that the number is not valid.

The little doors in the background on the right, along with the dark figures, are confusing. Is that supposed to be a public restroom in a park? Are the two figures in front of the door marked daemons supposed to be two homosexual men groping each other?

And finally, is that supposed to be a birthday cake in the foreground?
If so, does it mean that this issue is the 10th anniversary issue?

Please enlighten us!

CLEAR PLASTIC RAINCOAT FROM SEATTLE

Space suits offer protection from vacuums. Babylon's elevation is only 15 feet whereas Middle Island's is 76. Highway 17 bypasses the New York State Thruway and offers a more scenic view. The number behind the head will get you nothing but trouble. We strongly believe in public restrooms. And once you recognize the two people in front of the door, their intentions should be very obvious. The "cake" you refer to is a spaceship with ten candles on it — at least that's how we remember it. The fact that it's our tenth anniversary is completely irrelevant. We hope we've been helpful.

Now what the hell is "Clear Plastic Raincoat from Seattle" supposed to mean?

1996

Dear *2600*:

> *I used a trick I found in an old issue. A laundromat near my place has an old bill/coin changer, so I photocopied a $10 bill and fed it in the slot. I made myself about $200. The guy who owns the place must be on glue because he hasn't caught on yet. Whenever I'm broke, I just photocopy $10 bills and take 'em down and get the quarters, then take the change to the arcade and get bills. Also, for anyone traveling in Vancouver, Canada, the phony bills also work in the Skytrain terminals, a great way to travel for almost free. Also, if you buy a one zone fare with a 10, you get $8.50 change. Thanks guys, I love my 2600.*

THE MIGHTY PANTHAREN
N. VANCOUVER
CANADA

Let's get this straight. You're photocopying money, telling everyone in the world about it, announcing your location, and going back to the same places wondering why nobody's catching on? And on top of all that, you're saying that we were the inspiration for all this? It's all very interesting but most people probably want to know when exactly you landed on our planet.

Dear *2600*:

> I just wanted to inform you that you've got wrong guy. I am talking about Phiber Optik. He doesn't deserve that name. I am the true Phiber Optik. I thought of the name and asked someone on IRC if they liked it. He must have seen. You are a big fake! All that stuff in your "MOD" book was bull. You can't do any of that crap you did in the book. I can, so watch it, you fake. I want my name back, and you're gonna give it to me. Or else, and you can try to do anything to me cause I know your a fake, and I'm gonna tell the world. I am elite. Your knowledge of computers is a speck of dirt compared to mine. Don't get me wrong 2600 is OK but you guys are kind of dumb. Your mag is full of crap. Anyone who has anything to do with 2600 is a geek. Even if your dumb enough to read it.
>
> Here's my info I am sure you are bull so try to convince me losers.
>
> NG
NEW JERSEY

You're either a real cocky ninth grader or the guy whose name, address, phone number, and school you posted is a ninth grader you've had a falling out with. Either way we will investigate your claim and an adjuster will be in touch soon.

1997 ⎯⎯⎯⎯⎯⎯⎯⎯⎯⎯⎯⎯⎯⎯⎯⎯⎯

Dear *2600*:

> I do not have Caller ID, and I am not paranoid as some of your read-ers may be. I am about as clean and law abiding as they come. I just like to understand these technologies. Well, not 20 minutes after I set 2600 down, I got a phone call where there was silence and no one re-sponding. So I hung up and dialed *69. I got the three octave tone that indicates you did something wrong and a recorded message stating that

this call could not be called back. This tells me one of two things: the phone call was originated from Bell South, or Bell South authorized a government agency to do this. Can anyone tell me what they are looking for or if it could be a really sophisticated phreak?

PROCELL

You read our magazine, get a phone call, immediately believe the government is behind it, and consider yourself not paranoid?

Dear *2600*:

I was wanting some advice, needing a hacker who could hack into my brain and get my mother out of there. Although the experience has been the trip of a lifetime, it's caused me to lose the things most precious to me. I wouldn't necessarily suggest it for the future. Any advice on how to get it to stop would be great! I'm not the only person this has happened to. Be careful who you talk to about what. That's my suggestion!

HEAD-ACHES IN ARLINGTON

Well, we're sure glad you chose to talk to us about this. Maybe now your mother will stop calling us.

1998

Dear *2600*:

I want to write you guys (ask you a question, to be printed in the magazine), so where do I send the question?

DAVE

You seem to have sent it to the right place because your question is now being answered. Of course, you realize we never accept more than one question from any reader. Thanks for playing.

Dear *2600*:

> *I have several of your magazine. Which I enjoy reading very much. My question is why do you have telephones from every place on the globe on the back cover. I have nothing against it, I just thought it was something slightly out of the ordinary. Any clarification would be helpful.*
>
> MEGLOMANIAC

We are under orders. More than this we cannot tell you. Enjoy your day.

Dear *2600*:

> *Do all of your letters really start with "Dear 2600:" or do you just add that in there for consistency?*
>
> SALT

Yours did. Actually, you had a comma instead of a colon, which we fixed free of charge. Most letters do start that way or are very close. The letters with the really interesting salutations contain mostly profane words and usually stray off-topic.

Dear *2600*:

> *I've seen your page and I noticed that in the Europe map you have placed a country named MAC. I assume that this mistake was not on purpose but misguidance and I hope that you change the name to the official U.N. name that is F.Y.R.O.M (Former Yugoslavik Republic of Macedonia).*
>
> CHRISTOS PARASKEYOPOULOS

You guys really need to lighten up over there. Unless going around calling countries names like FYROM is your idea of humor.

Dear *2600*:

> *Why don't you try to get into the prison computer system, open every door in the entire compound, which would create complete chaos, so that he could get out?*
>
> CANDYMAN

We can only assume you're talking about Kevin Mitnick which would make this about the dumbest idea we're ever heard. You're welcome to give it a shot though — just make sure to tell all the other hardened criminals he's locked up with to stay put while he quietly makes his escape.

Dear *2600*:

> *You don't know me, I don't know you, but if you are a half decent hacker, you will find who I am soon enough, so enough with the pleasantries. Let me break it down for you. I want to learn to hack. Enough Said. Goodbye.*
>
> DRAMADAME

Dear *2600*:

> *HOW STUPID CAN BE A HUMAN BEEING LIKE YOU GUYS??DO U WANT THE ANSWER?VERY STUPID. YOU HACKED A SANT HOME PAGE WHICH SPEAKS ABOUT PEACE AND JESUS.YOU THINK THAT YOU ARE INTELLIGENT BUT WITHOUT THE COMPUTERS YOU ARE NOTHING. YOU HAVE TO KNOW THAT JESUS IS NOT MAD WITH YOU HE GIVES YOU A CHOISE TO REGRET ABOUT YOUR ACTIONS. I LIKE HACKING AND ALL THE PROGRAMMES ABOUT HACKING BUT NOT LIKE THIS. TIME TO REGRET.*
>
> HARRIS
GREECE

And heaven is going to be filled with this?

Dear *2600*:

> *why can u not answer??? how can i get in touch with someone who can answer my question about hacking into a schools computer and changeing your grade... i will subscribe to your cool magazine if u can tell me how or who i can contact to get this information... well thanks for your time...*
>
> VxPLaToNiUM

Just one of many lamebrains who gets into arguments with our email auto-reply that says personal replies aren't possible.

Dear *2600*:

> *I just love your webpage it's kool. i wanna get the 2600 magazine. i don't really understand what you do. are you hackers or what?*
>
> Malbushsa

Oh no. We're not falling for that again. You feds think you're real clever, don't you?

Dear *2600*:

> *I've read a letter by Christos Paraskeyopoulos about the country FYROM which you placed as Macedonia with the abbreviation MAC. I also read your answer which I found rather disturbing (for me at least) and a bit ironic. I guess you don't care how the U.N. decides each new country's name and you call it with the name you decide. I would like to ask you to change the abbreviation MAC with the correct one, which is FYROM. And as far as the part which says: "Unless going around calling countries names like FYROM is your idea of humor," I would like to inform you that our idea of humor is going around calling countries names like USA.*
>
> Varelides Marios
> (An angry Greek)

That's actually pretty funny. But the thing is, we call people in our country Americans because it's part of the USA name. Macedonia is part of the FYROM name yet you don't want us to call them Macedonians. You're mad at us for the wrong reason. If the country was called the Former Yugoslav Republic of Idiots, we would call them Idiots but we wouldn't call them FYROIs. We'd really like to know — what do you call those people who live in that place you don't like to say? And keep it clean.

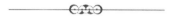

Dear *2600:*

Is there anything I can do with a mac.

NAME

Somehow we doubt it.

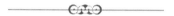

Dear *2600:*

I read your magazine and enjoyed most of the information. In light of the attitudes and commentary, I have several comments.

In the Bible, James 1:16-17 says, "Don't be deceived, my dear brothers. Every good and perfect gift is from above, coming down from the Father of the heavenly lights, who does not change like shifting shadows."

Is hacking a good thing? Are those involved gifted in their computer pursuits? Is the government fickle in the application of the law? Your readership says yes, I believe.

If hacking is inspired and the seed for all our gifts planted by God, why not take the next step and seek the source of the wisdom, knowledge, and understanding you possess?

PATRICK

Good idea. When they come for us, we'll just say God is the ringleader of the conspiracy. Get us some more Bible quotes so we can justify this.

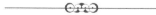

1999 _____

Dear *2600*:

> First off, let me say that I am a Christian as well as a (beginning) hacker. I have noticed a disturbing trend: "Christians" writing to computer magazines and spewing a holier than thou routine. I feel that 2600 is a place to spread information, not biased opinions. If you don't like it, flame on Usenet but not in 2600. I've seen the "kiddie xxxx" books at B&N and I've seen the hacked web page. Both have their good points and their bad ones, but it's now time to leave religion out of 2600. Just remember, you are entitled to your beliefs and so are we. On a side note, God of Dirt will never have an outdated arm, it will serve as a chilling reminder of the injustices done by our government.
>
> JOE SIXPACK

You were doing so well before you got to the God of Dirt.

Dear *2600*:

> Did you have any trouble with the federal regulations people when you published nudity on your recent cover?
>
> PHRED

No. Did you have any trouble when the drugs wore off?

Dear *2600*:

> I'm a new reader. I would like to write a letter to 2600, but I don't know what to write about. Do you have a cool letter that you would like sent? How about some ideas for cool letters?
>
> ROUTER

You're a natural.

Dear *2600*:

> *This letter is in response to the letter ccure wrote in 15:3. The reason people more experienced don't like 2600 is because it gives cluebag people (namely foreigners like Brazilians and Malaysians) the idea that by reading your magazine it makes them a "kr4d 31337 hax0r" and they go into hacker channels (where they don't belong) and ask stupid questions like "TEACH ME HOW TO HACK, IM BRAZILIAN." I have actually seen someone say that. And that is why people don't like 2600. You can catch me on IRC if you want #narqs-r-us@Efnet and #krad@Efnet.*
>
> DDHD

You never make the connection as to just how we're responsible for all of the newbies who are invading your turf. It pains us greatly to know that your "krad" channel is being overtaken by people who think they are "kr4d" but we're not the ones sending them your way. Maybe there's some other reason why you attract them. What we do is print a magazine and anyone capable of reading is welcome to pick it up. To please you, we would either have to password protect each issue or not come out at all. As Neil Young would say, it doesn't mean that much to us to mean that much to you.

Dear *2600*:

> *Can I file a restraining order against the government? They are always following me.*
>
> JOHN DOE

You are the government. Next time you see anyone following you, be sure to tell them this while running and flailing your arms. Works for us.

Dear *2600*:

> As I was reading your magazine the other day I remembered the U.S.
> Navy Seals and everything they do for us. Please have a section honor-
> ing the U.S. Navy Seals. Thank you.
>
> BLACK KNIGHT

*We'll devote a whole issue to them if you tell us how in hell we reminded you
of them.*

2000

Dear *2600*:

> I have some work for a good hacker. Would you place an advert in
> your newsletter? How much? When is copy date? Can you email me
> sample copy?
>
> WOLF

*You win the prize for the largest number of misassumptions in a short letter. First,
hackers don't go out getting hired simply because they are hackers. We don't take
advertising except in our marketplace and that's only for subscribers. We don't
charge for this. We don't have "copy dates." And we come out on paper, not via
email. A sample copy is $5.*

Dear *2600*:

> I just got my first 2600 mag ever and my friend tore it up because I
> spilled juice on his new Playboy. I cried for hours. By the way I love the
> new Windows 2000. It's super. Lenix and UNIX suck with a capitol
> "s" because they are too hard.
>
> SUPERHACKER@AOL.COM

You just can't make this stuff up.

Dear *2600*:

> To answer the question "Was God a hacker?" do the math. A=1,
> B=2, etc. "Computer" - (C) 3*6=18 (O) 15*6=90 (M) 13*6=78 (P)
> 16*6=96 (U) 21*6=126 (T) 20*6=120 (E) 5*6=30 (R) 18*6=108.
> The sum is 666. Revelation 13:17-18: "so that no one could buy or sell
> unless he had the mark, which is the name of the beast or the number
> of his name. This calls for wisdom. If anyone has insight, let him cal-
> culate the number of the beast, for it is man's number. His number is
> 666." Thoughts? Coincidence or Coder Supreme?

DAN

*That's a nice little trick but the actual sum of the numbers is 111. You simply multi-
plied everything by 6 for no reason other than to get the number you wanted. Now
if you take the letters associated with the word "hackers" and multiply their value
by 40, you'll see some real prophecy at work.*

2001

Dear *2600*:

> Does 2600 need cracker? Maybe I am a cracker not a hacker. I want
> to write some essays about crack. Does 2600 accept it? How could
> one join 2600? Has 2600 some persons who have high technique of
> computer?

STUDIN

The seeds planted by the mass media have begun to sprout.

Dear *2600*:

> I have always wanted a subscription to 2600, but I was poor and
> no one would ever buy me one. Now, thanks to your magazine, I
> hacked the crap out of Citibank and now I've accumulated over

$1,000,000,000 to spend on not only a subscription, but a bunch of other useless crap!!!! Thanks you guys!!!!

Just playin'.

SATE

You're a real funny guy.

Dear *2600:*

I ain't no hacker or cracker. But I know some crap about some crap. I know u could get my p-word or other crap like that. But I just got back into the scene. Legal trouble u know — amateur hacker gets screwed. Yeah that was me. But what happened to Minttic was Bull. Sorry I am a little drunk. Screw the US. Screw tha gov. What is it for what is it to live for.

GOOD BYE DUMB ASS SPYIN US GOV.

KHD

No, this did not come from China. But we got his p-word. And Minttic says hi.

Dear *2600:*

There is a matter of utmost importance that I must relay to you immediately: I can eat 50 eggs.

GIL YOUNG

No man can eat 50 eggs.

Dear *2600:*

How do you know when the subscribers die? You could waste money sending copies of your magazines to dead people.

GRANT WELCH

Great. Something else to worry about.

———— ❦ ————

Dear *2600*:

> *How do you say "2600?" a) "Two thousand six hundred," b) "twenty-six hundred," c) "two six zero zero," d) something else? Please write back soon, we have a bet on this.*
>
> Mikko

Would you believe it's never come up? Being magazine people, we don't have to actually speak out loud.

———— ❦ ————

2002 ⎯⎯⎯⎯⎯⎯⎯⎯⎯⎯⎯⎯⎯⎯⎯⎯⎯⎯⎯⎯⎯⎯

Dear *2600*:

> *We enjoy wearing brown pants and sniffing your magazine on Wednesday evenings while composing music with our Tandy 1000. You too are wearing brown pants!*
>
> Two Avocados

And this is as strangely haunting as a David Lynch film.

———— ❦ ————

2003 ⎯⎯⎯⎯⎯⎯⎯⎯⎯⎯⎯⎯⎯⎯⎯⎯⎯⎯⎯⎯⎯⎯

Dear *2600*:

> *I am in Germany working for the Army. What do I need to do?*
>
> Henry

Proceed with the original plan. You'll be contacted.

———— ❦ ————

Hi,

> *You have contacted the RunCoach Mailing List. You request has been passed to a human for interpretation. A response should not take too long.*
>
> REGARDS
LIST ROBOT

We've done no such thing. How dare you accuse us of contacting you. If you weren't merely a robotic script, we might entertain the notion of exacting some sort of revenge upon your ass. Fortunately a human will interpret this "request" and see it for the charade it is.

Hi,

> *You have been subscribed to the RunCoach Mailing list. This is a very quiet list. The next announcement should be in a few weeks regarding the next beta release.*
>
> REGARDS
PAUL

Now you've done it, Paul. You share the same DNA as the humans on our staff, yet you act as if you were an automated process working as an agent of the robotic script. This to us is nothing short of treason. Had you read our automated response, you would have seen no indication of any interest in your lameass mailing list. Yet, you betrayed your humanity and signed us up anyway. We cannot forgive this. Our readers cannot forgive this. What's more, the human race will never forgive this. Prepare for what lies ahead.

Dear *2600:*

> *I don't read your magazine, but my brother's letters got published twice. Please stop.*
>
> ERIK

He told us you'd say that.

2004

Dear *2600*:

> I expected an April Fool's prank, somewhat in the same vein as last year's where the government "commandeered" your site, but this year I was pleasantly surprised with the old-school games, such as Tetris and Pac-man, that you had on the site. Excellent job.
>
> MG48S

If you're referring to our site somehow being patched into an Atari 2600 on April 1, let's just say the investigation is continuing.

Dear *2600*:

> I have the Secret Service following me everywhere I go. They have bugged everything I own. Ruined every relationship I have. They are messing with my bank account, etc. I have proof! I desperately need advice. I don't know why they are on me but I am way out of my league.
>
> CHARLES

And yet you don't show us the proof.

Dear *2600*:

> I have a serious complaint against you. The apartment next to mine has had hacker meetings for some time and things have gotten out of hand lately. I know it's 2600 because they hang a sign on the door.
>
> I know they're hacking my cable modem because my connection dies every time they get together and I'll be offline all night. I get viruses, too. They know my phone number and prank me with breathing and hang-ups until I disconnect my phone. These people even write stories about me and post them online. While they're doing all of this they blast their computer music at full volume and put the speakers up

against my walls. The last straw was finding human feces in front of my door after their last meeting.

I bought a copy of your magazine to figure out their behavior but I'm still clueless. I thought you were about computers? I've lost my patience with this crap (literally) and I'd appreciate a response. I'd hate to have to involve the law.

VLADINATOR

We would love for you to involve the law. We would love to be held accountable for every group of people in the world who writes the number 2600 on their door. Because, as we all know, that's all it takes to prove that this is a tightly knit conspiracy. In all seriousness, if you want to deal with this problem, it sounds like you already know who the perpetrators are. There must be some way you can deal with them locally. If you really read the magazine, you would see that our meetings don't take place in apartments but rather in public places for all the world to see. So don't go assuming that anyone who writes down our name is somehow affiliated with us. Would you be complaining to the White House if they stuck an American flag on their door instead?

Dear *2600*:

I love you Natalie. I'm sorry, I always will, and saying what I said to you was the worst mistake of my life. You're the most beautiful thing that ever happened to me, and calling you a bitch was my own death sentence because you're the only friend I ever had. I could never do enough to apologize. But I'm doing my best. I can't say anymore or I'll break down right here in the Apple store. I'm sorry.

THOMAS

We believe you're sincere but what's important is that Natalie believes this. And for that to happen, you need to learn how to enter her email address properly, especially in a store where other people have been using the computer. Your "best" just isn't good enough at this point, Thomas, and we say this with all due respect. We want to help. You should consider yourself lucky that you sent this to us and not someone who could have really embarrassed you.

Dear *2600*:

> *For four and a half years I have been hearing voices from people who claim to be in the Secret Service and they tell me things that come true. I only started hearing the voices after the FBI visited my home. Has anyone mailed with this same complaint?*
>
> TABETHA

You wouldn't believe how many complaints like this we get. We don't know how helpful we can be but we can tell you that in all likelihood those aren't the voices of the Secret Service. You say what they tell you comes true and we know that anything the Secret Service might tell you usually winds up being a lie.

Dear *2600*:

> *So I got my first issue of* 2600 *about a week ago. As I was reading the story "Decoding Blockbuster" by SDMX on page 43 (21:3), I could not help but stumble upon a secret message hidden in the article. That's right, a secret message. On the bottom left of page 43 above the "Write for 2600" box and below the text "...quick cut and paste...", I read the text "there is nothing in this box" printed in small, light gray letters. I immediately began to wonder. What box? Why is there nothing in this box which I am unable to locate? Perhaps somebody forgot to place the necessary contents in the box?*
>
> *Seeing as I am rather unfamiliar with the particular details of your publication, I realize that I may be sadly mistaken. Perhaps this is something that you hide in every issue or a simple (yet strange) mistake on the part of the publishers. On the other hand, could it truly be a secret message and I may have won a prize (new CPU maybe)? In either case, I couldn't help but write you this letter.*
>
> SHELLCODE

It's quite a bit of a waste to spend this much time talking about nothing inside a box that doesn't exist.

2005 ⎯⎯⎯⎯⎯⎯⎯⎯⎯⎯⎯⎯⎯⎯⎯

Dear *2600*:

> Would this be the correct address to write to if I had a question about hacking?
>
> CalebLeo1

Depends. If that was the question, then yes. For all others, no. We hope that helps you.

Dear *2600*:

> The truth. What is there to know? Sometimes true, always lying. It splatters, affecting, or rather, infecting everything and everyone. Locusts of the real world, sound to the deaf, pictures to the blind. More than knowledge of the unknown, lies of the unsaid. Lies are what exist, they exist to create; to create, to destroy, to maim. Governmental ploys to shield us from the truth. The truth that the only real thing out there, the only real and true thing, is ourselves. Ourselves and our freedom to express. Express our undying — never ending — hate for the brotherhood known only as the "government." A shell, a meaningless organization used to suck every penny and minute of labor out of us, whilst using that liposuction, fat-filled, bilious money to fund its own people and dummy corporations — all for one. Feeding off the sweat of others. This is only the beginning — this is where you come in. The truth is nothing... without you to hear it.
>
> PH4N70MPHR34K

You may well have a career as a thrash metal lyricist.

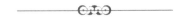

2600

> Greetings to the Fifth Hope Mission:
> I am so happy when I could visit your net. You had good plans. We are thrilled about your Hope. Please accept my heartiest congratulations

for conducting good programming. May God continue to grant you similar successes all through your plans. God has duly rewarded your sincere prayers.

I learned about your youth Hope, your speakers, locations, etc. Oh! It is very great.

I am N. Rajasekharam. We had youth ministry. I am working for youth. I think I will be introducing my youth members to your Hope. Please cooperate me. I will join as a volunteer in your Hope. I will join, I will do work in your mission with your "Jesus compassion." I will not pay for cost of registration. Please understand me. I will give my bio-data. Please accept me. Please introduce my ministry with your dearest friends.

I will pray for "our Hope." Pray for my ministry and me. Send me your information. You will do registration in Hope in my name.

Thanking You
In Hope
N. Rajasekharam

OK, we have no idea what any of that was about. It came to us in a registered letter from India from someone who was obviously looking at the Fifth HOPE website. True to his word, he sent us his "bio-data" which was his family history and date of birth along with every email address and handle he's ever used. We ought to drop the whole hacker angle and just set up a religion. We already own hope.net so we're halfway there. And if we can get testimonials like this without even trying, imagine what we could do if we really put our hearts into it.

Dear 2600:

In response to Black_Angel's question in 22:3, maybe the question isn't who the man on the cover is but what does he represent? Maybe what is important is the symbolism of a single man who is trying to look inconspicuous and is traveling the world with a briefcase with a biohazard symbol on it. Now that symbol could just be a reference to the band Biohazard but I'm pretty sure that's not it. So back to the topic at hand. What does the guy stand for, what does he represent? Is he supposed to be this so-called "terrorist" that our government

(America's to be exact) has led us to believe is out there and is going to get us on an unknown date at an unknown location? Is he just a man trying to get the word out or trying to get noticed? Or have the last few covers been a representation of how our mainstream media misleads us into looking at "the wrong hand in a magic trick" or just the latest mainstream media attack on hackers and all that they are afraid of? Also, on the cover of 22:3 there is a shadow above the low hover platform of what I'm guessing is a cruise ship, yacht, or some sort of luxury vessel, judging by the lounge chairs and tennis/basketball courts in the background. I have come to the conclusion that this shadow is that of the famous McDonald's fast food sign. So what does this mean? Has McDonald's taken over? Is McDonald's funding these alleged terrorists? Is Fast Food in general taking over or is it up to no good? I guess these are the truly important questions that we should be asking. I just checked the 2600 website after writing all of this and looking at the new cover of 22:4 (I don't have enough cash to buy it yet). I think my previous statement is true and to expand on it maybe the McDonald's sign represents "Big Business" and corporations and the "terrorist" is the government and the device being armed on the plane is their weapon against the underground and the hacker community. But who knows? I'm just a 16-year-old high school student.

WISECRACKER

Dear *2600*:

I realize that no one is perfect. When you have a large group of people, there is a lot of imperfection. When you run a business, however, the glaring imperfections should not include pricing things stupidly. For instance, the local Pizza Hut prices things goofy. One order of cheese sticks (which includes five sticks and one marinara sauce) comes to $3.68 around here. An individual order of cheese sticks (which includes three sticks and one marinara sauce) comes to $1.60. That's less than half. Two individual orders comes to roughly $3.38. A little math and you'll conclude that you can save $.30 if you get two individual orders instead of one single order. Not only that, but you then get an extra *stick and an extra sauce. Extra sauces cost $.35. You're definitely saving money. This goes to show how much money you can save by asking stupid questions like "what if I want two individual orders instead of one single order?" It also shows how easy it is to make a stupid math mistake and, when it becomes public, potentially lose money. Hacking isn't always about technology.*

ZACHARY

Of course it's also possible that their cheese sticks suck and getting people talking about them like this is all part of the master plan to have lines out the door for the individual orders that nobody would have wanted in the first place.

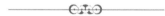

Dear *2600*:

> *My haiku for you,*
> *Wonderful blissful pages*
> *Of knowledge and fun.*
> *Twenty Six Hundred,*
> *You are my one drug of choice.*
> *Happy addiction.*

VYXENANGEL

It's a double haiku and a self-referential one at that!

Dear *2600*:

> *Last night I had a dream that I ran a small, independent magazine similar to 2600. It was really hard and I woke up in a sweat. I can only imagine what the real thing is like. I want to thank you guys for your years of continued hard work and support of the community. The dreamers are behind you.*

JEREMY

Dear *2600*:

> Just thought y'all might want to know that the production of boots is
> up this year.
>
> RUNSETUID.ROOT

And just what we're supposed to do with this info is going to be the topic of discussion for some time.

Dear *2600*:

> I recently purchased the spring issue (23:1). While innocently reading
> your magazine, I received what I would call an assault. Your maga-
> zine cut me. Normally I wouldn't complain, but as I feel that I have
> the right to make you listen to my opinion, I must alert you to the
> fact that your pages can cause quite an irritating cut. I don't feel it is
> necessary to involve the authorities in this matter. However, to spare
> innocent hands and fingers and possible litigation, I do feel it necessary
> to advise you to put warning labels on your magazine suggesting that
> possible injury can be derived while reading your magazine. I hope
> you heed this advice and I look forward to reading your publication
> in the future injury-free and duly warned.
>
> WEBBLES

The only problem we had with the warning labels was that people were peeling them off and then attempting to smoke them. The chemicals that were then released necessitated our issuing another warning for the labels. If your issue doesn't have these warnings prominently displayed, put it down, walk away, and alert the authorities.

Dear *2600*:

> We would like to purchase payphone booth like the one in Saint
> Petersburg, Russia. So could you please send more information and
> price of that booth.
>
> AHMED M ATTEF
MANAGER PAYPHONES
SPECIAL BUSINESS UNIT — HQ
SOMEWHERE IN QATAR

We don't know what you're up to but we fear you misunderstand what we're all about. We don't sell payphone booths or even payphones or for that matter phones of any kind. You've given us some ideas though. Best of luck in your pursuit.

Dear *2600*:

> *To my fellow conspirators, countrymen, and whom it may concern. Guide of contents, in these pages. Of what is contained within? Indeed. What's inside? Take a look. Ingredients: internal organs, innards. Both: Collateral and junk. Trouble indeed may be held within these discoveries of ways and means. Toward the path to knowledge, for fair visions of future far off, or evil wonders to behold. Only the following years shall hold. The contents, here within in these pages will be the ingredients and the path toward great knowledge, the wonder of which we shall see, when we've all grown. The great deeds we have sown have come upon us and it will matter not what have known. Here's to 26 more years of hacking!*
>
> *Do what you want with this, whether you edit it, use it, or simply despise it. Also, speak as freely as you wish with me, for I do not hide communications from others (my own devices and will for this should be obvious, so I will not say) if it can be helped, but will do so if you wish.*
>
> SOHO

What's scary is how much of this we actually understood.

Dear *2600*:

> *Hi,*
>
> *I was just hoping to see my name in print in the letters section.*
>
> WAVE _ RIDER _ 1899

And everything we've done up to this point has been orchestrated to get you to contact us. Now we can begin.

Dear *2600*:

What's up with page 44?

LENNY LOVE THE HOBO

It's just doing its job.

2007

Dear *2600*:

A local bar owner I know uses UNIX and has a long beard and wears thick glasses. He is also very fat. When he gets drunk, he talks about the good old days of Commodore bulletin boards and flat databases. Additionally, his bar is quite filthy. Therefore, I believe he is a hacker.

I really need to become a hacker and this man is my only hope. My question is how do I approach him about mentoring me? I keep showing up at his bar but he gets drunk and yells at me for loitering. Sometimes he falls asleep. One time I tried to show him a few tricks in Windows with TweakUI but he told me never to use his computer again. He even made fun of me for not knowing Linux and owning a Mac.

Thanks for any information you can give me about social engineering this guy!

HAROON THE HACKER

If you can't become a hacker by pestering a big, fat, bearded slob of a bar owner into teaching you the tools of the trade, there really isn't anything left that we can think of. We can't imagine what you're doing wrong; that approach usually works.

Dear *2600*:

Good Day!

Barrister John Ibe is my name and a Senior Advocate of Nigeria. I have a proposal to discuss with you concerning one of our Deceased

customers who is a national of your country. As soon as I hear from
you and once we are in agreements. I would be needing your assistance
in making a business investment in real estate, oil & gas and any other
lucrative sphere of business in your country.

Owing to the urgency of this transaction, I would appreciate an im-
mediate response from you to confirm the receipt of my mail. As soon
as I get this response from you, I will furnish you with details of the
transaction and the urgency at which I need to get the funds trans-
fered out of Nigeria to you. Your earliest response to this letter will
be appreciated.

JOHN(SAN)

We really want to do business with you but feel uneasy because of the grammar and
capitalization issues we've previously written to you about. One of your colleagues
even sent us a letter that was completely in capital letters! We simply cannot abide
that as it makes us feel quite small in comparison. Once we have the protocol sorted
out, we would be most happy to supply you with all of the information you need and
more in order that we may help to secure the transfer of the funds from Nigeria. It is
indeed disturbing how much money has been tied up in your country over the years
simply because there aren't enough people in the world who can give out their bank
account numbers and transfer codes. Please count us in as concerned parties who
want to help. Yours truly, etc.

2008

Dear 2600:

I think I am being "watched," as my cursor is "fluttering." But I got
this address from someone and would like to know more of what you
have to offer. Information, direction? I am in need of "advice" on
certain computer "applications," and/or email "applications." If you
could either direct me to a source of information, or otherwise, I would
sure appreciate it.

GRANNY

A fluttering cursor is a sure sign that you're being monitored, either by your next door neighbor or an anonymous foreign power. Use of excessive quotation marks has been known to strengthen the power of the monitoring virus which lives in your keyboard. Avoid using computers altogether until you know what you're dealing with. We suggest going to a local bookstore or library and researching the subject matter you're interested in as thoroughly as possible before going any further. Spend hours over there reading and learning. Just be sure to face the door in case you were tailed.

Dear *2600*:

> *I've felt that this hurts more than anyone could hurt me for saying it for a long time. With stating it being the least of the pain I've felt from fellow PTA members heckling me, I'm surprised catharsis in this fashion isn't illegal. That FBI would use covert interrogation and other illegal methods while putting a child in what those BDSM people call "subspace." Then, I find it hard to believe that these jerks would pretend to be a business and watch someone's every move. I make no mistake in saying that articles appear often on the Internet just as soon to disappear and their writers discredited.*
>
> *It's almost as if the English writers are speaking in code. That would mean that when other people pick up these codes intuitively and repeat them they phonologically must be typed as "mentally ill."*
>
> A Depressed Soccer Mom

The FBI and the PTA have always been in cahoots. Everyone knows this. Thanks for the coded message which our lab is now processing. You will receive our reply through the usual channel. Namaste.

Dear *2600*:

> *Hi. how are you Doing? my name is marie Almaleeq, please i want to you to Recover some money my father left in bank here, please is very important you get back to me we shall talk on percentage*
>
> Regard
marie

How very lucky for us your letter came when it did. We are always happy to help people with such matters and it seems as if more and more of them need our help every day. We are delighted to give you our banking information along with all sorts of our personal identification items if this will assist you to get access to the money which is rightfully yours. There's no need to talk about percentages — we feel it's the least we can do and we hope that everyone out there who happens to get a letter like this expends all efforts to help out. We have already written to you with an offer to extend a loan for the full amount while you wait for your money to be released. Our philosophy is that if more of us would only step up like this, the world would surely be a much nicer place.

Dear *2600*:

> *Urgent! I need a new identity for me and my daughter because we are victims of abuse illegally. Send me information please.*
>
> Eva

Do you really believe that emailing total strangers is the best way to start a new life? We're not the witness relocation people but even if we were, it's not the kind of thing you do casually. You can find a whole lot of tips on the net about how to hide and/or protect your privacy. Advertising your problems to anyone who will listen is probably the first item on the list of things not to do.

Dear *2600*:

> *let me in... so what do i have to do to get in? im trading code to this guy for nice computers. usenet would nice. it would be nice. im going to have a mindset with nuemonic reach and a storage partition of a 100 gb with terrar process. but i dont have any other*
>
> Phobus

No, you certainly don't.

Dear *2600*:

> Stop your inresponsible word! *Tibet is, was and always a part of China, that no doubt of it, please stop your ignorant words if you know nothing of China. China is a beautiful, great country, welcome to China to see every thing with your own eyes and get your own conclusion. We can't tolerance someone split our country, we can fight to the death!*

> INDIANA _ LAU

How about you go and fight to the death and we can try and figure out just what in hell you're going on about and why you think it has anything at all to do with us.

Dear 2600:

> hack the election and overthrow the shadow systems rigging of elections that have been farced for the last 70 years. those that have elected all of our presidents. i know, and i have been witness to the last few. you need to start everyone on electing a small party candidate (the system needs to be hacked). the red and blue are truly connected. do not let the corporations and special interest and all of americas other evils select who runs your country. and do not let them rig another election with equipment that you wouldn't let your grandmother use. do not try to trace this message. i have ghosted an aol account.

> my apologies for not signing

> please heed my advice

> thank you

> [ANONYMOUS]

Anyone who can ghost an AOL account clearly knows what they're talking about. The hackers of the world will take this solemn duty most seriously.

Dear *2600*:

> good day i hacked www.yahoo.com it was not mafia boy aim a muslim i leave in the netherlands city: heerhugowaard aim now a good Muslim you can believe me or not but i really dit it but mafia boy was a friend of me we here little kids do bad thing who don't no really that time what we doing you most now i have hacked his school with netbus but oke i don't lie believe me so that was my story now i don't hack any more
>
> why i don't tell it before i don't no i was just a little kid 13 years old now aim 19
>
> Swinger

We can only wonder what a letter from you when you were 13 would have looked like. Thanks for all of the identifying information (including your phone number) that you sent us, but we think it's utter nonsense. That's right, we don't believe you could hack a typewriter, much less Yahoo. Of course, if you were really good you'd hack Google or maybe even the government. But we don't think you've got what it takes. No skills whatsoever. Of course, if we were wrong, we'd sure look stupid and you'd look totally awesome. But we're not. We're right and you're lame.

This should be fun.

Dear *2600*:

> I feel kinda bad. I am a homeless hacker and I have been reading your mag since I was building desktops out of the dumpster. I love your mag, great content. I only wish I didn't have to steal it to read it. I guess I could just read it online, but there's nothing like a new copy. I'm addicted!
>
> Homeless Hacker

Well, as an addict, you should realize the importance of paying for your next fix. You don't want to anger the supplier.

Dear *2600*:

> Hi. I'm an 11-year-old boy in Sweden. I've heard about a new hacker
> that calls himself Zero Cool. He's also 11. His father is from Kosovo
> and now he's at war with some other Albanian hackers: Dr.Go, @
> nti-Viru!$, Matrix, Unicracker, and Granit.
>
> Dr.Go is 15-16 years old, he's the only one of these crackers who's got
> a heart. His friend is @nti-Viru!$, he cracked an FBI page a few days
> ago, he used to be friend with Matrix but then they became enemies,
> and he's about 180 cm.
>
> @nti-Viru!$ is also 15-16 years old, he's the one who has the coldest
> heart, he made Matrix's nose get bloody — haha it's really funny. I
> can tell you about it in the end. He's about 164 cm.
>
> Matrix got his nose bloody from @nti-Viru!$, he used to be friends
> with Dr.Go but it didn't get so good. He's about 180 cm and he's
> friend's with Unicracker. Matrix is ranked Number One on the hacker
> list in Kosovo.
>
> I don't have any info on Unicracker.
>
> Zero Cool is 11 years old, he's 163 cm., and lives somewhere in
> Sweden.
>
> Here is the story about @nti-Viru!$, Dr.Go, Matrix, and Matrix's
> little brother: @nti-Viru!$ gave a lollipop to Matrix's little brother
> and his phone to record when they beat up his brother. (Matrix's little
> brother is 11-12 years old.) @nti-Viru!$ hit Matrix with his fist and
> broke his glasses and then Matrix started bleeding from the nose and
> Matrix's little brother looked at them with confused and surprised
> eyes. Then @nti-Viru!$ looked at Dr.Go and said, "What the hell are
> you doing?" (they are really just speaking Albanian at the time) and
> he kept saying, "Why did you hit him?" Then @nti-Viru!$ kicked him
> and Matrix started running and @nti-Viru!$ and Dr.Go ran after
> him (also Matrix's little brother). Then when Matrix was about to go
> into his big house (first he had to pass the gate to come to the yard), @
> nti-viru!$ kicked him in the ass, then Matrix let his little brother go in
> and they started swearing at each other (Matrix on one side of the gate
> and @nti-viru!$ on the other). Then Matrix started with, "I f*cked
> your mum, I f*cked you up." Then @nti-viru!$ said, "Well come out

then!" Then Matrix said, "No way, I'm never going outside again."
Then Matrix turned to his little brother and started swearing at him
and at his lollipop like: "You and your f*cking lollipop!"

CRACKER SPION

Well, there's at least one book here and without doubt a major motion picture as well.
It's clear to see what makes these people the talented hackers that they are. Why
can't the rest of the world understand this? We hope in the next installment to find
out why Zero Cool went to war and who the hell Granit is. Truly fascinating stuff.

Dear *2600*:

How do I get a hold of you? Need sales to angrylou.com. Any
suggestions?

LOUIS MARTINEZ

We have suggestions but they're not really printable. Sometimes it seems as if
most of our mail is from people who have no idea what it is they're mailing. And
that's not even counting the spam.

Dear *2600*:

I have a number of clients within our network looking for portable
toilets. I was just looking at your site, and I am seeking to work with
one company exclusively. I'm simply looking to direct my clients to a
relevant site when they're looking for portable restrooms.

Your site looks like it could make a strong fit for what they're looking
for. Call me today for a demonstration of how we can connect you to
these clients. I am looking to work with one company as soon as pos-
sible, so I'm hoping the decision maker is available to talk sometime
today. Give me a call at your convenience.

THANKS IN ADVANCE.
ELIZABETH GREER
949-379-2022 OR 949-300-3953

It takes a lot to get us angry. Unsolicited emails that make little sense don't really get us upset in the least. Nor does having someone say that they've visited our website and the first thing it made them think of was portable toilets. That's a valid critique and we will defend to the death the right of someone to express it. We are a little frustrated that such an opportunity has apparently landed at our doorstep and we find ourselves with absolutely no contacts in the world of toiletry to even attempt to bluff our way through this and finally realize our dream of supporting ourselves through the production of human excrement. But whatever.

None of that made us angry. What made us lose our cool here was something that happened after our auto-response was sent to the email address listed. See for yourself:

> "From: Elizabeth Greer <elizabethg@inbox.com>
>
> Subject: My spam filter requires verification of your email address
>
> Hello,
>
> You have reached Elizabeth Greer.
>
> I'm protecting myself from receiving junk email by using Challenge/Response Spam Protection.
>
> Please follow the directions below to make sure I receive the email you just sent me."

This was followed by all sorts of directions that needed to be carried out to the letter in order for our mail not to be discarded. Now we're not especially big fans of jumping through hoops in the first place, regardless of the end goal. But the irony of spammers protecting themselves from spam and then bragging about it to the people that they just spammed while subtly implying that those very people may in fact be the true spammers was a bit much for our relatively level heads. We've already been in touch with some of the highest authorities in the toilet industry who don't like to see their overwhelmingly positive image tarnished by such behavior. Needless to say, this isn't over.

Dear 2600:

> Hi my names Greg but my nick is feretman i read your relly old 2600 but i was jut telling every one a windows xp egg go in to note pad

and type Bush hid the facts you should ether get squares or just some japenes jibbery joob

P.S. IM 12 LOL
GREGGG

In a few years, would you be kind enough to revisit this letter and tell us just what it meant? It might prove to be a fascinating study of some sort. It might also prove fruitless as we know a number of middle-aged people who also speak this dialect.

2009

Dear *2600*:

I wish to contribute as well as subscribe to 2600 Magazine and The Hacker Quarterly. *Could you thus ship me specimen hard copies for evaluation? Thank you.*

DANIEL OBORI
NIGERIA

For some reason, we get at least one letter with this exact phrasing every week and almost always from Nigeria. There are those who would say that this is somehow part of some kind of a scam, but we just don't buy it. It's one thing to hand over one's banking information (which we are sending you as a courtesy), but to simply ask for specimen hard copies seems harmless enough. We have therefore sent you one copy each of all issues of both 2600 Magazine and The Hacker Quarterly in the hopes that you will evaluate them and let us know of your decision. And now the wait begins.

Dear *2600*:

Thanks your website. please hack these id we shall be very thankful to you. [deleted]@hotmail.com, [deleted]@yahoo.com, Ashe is not good lady she is money maker and just communication for money after that she use for wrong work. with thanks.

FAROOQ NOOR

And somehow you heard that we were the people to come to when something like this happens. That alone is incredible. We're intrigued, though, as to what "wrong work" consists of.

Dear *2600*:

> HAVING BEEN UNCEREMONIOUSLY DUMPED, I WOULD LIKE TO TEACH MY EX A LESSON HE SOON WON'T FORGET, AND AM WILLING TO PAY FOR THE PRIVILEGE OF SENDING HIM A VIRUS OR TWO, AS WELL AS DISABLING HIS WEBSITE, SINCE AFTER PROPOSING TO ME HE DECIDED THAT MAKING JEWELRY AND MONEY WERE FAR MORE IMPORTANT TO HIM THAN I WAS, AND IN THE PRESENT STATE OF THE WORLD ECONOMY HE TOLD ME THAT'S ALL HE HAS TIME FOR, AND MAYBE ONE DAY WHEN THINGS GET BETTER HE'LL GET BACK TO ME...

> I'M WILLING TO PAY A COUPLE OF HUNDRED DOLLARS I CAN ILL AFFORD AT THIS TIME, BUT AM WILLING TO PART WITH IF YOU CAN PUT ME IN TOUCH WITH SOMEONE WHO CAN HELP ME WITH MY REQUEST.

> I'M NOT A COP/CYBER SURVEILLANCE ANYTHING — JUST A GIRL WHO'S HAD HER HEART BROKEN, AND IS TRYING TO MAKE THE PAIN OF HER SITUATION LESS UNBEARABLE...
>
> ANGELIQUE

We can't imagine what this guy was thinking. He's walking away from quite a catch, no question there.

Dear *2600*:

> PLEASE I NEED TO KNOW IF YOU HAVE TO CALL TO CUBA, GOOD RATE.
>
> NICOLAS

Why on earth do you think we're the people to ask about this? Go shop around, ask Google, visit a corner grocery that sells phone cards, participate in online forums where people actually discuss this stuff, or ask random people on the street. You also might want to find a way to unstick your Caps Lock key. Good luck.

Dear *2600*:

> *I have read on your site very nice things but I can you help me please with some hacking. Its about a betting site and they have in every betting house a TVs on them are going recorded dog bets 1-6 my question is can we hack them to see whats next bet on dogs there is a lot of money to win can you answer me please bye :)*

> ARNEL

You want us to somehow help you hack dog betting? Other than fixing the races (let's hope you're talking about races), what precisely do you think we can do? We'd like to say this is the most unclear letter we've ever gotten but it wouldn't be true — not for this issue and not even for the day that this was received. We seem to have become the clearinghouse for the dazed and confused.

Index